S0-BNH-063

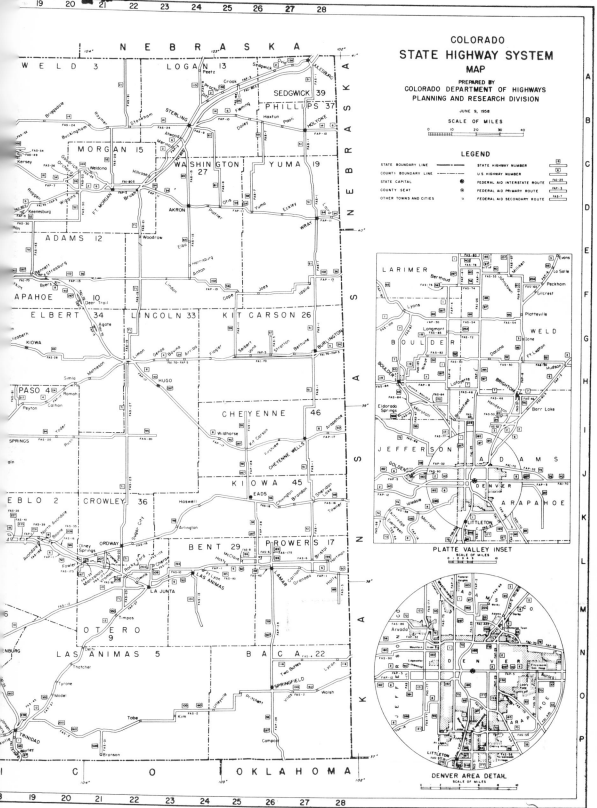

COLORADO
# STATE HIGHWAY SYSTEM
## MAP

PREPARED BY
COLORADO DEPARTMENT OF HIGHWAYS
PLANNING AND RESEARCH DIVISION

JUNE 9, 1958

SCALE OF MILES

0    10    20    30    40

### LEGEND

| | |
|---|---|
| STATE BOUNDARY LINE | STATE HIGHWAY NUMBER |
| COUNTY BOUNDARY LINE | U.S. HIGHWAY NUMBER |
| STATE CAPITAL | FEDERAL AID INTERSTATE ROUTE  FAI-25 |
| COUNTY SEAT | FEDERAL AID PRIMARY ROUTE  FAP-3 |
| OTHER TOWNS AND CITIES | FEDERAL AID SECONDARY ROUTE  FAS-7 |

PLATTE VALLEY INSET
SCALE OF MILES

DENVER AREA DETAIL
SCALE OF MILES

GUIDE TO THE COLORADO
GHOST TOWNS AND MINING CAMPS

# GUIDE
## to the
# COLORADO
# GHOST TOWNS
## and
# MINING CAMPS

## PERRY EBERHART

SAGE BOOKS
1959

To SANDY, tops in my book

# LEGEND

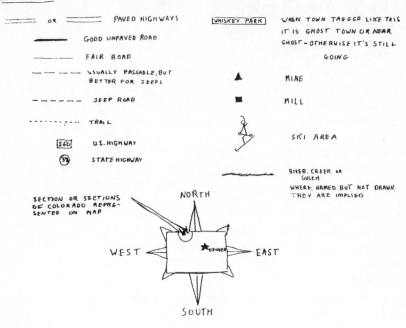

======= OR ======= PAVED HIGHWAYS

———— GOOD UNPAVED ROAD

———— FAIR ROAD

—— —— —— USUALLY PASSABLE, BUT BETTER FOR JEEPS

— — — — — JEEP ROAD

· · · · · · · · TRAIL

[560] U.S. HIGHWAY

(3½) STATE HIGHWAY

[WHISKEY PARK] WHEN TOWN TAGGED LIKE THIS IT IS GHOST TOWN OR NEAR GHOST – OTHERWISE IT'S STILL GOING

▲ MINE

■ MILL

SKI AREA

RIVER, CREEK OR GULCH

WHERE NAMED BUT NOT DRAWN, THEY ARE IMPLIED

SECTION OR SECTIONS OF COLORADO REPRE-SENTED ON MAP

NORTH

WEST ★ DENVER EAST

SOUTH

## NOTES

All of the important gold and silver areas are represented on the maps. There may have been a few isolated and lesser camps off the beaten track that are not represented. Coal camps are scattered throughout the state and were not included in this study. Those shown on the maps just happened to be in the right place to be included.

Road conditions change frequently. The bulk of the back roads leading to the mountain ghost towns are impassable in the winter. During the summer months, a sudden storm may wash out a road or otherwise make it impassable. On the other hand, old roads are being graded or improved upon all the time. The symbols used on the maps represent the general or latest condition of the roads.

Not all of the gulches, creeks, mountains and roads are included on the maps. In many cases the unnecessary details might confuse the search for the ghost town. However, the important features of the area, and all those necessary for locating a town, are shown on the maps.

## PREFACE

This is not a history book. Rather it is a directory of towns, and compilation of known information about those towns. In undertaking the study, I was amazed at the amount of legend and contradictory information Colorado history has collected in just one hundred years. Who was it that said: "History is the perpetuation of saleable gossip"? (Perhaps, nobody has said it yet. In that case, it's mine, all mine.)

In an effort to avoid taking sides in the battle between historians, I have attempted to label all legend just that. When I label something as "story," I mean it to be the popular version, but it too could be legend. In fact, much information I cite as fact, could well be "accepted gossip." Colorado's "guardian of truth" has been lax lo these one hundred years. Even some contemporary students of Colorado have become so afraid of its history they will not label as fact anything they have not discovered themselves. At least, I hope I am fair with the gossips in printing both sides of a disputed story.

So much for that.

As of this moment, this is the most complete compilation of Colorado mining towns — ghost or going — available. As far as I can determine, I have mentioned just about every town of any consequence in the mountain mining sections of the state. But there were hundreds more that were inconsequential. Whenever a new boom area opened up, the landscape was dotted with several tent settlements, one right after another. And about the first thing the settlers did was give their camp a name, often a very sophisticated name in the hope their camp would emerge as a permanent city. Few did.

I have sidestepped the bulk of these camps "that didn't make it." For one thing, their history is too obscure to recall with any authority and they would be almost impossible to plot. I say this with a sadness, however. These "fly-by-night" camps, at one time, were important to some people. We poor moderns may never know thousands of names, interesting names, that have been bandied about in the Colorado hills.

In case I have neglected some towns, however, that do merit mention, I apologize. I would appreciate information on them, if any is available. In fact, any information of any nature whatsoever would be greatly appreciated.

PERRY EBERHART

# TABLE OF CONTENTS

# TABLE OF MAPS

# TABLE OF ILLUSTRATIONS

# 1. A HANDFUL OF DUST

      The mountains were there when man came west.
Shoulder to shoulder, they marched tall out of the plains,
Their silent profile born of unheard fury and sound,
Their wrinkled brow washed by the snow of ages,
And whipped by the unheard winds of the millenniums.
Here volcanoes roared,
Storms were born,
First life crawled onto shore,
Mighty beasts lumbered over the land,
First man felt the sun's warmth briefly, and died.
Here in the mountains
All things lived and died.
      The mountains were still,
The trees were green and full,
There was the same blue sky
When the red men came .
Their bronzed bodies walked through the centuries
And through the trees.
Here was their happy hunting ground,
A pagan playground for the sober ritual of living and dying.
      Long ago the Spanish came,
In shining armour and with fine, black horses.
Somewhere in that snow-capped jungle
Is Eldorado, the city of shining gold.
The Spanish had their moment,
And were gone.
      Eldorado remained.
      Then came the explorers.
One by one they fought their battle with the mountains.
They lost, or won little victories.
Cautious Stephen A. Long walked over what he called "the great
    American desert" to the foot of the mountains .
He looked up.
Invulnerable, he said.
Of course, the mountain men didn't believe him.
Kit Carson, Broken Hand Fitzpatrick, Charles Baker, Jim Beckworth
    and others didn't believe him.
      A young fellow named Fremont,
John C. Fremont, didn't believe him.
He walked to the top of the mountains

13

And looked down . . . .
A matter of perspective.
He and Kit began cutting the mountains down to size,
Moving them apart.
        But when the gold was discovered in California,
When the wagons started rolling,
They cursed the mountains and went around them,
Leaving them to the savages, the mountain men, and John C. Fremont.
        They knew there was gold in Colorado.
The Spanish said so.
Pike said Purcell, or Pursley (What was his name? Who was he?) . . . .
He found some . . . . in 1806 or 1807.
The mountain men told of gold.
Fremont said "Parson" Bill Williams found it in South Park in 1846.
"Buck" Rogers found a mountain of it on the way to California.
Col. William Gilpin, in 1849, searched the mountains for Indians.
And found gold, or evidence of gold, in five areas: South Park,
        Pikes Peak, Cherry Creek, Clear Creek, and the Cache La Poudre.
Georgia hunters told of gold they found on the Cache La Poudre.
The Ralston brothers found gold on the South Platte in 1850.
Another California-bound prospector named Norton found gold in 1853.
Mexican miners from Sonora panned gold above Cherry Creek in 1857.
Fall Leaf, the Delaware Indian guide, displayed the gold he found.
        But the mountains were still too formidable.
Besides, there was enough gold in California and Nevada for everyone.
        William Green Russell was more a symbol than a beginning.
He was a symbol of the end of the California and Nevada romance,
Of hope of prosperity after the depression of 1857,
Of escape from the burning slavery question.
He represented a need . . . .
A need for a new gold rush.
        He didn't find much . . . .
Just a handful of dust on Cherry Creek,
But his find, traveling through the troubled air,
A handful of gold dust in a depression
Became a new Eldorado back east.
        There was gold in Colorado . . . . gold in Colorado!!!!
        There was gold in Colorado!!
        And they started coming.
In wagons, wheelbarrows, or walking,
From the far pockets of humanity,
They started coming.

Maps and guidebooks to the new wonderland sold at a premium.
The guidebooks were all wrong . . . .
But they sold well.
Except for bits and snatches,
What did they know of the mountains?
To an easterner all Colorado lay in the shade of Pikes Peak.
Pikes Peak was three mountains . . . .
All the mountains rolled into one.
But the guidebooks were more than that.
They were tickets to the new Eldorado,
A fresh start, new hope, a chance on a fortune, a ticket to heaven.
  And by thousands they came.
Starving, ragged, stumbling and dusty they came.
Their eyes on the horizon;
The Mountains were their goal.
Many didn't make it.
Many died on the way to Eldorado.
Many tarried along the road . . . .
The dream was too much for them.
The Parade couldn't wait.
Here came the farmers, lawyers, doctors, ne'er-do-wells.
Here came the best and the worst,
Southerners, northerners, the English, French, Chinese.
There were the cannibals, the slaves, the barons,
But mostly just average men after an honest fortune,
They were all in the parade.
  There was George A. Jackson, Gregory and A. D. Gambell.
They find more gold in one week than Russell found all last year . . . .
Just in time, too.
They put an end to talk of a "Pike's Peak Fiasco."
Here came Rose Haydee, the first "pinup" girl in the mountains,
Jack Langriche and "Drinking" Ed Daugherty,
They saw the mountains as a stage.
Silver Heels and her flashing feet,
She lost her beauty but gained immortality.
Here came H. A. W. Tabor whose dreams were as big as the mountains,
Too big to see beyond.
Others found gold,
Pat Casey, John Morrissey, Tom Bowen, methodical Winfield Scott
  Stratton, Thomas Walsh,
Some illiterate, some carpenters,
All dreamers.

For some the dream was never finished,
For "Chicken" Bill, Dick Irwin, "Cowboy" Bob Womack,
    and "Commodore" Stephen Decatur.
Some dreamed too much,
Take Mark M. "Brick" Pomeroy, for example.
To some not even the mountains were too big,
Like Otto Mears,
The little man who could see over 14,000-foot peaks.
And there were Hagerman, Rollins, David Moffat, and others,
Who weren't afraid.
        The Mountains had room for everybody.
A widescreen stage for the Reynolds farce,
A hiding place for the "Bloody" Espinozas.
A burial plot for Bob Ford, "that dirty little coward."
There was even room for "Mr. Howard" in California gulch.
There was elbow room for Soapy Smith, and plenty of suckers.
There was a stage, a boudoir, a rose-covered castle for the ladies,
For Augusta Tabor, afraid to dream;
For Baby Doe, who dreamed enough for both.
There was "Silk Stockings,"
Who found respectability in a parlor house;
There were the dealers in human flesh:
Mollie Purple, Mattie Silks, Six-foot-two Rose Vastine,
        Better known as Timberline.
There was "Calamity" Jane, smoking a stogie;
The "Unsinkable" Mrs. Brown,
Who found Denver society too small to handle her.
        There were the men behind the badge,
Good men and gunslingers.
There was Sheriff Billy Cozens, Matt Duggan, Jim Clark and Matt Dillon.
There were the men of God,
Father Dyer, Bishop Macheboeuf, two-fisted Reverend Uzzel and
        Sheldon Jackson,
Their eyes on Heaven,
Their feet in the mud.
There were the chroniclers, the poets,
  Cy Warman, David Frakes Day, Eugene Field, Damon Runyon.
        There were others, many others,
Big and little people,
As mountains are big and little,
As hopes and dreams are big and little.
They cut impossible trails through impassable mountains and forests.

They gave life to such temporary towns as Buckskin Joe, Tin Cup,
    Caribou, Slabtown, Camp Bird, Rosita, Irwin, Gothic, Royal
    Flush, Silver Heels, Whiskey Park, Crazy Camp and Poughkeepsie.
Each sought God on the mountain tops.
Their search was furious,
But short.
They are dust now,
Their names, their dreams, are but dust . . . .
Scattered in the mountains.
    Some found their gods,
Some didn't.
Maybe the Indians were right.
Maybe the mountains are the real gods, after all.
More than a happy hunting ground,
More than Eldorado,
More than gold and silver . . . . and uranium.
More than a handful of dust,
But hope and dreams and fear,
Loving and laughing,
Living and dying . . . .
And more . . . .
Because when the hoping and dreaming,
When the loving and laughing,
The living and dying are done,
When the echo of the gold is gone,
The mountains remain.


*MAP ONE*

## THE KINGDOM OF GILPIN

Central City
Mountain City
Hoosier City, Springfield, Quincy, Gregory, Gregory Point,
    Eureka and Dogtown
Bortonsburg, Hughesville and Mammoth City
Nevadaville (Nevada, Nevada City, Bald Mountain)
Missouri Flats (Missouri City)
Black Hawk
Russell Gulch
Lake Gulch

17

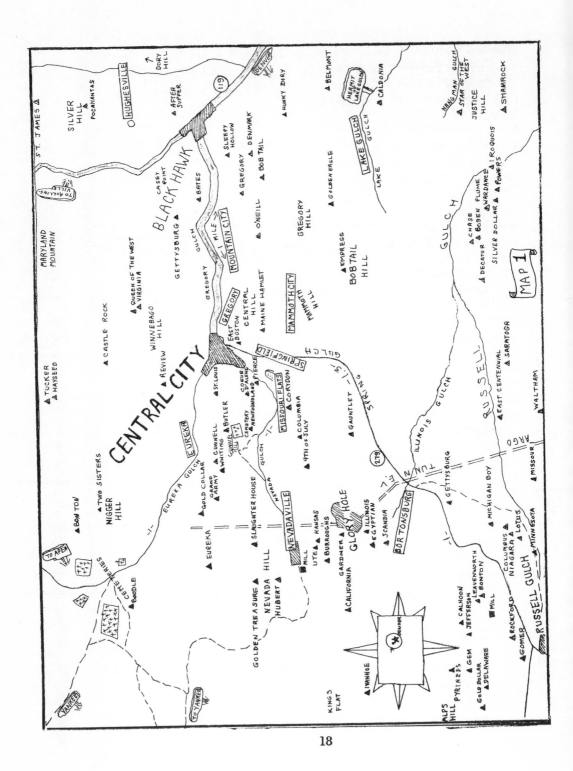

18

## CENTRAL CITY

Colorado was born in Cherry Creek.

White men in the Colorado wilderness numbered about two hundred. The shabby little settlement along Cherry Creek was no more than a way-station. It had nothing on which to sustain itself. It would soon die out . . . unless something happened.

William Green Russell, a determined prospector, found a little bit of dust in Cherry Creek in the late summer of '58. His strike was barely enough to make his expedition worthwhile. It was far from enough to support a gold rush.

But the nation was ready for a new gold rush. The excitement and prosperity from the California and Nevada gold rushes were wearing thin. The country was caught up in the throes of a depression. Thousands were unemployed and hungry. The nation was restless and irritable over the slavery question.

The new, the welcomed, rush was on.

One of the first in the mountains was John H. Gregory. Just about the time the Pikes Peak Gold Rush was turning into a fiasco of disappointment. Gregory hit a rich strike in the mountains. In the first week, he panned more gold than Russell panned the entire summer before.

Within weeks, thousands of people who had been scattered all over the mountains in search of the elusive "Pike's Peak Gold," were concentrating their search in the hills and valleys around Gregory Gulch. Other strikes were made. New York newspaperman Horace Greeley came out to look for himself.

Miners salted a worthless claim with gold dust and allowed Greeley to pan it himself. Greeley was impressed. He said:

"Gentlemen, I have washed with my own hands and seen with my own eyes, and the news of your rich discovery shall go forth all over the world as far as my newspaper can carry it."

And the news did carry throughout the world. The rush gained momentum. There came every sort of American. There came the Germans, the English, Chinese, Russians, Scotsmen and Canadians.

A month after the Gregory find, Mountain City was laid out near the strike.

But the thousands of prospectors were not to be contained in one small settlement. Tent cities and camps blanketed the hills. Prospectors pushed on throughout the "Kingdom of Gilpin," into Boulder County, into South Park to make new strikes and start new cities. Gilpin County soon had several aspiring cities. Adjacent to Mountain City was Central City. It soon overshadowed or absorbed most of the other camps in the Kingdom.

Central City became the largest city in Colorado Mountains. It rivaled Denver for several years, and, for a while, was considered a possible capital in the territory.

The hills around Central City have produced more than 125 million dollars in precious metals. Gilpin County has produced nearly a half-billion dollars.

Central City was not only Colorado's first major boom city. It was, and always will be, the state's most typical mining community. It represented all the lush and lavish qualities of Colorado's mining boom.

It was a busy city. Living was hard, but interesting. It had its unruly element, but was comparatively well-behaved for an early mountain mining community. Central City had more than its share of characters, produced more than its share of Colorado leaders.

But more important than its status as a representative mining town, perhaps of more lasting value to Colorado than the millions of dollars worth of precious metals it produced, were the cultural aspects of the city.

Colorado's culture was born in Central City. The top entertainers in the world performed here. They are still coming.

Jack Langrishe, more than any one man, was responsible for bringing enlightenment to the harsh, uncultured Colorado mountains.

While Central City was still an infant, Langrishe formed a stage group. It gave its first performance in 1861 and was an immediate success. Langrishe took advantage of the talent in the mountains. He developed miners and dance hall girls into polished performers. The most notable example was Mike Dougherty. Langrishe discovered him and molded him into a top stage performer in a few short months. He was the favorite of the territory by 1865, when he died of drink.

Langrishe didn't confine his performances to Central City. He developed traveling troupes which played in mining towns throughout the Colorado mountains. Everywhere, his performances met with overwhelming success. In many mining towns, a visit by Langrishe and his troupe was a highlight in the community's history.

Other stage groups in Colorado were modeled after Langrishe's troupes. Other operahouses and playhouses were built along the lines of those in Central City. Some towns, in the uncivilized pockets of the mountains, actually built theatres to lure Langrishe and his group.

The success of plays and musical performances in Colorado encouraged visits by the star performers of the day. They all came to Colorado.

Central City opera and stage plays were revived in the early 30's, due largely to the efforts of several prominent Denverites.

And the top stars began coming to Colorado again. One of the first of these latter-day performers was Lillian Gish. Others that followed included

20

singer Eleanor Steber, Louis Calhern, Maurice Evans, Cyril Ritchard, Faye Emerson, Frank Fay, Helen Hayes, Shirley Boothe, and Gladys Swarthout—to mention but a few.

World-famous plays and operas are performed, and many original plays, written by Coloradans, have been staged here too.

The fame of the Central City summer festival has spread over the years. Today it is a highlight on the summer theatrical calendar from Maine to California. Hundreds of nationally-known personages have attended the performances. And they come back year after year.

A lion's share of the colorful history and legend of Central City revolves around its early theatres and the proud old Teller House.

One of the best-known stories concerns "Pat Casey and his Night Hands."

Pat was an illiterate Irishman who struck it rich while digging a grave near Central City. His elaborate display of wealth, his burly body-guards, and he, himself, were sources of much of the legend of the mining town. It seemed only natural an original play should be written about him. The play was called "Pat Casey's Night Hands," and Langrishe scheduled it for April 27, 1863.

When Casey heard about the play he was fit to be tied. He let it be known the play would be performed over his dead body. Pat bought plenty of tickets for the premiere performance with the intention of filling the theatre with his men who were instructed to break up the performance—and much of the theatre.

But the night of the premiere, Captain Frank Hall and fifty men from the local militia were also in attendance, armed with rifles and bayonets. There was no violence, and when the final curtain came down, Pat Casey and his night hands were laughing and cheering the loudest.

The play was put on in the Montana Theatre, Central City's first authentic theatre, which opened just a few months before. The Montana was owned by George W. Harrison, a popular man-about-town.

The day before the grand opening, on July 31, 1862, Harrison pumped 35 shots into swaggering Central City boxer Charlie Swits as the latter stepped from the Barnes Pool Hall.

At the murder trial, Harrison's defense was based on the fact he didn't like Swits. The jury didn't either. It did like Harrison, so the theatre owner was acquitted.

Harrison later became a state senator and a publisher in Idaho. The Central City fire of 1874 burned down the Montana theatre.

Central City didn't confine its theatrics to indoors. As hundreds of Gilpin County residents jammed the streets below, Madame Carlisa walked across the main street on a tightrope.

One of the favorite female actresses in early-day Central City was Rose

Haydee, who appeared in Central City's first stage play, the "Cross of Gold," performed in January of 1860.

Every miner in the Central City region worshiped Rose, lovely virginal Rose Haydee. It was sort of a fatherly love. When gambler Tom Evans finally persuaded Rose to elope with him, the whole city was up in arms, and set out to lynch Evans. The murder was prevented when Sheriff Billy Cozens interceded.

Cozens was, perhaps, the major reason Central City never succumbed to the unruly element. Cozens was a fair but hard working sheriff, one of Colorado's best, if not *the* best. He was so dedicated to his job that he had two prisoners chained to his bed posts on his wedding night. The jail was under construction and there was no place else to put them.

Testifying to the relative lack of lawlessness in Central City was a note left on the jailhouse wall by a prisoner just before he escaped. The pensive prisoner said he had to take this way out, he couldn't stand being alone.

Another jail escapee penned the following note on the wall of his cell:

> Perhaps I'm on the land,
> Perhaps I'm on the sea,
> Perhaps I've gone to Brigham Young
> A Mormon for to be.

Central City, then as now, had many distinguished visitors. Perhaps its greatest early visitor was President Grant. No Colorado mining town accorded the colorful figure a more gala welcome. Gold was too common around Central City in those days (1873). So, the city fathers sent up to Caribou for some silver bricks and lined the entrance of the Teller House with them so Grant would walk on pure silver after alighting from the stage.

Grant, earlier, had visited most of the boom areas in Colorado. He traveled by wagon, stage, and white mule. But he said none of the jaunts was more harrowing than his ride from Central City to Golden aboard Billy Opdyke's "hot-rod" stage.

Billy knew every inch of the road and he never lost a second making that trip, flying most of the way. The ride had already scared the wits out of many a distinguished visitor before Grant came along, men like Mark Twain and Horace Greeley.

But the ride was too much for Grant. He told Henry Teller he'd better build a railroad into Central City to save wear and tear on the visitors.

That was when Grant was just a general. The railroad was built when Grant returned as president—when he walked across the silver bricks.

Teller was just one of the many important figures produced by Central City. Teller was a mining man and a railroad man, who later served 29

22

years as a senator. He was called "the grand old man of Colorado" and several early mining towns were named for him.

He was Colorado's first senator, along with Jerome Chaffee, another Central City product.

Henry Wolcott, Central City area milling man, was another Colorado senator and Republican leader. (See Summitville for his battle with Tom Bowen.)

George Pullman got his start here, clearing $150,000 in a short time, not by mining, but by lending money at twenty per cent interest per month. They say he got his ideas for pullman cars from the bunk arrangement in Colorado mining camp cabins.

Another Central City figure was James Belford, called the "redheaded rooster of the Rockies." He was a member of the Colorado territory Supreme Court, was later a Colorado state legislator and helped shape many of the mining laws of the nation.

W. A. Clark, operator of the Bobtail mine near Central City, later became a copper king in Montana and a senator.

Central City was never deserted, although it had its ups and downs. Several old mines have been reopened in recent years and new mills have been built. The mines usually average more than a half-million dollars in precious metals per year. Some uranium has been found here.

The population is increasing and the area now has about 800 year-round residents. It is one of the busiest and most colorful places in the state during the summer season.

GOLD DUST: The Central City fire of 1874 which burned down the Montana Theatre also destroyed most of the business district . . . . near the center of the city is a great yellow mound of mill tailings from the Glory Hole on Quartz Hill . . . . some of Colorado's first mining laws were written here, and were used as models for laws in mining districts throughout the state. The first laws stated that no miner could hold a claim on more than one creek or mountain. A claim had to be worked within ten days in order to keep it. Placer claims were limited to 100-feet square and lode claims were limited to 100 feet in length and 50 feet in width . . . . most of the placer mining gave out about 1864 and the area was threatened with extinction for a short while before good lode claims were found and Professor Hill built his amazing mill (see Black Hawk) . . . . the now-famous "Face on the Barroom Floor" was painted in 1936 by Denver artist and newspaperman Herndon Davis who recited the poem and drew the picture for, and of, lovely sculptress Challis Walker, while the two were attending a Central City summer performance . . . . other than the fire, Central City had other tragedies. The surrounding farm area was almost destroyed by grasshoppers in 1874 and 1875. A diphtheria epidemic in 1879 killed hundreds of residents. Most of the victims were children . . . . the city was snowbound for two weeks in 1913 . . . . the Central City mineral belt extends four miles long and two and one-half miles wide, with Central City at its center. Ten mines in the area produced 60 million dollars by 1903 and all the mines produced 100 million dollars . . . . Central City was platted by William N. Byers, long time editor of the *Rocky*

*Mountain News* . . . . Dougherty's most famous role was that of Skaterer, the mountain thief. When he died of drink in 1865, the Masons buried him and virtually all of Central City attended the funeral. . . . Langrishe not only toured Colorado mining towns, but Montana areas as well. Babcock's three-piece band was a part of Langriche's company. . . . Lillian Gish played the title role of *Camille* in 1932. *Camille* was the first show put on in Central City by Langrishe, on March 16, 1861. . . . Harry Richmond, one of Langrishe's performers, participated in the Sand Creek Massacre and brought back Chief White Antelope's headdress for a stage group. . . . the Teller House was opened in 1872, and was operated by members of the Teller family until 1935 when the Opera House Association took over . . . . the Clear Creek Canyon road from Golden to Central City was dedicated in 1952. It is 18 miles long and cost five million dollars . . . . the Mammoth Vein was considered the richest vein in Gilpin County. It runs west through Quartz Hill and was called "the richest square mile on earth." . . . . much gold, silver, lead, copper and even pitchblende and uranium have been taken out of the Diamond Lil tunnel which almost intersects the Mammoth Vein . . . . the Glory Hole, near the summit of Quartz Hill, is a man-made crater which produced more than four tons of gold. The first mining was done from the top of the hill, using systematic cave-ins to locate the ore . . . . Broadway and Hollywood actress Julie Harris owns the Wolverine mine high above Central City . . . . one of early Central City's well known characters was "Aunt" Clara Brown. Aunt Clara, born in slavery, came to Central City in 1859 and opened up a laundry. By the end of the Civil War she had saved $10,000. She returned to the South and located some 34 relatives that had been sold in bondage, including two of her own children, and brought them all to Colorado . . . . Gregory's first pan yielded four dollars in gold. He panned $60,000 from February to August in 1863. The various claims on the Gregory diggings produced more than sixty million dollars . . . . on discovering gold, Gregory reportedly said: "Now my wife will be a lady and my children will have an education."

## MOUNTAIN CITY

Mountain City, which later became the eastern portion of Central City, was one of the first communities in the Kingdom of Gilpin and boasts many firsts in the Colorado Mountains.

It had the first church sermon in the Central City region—on June 12, 1859. The next January, Mountain City was the scene of the first show in the Colorado Rockies—Hadley Loft's "Cross of Gold." It had the first newspapers in the mountains—*The Rocky Mountain Gold Reporter* and *Mountain City Herald*. It had the first Masonic Temple, and perhaps most important in those days, it had the first saloon, a crude thing—little more than a log bar—where unwashed tin cups were used instead of washed glasses. Credit began the first day, by the way, and some of the bills still aren't paid.

Mountain City was founded near the site of the original Gregory strike in the spring of 1859. It was the first city in the Central City group. Some reports say Central City and Black Hawk were started when Mountain City ran over, and Central City eventually overran Mountain City. Other reports

24

say Central City was simply another camp that outgrew, and eventually absorbed, Mountain City.

During the summer of 1859, Mountain City grew at a fantastic rate. Within weeks there were a large tent hotel, a log theatre, several businesses and saloons, and some 200 tent and cabin residents. By the end of the summer Mountain City took on an air of permanency. Cabins were replacing the remaining tents as nearly 1,000 residents prepared for winter.

Most historians say Mountain City was absorbed by Central City around 1880, but a Mountain City was mentioned by newspapers long after that date . . . as late as 1905. The merger of the two towns must have been a subtle thing . . . too subtle for historians to handle.

## HOOSIER CITY, SPRINGFIELD, QUINCY, GREGORY, GREGORY POINT, EUREKA and DOGTOWN

Seven of the original camps up and down the gulch that sprang up shortly after the Gregory strike.

Hoosier City was apparently the largest and most progressive of these temporary camps. Horace Greeley mentions the camp during his visit to the Central City area. And a story is told of some miners whooping it up at the Hoosier City Hotel—if not the first hotel in the area, at least one of the first.

Eureka was a fast-growing camp in Eureka Gulch about a half-mile west of Central City. The naming of the gulch and camp was another one of the "Eureka! I have found it!" sort of things.

Springfield was in Spring Gulch and Gregory was in the grove where Spring, Nevada and Eureka Creeks came together. The other camps are somewhat obscure, although one source says a pack of dogs used to hang out in Dogtown.

All the camps were within two miles of each other. The camps expanded so rapidly they began running over into other camps. That's when the permanent cities began to take shape.

## BORTONSBURG, HUGHESVILLE and MAMMOTH CITY

Three small camps around Central City and Black Hawk that didn't last very long.

Bortonsburg was located in Illinois Gulch below Central City. It was founded in 1861 when a Colonel Bortons hit paydirt in the gulch. A few foundations remain but a hike is required to see them.

Hughesville was located on Silver Mountain northeast of Black Hawk. A silver strike in the 70's brought new excitement to the Central City area. The town grew around the Hard Money mine located on property owned by Patrick Hughes.

Mammoth City was a small camp on Mammoth Hill south of Central City. Two tunnels, the German and the Centennial, were built into the hill.

## NEVADAVILLE (Nevada, Nevada City, Bald Mountain)

In 1859-60, when much of the population of this section lived in one steady stream through the mining area, a large part of these miners were concentrated along Nevada Gulch two or three miles above the site of Central City.

The camp that emerged was named Nevada City for the gold camp in California. The post office department, fearing confusion with the other city, changed the name, and Nevadaville was finally accepted by both the residents and the post office.

During those early, confusing years in the area, Nevadaville threatened to be *the* camp in the district. The population topped the 1,000 mark and scores of prosperous businesses lined the gulch. Nevadaville boasted one of the first schools in the area, attended by some 150 students.

When residents in one section of the city threatened to secede and form their own community, the newly-elected officials were quickly arrested and charged with "secession."

Contrary to some histories of the area, Nevadaville never faded completely until recent years. It had its ups and downs, however. It flourished in the early 60's, again in the late 70's, was almost emptied by the panic of '93, but renewed activity in the late 90's brought new prosperity and a peak population of 1,200.

There was some activity here just before the first World War and again in the 30's. But Nevadaville has been a ghost since World War II. Many cabins remain, some of them occupied. The old cemetery that served Nevadaville and Black Hawk is visible, full of headstones and weeds.

During its day, Nevadaville was the scene of much of the winter sports activities in the Central City area. The snow run between Nevadaville and Black Hawk, dropping 500 feet in two miles, was famous. The run was in almost continuous use for sleds and snowshoes, similar to present-day skis.

The Glory Hole has always been a tourist attraction, and still is. The mining hole is more than 300 feet deep in spots and is 1,000 feet long.

The California mine here had the deepest shaft of any mine in the area—2,230 feet.

GOLD DUST: Lack of water, and its high, uneven terrain were the two main reasons Nevadaville never achieved the prominence of Central City . . . . but the early citizens were positive their city would be tops in the area. They built many of their buildings in brick, including a city hall . . . . "Nevada" is Spanish for snowclad or snowy land . . . . Nevadaville had several quartz mills . . . . Central City character Pat Casey had a mine here . . . . in addition to its winter sports activity, N͏evadaville was noted for its rock-drilling contests and had some of the best drille͏ in the

26

region . . . . pitchblende, from which radium is extracted, has been mined here in recent years.

## MISSOURI FLATS (Missouri City)

High above Central City looking down on the scene below is a lonely tombstone. It says:

Clara A.
Dau. of F.S. and D.F. Dulaney
Died July 5, 1865
Aged 1 yr 12 days

The tombstone marks the remains of Clara A . . . . and Missouri Flats.

Missouri Flats roared into being in 1860, a short distance southwest of Central City. Missouri Flats closely rivaled Central City and Black Hawk, and was once considered as a possible county seat.

But Missouri Flats couldn't keep up the pace. The city fathers petitioned the Leavenworth and Pikes Peak Stage and Express Company to make Missouri Flats a stage station. Petition denied.

Central City was a more convenient location. Water and transportation came easier there. One by one the residents of Missouri Flats drifted down the hill . . . . and gave up the ghost.

## BLACK HAWK

Black Hawk takes its place among Colorado's leading mining towns, not so much for the mining done here, but for its mill.

Colorado's hard-rock mining industry was dying on its feet for lack of a smelter. The makeshift smelters built before 1867 could only handle the best ores, and not too effectively at that. Most ores had to be shipped great distances—as far away as England—eating up much of the profit. Lower grade ores were not worth the effort at all.

Professor Nathaniel P. Hill of Brown University came to Colorado in 1864. He saw the problem and set out to conquer it.

The professor, after studying the milling methods in the east and in Europe, built the Boston-Colorado smelter, employing the latest milling methods known at the time.

The smelter was an immediate success, and the flourishing Colorado mining industry was back in business again. The mill worked night and day processing the ores for the "Kingdom of Gilpin" and the Boulder area. Within a short time, mills modeled after the Boston-American were built in boom areas throughout the state.

Hill had saved the hard-rock mining industry in Colorado and he made a fortune besides. He later built the fabulous Argo Mill near Denver, using much of the machinery and material from the original smelter. In addition,

27

Professor Hill became a leading figure in early Colorado history, topping off his great career as one of the state's first senators.

The smelter made Black Hawk a key city in Colorado's early boom. The first narrow gauge railroad, the Colorado Central, meandered up Clear Creek from Denver to Black Hawk in 1872, making the twin city to Central City a great shipping center for a short time.

Shortly after the Colorado Central spun its way up to Black Hawk, one of the company's two engines slid into Clear Creek. The company went broke trying to fish the engine out. The Black Hawk railroad station was washed away by a flood in 1936.

The first strike in the area, the Gregory strike, made May 6, 1859, was located midway between Black Hawk and Central City. Many of the subsequent, and best, strikes were made near Black Hawk. Tents, huts, and rude cabins blanketed the region.

The Lee brothers and a man named Judd laid out the city, stretching it along Clear Creek Canyon. They named the site Black Hawk for the famous Indian chief. More than 2,000 persons lived here during the 60's. Had not the canyon been so narrow, Black Hawk may well have surpassed Central City. As it was, it rivaled Central City for several years. It still owns an identity of its own.

Black Hawk had many other "firsts" in the Colorado Mountains. In addition to the mill, the first mining machinery foundry in Colorado was established here by the Hendrie Brothers. Black Hawk also had the first cemetery in the state, on Dory Hill.

Black Hawk was a rip-roaring town, with its share of all-night gambling and "girlie" dens. It was noted for its rock-drilling and wrestling contests, and it shared the winter sports spotlight with Nevadaville. The area's most popular ski (snowshoe) and sled run connected the two cities.

One of the first churches in the state was built here in 1863.

Geologists say there are still valuable deposits in the Black Hawk region. Some old mines have been opened and new mills have been built in recent years. In addition, Black Hawk, with its famed Gingerbread House, is sharing some of the latter-day tourist glory of Central City.

GOLD DUST: The site of the Gregory strike is marked by a monument between Black Hawk and Central City. Gregory mined $900 worth of gold from the strike before selling his claim for $21,000. His claim became one of the richest in the state . . . . between Black Hawk and Central City is a sharp promontory named Casey's point, named for the notorious Central City character Pat Casey (see Central City), who came to the Kingdom of Gilpin as a roustabout, struck a rich lode and became a millionaire. He was illiterate and crude, and many stories have been told about him. One of the most popular was his statement: "I use up tin pencils a day and thin don't get half through me business." Pat Casey couldn't write . . . . among the most celebrated lodes was the Bobtail, so named because the first ore was hauled to the sluices by a bob-tailed ox, harnessed to a forked limb over which raw hide was stretched . . . . some early records list a small camp named *YANKEE BAR* on the hills above Black Hawk. Its exact location and any history about the camp have been completely obscured by time.

## RUSSELL GULCH

Scene of the second discovery by William Green Russell, in the spring of 1859.

Before the summer was over, nearly 1,000 prospectors were here and gold production averaged $35,000 a week.

During the winter, the residents, unable to do much mining and prospecting, organized the town and the district, drawing up some of the first mining laws in the territory. They were progressive laws, too. Women had the same rights as men, and only children under ten were prohibited from holding claims.

When spring came the following year, so did hundreds more fortune seekers. Soon, Russell Gulch was bulging with 2,500 citizens. A federal hall, brick school house, a church, and dozens of business houses were built.

But most of the gold was gone in four short years, although some mining continued for another twenty years, and off and on since. Some uranium was found here in the 20's, but was almost neglected until recent years. There were several metals mined during the 20's and 30's and the population topped 100 much of the time.

Russell Gulch is noted for its gala Fourth of July celebration during its first year (1859). The Fourth was an explosive holiday in those days, and Russell Gulch outdid itself. Center of the celebration was a giant flag, made from overalls and red flannels.

Russell left the area in 1862 to join the Confederate Army. He was arrested in Santa Fe, but soon released. He returned to Colorado and remained until 1875 when he joined the Cherokees in Oklahoma. His wife was a Cherokee squaw.

Russell Gulch became notorious during prohibition days as many bootleggers hid away in the mines, using some of the deserted mine shafts as warehouses for their merchandise.

Much of Russell Gulch remains.

## LAKE GULCH

The most remembered thing about Lake Gulch was its hermit, called, strangely enough, the Hermit of Lake Gulch.

Nobody knew much about him, and he apparently liked it that way. He usually wasn't around when anyone came near his crude cabin.

About the only contact he had with the outside world was his rare visits into town to pick up supplies.

The story is told of one of his trips to Idaho Springs during World War II. He ordered his food supplies and slapped the cash down on the counter.

The grocer said ration stamps were needed for some of the food. No ration stamps, no food!

The Hermit didn't know anything about ration stamps, but it didn't throw him. He merely pulled out his gun, picked up his groceries, paid the tab and walked out of the store, back up to Lake Gulch.

Lake Gulch's history paralleled that of Missouri Flats. It started about 1860, flourished for a few short years, then lost out to Central City.

Jerome Chaffee, one of Colorado's first senators, had interests here. He was a partner of Eben Smith, who also became a prominent Coloradan, hitting it richer in the Aspen boom.

Chaffee owned the Lake House, overlooking the lake at the head of the gulch. The lodge was a favorite boating and party rendezvous for the elite of Central City.

About the two best mines in the Lake Gulch region were the Empress and the Williams.

All that remains of Lake Gulch is an old brick building up a steep hill. It was once a school house but is now a private home.

## II. COLORADO'S FABULOUS FAILURE

Eighty years ago, before there was magic machinery to bore through mountains and before there were government millions for such a project, the entire nation and much of Europe were excited over the possibilities of building a tunnel under the Continental Divide.

More than ten thousand people from Maine to California and in England and France invested their dollars in the plan. When the money ran low, many of them dug down into their pockets and shelled out some more. Some of the nation's top engineers, mineralogists, civic leaders and political figures were involved in the project.

And they weren't timid in those days about rolling up their sleeves and pitching into such a momentous task. They bored nearly a third of the way through the mountain. Only after about twenty years of trying and after untold millions had been spent did they abandon the job.

This enthusiasm, this belief that the impossible task (for that time) could be done was primarily generated by one man, one of the most talked-about men of his day and certainly one of Colorado's most colossal characters.

Yet few people today recall the name Mark M. (Brick) Pomeroy, Colorado's fabulous failure.

Yes, Brick Pomeroy was a failure, not just once, but time after time. He was the all-time champion of lost causes. It was said at the time that the only honest dollar he ever made in his life was in newspaper work. When he devoted his talents exclusively to journalism he was the best in the country. The first issue of the newspaper he put out in Denver enjoyed greater sales than the combined circulation of every other newspaper in the state. Brick Pomeroy wasn't satisfied. He began branching out, and his newspaper failed too . . . . in just a few short months.

Brick Pomeroy was not impressive in appearance. He was of average height (5′ 9″ tall), slightly stocky, a little handsomer than most. He wore a handlebar moustache much of the time, but then almost everybody did. Some say he was a mental giant; others say that's going too far. His most notable characteristics were that he was a dynamo of enthusiasm, he had the gift of gab, and an abundance of ideas, big ideas. He was eccentric in some ways. He didn't drink or smoke and refused to hire men who did. He wasn't a religious man, yet he spent thousands of dollars the last years of his life trying to win his way into heaven through any spiritualist that came along. About his only personal vice—unless over-enthusiasm can be called a vice—was women. He went through two torrid marriages and several affairs before he found his true love.

31

Brick was born in Elmira, New York, in 1833. He was raised on a farm by relatives after his parents died when he was two. He entered journalism through the back door . . . as a printer. His first newspaper was the *New York Sun*. It wasn't a financial success but it did give Brick a chance to work the kinks out of his journalistic talents. In 1860, he and a partner started the LaCrosse, Wisconsin, *Weekly Democrat*.

When the Civil War broke out, Brick became one of the most spirited and articulate "copperheads" in the north. So pointed was his criticism of President Lincoln, his administration and the Civil War, that a Union soldier, home on leave, stormed into Brick's office one day—gun in hand—with the expressed intent of ridding the world of a "traitor." After two hours of quiet talk behind closed doors, Brick and the soldier emerged from the office arm in arm and smiling. The soldier became a devoted friend of the man he had intended to kill.

The *Democrat* was under constant fire during the Civil War. It stirred up much resentment and had its tussles with Dame Fortune, but by 1868 it was sailing smoothly with a circulation of more than 100,000. Brick, however, was never one to be content with one major undertaking—a characteristic he displayed throughout his life, and, perhaps, the reason for his being a failure.

That same year—in 1868—he began publication of the *New York Democrat* and the *Pomeroy Democrat*, a weekly, published in New York and later in Chicago.

During this period he also began his career as a lecturer and after-dinner speaker. In 1867, Brick published a book called *Sense*. It was merely a series of conversations between a boy and his father, but they expressed Brick's liberal, sometimes radical, viewpoints on nearly every aspect of life. Despite its being panned severely by conservative newspapers throughout the country, the book was an immediate success. Enough so that Brick felt compelled to publish a second book, *Nonsense*, that same year. Within the next few years he came out with *Gold Dust* (1871), *Brick Dust* (1871) and *Home Harmonies* (1876). His books were mostly random essays on this and that, many of which he lifted from the columns of his newspapers. All were panned by conservative critics. All were successful.

The man was already nationally known when he organized an "anti-bond greenback" group. In four years he established some 8,000 clubs throughout the country and distributed millions of circulars and documents conveying liberal ideas on finance and the legal power and management of financial affairs by government. The campaign made for him hundreds of bitter enemies but thousands of ardent followers.

Brick was already spread pretty thin. Many of his far-flung enterprises were beginning to suffer from lack of attention. This would be a time most

Ruins of Nevadaville including the old city hall. *U. S. Forest Service photo.*

Blackhawk at the turn of the century. Picture looks south. *U. S. Geological Survey photo.*

The old mine at Lamartine, one of the more difficult towns to get to. The town is located just over the hill, to the south. *Photo by Jim Ward.*

Last of Waldorf, nestled high above Georgetown at the foot of once-famous Argentine Pass.

New look to old Idaho Springs, showing the new bypass. Once a great mining and milling town, Idaho Springs is now a popular resort town. Note the famous Argo mill at right-center of photo. *Colorado State Highway Department photo.*

The Maxwell House in Georgetown, one of the ten most outstanding examples of Victorian architecture in the nation. The house received its bright colors during a recent town-painting crusade by a group of Denver citizens.

High bridge on the Georgetown Loop. Countless thousands thrilled to the ride over the years. *State Historical Society of Colorado photo.*

Apex, one of the most delightful mining camps in Colorado during the last years of the last century. The taller building near the center was the famous Apex Dance Hall.

Colorful Baltimore. Two of the many relics of yesteryear.

The Snowshoe Itinerant, Father John L. Dyer. *State Historical Society of Colorado.*

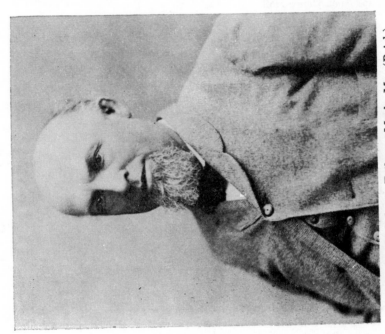

Colorado's Fabulous Failure, Mark M. (Brick) Pomeroy. *Denver Public Library Western Collection.*

Eldora shortly after the turn of the century. Picture looks west. *U. S. Geological Survey photo.*

Caribou in 1886, the town where the winds were born. *State Historical Society photo.*

Tungsten in 1917, during its boom. Tungsten Company Production Mill at left rear and Vasco mill at right. Vasco workings can be seen on hillside. *U. S. Geological Survey.*

Fashionable house in Gold Dust, just down the gulch from Perigo.

successful men might pause to recoup their footing. Brick saw it as a time to spread out. He sold his *Weekly Democrat*, whose circulation had begun to lag, and came to Denver in 1879. He launched his Colorado career by publishing *The Great West*, a weekly newspaper. Before the first issue was off the press there were 47,000 subscribers, more than the combined circulations of every other newspaper in Colorado. Some say Colorado conservative forces united to nip this upstart liberal in the bud. Others claim Denver postmaster William N. Byers merely couldn't believe Brick's newspaper had such a following and that it was all some promotional stunt. Whatever the reason, Byers refused to let *The Great West* enter the mails. Brick took the news calmly. He simply wired a friend in the postoffice department in Washington. Byers got his comeuppance by return wire, and *The Great West* was sent far and wide.

During its first few months, the newspaper enjoyed unprecedented popularity. Brick's crusades were the talk of the Rockies. *The Great West* had the widest readership of any newspaper in the west. Anxious readers would wait in line on Saturday to get the paper as it hit the newsstands.

Even Brick's enemies admitted the man's journalistic genius. Years later, *The Denver Republican* said that for caustic wit and colorful writing Brick couldn't be matched. Pomeroy championed the little people. He fought their battles. His newspaper career was marked by one continuous crusade against graft and corruption in government. His sparring partners were always men in high places, and Brick usually came out on top. His newspaper was the ideal of smaller liberal publications, and they often joined in Brick's crusades.

As a boss, Brick couldn't be matched in this respect either. He always treated his workers fairly, like a father. He paid the highest wages in town and insisted on a union shop—at a time when "union" was still a naughty word.

Why, then, did *The Great West* fail? Well, sir, that's a good question, a darned good question . . . because that's where our story begins.

*The Great West* was still going strong when Brick started to get these other ideas. He opened another office in Denver to handle and promote the many schemes that he had. Before long his newspaper had degenerated into little more than a stock report and come-on for Brick's other business ventures. The circulation fell off, until it was down to 5,000. Within months of its birth, it died quietly.

Brick, however was busy, busy, busy.

The Atlantic-Pacific Tunnel, as it was called at the time, was just one of Brick's far-flung business adventures. A short list of his promotional enterprises, his first few years in Denver:

41

Idella Tunnel Company
Black Hawk Mining and Milling Company
Buckeye Mining Company
Greater Gold Belt Tunnel Company
Climax Mining Company
Great West Mining and Milling Company
Georgetown Brick Manufacturing Company
Kaloo Powder Company
Flemming Electric Drill Company
Working Men's Prospecting Company
Highlander Mining Company
Len A Wee Tunnel Company

Although many of his enterprises dealt with some phase of mining or milling, Brick didn't limit himself to any special field. He promoted a Denver transportation company, an artesian water company, and a shipping firm. He was ready to manufacture just about any new gimmick anyone brought along. He liked chicken, so he bought the largest poultry farm in Colorado at the time.

Brick was a great one for brick. They say that's how he got his nickname. In fact, oldtimers say he was called "Brick" because he built the first all-brick house in Denver. Earlier press notices show, however, that he was called Brick before he came to Denver, and he didn't build the first all-brick house in Denver. Some buildings and a few houses made use of brick, for the foundations and such, but brownstone was the thing in those days.

Not for old Brick. He had ox-cart after ox-cart of bricks shipped in from Omaha. He spared no expense in the construction of his "castle" (on what would now be 37th and Federal Boulevard). The house even had a theatre in the attic, complete with dressing rooms and drop curtains. All told, he spent more than $65,000 building the house, equivalent to a few hundred thousand at today's prices. It was considered one of the finest homes in Denver—if not *the* finest.

That's why it was called "Pomeroy's Folly." He spent so much money on it, took such pains to have everything just right. And then he only lived in it for a few months.

For his most grandiose undertaking was just getting under way.

The Atlanic-Pacific Tunnel, as the giant project was called, probably wasn't Brick's idea. Even then people knew it was needed, but it was more or less considered a far-off idea, something they might see in the future— that is, if they lived long enough. This kind of situation was Brick's meat. Now was as good a time as any to old Brick. Once he latched on to the idea, there was no stopping it, and under Brick's able guidance, half the world was caught up in the momentum.

The plan was to bore through Gray's Peak near Georgetown, thought to be the narrowest point in the front range. The tunnel was to be 25,200 feet long, and large enough for a train to travel through. The tunnel would slice one hundred miles off the traveling distance between Denver and Leadville, Colorado's second city, and three hundred railroad miles from the distance between Denver and Salt Lake City. The tunnel was also a mining enterprise. It was expected to cut through 200 "known" fissures.

Newspapers from San Francisco to Long Island trumpeted the possibility. One New York newspaper called the plan "the most stupendous mining enterprise in the world." Another paper called it "the most spectacular tunnel plan of all time."

Brick journeyed to London, then the financial capital of the world, to win support for the plan. He got some there. But the main body of support came from Mr. and Mrs. America, from Maine to California, from every state where Brick's tantalizing circulars were distributed. The Atlantic and Pacific Tunnel Company sold shares to the public at $2.50 each, and the company couldn't print them up fast enough. Some ten thousand people in every state in the union, and in England and France, dug into their pockets to help build the Colorado tunnel. The amount of money accumulated through the sale of stock has been estimated at from two to four million dollars.

Said one journal: "Never in the history of finance was there so large an issue of stock for any one enterprise."

Brick was made president of the Atlantic-Pacific Company in 1890, and he set up his offices in New York. Some say he moved to New York because he was already beginning to be plagued by his business failures in Denver. Brick indicated, however, that since the tunnel was a nation wide, and even an international, enterprise, New York would be more convenient to all the stock holders.

Anyhow, work on the tunnel got off to a great start. They started drilling on both sides of the divide. They did find some good ore on the way. By 1892, workers had pushed a nine-by-ten shaft nearly 4,000 feet into the mountain from the east side and 1,400 feet from the west.

But work was already beginning to bog down. There were many technical difficulties, and the money problem was starting to show through. The financial panic of 1893 stopped work on the tunnel altogether, and marked the beginning of the end for Brick Pomeroy—who, by the way, had whiled away his spare time in New York by publishing a news monthly, *Advance Thought*.

Some alert, or nosey, citizens began to wonder where all the money invested in the tunnel had gone. A stockholder in Denver asked to see the books. Brick refused. The Denver party took it to court and the court demanded that Brick show the books. Brick refused—New York was a long ways away. Brick was indicted for malfeasance in office by the Colorado Grand Jury. Extradition apparently wasn't worth it in those days. Brick wasn't brought back to Denver—he came of his own free will. It was months later, but the indictment was still waiting for him. Why he came back in the face of the indictment no one is quite sure, but we do know Brick wasn't afraid of anything or anybody. The case never came to court. The indictment may still be tucked away in some little pigeon-hole in the state house. They say there were too many big people, politicians and civic leaders, involved in the tunnel affair. They didn't want it all brought out in a public trial. Anyhow, many of the witnesses weren't around.

However, Pomeroy did have to sell his house and all of his holdings to help cover his backruptcy expenses. This only covered a small portion of the debts Brick Pomeroy had accumulated. Suits by stockholders began to pile up. Brick Pomeroy was a broken man. His enthusiasm had deserted him. He died in Brooklyn in 1896. His faithful wife, Emma, seven months pregnant, was by his side.

Although forgotten now, Brick Pomeroy was subject of debate long after his death. Despite the many lawsuits brought against him and despite a few off-hand accusations that Brick was a scalawag who pocketed the investor's money, all of his projects were legitimate business enterprises. It has not been proved otherwise. Virtually all of his ventures failed, quietly, ignobly, to be replaced by others. His investors never made a dime on their investments. Yet, many of them dug down into their pockets and shelled out for one of Brick's schemes after another.

It doesn't seem reasonable that Brick could be dishonest. A dishonest promoter would be wary of others' schemes. Not Brick. He was the softest touch in Denver, New York, or wherever he was. His office was the busiest place in town. A steady stream of people, from top state officials down to the newsboy on the corner, paraded through his office door. Brick heard them all. He fell for just about every hard luck story and far-fetched scheme that came along. They say that Brick grubstaked scores of prospectors. Many of them located some of the best mines in Colorado. Brick didn't know about it. As far as he knew, he was never attached to a well-paying mine in his life. It would have been out of character.

Through all his enterprises, whether investing himself or attracting investments from others, Brick was a top source of Colorado's economy. Said the once-critical *Denver Republican* shortly after Brick's death:

"It is safe to say that no man ever brought more money into Colorado or scattered it more broadcast over the state."

Brick remained in the headlines for several years after his death, as his fellow men attempted to explain his failures. They said Brick spread himself too thin, even for a man of such tremendous capacity. They say he was born too soon, the world was unprepared for such advanced ideas. All the newspapers, even those that had been opposed to him and his ideas while he was alive, said what a great man he could have been.

Another era had ended with Brick's death, an era of enthusiasm, in a world lacking enthusiasm. The millions upon millions of dollars that passed through Brick's hands have returned to dust. Nobody now is any richer or any poorer because of it. Brick himself is now dust. The world, for a while, was a slightly more exciting place for his having been on it. But the excitement is passed. Time has covered over the tracks Brick Pomeroy made through the pages of history.

His palatial home, once the finest in Denver, is no more. It was a private home and showplace for a few years, and then served as an orphanage. In 1935, it was torn down to make room for a "modern" dwelling—and a service station. Just a few weeks before it was destroyed, Brick's daughter, Mrs. Douglas W. Card, who was born a couple of months after her father's death, saw the house for the first time while attending a convention in Denver.

Time, dirt, underbrush and dust have obscured the openings of the incompleted Atlantic-Pacific Tunnel. The project wasn't abandoned for several years after Pomeroy's death. For several more years after it was abandoned, certain parties attempted to get the project going again. But they lacked Pomeroy's enthusiasm. Some still haven't given up hope of a tunnel through the heart of the Continental Divide.

In 1896, after work on the Atlantic-Pacific had been halted for three years, it was taken up again. The second attempt sputtered and died. In 1905, the Denver and Salt Lake Railroad formed a new corporation, sold 100,000 shares of stock. They bored a few thousand more feet into the mountain. Then work stopped completely.

The tunnel has became mining property.

There were those who kept hoping, however. Said the *Mountain States Monitor* a few years later:

"It is believed that 1923 will see the beginning of the work that will justify the hopes and result in the completion of the plans that Brick Pomeroy and David H. Moffat (promoter of the Moffat Tunnel) carried with them to the great divide which they have crossed. Mankind would make slow progress without men of this type."

## FROM GEORGETOWN TO APEX

Georgetown (Elizabethtown)
Silver Plume
Brownsville
Pomeroyville (not on map)
Silver Dale
Bakerville and Graymont (Graymount)
Sidneyville
Waldorf
Santiago
Hill City (west of map)
Empire (Valley City, Union City)
North Empire and Empire Station (Empire Junction)
Lawson
Silver Creek
Red Elephant
Downieville (Downeyville)
Dumont (Mill City)
Idaho Springs (Idaho, Idaho Bar, Idaho City, Jackson's Diggings,
    Payne's Bar, Sacramento)
Spanish Bar
Lamartine
Freeland
Bonito
Fall River
Alice
Silver City
Yankee (Yankee Hill)
Apex
American City and Nugget

*And Then There Were* . . . . Ofer (Ophir), Green Lake, Yankee Bar (not on map),
Twelve Mile (not on map), Pine Creek (not on map), Elk Park, Kingston, Pile Hill,
Ninety-four and Magnet (Magnet Park).

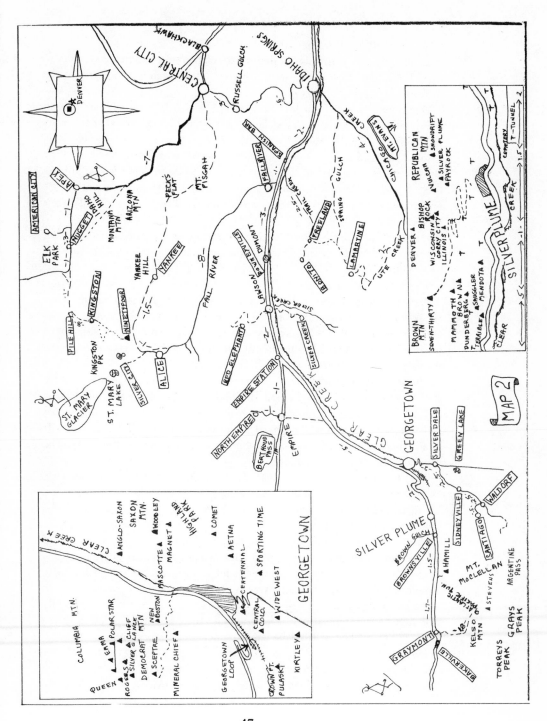

47

## GEORGETOWN (Elizabethtown)

Louis Dupuy was, without a doubt, one of the most unique characters in early Colorado. He was *the* figure of Georgetown. He set the tone of the distinct personality of this city.

Dupuy told so many stories of his background it is impossible to give an accurate account. It is believed he deserted the French Army, then, later, the American Army. He did many things on his way across the country, before he turned up as a miner in the thriving city of Georgetown.

They say he was injured in a mine accident while saving a fellow miner's life. A hero, but unable to work again as a miner, Dupuy started a store on the money collected for him by other miners. The store eventually grew into a hotel.

Dupuy finally found his calling in the hotel business. Under his stern but unpredictable guidance, his hotel became the center of Georgetown and the talk of the nation.

The hotel, of course, was the Hotel de Paris.

A perfectionist, Dupuy insisted on the best in furnishings, food and wine. He is called the father of Domestic Science in the United States. It was not a haphazard title. Dr. James Russell of Columbia University began the first course in the field shortly after visiting Hotel de Paris and studying the science under the old master, Louis Dupuy.

The incongruities in Dupuy's character added to the lustre of his hotel. He hated women and most men. He insisted on decorum and good taste. But his moral beliefs seldom conformed with those of the day. He would rather let a room to a well-behaved harlot than a dowdy, ill-mannered wife of a carbonate king. He was known for turning away or evicting those who couldn't live up to his standards.

They say he loved children best of all people. Men were to argue with. He loved to argue—any subject, any side, just for the sake of an argument. He loved poetry and was the father of philosophy in Georgetown. His philosophic gems, although seldom penetrating, were at least different.

Dupuy refused to pay taxes. In fact, he boasted of keeping a loaded shotgun handy to shoot anyone who attempted to collect taxes from him.

The final incongruity in his character concerned his friendship with Madame Galet. Although an avowed woman-hater, he permitted her to move in on his life and dominate it. Although he frequently argued loudly with her, he worshipped her. She gradually took over the operation of the hotel. When he died in 1900, he left the hotel—lock, stock and rare wines— to her.

In its heyday, under Dupuy, the top figures of the day, including General Ulysses S. Grant, stayed at the hotel and were thrilled at the exquisite cuisine and rare wines.

Hotel de Paris was the social center of Georgetown, and the main reason for the aristocratic name Georgetown had among Colorado mining camps. It had its boisterous side, its roaring red light district, its murders. But all this was overshadowed by a queenliness, distinct from any other city in Colorado.

Another important figure in early Georgetown was William A. Hamill, mine owner, lawyer, brigadier-general in the state militia, and Colorado political and civic leader.

Hamill purchased the Watson House in 1872 for only $4,500. After that, Hamill spared no expense in developing the property until it became one of the most luxurious homes in the state. Highlights of the house, still standing, include diamond dust mirrors; gold, silver and camel's hair wallpaper; carrara marble and onyx fireplaces; walnut and maple woodwork; curved glass conservatory, and even an elegant out-house.

The house is now the Alpine Lodge.

The first buildings displayed a feeling of permanence. Their architecture, although of different schools, was of high taste. This personality is alive today in the brightly-colored, beautifully situated city of Georgetown.

But it always was a mining town. Before Leadville appeared on the scene, Georgetown was the most important silver mining town in Colorado. It has remained, even after Leadville, one of the richest mining towns in the state. It has been estimated, as much as 200 million dollars worth of precious metals have been mined from the hills around Georgetown.

They say George Griffith, tired from prospecting, laid down in the shade to rest. Some say he discovered rich ore when he used a rock to brace himself as he got up. Part of the rock broke off, uncovering rich ore. Others say Griffith merely noticed evidence of pay dirt as he rested on the ground. At any rate, we know he discovered pay dirt . . . and he was tired.

That was in 1859, when the Pikes Peak gold rush was in full swing. But most of the 59'ers were centered around Central City. Not many of them had gone as far into the mountains as George Griffith.

Griffith went back for help. He returned to the spot with four others. The five dug out $500 in ore in a short time. They then set up shop and called the site Georgetown for George Griffith.

Winter came. The party returned to civilization. Griffin came back to Georgetown in 1860 with his wife, brother and father. Others followed. Georgetown began to show signs of life.

But the ore was poor in gold. It had plenty of silver, but silver wasn't worth nearly so much as gold—unless one found enough to make it worth while. The prospectors returned, bringing others with them.

By the mid-60's, more than 2,000 lived in the area. They lived in two camps. The other one was named Elizabethtown for George's sister. In

49

1866, the area was granted a post office and the camps merged. They needed a name. George magnanimously wanted the merged camps to be called Elizabethtown, but he was outvoted. Georgetown it was.

George set a precedent by bringing in his family early. Unlike most other mining camps, families became an integral part of Georgetown from the beginning. They used the natural beauty of the area, leaving the trees where they were. Good, substantial houses were built, embodying the latest of eastern architecture. Churches and schools were put up early.

But no mining camp could keep out the other element. Georgetown was as rough a town as any.

They laid out a cemetery and were anxious to get it going. But nobody condescended to die. So they had to hang a man.

Georgetown had one of the most notorious "gaming" streets in the state— Brownell Street. The street had five high-class parlor houses and a bevy of saloons and "gambling hells."

Mollie Dean and Mattie Estes were the leading madams. Mollie was murdered by her jealous lover after she stepped out with another man. Another madam, Jenny Aiken, was burned to death when her parlor house burned down. Shortly before, a miner had been shot to death in her "shop." Another miner was shot and killed in a jealous argument over a shady lady.

A man who couldn't read opened up a saloon. He hired a sign-painter to paint a sign. The sign painter didn't like the saloon keeper so he painted the sign to read: "We sell the worst whiskey, wine and cigars." But the plan backfired. The sign attracted so much patronage, the saloon keeper left it up, even after he found out what it meant.

There were other social activities.

McClellan Hall, used for all sorts of meetings, was built in 1867. Two years later, the Opera House went up. It was one of the best in the territory and played many big names before it burned down in 1892. It used to stand next to the Hotel de Paris and is now a vacant lot.

Georgetown had one of the classiest fire-fighting brigades in the state. It took the state championship in 1877 and 1879, and placed high in the competition for several years. Georgetown played host to the state tournament in 1888.

Georgetown declined with the decline in silver prices in the 90's, but kept going on its gold and other metals. It's been producing through the years. Business picked up with the increase in silver and gold prices in the 1930's.

A couple of coats of brightly-colored new paint have been slapped on the city in recenty years. And Georgetown is experiencing its greatest tourist boom. It's still a beautiful and proud town, and certainly an interesting one. She's a prim and proper old lady waiting for visitors, anxious to tell the stories of her past.

50

One of Georgetown's most famous attractions was the fabulous George-town loop. It was one of the most daring and difficult railroad projects in the state, and during its heyday as many as seven trains a day carried tourists back and forth between Georgetown and Silver Plume. The trip was popular not only for the beautiful scenery but also for the thrill of making the Loop.

The Union Pacific began construction of the Loop in 1882, under the supervision of Robert Blickensderfer. The narrow gauge road ran about four and a half miles between Georgetown and Silver Plume, climbing 365 feet between the towns. There were 14 curves with a curvature of 18 degrees or more. Some of the curves were almost directly over similar curves below. The curves were constructed in a spiral fashion to enable the train to gain momentum for the steep grades on the straightaways. It was the closest thing Colorado had to a roller coaster for several years.

Amid much clamor for and against, the Loop was dismantled in 1939; the tracks were torn up and used in the nearby mines for supports. The scar of the famed railroad run is still visible.

GOLD DUST: Georgetown was called "the Silver Queen of the Rockies" as opposed to Leadville, the Silver King . . . . the first Episcopal church in the state was built here in 1867. It blew down the same year, but was rebuilt and is still standing. Two other early-day churches are still standing . . . . as part of its unique character, rockers were installed on the jury chairs in the courthouse, so those on jury duty could withstand the experience in the most comfortable fashion . . . . General Grant made three visits to Georgetown . . . . Georgetown is a favorite rendezvous for skiers . . . . the peak population of Georgetown has been estimated as high as 25,000 to 30,000 during the mid 70's.

## SILVER PLUME

The story goes that Owen Feenan discovered the Pelican lode way back in 1868.

He didn't patent the claim. He kept it a secret. But a few months later he became deathly ill, and, on what he thought was his death-bed, he told two friends of his rich strike a few miles above Georgetown.

In 1871, when Feenan was able to climb out of his "death-bed" and return to work, he found his claim was working full force and a camp had arisen nearby.

The camp, of course, was Silver Plume. Feenan's "friends" had taken over the Pelican and Feenan had been cut out entirely.

The Pelican and the Dives were the two big mines of Silver Plume. The two apparently tapped the same vein. Therein was the problem.

The early history of Silver Plume is rife with the squabbles between the two mines. At one time there were more than twenty suits and counter-suits pending between the two mining companies. It almost ended in a shooting war. In fact, a man called Snider, owner of the Pelican, was shot and killed by a Dives employee in 1875. In the courtroom, the judge was forced to check the guns of all the participants and he kept a gun handy on his bench.

The Pelican finally won out. But the Dives had the last word. Before ending work on the vein, miners in a sad procession came out of the Dives carrying six coffins, said to contain the bodies of Dives miners killed in a mine accident. The coffins were particuarly heavy. They contained high grade ore.

Hamill eventually took over ownership of the Pelican. He purchased the Dives property for $50,000. A short time later he sold the Pelican-Dives for five million dollars and became the richest man in the region.

There were other mines around, good mines. Clifford Griffin, the Silver Plume character, owned and operated the Seven-Thirty mine. He came to Colorado to forget his sweetheart who died the night before their scheduled wedding. Griffin kept to himself. He owned a cabin high on the mountain above Silver Plume and spent the evenings playing a wistful tune on his fiddle. On clear nights, the lonesome music could be heard in the town below. He eventually commited suicide.

As the mines poured forth, Silver Plume thrived. It was a bustling city during the 70's, when more than 2,000 persons lived here. There were a theatre, two churches, a schoolhouse, post office and several stores.

Stages connected the city with Georgetown to the east, and Graymont and Bakerville to the west. Then, in 1877, the railroad came to town. A few years later the famous Georgetown Loop was constructed nearby, lending importance to Silver Plume.

In addition to the millions in silver, gold, lead, zinc and copper mined here, high-quality granite was quarried near Silver Plume. The granite is used for most state historical markers.

Silver Plume slowly faded through the years. It never became a complete ghost, although it hovered on the brink several times.

Many of the old buildings are gone. The Odd Fellows club, an important social center in early Silver Plume, was destroyed in a mud slide and never rebuilt.

However, the buildings that are left, many of which are occupied, give a representative picture of a typical early-day mining town in Colorado.

Mining is still carried on nearby.

GOLD DUST: A student of place names could run riot in Silver Plume. There are no less than five versions of how the name came to be. Some say it was named after an Indian; others say it took the name of a mine; still others claim it was named for James G. Blaine, former candidate for President known popularly as the "Plumed Knight," and there are some who say Stephan Decatur named the town for reasons of

52

his own. However, the most accepted version is that the town was named when some of the first prospectors discovered some silver in the form of a perfect plume. Decatur may have been in on that, he was in on a lot of things . . . . power drills made their first appearance in mining at the Burleigh Tunnel here in 1869 . . . . Silver Plume's jail, the original band stand, and one of the few hand pumpers of the volunteer fire department are still available for inspection . . . . promise of new life was breathed into the mining camp in April of 1964 with the discovery of a rich lode in the Johnny Bull Claim. The discovery, which runs up to $6,000 a ton, was the result of a 20-year search by Mrs. Vivian Rowe Tonini and her husband Francis Rowe.

## BROWNSVILLE

Much of the history of Brownsville was involved in the Atlantic-Pacific tunnel. There was some mining in the neighborhood, but the town was primarily a construction town for workers on the tunnel. The fortunes of the town generally followed the ups and downs of the work on the tunnel.

Because Brownsville was so closely allied with the tunnel, it may have once been called Pomeroyville.

Brownsville was platted a short distance west of Silver Plume. It was little more than a suburb of the larger town.

A mud slide early in Brownsville history destroyed much of the town and little was rebuilt.

## POMEROYVILLE

A Pomeroyville was mentioned frequently in newspaper accounts as a suburb of Georgetown.

Since the mention is made of the town during the erratic construction periods of Brick Pomeroy's Atlantic-Pacific Tunnel, the town was most likely a construction camp at the opening of the tunnel.

If development of the town was as erratic as the development of the tunnel, the town had a haphazard existence, to say the least. But, if Pomeroyville was the construction town for the tunnel, it could well have had a large population when the tunnel construction was going full blast.

The town was named for Brick, naturally.

Pomeroyville could possibly have been another name for Brownsville.

## SILVER DALE

Silver Dale was a small but active little silver camp about a mile and a half south of Georgetown, at the junction of Leavenworth and South Clear Creek.

The Colorado Central, Equator, S. J. Tilden, Robinson and Curtly mines were here.

There were at least three tunnels. The most important was the Marshall Tunnel which cut through a number of valuable deposits. The Robinson and Curtly were two other tunnels.

The population of the camp was never more than one hundred. There were a post office and a store or two.

## BAKERVILLE and GRAYMOUNT (Graymont)

Two smaller, although rather important towns, beyond Silver Plume, on the approach to Loveland Pass.

There was some good mining at both towns. They were also important stage stops, and when the railroad was extended from the Georgetown Loop, station stops and resort centers. The railroad came to the towns in 1873.

Bakerville was named for John Baker, who, with two others, discovered gold on Kelso Mountain in the summer of 1865. When the gold played out, the town became more important as a stage and railroad stop. Now it is a summer resort roadstop.

Graymount, often shown as Graymont on early maps, was named after the peak above the town. When the railroad arrived here it brought many tourists, who would rent horses here and ride up to the top of Gray's Peak. The best mine here was the Stevens.

## SIDNEYVILLE

Sidneyville was primarily a station on the old Argentine Central, although there was some mining done here.

It was located in Leavenworth Gulch, about five miles above Georgetown, and was named for Matt Sidney, who located the Sidney Silver Mine.

## WALDORF

Waldorf sleeps serenely near the top of the Continental Divide. It was an important mining camp in its day, but its day has long since passed.

The Big Stevens mine was located in 1868. Within the next few years, some 75 locations were staked out. Of these, nine were important and produced millions in gold and silver.

The Waldorf Mining and Milling Company took over many of the claims and made some four million dollars.

Waldorf also served as an important stop in the stage run over Argentine Pass. Later the Argentine Central was constructed to the top of the pass, the highest steam railroad route in the world.

Although the railroad was designed for the mining at Waldorf, it served another purpose. It opened up a superb view, and the thrill of curves up to 145 degrees plus a grade up to 10 degrees soon brought a flood of tourists. The tourist revenue soon outstripped the freight revenue ten to one.

It claimed to be the highest and most scenic ride in the world. Its slogan was "a lifetime in a day." One-sixth of the state can be seen from the summit of the pass.

The mine tunnel atop Mount McClellan was a tourist mecca. It was called the "ice palace" because icicles lined the roof of the tunnel the year-round.

It is said the early miners attempted to roll the ore down the hill in sacks from the mines, but too many of the sacks broke open and the plan proved unprofitable.

Much mining and milling were carried on here for several years after the turn of the century, but the city began to die and has been deserted for several years.

The altitude (11,666 feet) and the long, hard winters have helped preserve the city and much of it is left.

## SANTIAGO

A small camp that grew around the Santiago mine on the hill above Waldorf.

The site can be reached by a short climb or by driving over a winding road from Waldorf.

Some mining has been carried out here in recent years, but only the mine shaft and one cabin remain.

## HILL CITY (west of map)

Another city that began big, but faded out in about a year.

Hill City erupted in 1881 near the headwaters of Williams Fork Creek, southwest of Berthoud Pass, on the old Hayden Wagon Road.

Several hundred men scurried to the spot when some placer gold was found here. But many of the fortune seekers turned around and left within days or weeks.

The site was named after Professor Nathaniel Hill (see Black Hawk).

## EMPIRE (Valley City, Union City)

Early prospectors in the Central City area traveled by here over old Union Pass in the early 60's. It wasn't until 1864 that they paused long enough to find some ore.

Prior to that time, Empire had been the important stop on the pass. A hotel, blacksmith shop and combination grocery and post office were constructed. With the discovery of gold, several more cabins and buildings were built.

The site was originally called Valley City. For a short while, it was also known officially as Union City to demonstrate the residents' sympathy for the northern cause in the Civil War. "Empire" comes from the nickname of New York, home state of many of the early residents.

Fifteen hundred people were here during the early boom, but lack of water and good ores soon drove the residents to other boom towns.

The camp also suffered from its isolation. Supplies were hard to come by and expensive. Butter ran as high as three dollars a pound, eggs three dollars a dozen, and hay 200 dollars a ton. The situation was alleviated somewhat when good hay meadows were found over an old Indian pass in South Park.

The pass was improved upon, as were the roads from Georgetown and Central City. And, although Empire was kaput as a mining town, it became an important stage and supply town, feeding the booming cities over the pass.

The city never died out completely, although it had more than its share of ups and downs. Generally, however, the population has ranged between 100 and 200 through the years. There was some mining here this century, but not much. Empire is currently experiencing a tourist and winter sports boom, which promises to increase through the years as the endless recreational facilities of northern Colorado continue to be developed.

## NORTH EMPIRE and EMPIRE STATION (EMPIRE JUNCTION)

Two "suburbs" of Empire when the latter was booming.

North Empire was a mile above Empire, and connected to it by a good road which served as the main street of the suburb.

The Negus Placer Mine was the big mine at North Empire. It produced about $50,000 in 1878-79. There was also a mill here.

Empire Station was a mile below Empire near the Georgetown cutoff. It was a railroad siding and station for Empire.

## LAWSON

Alexander Lawson built an inn here in the early 70's. It was a lavish place he called "Six Mile Inn" because it was six miles from Georgetown. Lawson prospered as his place became a popular stop along the well-traveled road.

Lawson soon went into the freighting business. His wagons were in constant use throughout the region. He also ran a stage line between Georgetown and Silver Plume. He was making all kinds of money.

And his business wasn't hurt any when gold was found in 1876 on nearby Red Elephant Mountain and Silver Creek.

A town sprang up around Lawson's Inn. Lawson, that's what the town was named, was a prosperous, busy place through the 80's and part of the 90's. The population topped 500 most of the time and many other business-men moved in to get some of the Lawson gravy.

But eventually the mines closed one by one, and the residents drifted off. Lawson is undergoing a revival which began a few years back and depends on the resort and tourist trade.

56

## SILVER CREEK

Silver Creek was active as a mining and resort community for several years. It was still mentioned prominently as late as 1905.

Several groups from Denver and Cripple Creek owned lodges and cabins here. There were many elaborate parties and society outings.

Some Illinois money was invested in the mines. There were tunnels built to the Mary and Starling mines, and one was considered to the Metropolitan group of mines.

The community had a hotel, a number of lodges and cabins, a school and a post office. Now only a few cabins, mostly of the sportsmen variety, and a few mine dumps remain of the site.

## RED ELEPHANT

A small camp located around the properties on Red Elephant Mountain, one mile above Lawson.

The Red Elephant Mining Company operated extensive holdings here, and the camp was primarily a company town. There were a post office, commissary, and several miners' boarding houses and cabins. Peak population was about 300.

Mining continued off and on for several years, but after a time most of the miners moved down to Lawson.

## DOWNIEVILLE (sometimes Downeyville)

Downieville was a stage and freighter station that went big time. It became quite a social center.

It had a roadhouse, a large one, and had a theatre that won considerable fame in the region.

A scandal occurred when the daughter of the roadhouse owner ran off with a Lawson big-wig.

The two-story stage station was the third stage stop from Denver. The building was later turned into a poor farm.

A roadhouse marks the spot today.

## DUMONT (Mill City)

Dumont was an important smelting center and stage station, as well as a mining town.

It is said to have had the first mining in the region, the first school west of Denver in the Rockies, and the first sewing machine in the territory.

Some records show Mill City was actually located a short distance away, between Dumont and Downieville. But it is generally believed Mill City was the predecessor of Dumont.

The city was laid out in 1859 and soon became a smelter and milling center.

The famed Mill City House was built in 1868, one of the more elaborate buildings in the mountains. Many of the furnishings came from back east. The building was a stage station and toll house. It had a large and lavish bar and billiard room. It had a piano, and the upper floor was used as a meeting hall and opera house.

It got to be that the Mill City House was just about the only *raison d'etre* for the town. The nearby mines didn't live up to expectation, and although mining was carried on here for years, most of the smelters closed down.

John M. Dumont, owner of the Whale, Freeland, Lincoln, and other nearby mines, came along and attempted to revive the city. He didn't do much good, although he did rename the site Dumont. He later went to Empire and helped keep that city alive.

Part of the Mill City House was destroyed by fire.

Much remains of Dumont, including people.

## IDAHO SPRINGS (Jackson's Diggings, Sacramento, Idaho Bar, Payne's Bar, Idaho City and Idaho)

George A. Jackson scraped about nine dollars worth of placer gold from frozen ground at the head of Chicago Creek in January of 1859. It was just a few short months after the Russell discovery and five full months *before* the Gregory strike.

Jackson made a detailed map of his location, then trudged back through the snow to Denver to await spring.

He kept his find a secret, but quietly took on some partners and organized the Chicago Mining Company. Activity of the group stirred up some curiosity, and when the company returned to Chicago Creek in May, a handful of prospectors was close on its heels. Jackson and his group washed out $1,900 in gold the first week. Word spread, and more and more prospectors entered the area.

A camp was laid out on level ground a short distance from the original strike. The first haphazard camp was called simply Jackson's Diggings. But within weeks, as more and more prospectors flocked into the region and the site took on an air of permanency, the settlers began casting about for a more sophisticated name.

They came up with many before finally settling on Idaho Springs.

Taking their cue from the rich gold fields in California, the settlers first hit upon Sacramento or Sacramento City as a name. There was evidence that the names Payne's Bar and Jackson's Bar were also tried out somewhere along the line. Later, when there was some talk of calling the entire region Idaho territory, the name of the city was changed to Idaho or Idaho City. The settlers hoped vaguely that the booming community would be made capital of the territory.

58

When the region became part of the newly-created Colorado territory, Idaho City became merely Idaho. And later still, when the medicinal hot springs here became more and more famous, Springs was added to the name. Idaho is Indian for "Gem of the Rockies."

Clear Creek County was one of the original 17 counties created in 1861 by an act of the first Colorado territory legislature. Naturally, Idaho Springs, or Jackson's Diggings, was made county seat. By 1868, however, when Georgetown became the chief city in the region, residents in the county elected to move the county seat to the thriving silver city.

The medicinal benefits of the hot springs near Idaho Springs were recognized as early as the 60's, and the community became a health resort from the start. Hundreds of tourists journeyed to Idaho Springs for health treatments. In addition, the mineral water was bottled and sold throughout the world.

Mining was carried on here without let-up through the years. Much mining is still being done. Idaho Springs has served as a dual health and mining center from the beginning but is more known for its hot springs today than for its mining.

Along with its mining activity, Idaho Springs was, and is, a smelting center. Its smelters handled ore from mines in all directions. By 1903, there were nearly 30 large and small ore treatment plants in and around Idaho Springs.

Almost immediately after the city was founded, roads were cut to connect Idaho Springs with Denver and the boom center, Central City.

The Virginia Canyon road to Central City was one of the first roads in the mountains. It was well traveled in the early days, and is still being used . . . not by the squeamish, however. Another road went up the Fall River and over Yankee Hill into Central City. Shortly after the founding of Georgetown, the roads to Idaho Springs were extended to connect with the silver center. Stages rumbled over the roads with regularity.

The Colorado Central Railroad completed its narrow-gauge line from Golden to Georgetown along Clear Creek by 1877, and Idaho Springs became the important stop on the run.

The peak population of Idaho Springs, during the 60's, has been estimated as high as 12,000. It fell to around 4,000 a few years later, and stayed about there for several years. Now, the population is a little less than 2,000 but thousands more pass through the city each month.

Most of the characters of Central City and Georgetown were familiar in Idaho Springs, too. General Grant visited here in 1873 when he toured the Colorado gold camps. Mark Twain was said to have passed through here.

The hospitality center was the once famous Bebee House Hotel, operated for several years by F. W. Bebee.

Idaho Springs has taken on a new appearance in recent years. It is still a mining and resort center, thousands of tourists stop and linger here. But a new highway by-pass carries thousands more around the city. The by-pass was completed in 1958 to alleviate the almost constant traffic jam on the old highway.

Idaho Springs will long remain an important tourist stop.

GOLD DUST: A monument has been erected in honor of George A. Jackson near the site of his original discovery, about a quarter of a mile up the Chicago Creek road (Colorado Highway 103) . . . . in 1892, two drainage and transportation tunnels were constructed to aid mining in the area. The Newhouse tunnel, now called the Argo, runs five miles through the hills from Idaho Springs to Central City and cost ten million dollars to construct. It is the largest tunnel of its kind in the world . . . . the Idaho Springs area mined mostly gold, although several other minerals, including uranium, have been found near here . . . . good quartz lodes were located nearby long before the placer finds were exhausted, so Idaho Springs never suffered the early precarious existence of Central City . . . . the first narrow-gauge engine into Idaho Springs has been kept and maintained by the city, and is a favorite tourist sight . . . . the early miners lost little time placing names on the nearby mountains (a favorite miner pastime, in all the camps). Most of the early names took hold. The mountain behind the city was named Squaw Mountain. Scenic Squaw Pass running from Echo Lake to Bergen Park is another Idaho Springs by-pass that was constructed several years ago. It is a popular picnic route and well worth the trip . . . . another theory on the name comes from a legend about a Chief Idaho who brought his sick and wounded warriors here to recuperate at the hot springs . . . . Idaho Springs had a big strike during the Colorado labor unrest in 1903. The miners struck for an eight-hour day. There was much violence and the miners were accused of dynamiting many mine buildings. Finally, the citizens drove the union leaders out of town and the strike was settled in favor of the mine owners.

## SPANISH BAR

Two miles west of Idaho Springs on south Clear Creek is the site of Spanish Bar.

The place was named for or by the many Mexican prospectors who worked the area in the 60's. Some good gold was found here.

The area was worked off and on for years. A big revival took place around 1880 when the population was nearly 400, and there were several active mines and mills. The big mill was the Freeland.

Mike Dougherty, early Colorado's favorite character, claimed he was the first "to discover grass on Spanish Bar."

## LAMARTINE

A Denver jeepster claims there are two or three jeep trails to this well-hidden old town. He admits, however, that none of the trails is well marked.

For those interested, he says the best route is five miles up State 103 along Chicago Creek, then a steep old road to the west up Ute Creek Canyon, then due north over Meadowland to the town. Anyhow, it's near the top of the hill.

The town grew around the Lamartine mine, which got off to a slow start but produced several millions in gold, silver and lead before it was washed up in the early 1900's.

It seems that evidence of gold was found here early, but the claims weren't developed. A fellow named Himrod eventually bought all the claims for about $280. He spent thousands in developing the claims but got little back. When he died, the ownership was passed on to his son, who also spent plenty of time and money without realizing any profit.

He eventually sold out for $360, and the new owners—almost immeditely—began to make money hand over fist.

This was when the town was built. It flourished during the 80's, 90's and early 1900's—as long as the Lamartine continued to pay off. The peak population of the town never exceeded 500.

The Lamartine Tunnel further developed the property.

Much is left of the town—if you can find it!

## FREELAND

A frightening four-mile drive over a ledge road, made more for jeeps than standard autos, will take the interested to the ghost of Freeland.

The route is lined with shafthouses and mine dumps, once the source of prosperity for the mining camp.

Freeland was born about 1880 with some rich strikes made nearby. It soon had a population of more than 400, had some 80 cabins and frame houses, two stores, a saloon and a public school.

It was a peaceful, industrious little community. It depended upon the Freeland, Lone Tree and other mines. When they faded, so did Freeland.

About the only distinction ever achieved here was an interest former New York Senator Lehman had in one of the mines.

## BONITO

A small community that grew around the smelters and mills that treated the ores of nearby mines.

The largest smelter was the Bullion, built in 1884, to treat the ores from the Freeland mine. The smelter employed some 25 men in its day.

Some ruins of cabins and mills remain at the site.

## FALL RIVER

Mines, mills and cabins once lined Fall River, from Clear Creek to St. Mary's Glacier.

In this hodge-podge, however, only two or three camps emerged clearly: Alice, Fall River and Silver City.

Fall River, which began near the junction of the Fall River and Clear Creek, ran quite a distance up the narrow valley. It had two large mills and several smaller ones, dozens of cabins and prosperous businesses.

The camp reached its peak in the early '80's. Ten new discoveries were made in 1880, four of which were said to be "unusually rich" in free gold. All the new strikes were owned by a Comodore Kane and his associates of New York City. The Kane company constructed a tunnel to cut into each of the new diggings.

Foundations of the mill and several old cabins remain at the site.

## ALICE

Alice was the largest of the many camps along the Fall River. During the boom, cabins were spread throughout the pocket at the end of the valley, below St. Mary's Glacier.

There were many claims here, but only a handful were developed to any extent. The Alice and the Kaminky were, perhaps, the largest of the mines.

The region was settled in the early 80's when some placer gold was found along Fall River. More than $50,000 in gold was taken out of Alice those first few months. A stamp mill was erected; later, some lode mining was done; and Alice took on most of the appearances of a permanent city.

The Alice Mine and other properties were sold on hand for a quarter of a million dollars in 1897. The deal called for a cash payment of $50,000 and two yearly payments of $100,000. The new owners planned to enlarge the 200-ton concentrator mill and bring into use several large air drills. There were already several tunnels built, the largest 600 feet.

Apparently, however, about the time the last payment was due—in 1899 —the mines closed, and Alice was soon deserted. There has been a little mining activity here since, but not much.

Ruins of many of the cabins can be seen, scattered amid the pines. However, signs of past mining activity are fast being replaced by evidence of increasing summer tourist activity. A huge lodge covers much of the cup at the end of the valley. Tourist cabins dot the road.

Overlooking the scene is St. Mary's Glacier, one of Colorado's most famous glacial formations. Here is one of the few spots in the state which holds enough snow the year round to permit summer skiing.

The glacier rests on Kingston Peak (12,136 feet). At the foot of the glacier is St. Mary's Lake. Nearby is Silver Lake. Alice also has its Glory Hole, a 150-foot deep mining excavation, a short distance off the main road.

Alice was once an important stop on one of ·the main roads between Central City and Idaho Springs, over Yankee Hill. Central City is just a short distance away on this route.  But although jeeps can generally make it today, the road is difficult and becoming more so by disuse.

## SILVER CITY

One of the shortest-lived communities in the area, Silver City at one time had a population of about one thousand.

But the site consisted of little more than tents and brush huts, and the miners soon pulled those down when they discovered the ores around weren't worth the trouble to take out.

Silver City was located on the upper Fall River.  Virtually all of its life span was contained within the year 1860.

## YANKEE (Yankee Hill)

A jeep now and again travels up Yankee Hill to the old site of Yankee. A few cabins and mine holes remain as souvenirs of the past activity here.

Time was when Yankee Hill was a well-traveled route between George-town and Central City.  It was certainly the shortest route.

Yankee, located at the top of the hill opposite Alice, was an important stop on the route, as well as being a mining town.

The mining was never developed to any great extent, but the site was occupied for several years.  A new concentrate mill was built here in 1905 to handle the ores from the Gold Anchor Mine.

Yankee Hill was named during the Civil War by Northern sympathizers. The town was named for the hill.  Some sources say it was vice versa.

## APEX

Sledders and skiers zoom down the road past Apex and the Palace Dancehall and Saloon now.

Time was, Apex and the Palace were famous, bustling and prosperous.

Apex was the center of the Pine Creek Mining District that came to life during the 90s.

The best mine at Apex was the Mackey, and it has a curious history.

The mine was originally owned by Dick Mackey.  It was taken over by a fellow named Mountz and his partners.  They had hardly begun work on the mine when the partners ran off with $30,000, leaving Mountz with a grand total of $400 in working capital.

Mountz did all he could, working carefully and frugally.  He drove in a tunnel.  No good.  The money ran out.  In disgust Mountz planted dynamite to blow up the whole mess.  The blast uncovered a rich lode.

Mountz ordered a bundle of ore sacks from Denver—on credit.  He ordered two four-horse teams and wagons from Central City—on credit. He was in business.  The first ore assayed at $1,800 a ton.  Mountz paid up his bills and didn't need any credit after that.

There were several good mines within a radius of four to six miles of Apex in all directions.

There was the Schultz Wonder, a mile and a half south of Apex. Next to it was the Wetstein with an 1,800-foot tunnel. On Nevada Hill were the Jersey City, Rooster, Evergreen, and other good mines. A mile east of Apex was the Tip Top, which was not only a good mine but also its opening afforded a magnificent view of the countryside.

Apex, although never very large, was one of the most sophisticated towns in the entire region. The Apex Hotel, one of the two hotels here, was one of the best in the county and did a thriving business. The big Palace Dancehall was always busy. The newspaper, *The Apex Pine Cone*, was one of the most popular newspapers in Colorado. There were a school and a couple of churches. At its peak, around the turn of the century and a few years after that, Apex had a total of about 100 businesses. The population, however, never got much over the 1,000 mark.

In recent years, some private parties have taken over some of the remaining cabins at Apex and have improved them. But the old Palace is just about the way it was when the miners went off and left it . . . a little the worse for wear.

Up the road that cuts through town, and up a winding mountain road, is the Tip Top. Midway through town, just beyond the Palace, is the cut-off for Nugget and American City.

Down the road is a beautiful view, one of the main reasons Apex was so popular.

### AMERICAN CITY and NUGGET

American City was the larger of these two towns a short distance apart and north of Apex.

Both towns thrived in the late 90's, then Nugget faded, and American City took over.

Several companies were headquartered at American City. There were the Boston-Occidental Mine and Mill; Imperial Mining and Milling; Evergreen Gold and Copper Company; Missouri-Colorado Milling and Mining; Mantz and Palmer Mill. Some of the best mines were owned by these companies. In addition, there were the Sarah Jane, Mackay and Mascot Mines.

The town had a rather sophisticated hotel for the type of environment— the Hotel Del Monte. It was a popular stopover for travelers and did a good business the early years of this century. American City also had a school, and it is believed the children of Nugget, when that town was alive, journeyed to American City for their schooling. ·

One or two ruins a short distance apart mark the two towns.

*And Then There Were . . . . OFER CITY* (Ophir) — (not on map) — named as the principal camp in the Empire district when it was set up in 1860. It may have been a predecessor to Empire. At any rate, after its first prominent mention it was not mentioned again . . . . *GREEN LAKE,* a small resort village on the lake south of Georgetown and popular during the boomdays . . . . *YANKEE BAR,* (not on map), a small camp in the hills above Black Hawk . . . . *TWELVE MILE, PINE CREEK* and *ELK PARK* (not on map), three areas in the Pine Creek Mining district near Apex. By reports of the time it is not clear if these were official towns. They were mining areas, and were frequently mentioned as if they were actual camps. As might be the case, they were mining areas with several cabins but no town platted. *TWELVE MILE* was the most frequently mentioned of the three. Reports often said: "the place known locally as Twelve Mile." Its location was described once as "up the creek from Apex where the main branch of Clear Creek finds its headwaters." Another newspaper said: "Between North Clear Creek and Elk Creek are Arizona and Montana Hills, while between their western slopes and Baltimore Ridge are embraced the Valleys known as Twelve Mile and Elk Park." Twelve Mile and Elk Park were apparently close together, and may even have overlapped. At least the mines mentioned in conjunction with their names often overlapped. The mines were the Wolverine, Plateau, Lulla Bye, Mattie S., Moose and Portland. An Elk Park referred to in very early reports from this area has later been identified by some historians as present-day Bergen Park, but this wouldn't be the mining area in the Pine Creek district. Pine Creek, other than being the name of the district, may also have been a small camp not far from Apex. At least some newspaper descriptions indicated as much. A couple of mines mentioned frequently in conjunction with Pine Creek and which are not attached to other camps are the Manchester and Nancy Lee . . . . *KINGSTON,* a small camp on the trail between Nugget and Alice. The primary mine was the London. Other mines were the Moose, Illinois and a few other workings on Pile Hill. There were also some cabins on *PILE HILL . . . . NINETY-FOUR,* a camp around the Ninety-Four Mine in the Silver Lake area. The camp also served the Princess Alice and Lalla. Ninety-Four was so named because it was located in 1894 . . . . *MAGNET* (Magnet Park) was a small camp around the Magnet Mine, a short distance east of Georgetown. Ruins can be seen on the hike between Silver Creek and Georgetown. There were other small camps in this general neighborhood, between Lamartine and Silver Creek and Georgetown. Evidence of these towns can be seen along the many half-hidden roads through this rugged area. Most of the towns took the name of the mine, or the mine owner.

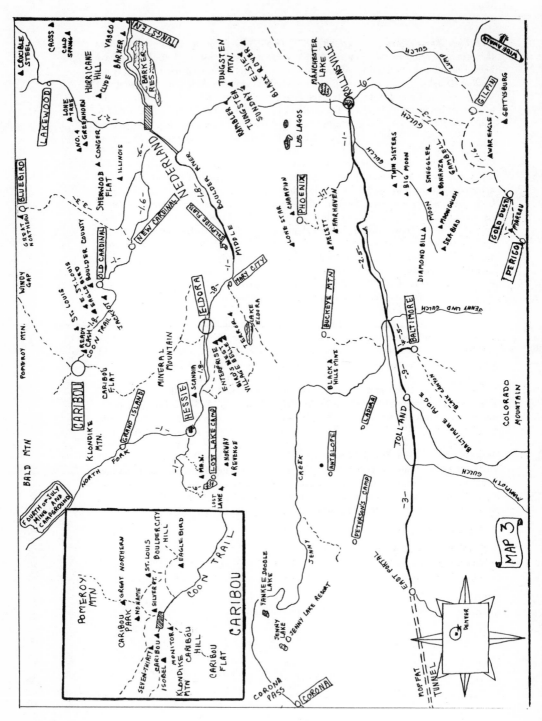

MAP 3

# III. CARIBOU AND CORONA PASS

*MAP THREE*
## CARIBOU AND CORONA PASS

Nederland (Middle Boulder, Brownsville)
Tungsten (Steven's Camp, Ferberite)
Lakewood
Caribou
Cardinal (New Cardinal)
Cardinal City (Old Cardinal)
Eldora (Eldorado Camp, Happy Valley)
Mary City and Sulphide Flats
Hessie, Grand Island and Lost Lake Camp
Fourth of July Mine (north of map)
Rollinsville
Tolland (Mammoth), East Portal and Corona
Baltimore
Deadwood Diggings (not on map) and Gambell Gulch
Perigo
Gold Dirt
Gilpin

*And Then There Were* . . . Bluebird, Phoenix (Phoenixville), Buckeye Mountain, Antelope, Ladora, Jenny Lake Camp, Peterson's Camp, Wide Awake, and Mammoth City.

*NEDERLAND* (Middle Boulder, Brownville)

Helen Hunt Jackson called Nederland "that dismal little mining town."

True—the town was too busy to dress up for all its visitors. It was too busy being a mining center for one of the richest gold and silver areas in the state, and then one of the richest tungsten centers in the world.

But it's had a chance to catch its breath in recent years and is developing into quite a tourist center.

Though it still looks like "that dismal little mining town."

A mill was built here in 1870 to handle the ores sent down the mountain from Caribou. It was from this mill silver bricks were made to serve as a walk for General Grant's visit to Central City in 1873.

Nederland thrived all through the 80's and 90's as a supply, smelting and shipping center for the mining camps about. With the discovery of tungsten at the turn of the century, activity increased. But it wasn't until the outbreak of World War I, when tungsten prices skyrocketed, that the find brought the stampede.

67

Wartime Nederland was like wartime Washington. Lots were at a premium, a place to sleep was worth its weight in tungsten. Hotel beds were rented for eight hour shifts. Men rented beds in barns and were glad to get them. Restaurants allowed guests only 20 minutes to eat. Bars were extended and extra swinging doors were put in to accomodate the customers.

However, the boom couldn't last. As the tungsten price soared, buyers eventually were able to import the mineral from South America and Japan at less cost. The bottom fell out of the market overnight. The end of the war shortly thereafter sealed the doom of the Nederland tungsten boom.

Tungsten is still produced in the Nederland area and some of the other mines are working. But it's nothing like it was.

GOLD DUST: The first camp was called Brownville for N. W. Brown, the first settler. In 1873 the name was changed to Middle Boulder for the stream that furnished the water power. In 1874, a Dutch company took over some mines in Caribou and the mill, and renamed the city for their homeland . . . . the Primos Mill at Lakewood, three miles from Nederland, was the largest tungsten producing mill in the world . . . . several buyers from Europe inspected the tungsten mines and mills at Nederland during the early years of this century . . . . tungsten is used to harden metals and for filaments in electric lights.

## TUNGSTEN (Steven's Camp, Ferberite)

Looking down from Boulder Canyon on the ghost of Tungsten, one wouldn't believe the site was the busiest and richest city of its size in the state during World War I.

It was.

During the war, when tungsten was more valuable than gold and silver, the city had a peak population of 20,000, and thousands more slept and ate wherever they could in Tungsten, Nederland and other nearby places. Seventeen mills were working around the clock. The traffic was so heavy along Boulder Canyon road that guards were stationed at most curves to prevent accidents and trouble. Production reached nearly six million dollars in 1917 alone.

Tungsten produced here broke a monopoly held by an eastern firm, and the area established its own monopoly of sorts before the price got so high that users found it was cheaper to import tungsten, and did so. When this happened the market fell overnight and Tungsten, the city, died almost as quickly as it had roared into existence.

For years miners and prospectors trampled over what they called "that damn black rock" found in abundance here. Some were curious about the unusual stones and tarried awhile. But when they found it held no silver or gold, they trudged off.

The metal was found to be tungsten around the turn of the century, but hardly anyone needed it then, and the area was deserted until about the start of the war and the tungsten boom.

The tungsten area covered 12 square miles and extended as far down Boulder Canyon as Magnolia. Tungsten, of course, was the center of activity, although prosperity from the boom was felt at Nederland, Boulder and throughout Colorado.

The bustling community was first named Steven's Camp for Eugene Stevens, an early miner. But the growing camp soon took the name of the metal that made it famous.

The Tungsten mill at neaby Lakewood was the largest in the world. The Boulder Tungsten Production Company was formed at a cost of $30,000, but paid for itself within a month.

Activity dwindled after the market crash, and all but stopped following the war. But a little mining has been done off and on since.

Most of the mills and other establishments are gone. Many were lost to Barker Reservoir, now covering the "Barker Meadows" where horses and burros grazed during the boom.

## LAKEWOOD

Site of the largest tungsten mill in the United States during the tungsten boom.

The community was built around the mill, and the residents were the mill workers.

The mill closed shortly after the tungsten boom was over, and the community faded almost overnight.

The site is—or was—exactly 2.6 miles north of Nederland on the Peak-to-Peak Highway, but only a trace of the once-important center remains.

## CARIBOU

Sam Conger of Central City noticed peculiar stones while hunting in the area in 1860. He thought little more about them until eight years later when he happened upon similar stones in a railroad car in Wyoming. He stepped closer to inspect the rocks, but a guard told him to stay away—it was valuable ore from the Comstock lode in Nevada.

"Hell," said Conger, "I know where there's a whole mountain of that stuff."

He finally located the spot where he had seen the stones more than eight years before. Conger had the ore assayed, and it proved rich in silver. He took five partners, the six of them working through the winter, storing the ore for a spring shipment to the smelter. But their secret leaked out before their task was finished. By spring, other fortune seekers were in the area, other rich locations were made, and before long the area was swarming with prospectors.

And Caribou was born—one of the richest (but one of the most ungodly) places to live in the state.

Situated on a barren mountain nearly 10,000 feet high, strong, usually biting, winds roared continuously through the camp. It was known as "the town where winds are born." Severe storms were also born here. Drifts as high as 25 feet blanketed the site during the winter, often requiring residents to enter and leave their homes through second-story windows. Fires, in 1879 and 1900, whipped across the city, leaving it in smoldering ruins. Scores died in two major epidemics, scarlet fever and diphtheria.

But to some, the advantages were far geater than the disadvantages. For several years, Caribou was one of the richest camps in northern Colorado.

The city was platted in 1870, and within months more than 3,000 people were living at Caribou. Some 60 businesses—all types of businesses—prospered. Some 20 mines were paying off in the thousands. The camp produced nearly a half a million dollars in gold and silver in 1875 alone.

The camp started fading in the 80's. The panic of '93 struck another blow from which Caribou never fully recovered. Then the fire of 1900 virtually wiped Caribou off the map. Little rebuilding was attempted.

The city has been all but deserted since. Some lease mining has been carried on in recent years. The last permanent resident—"the Hermit of Caribou"—died in 1944.

In 1946, the Consolidated Caribou Silver Mining Company completed the 3,500-foot Idaho tunnel, which had been abandoned 50 years before. By direct telephone from Rockefeller Center in New York, the company president gave the signal for the final blast opening the tunnel.

But although the blast was heard in New York via telephone, it was not loud enough to wake the slumbering city.

BEST MINES: Caribou, Conger, Poorman, Sherman, Idaho, Boulder County, No-Name, Spencer, Sovereign People, Seven-Thirty.

GOLD DUST: Another thing that helped cause the downfall of Caribou was the lack of direct railroads. The railroad was only built as far as Cardinal. During its heyday, a constant stream of ore wagons rambled down "coon trail" to the railway . . . . the Caribou city fathers had frequent pangs of conscience. During these periods they ran the shady ladies out of town. The ladies set up shop in Cardinal for awhile and then drifted back to Caribou . . . . the Caribou was the top mine, producing between six and eight million dollars in silver and gold. But there were many other good mines. The first 20 feet of the Idaho shaft brought $20,000 . . . . the Caribou changed hands many times until a Dutch company paid three million dollars for it in 1873 . . . . an exhibit of Caribou silver ore at the Philadelphia Centennial Celebration in 1876 brought widespread attention and additional investment in the camp . . . . Caribou had several newspapers through the years. The first was the *Caribou Post* which was published from 1870 to 1872 by editors of the Central City newspaper . . . . the interesting Caribou Cemetery is over the winding road from town. Only a few cabins are left in the town, but the hills are splotched with evidence of past activity.

## CARDINAL (New Cardinal)

Although Cardinal was a mining town, it was important as a terminal for the Caribou railway branch, and was most remembered as a frequent refuge for the shady ladies of Caribou.

Reformers frequently rose to the fore in Caribou and the ladies were run out of that town. The gals set up shop in Cardinal, greatly bolstering the commercial value of the city below Caribou. Eventually the ladies would drift back to Caribou, only to return to Cardinal now and again.

Much to the dissatisfaction of Caribou residents, the railroad only went as far as Cardinal. This kept Cardinal happy and busy for a time. But the shady ladies and the railroad couldn't sustain Cardinal more than a few years. The boom lasted from 1878 to 1883, and the peak population was 2,000. After that, the miners and businessmen drifted off or discovered they could live as well in Caribou.

Cardinal's top mine was the Boulder County, which is still producing. The mine and a few scattered ruins are all that are left at the site.

## CARDINAL CITY (Old Cardinal)

Cardinal City or Old Cardinal was founded two miles below Caribou in 1870, several years before New Cardinal came into being.

By 1872, more than 200 persons lived here, and the city had a post office, several saloons and other less lucrative commercial enterprises. A courthouse was planned but never built.

It is not clear why the city was moved to a new site closer to Nederland, but it is believed the railroad had much to do with it, and may have been the sole reason.

New Cardinal soon replaced the old location, and now nothing remains of the old community.

## ELDORA (Eldorado Camp, Happy Valley)

Eldora prospers anew—as a summer recreation mecca. Traces of the old Eldora have disappeared or are well-hidden by the new.

Eldora got off to a slow start, but once it caught on, it was thought to be another Cripple Creek. It wasn't, of course.

Some prospecting was carried on here and some locations made in 1860. The Grand Island mining district was organized the following year, but little was done to develop the area until Sam Conger located the Caribou mine in 1869. In 1875 the Fourth of July mine was located near the Divide.

There was activity all around Eldora, but nothing nearby until 1891 when a group of Central City miners located the Happy Valley placer in 1891. The camp that resulted was called Happy Valley. A rival town company set up townsite within the Happy Valley land grant. Litigation followed, and eventually the court ruled in favor of the original town company.

The site came to be called Eldorado Camp, but the post office department complained of the confusion caused by a similar name in California. So the citizens dropped the final syllables of the name.

Eldora prospered all through the 90's. Although it had a mining life of its own, it also served as a supply center for the camps beyond, and a railroad shipping center for the camps in the area. The first time the manager of the Bailey Chlorination Mill missed a payday, the workers shot him and burned down the mill.

Eldora was a sociable and lively town. The many dancehalls and gambling houses ran night and day. The sporting district was across the creek. The Miners Hotel was the hub of the elite social activity, and many lavish—and boisterous—dances were held there.

However, the ore started giving out after the turn of the century. Some residents continued to make money by selling worthless claims for fabulous fees. Some lease mining has been done in recent years, but for the most part, Eldora has settled back into a quiet, respectable tourist center.

BEST MINES: Grand Island, Happy Valley, Enterprise, Bird's Nest, Clara, Virginia, Virginia Belle and Revenge.

GOLD DUST: The mining district was 16 miles long and 4 miles wide, extending from Castle Rock in Boulder Canyon to the Continental Divide . . . . heavy snow in the winter frequently forced the mines to lug out ore on large sleds . . . . the Mogul tunnel drilled below the mines further developed the area . . . . the Eldora jail was just behind the Miners Hotel. A two-teacher school was nearby. Eldora had just about everything but a cemetery, boasting there was no need for one . . . . during the boom, four Boulder stage companies ran stages to Eldora . . . . "Old Bob" Stewart was a hermit for many years in the mountains near Eldora . . . .

## MARY CITY and SULPHIDE FLATS

Two camps that erupted in the 90's south of Eldora.

Sulphide Flats, because of its location beside an attractive lake, was expected to outdo Eldora. A two-story hotel was built along with some cabins, and other lavish plans were made. But the rush never came and the site quickly returned to nature.

Mary City had a more practical founding but as ignoble an end. It grew up around an expensive stamp mill, built to handle the ore of Eldora and other nearby locations.

But the mill was not adequately equipped and could not compete with the mills of Nederland. Mary City was soon empty and forgotten.

## HESSIE, GRAND ISLAND and LOST LAKE CAMP

Three one-time important camps beyond Eldora.

Hessie, two miles west of Eldora where the north and south forks of

Boulder Creek meet, was the largest of the camps. It once threatened to outdistance Eldora. There were some mining properties nearby, but the best mines were farther up Jasper Creek and around Lost Lake.

Grand Island was three miles beyond Hessie on the north fork of Boulder Creek. The camp boomed for a short time during the nineties, but the nearby mining properties soon played out. Only a wee trace of its past activity marks the site.

There were a number of fairly good mines around Lost Lake, southwest of Hessie. The camp had as many as two hundred persons during the summer months. The top mines were the Lost Lake, Ma W., Shirley, Revenge and Norway.

## FOURTH OF JULY MINE (north of map)

Don't confuse the Fourth of July camp grounds with the site of the Fourth of July Mine. The camp grounds, six and one half miles from Eldora, are at the end of the road. The mine is another two mile hike westward toward Arapaho Pass.

Many Indian trails were found in the mountains here. C. C. Alvord chose the Arapahoe Trail in 1875, and located some silver ore. The find was made in May and nobody since has quite explained how the mine got its name, the Fourth of July.

The mine was only worked for silver at first, and the silver ore, although fairly good stuff, was hardly worth the trouble and expense of taking it out. The location was soon forgotten. Twenty years later good copper ore was found here. The Copper Mining, Milling and Smelter Company was founded. Three million shares of stock were sold at a dollar a share.

The mine was worked for years, but it continued to be an expensive operation. Other than the transportation problem, drainage was a continuous headache. Eventually, the site was forgotten for good.

## ROLLINSVILLE

General John Q. Rollins was a prominent figure in the settlement and development of the Midwest and Rocky Mountains.

He had widespread interest in mines and mills, was a town builder, road maker, stage line operator, and had interests in farming, lumber and other business enterprises.

He was also an expert billiard player. Although he didn't allow gambling in Rollinsville, he himself won $11,000 in a Denver billiard match.

Rollins improved upon the old army pass above here, named it Rollins Pass, and ran it as a toll road. It was the first pass over the Continental Divide into Middle Park.

Rollins believed everyone wishing to enter Middle Park would have to

73

do so over his road. He laid out Rollinsville believing everyone would be obligated to pass through this junction and supply center.

For several years his theory held up. But eventually Berthoud Pass was improved and Rollins Pass lessened in importance.

Rollinsville thrived for several years. It was unique in that Rollins, who owned the townsite, didn't allow saloons, gambling, houses or dance halls within the city limits.

The community is still an important junction on the Peak-to-Peak highway.

### TOLLAND (Mammoth), EAST PORTAL and CORONA

Tolland was a stage station between Rollinsville and East Portal. Later, with the construction of the Moffat Tunnel, it became a railroad station. Although little used, the station still stands.

Tolland, once called Mammoth, was named by Mrs. Charles B. Toll for her family's ancestral home in England. Mrs. Toll operated a large hotel here during the early years of this century, and was also postmistress.

East Portal and Corona were primarily construction towns, busy during the construction of fabulous Corona Pass, and East Portal continued its importance during the construction of the Moffat Tunnel, while Corona disappeared. Nothing remains of Corona and there is little evidence of its history, but it was located at the top of the Continental Divide (11,600 feet) and was the highest station in the world at one time.

Corona Pass is again gaining in popularity. The scenic, although sometimes hazardous pass, runs from East Portal to Winter Park, a distance of 28 miles. It is one of the oldest and most historic passes in the state.

Long before the white men came, the pass was a favorite Indian trail. It is believed to be the trail the Mormons took enroute to Great Salt Lake. It was later improved upon and used by the U. S. Army.

General John Q. Rollins (see Rollinsville) greatly improved upon the road in 1866, and officially is still called Rollins Pass.

David H. Moffat began construction of a railroad route over the pass in 1901. The railroad line was completed in 1909, and continued in use until the Moffat Tunnel was completed in 1928.

The pass was frequently hazardous and was piled high with snow much of the year. Even today, it is open only from about July to the first big snowstorm in September or October. Long railroad snowsheds were constructed at strategic points, but some were destroyed by the snow and others burned down in the 30's. The old Denver and Salt Lake budgeted up to 41 per cent of its operating budget for snow removal.

Recent improvements have been made on the road by Boulder and Gilpin Counties, and by the Colorado Game and Fish Department, and the U. S. Forest Service.

74

Governor Steve McNichols presided at the official re-opening of the route in 1956. At that time he expressed the hope the road would some day be paved; and at these ceremonies it was called Corona Pass.

The improved road follows the railroad grade and is therefore gentle in slope, averaging about a four per cent grade. The road is usually open to two-way traffic but there are some narrow sections. The road crosses two of the original trestles near the summit and crosses gullies more than 1,000 feet deep.

The road gives access to Middle Park and about 20 fishing lakes, some located near the top of the Continental Divide.

The Moffat Tunnel, second largest railroad tunnel in the United States, was the dream of David H. Moffat. His railroad line over Corona Pass was too costly for profit, and he hoped one day to drive a tunnel through the divide. But he and his partners had spent too much on developing the railroad with much of the cost going to the development of Corona Pass.

He then led the lobby for the state's construction of the tunnel. As a result, the Colorado legislature created the Moffat Tunnel Improvement District in 1922. The Moffat Tunnel Commission was created and bonds issued to finance the project.

Original estimate of construction costs was set at $6,120,000, but when the work was completed in 1927, the price tag had topped 18 million dollars.

There are two tunnels, one used as a water diversion bore for the city of Denver. And the other is for railroads. The route became a part of the Denver and Rio Grande Western in 1947. It is used as a regular route of ski trains from Denver to Winter Park in the winter, and cuts 176 miles off the old D & RGW route to Salt Lake City.

## BALTIMORE

Baltimore must have been a prosperous and attractive mining community. But it apparently is one of the least known.

It is in a clearing a short distance off the highway—a beautiful location, rapidly developing into a resort area.

The ruins of the old city demonstrate that it was a large community. A big, two-story building, believed to have been a hotel, recently fell on its chin near the opening of the clearing, while several other ruins can be found back near the hills. Some ruins have stone foundations. Aspens grow now in the livingrooms of some of the roofless cabins.

Baltimore had an opera house that had some of the top shows of the region. It also had a lavish social club called the Baltimore Club. After activity began to fade here, the club's bar, curtains and other fixtures were moved to Central City.

## DEADWOOD DIGGINGS (*not on map*) *and* GAMBELL GULCH

A. P. Gambell located some placer claims here in the winter of 1859. After his discoveries, he journeyed to Denver for supplies. A stranger from the hills, buying supplies with gold dust, was always a subject of curiosity. When Gambell left Denver, he found he was being followed by a group of men, and no matter what he tried he couldn't lose them. In fact, the men soon overtook Gambell, roughed him up a little and forced him to take them to his gulch.

Thus was the nefarious beginning of Gambell Gulch.

One of the first claims after Gambell made the original strike was staked by a B. F. Langly. He named the spot Deadwood Diggings for the fallen timber in the area. Early records show his small camp later became Gambell Gulch. Both, apparently, were camp names, although Perigo and Gold Dirt were the two towns that emerged in the gulch. Perhaps Gambell Gulch was an earlier name for one of those towns. However, the name of the gulch has remained the same.

On Gambell Gulch there was the Colorado Tunnel, operated by the Colorado Mining Company, which made regular shipments to the big Argo Mill in Denver. The Penobscot Mining and Milling Company had a tunnel running to the Tip Top Mine, and were making plans just after the turn of the century to extend the tunnel 1,800 feet to meet several of the mines on Perigo Hill. There was also a Happy Hollow Mine on the Gulch, and the Mountain Monarch Tunnel.

The Star of Gilpin Mining and Promoting Company worked several properties on Lump Gulch. Two of the larger mines here were the Victoria and Gettysburg.

## PERIGO

Perigo was one of the more industrious towns in the region for several years. There were several mines and a few mills to handle the ores. It was quite a sociable town as well, and Perigo society attempted to make a name for itself on the society pages of the Central City and Denver newspapers.

There was a Perigo Social Club which sponsored several dances and outings. The "Society" attempted to lure many of the shows of Central City and Denver to Perigo, but met with very little success. They had to be content with making a big show about attending the social events, music and drama doings in the other nearby cities. The society columns of the day were frequented by Perigo matrons.

There were several mines around Perigo: the Free Gold, Golden Sun, and the Perigo itself, for which the community was named. The big deal at Perigo, however, was the 30-stamp mill. The stamps were extra heavy to treat the low-grade ore found here, and was one of the first of its kind in the state. The mill was taken over by the McFarlane and Company firm of Central City and Black Hawk.

Mining has long since died away here, but Perigo is still alive as a summer resort and small supply town. It still has a post office.

## GOLD DIRT

Gold Dirt, a mile down gulch from Perigo, produced more gold in its day—two million dollars—but was not the social town Perigo was. It wasn't as big, either.

Gold Dirt was primarily a project of John Q. Rollins. He set up a six-stamp mill here in the winter of 1860-61. The mill made nearly $1,500 the first week, so he enlarged it to 16 stamps and bought most of the claims around.

In 1864, Rollins went to New York and organized mining companies. He held a large share of stock in each. The companies operated around Colorado, and had wide holdings in Gambell Gulch. Some of the mines in which he had an interest were the Comstock, Ophir, Virginia and White Pine.

Rollins Stamp Mill was fed by a two and half-mile flume that touched many of the mines. It cost $15,000. Gold Dirt continued in existence for several years with varying degrees of activity.

## GILPIN

A short distance away from Gold Dirt and Perigo was the small camp of Gilpin.

Gilpin's life and good times pretty much paralleled that of the other two camps, although it is believed the mining wasn't as good here.

Summer cabins now mingle with the old miners' cabins at Gilpin.

*And Then There Were* . . . . *BLUEBIRD*, a small camp a short distance northeast of Caribou. About the only good mine was the Great Northern . . . . *PHOENIX* (Phoenixville) a camp between Rollinsville and Eldora in the center of three or four fairly good mines. The top mine was the Champion. Others were the Lone Star, Melett and Fairhaven . . . . *BUCKEYE MOUNTAIN* another small and temporary camp in the center of some minor properties on Buckeye Mountain. About the only property found to be worth development was the Black Hills property . . . . *ANTELOPE* and *LADORA* stations and switches on the railroad line over Corona Pass. The sites were on the old railroad bed and not on the present Corona Pass Road . . . . *JENNY LAKE CAMP* a popular resort during the days of the railroad run over Corona Pass. The camp is gone but the lake is still there and is still a popular spot for fishermen . . . . *PETERSON'S CAMP*, a small camp off the beaten track around some lesser mining properties. The camp only lasted a few months. . . . *WIDE AWAKE*, a mill, the post office an another cabin remain of this town, which paralleled the history of Perigo. The town had a population of several hundred in its heyday. The most important location was the Caledonia. Remains of the town about a half mile beyond Missouri Lake . . . *MAMMOTH CITY*, a small, obscure town that spent a few years on Mammoth Gulch, northwest of Apex.

# IV. THE NIGHT THE STARS FELL . . .

Captain Thomas Aikens, leading a party of Argonauts up the Arkansas River in 1858, scanned the blue mountains with a telescope, and noted:

"The mountains look right for gold and the valleys look right for grazing."

When the party arrived at the site of present-day Boulder, Chief Ni Wot (Left Hand) and a band of Arapahoes were camped nearby.

The Chief greeted the white men, then he asked Captain Aikens if he remembered the year the stars fell. The captain replied it was 1832.

"It was that year white men first came," the chief said. Then pointing to Donati's comet in the sky, Chief Ni Wot asked:

"Do you know what that star with the tail means? The tail points back to when the stars fell as thick as the tears of our women shall fall when you come to drive us off."

In slow broken English, the chief told of a dream he had. He said he saw the canyon (Boulder) flooded. The Indians were engulfed and the white men were saved. He warred the white men to leave or they would be killed.

The bluff didn't work. The white men didn't leave, and they weren't killed. Nor did the Indians leave at first. White men and red men lived side by side. One often helped the other. There was no bloodshed. Chief Ni Wot became a friend of the white men.

But, eventually, as the white men flooded his land in search of gold, the chief moved to a special Indian reservation at Sand Creek, set aside for the "good" Indians, while the white men sought out the "bad" Indians, chased them away or killed them.

On November 29, 1864, Colonel John M. Chivington and a large force of soldiers swooped down on Sand Creek. Before their work was finished, some 700 men, women and children were dead.

Among them was Chief Ni Wot, who had dreamed his land would be flooded and his people killed . . . and the white men would be saved.

## BOULDER (Boulder City)

The first school house in Colorado opened up in Boulder in 1860. A few improvements have been made here and there since, but Boulder has remained the educational center of the state.

Today the city is known for its university, but in past years it served as a gateway to one of the richest mineral sections of the state. It was, and still is, a supply center for the hills behind it.

In turn, the hills shipped more than 35 million dollars worth of gold, silver, lead, copper and several millions in tungsten. Some of the mines are

*MAP FOUR*

## THE BOULDER AREA

Boulder (Boulder City)
Red Rock and Boulder Diggings (neither on map)
Orodelfan (Orodell, Maxwell's Mill, Hortonville, Hunt's Concentration
    Works)
Sugarloaf
Magnolia
Sunshine
Crisman
Salina
Summerville
Gold Hill
Mount Alta
Sunset
Wall Street (Delphi)
Copper Rock
Altona (Modoc, Niwot)
Jamestown (Camp Jimtown, Elysian Park)
Balarat (also spelled Ballarat)
Camp Providence (John Jay Camp), Camp Enterprise (not on map),
    Glendale and Gresham
Rowena (Rockville)
Springdale
Gold Lake
Camp Tolcott, Quiggleyville and Puzzler
Ward
Camp Francis (Francis)
Williamsburg (Switchville)
Camp Albion

*And Then There Were . . . . EAGLE ROCK* (Wheelman), *SWITZERLAND PARK,
GOLD HILL STATION, JACKSON'S CAMP, CAMP LYON* (not on map), *TEL-
LURIUM* (not on map), *BLOOMERVILLE*, PRIMOS, and ALLEN'S PARK.

79

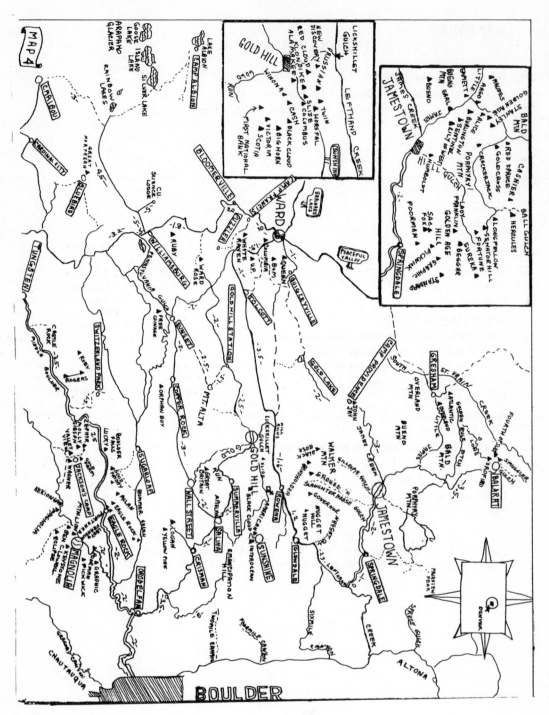

MAP 4

still producing and uranium has been added in recent years to the impressive list of minerals that still pass through Boulder.

## RED ROCK and BOULDER DIGGINGS (not on map)

Red Rock was the first mountain camp in the Boulder area. Some say it was the first camp of any kind here, but there is good evidence that the Argonauts camped first at the mouth of Boulder Canyon near the present site of Boulder.

Within a few days, however, they moved up the canyon and established a camp at Red Rock. Since Red Rock is shown (at various distances up the canyon) on several early maps, it apparently was a permanent camp for a few short years, serving as a headquarters for prospectors.

Since most of the first prospectors headed up Four Mile Creek in the direction of Gold Hill, Red Rock was most likely situated at or near the mouth of the creek, at the site of later-day Orodelfan.

Boulder Diggings is believed to be the first mining camp in the Boulder area. It was apparently around the site of Gold Hill and may be Gold Hill itself. About all the early histories say concerning its location is that it was 14 miles from Boulder.

The camp was mentioned prominently in 1859 and 1860 as the destination of a Methodist Episcopal Mission from Iowa. The mission, under the leadership of Reverend W. H. Goode, made the trip to Denver from Glenwood, Iowa, in four weeks.

After landing in Denver the group decided to split up, one half "working" Denver, and the other half taking the word of God to Boulder Diggings.

Come to think of it, the peaceful and religious-like beginning of Gold Hill lends more evidence to the theory Boulder Diggings, with the Methodist Mission on hand, was Gold Hill after all.

There was virtually no violence in Gold Hill and the first settlers voted against allowing saloons in the city . . . a rather pious beginning for a Colorado mining town.

## ORODELFAN (Orodell, Maxwell's Mill, Hortonville, and Hunt's Concentration Works)

This site, on Boulder Canyon Road at the turn-off toward Crisman, was once a camp around various mills built to process the ores that came down from the hills.

At various times it had a smelting works, sawmill, a post office and store. The name was usually taken from the facility in dominance at the time. But the name was eventually changed to Orodelfan.

Just before the turn of the century, some Chinese miners made a modest living by hand picking the gravels in the stream for placer gold.

Nothing is left of the site today.

81

## SUGARLOAF

In 1902, after the Sugarloaf area had been worked for 40 years, an old prospector named Niles crossed over a potato patch and chanced to notice some gold float on the ground. The prospector hired a team and scraped off the topsoil. Some gold was found just below the surface, and a little deeper he struck a rich vein of ore.

Within a short time Niles realized thousands of dollars from the Potato Patch Mine.

Some surface gold was found here in 1860, but it soon worked out and the area was deserted for more than ten years, until some tellurium was found. Many profitable mines were located. The area was busy for many years.

The U. S. Gold Corporation began construction of a huge mill in 1915. Its carcass still stands, although its machinery was removed during a scrap drive in World War II.

Now potatoes and some mountain peas grow once again where gold was so rich it could be picked up off the ground. There is also some ranching and tourism here.

BEST MINES: Livingston, which produced more than $300,000 in gold, and the Potato Patch.

## MAGNOLIA

Magnolia is another old gold-mining town that is developing into a resort area. Little of the old life is visible.

Magnolia came into being about 1875 when ore similar to that found in Sunshine was located here. The town was pretty much scattered all over the area, and Jackson's Camp was located a short distance away.

The mines were worked for rich ore, and then after a cyanide mill was built, the diggings were worked again for the low-grade ore that hadn't been worth the trouble before. After the turn of the century, some of the mines were worked by lessees for a third time, and some good ore was found.

The site can be reached over a steep, rough road, climbing two and a half miles off Boulder Canyon.

BEST MINES: Magnolia, Young Magnolia, Jefferson, Atlantic, Queen Victoria, Dunraven, Keystone, Mountain Lion, Lady Franklin, and Little Maud.

## SUNSHINE

Sunshine had many notable features, not the least of which was the fact it was one of the very few mining camps that closed its saloons on the Sabbath.

Other features included: an ore specimen which won first prize at two national expositions; and a dangerous gamble that paid off.

Hiram Hitchcock of New York, a man of many interests, had won and lost many fortunes on mines throughout the west. At the time, he was on the losing side. Profits from his Fifth Avenue hotel were not enough to cover his debts. But just on a gambler's hunch he purchased the American Mine in Sunshine for $17,500.

The mine had been located by George Jackson and Hiram Fuller. The two realized about $15,000 from a rich vein, but after this played out they considered the property worthless, and felt lucky to get $17,500 from the "eastern sucker."

The American, however, soon put Hitchcock back on his feet and more—much more. Within two years the mine produced nearly $200,000 in gold, and a million and a half more before it was through. It was ore from the American that won first prize at the Philadelphia Mining Exposition in 1876.

Long before Jackson and Fuller came here, other prospectors passed by the region and considered the area worthless. It wasn't until 1873 that a rich strike was made and Sunshine came into being. Several other good locations were made in the next few months.

Another sample of ore from the Inter Ocean mine won first prize in the mineral exhibit at the World's Fair in St. Louis in 1904.

The city, which was named for the first baby born here—Sunshine Turner—had a population of 1,500 men, women and children in its heyday. There were three good hotels: Forest House, Grand View Hotel and Howard House; a school house, newspaper and many other businesses. Among the distinguished visitors were "Commodore" Stephen Decatur (see Decatur) and Governor Routt, who spoke at a Republican convention here in 1876.

The newspaper, *The Sunshine Courier*, was published from 1875 to 1878, when it was taken to Boulder.

The mines produced well and some of them are still being worked by lessees.

Some new tourist cabins are found here, mingled with relics of the once-prosperous city that didn't sell liquor on Sunday.

A tiny cemetery can be seen alongside the road toward Bighorn Mountain. BEST MINES: American, Inter-Ocean, Sunshine, Little Miami, Grand View, White Crow.

## CRISMAN

The Logan mine, located in 1874, was said to be the richest mine in the county. They say its free gold was so pure it was put in a strong box and taken directly to the Denver Mint.

Other good finds were made about the same time, and the city of Crisman was platted near the mines. The site was named for Obed Chrisman, one of the early settlers and owner of an ore concentration mill.

A story is told about the Logan mine. It seems a tunnel had been drilled more than 2,000 feet in 1908, but nothing worthwhile was found, and the owners ordered work stopped. Superintendent A. S. Coan was permitted to lease the property. His first blast uncovered $1,500 in high grade ore, and the agreement was quickly revoked.

The town had a general store and post office in 1875.

Crisman was also noted for its wine cellar, built by Francois Pierre Ardourel, a former captain in the French Army and father of Alphonse Ardourel, former adjutant general of Colorado.

Francois Ardourel came to Colorado after service in the Franco-Prussian War in 1870. He located the Grand Republic mine on Four Mile Creek near Crisman.

Being an aristocratic Frenchman, he insisted on fine wines and built a lavish wine cellar under his home, which bored into the hill.

After the flood of 1894 washed out much of the Salt Lake and Pacific Railroad tracks along the creek, the tracks were relocated on higher ground behind Ardourel's house. This necessitated blocking off much of the wine cellar.

But the smaller wine cellar and Ardourel's house still stand in Crisman, mingled with the tourist houses built in recent years.

The Yellow Pine and the Logan were the top mines.

## SALINA

Salina, named for the city in Kansas from which many of the first settlers came, still lives, but is only a skeleton of its former self.

It took 14 years before prospectors first worked their way down the valley from the first strike on Gold Run in 1859. The first locations were made at Salina in 1874, and within a year nearly 100 claims were staked out, and a reduction mill was working to capacity.

The population exceeded 100 by 1875 and doubled in the years to come. Cabins dotted the valley, the Salina House Hotel was operating to capacity, and a school house was built and classes held. A toll gate was built here.

Within three years, however, the prospectors found only a handful of the claims were worth developing. And only those who were needed, stayed.

Salina lingered on for years, and some work has been done here in recent years. But most of the residents today are summer guests.

The large mill here was the West Reduction works, built in 1875.

BEST MINES: Black Swan, Melvina, and Shamos O'Brien.

## SUMMERVILLE

Halfway between Salina and Gold Hill on what was known as Gold Run was Summerville.

Some mines were located here in the seventies. Much of the ore was only average grade. When the pockets of good ore were emptied, Summerville was pretty much neglected until about the turn of the century when more efficient methods of milling made it profitable to treat the low-grade ore.

The best mine was the Black Cloud. Other mines were the Victoria, Cah, CQ, U. S. Band and Hoosier Ledge. There has been a little mining here in recent years.

A couple of the remaining cabins at Summerville are still occupied.

## GOLD HILL

Gold Hill was believed to be the first permanent mining camp in Colorado.

Rich ores were located here in 1859, and within a year some 1,500 gold-hungry prospectors covered the area.

The first quartz mill in Colorado was hauled through the wilderness by ox team and set up here in 1859.

The first gold was of the surface variety and this played out in a few months. Most of the residents pushed on, locating other strikes in the Boulder area, and starting other cities.

Some of the mines continued to pay off, but the others were deserted until 1869 when Professor Hill (see Black Hawk) set up a mill to treat low-grade ore.

Gold Hill's second boom reached its peak shortly after 1872, when tellurium was found. From that moment on, Gold Hill was for real and the city never died, tourists taking up the slack in mining in recent years.

One of Colorado's first organs and pianos was brought across the plains by ox-cart and was lugged into Gold Hill. The two instruments furnished the music for Gold Hill's dances, and there were many.

Gold Hill was one of the more sociable cities in the Boulder area. Other than its many dances and musicals, the city was known for its flower gardens and prize blooms. It had a large and busy roller skating rink. Sledding was popular and some of the first skiing in Colorado was done here. But perhaps its greatest claim to fame was its drill champions.

Machine drilling competition was a popular sport among the early mining camps, and Gold Hill was blessed with two champions, Jim Pittman and his brother-in-law, Dan Caughlin. The two took on all comers and won many a prize for Gold Hill.

Gold Hill had many hotels and newspapers in its day. The Miner's Hotel, built in 1872, is still standing and many of the original furnishings remain intact. The hotel, operated by Casey, boasted some of the nation's best cuisine and was immortalized by Eugene Field in his "Casey's Table D'Hote."

Gold Hill's second and worst fire occurred in November 1894. The fire roared through the dense timber from Ward, pushed on by a strong west wind. Within hours all of Gold Hill was deserted, most prized possessions hidden from the flames in mines. Much of the population climbed to the top of barren Horsfal Mountain, in the bitter cold, to watch their town being ravaged by the flames. After the fire had done its damage, the wind died and a snowstorm put out the embers.

Thousands of dollars in property went up in smoke. Relief came from Boulder and other nearby areas. A flood that same year helped complete the destruction. Much of the city was rebuilt, but Gold Hill was never the same.

Despite the extensive mining done here, Gold Hill experienced few mine disasters. Perhaps the worst disaster occurred in 1878 when two men drowned in the Cold Spring shaft. The entire city stopped its activity to attend the funeral, and the victims' families were well taken care of by the townspeople.

The camp's richest and biggest mine, the Slide, which still sits majestically above Left Hand Canyon, was one of the few big mines in Colorado that never had a fatal accident.

The Hill is still covered with cabins, but most of them are newer tourist cabins and lodges. Much of the past is gone.

GOLD DUST: Gold Run was named by the first prospectors who panned gold dust in the stream. The Gold Run road down from Gold Hill was famous for speedy runs made by stagecoaches and ore wagons which zoomed down the mountain in a cloud of dust . . . . Lickskillet Gulch, running from Gold Hill down to Left Hand Canyon, achieved the same notoriety . . . . Gold Hill's cemetery is four miles south of the city . . . . the original Gold Hill district was partially in Nebraska territory and part in Kansas territory . . . . the original site of Gold Hill was below the present site, which was laid out in the early 70's . . . . Hannah C. Spaulding was Gold Hill's first school teacher. She opened a school here in 1873. She later married James Guise, a miner, and the couple lived here in the same house for the better part of 52 years. They both died in December, 1929 . . . . $100,000 in gold was taken out the first year by simple "Hand Rockers" . . . . Gold Hill was another mining town which rejected saloons in a vote by early settlers.

## MOUNT ALTA

Mount Alta is still a good place to have a picnic, but nothing like it was. The site was developed by the railroad as a resort and picnic area.

It was a welcome stopover on the rugged trip over the Switzerland Trail, and it was a spot for an all-day outing. Trainloads of tourists would take the train to Mount Alta, spend the day there, and then catch the train on its return trip to Boulder.

The site had a large lodge and dance pavilion, other tourist traps, and some cabins.

The large stone fireplace is all that remains of the lodge. The ruins of the famed Mount Alta fountain are a short distance away.

### SUNSET

Sunset was an important junction of Denver, Boulder and Western Railroad. Here the line branched off, one branch going on to Eldora, and the other going to Ward.

The railroad brought considerable business to the community, but there were a number of mines here also. The most notable were the Scandia, Free Coinage and Poor Woman.

Sunset hit its peak in the mid-90's, when hundreds of persons lived here and more hundreds passed through daily. But slowly the city faded. Now, an old box car, with Sunset emblazoned on its side, a few scattered cabins and an old cemetery behind the site, mark the location.

High on the hill between Sunset and Gold Hill is an old white house. The house is called Honeymoon House and legend says it is haunted.

The story goes a young man, very much in love with his bride-to-be, built the house for her as a wedding present. But before the two were married, she died.

They say—"they" being the kind of people that enjoy saying things like this—on clear nights when the moon is bright and the wind whistles through the pines, making weird noises and moving the eerie shadows, that the young bride returns to the house to whisper her love for her young suitor, who is also a ghost by this time.

### WALL STREET (Delphi)

Wall Street booms once again—as a resort area. But during the 90's and early 1900's, it was one of the top gold producers in the area.

Several mines were located here as long ago as 1878, but Wall Street got its big lift in 1902, with the construction of the Wall Street Gold Extraction Company mill to handle the ore brought through the Nancy Tunnel.

The chlorination mill, one of the first in northern Colorado, was built at a cost of $175,000, but paid for itself many times over.

The Nancy Gold Mine and Tunnel Company was organized the same year the mill was built, and greatly aided in the development of many of the mines.

The Nancy mines included the Last Chance, Gold Eagle, Golden Rule, Grand View, Gillard, Wedges, Lion's Roost, Silver Eaglet and many others. Several other mines, including the South American, Mountaineer, Star and Great Britain, can be seen between Wall Street and Salina.

The Wall Street Mill still towers about the city where newer tourist cabins are mingled with the cabins of yesterday.

Wall Street, earlier called Delphi, was named for the New York money invested in the area.

## COPPER ROCK

An old log cabin with the designation of "Copper Rock" on a sign nearby, and a cabin back off the road, mark the site of Copper Rock—a small gold camp that mushroomed in the early 90's.

Copper Rock was also a station on the railroad.

A green copper stain can be seen on the mountains across from the town.

## ALTONA (Modoc, Niwot)

Altona was never a mining camp. It was meant to be much more. It began as an ambitious project, a mountain metropolis to serve all the camps in the area.

With its advantageous position near the mouth of Left Hand Canyon, it would be a supply and transportation center, perhaps surpassing Boulder and even Denver.

But the plan, dreamed up in the early 60's, didn't get very far.

It did, however, get a good start. It was the station of the toll road running through Left Hand Canyon, and it was a trading center for a while. Then, other roads were built into the area, and the railroad was built, ignoring Altona and its elaborate plans.

For many years Altona served as headquarters for the quarry men working the red sandstone deposits along the front face of the range.

But then, they too left, until the postmaster was just about the only man left in town. In 1918, after no mail had arrived at Altona for several months, he locked the door of the post office and never came back.

Now, the site of Altona is ranchland and only one old frame building marks the spot of the ambitious city that didn't come off.

It was first named Modoc, changed to Niwot in 1872, and then to Altona in 1879.

## JAMESTOWN (Camp Jimtown, Elysian Park)

Jamestown is one of the oldest mining camps in the state, and it is still busy. It has boomed and re-boomed and boomed again.

There are still minerals in the area, including uranium and radium and felspar.

George Zweck built the first cabin on the site in 1860 and prospected the area for three or four years before some galena was found and the first rush began. More than 400 fortune seekers worked the hills, but the boom only lasted three years and Jamestown was all but deserted for another ten years.

88

Only rubble remains of Lakewood. During the first World War the largest
tungsten mill in the world was here.

The last of Williamsburg, once believed to be another Caribou. The remains of the town can be seen just below the Peak to Peak Highway.

An old mine looking down on Salina. Note workings on the face of the mountains across the way.

Summerville, between Salina and Gold Hill. A couple of the cabins are occupied during the summer.

The Gold Hill Cemetery, four miles from Gold Hill on the road toward Sunshine. Despite its rundown condition, a couple of new markers have gone up in recent years.

Ward on January 23, 1900, just after the big fire. The town and the church are still going strong. *University of Colorado photo.*

A trappers cabin alongside Grand Lake in 1884. *Colorado State Highway Department photo.*

Not little ole New York, but Manhattan, Colorado, as it looked in 1888. *Denver Public Library Western History Collection.*

Hahns Peak, town and mountain. *U. S. Geological Survey photo.*

Pearl, near the Wyoming border. Picture looks west toward Davis Peak. *U. S. Geological Survey photo.*

Buckskin Joe about 1864, where Silver Heels danced. *State Historical Society of Colorado photo.*

Ruins of the last house at Mudsill, a short distance from Leavick.

South Park City, a "new" suburb of Fairplay. The buildings here were important in the early history of the South Park area and have been restored inside and out as authentically as possible. *Photo by Nels Nelson.*

Breckenridge today, a peaceful little mining town. That's Mountain Number Eight in the background.

Early Montezuma, the closest thing to a ghost town still going. *State Historical Society of Colorado photo.*

The first and only building in what was to be the elaborate town of Franklin, a mile and a half south of Montezuma. The house was a meeting and show place for officers of the Montezuma Silver Mining Co. *State Historical Society of Colorado photo.*

In 1875 some rich gold float was found and the second boom began. Another boom started in 1882.

Up until 1915, the Jamestown district produced more than five million dollars in gold, silver, lead, copper and fluorspar. Attention was turned to the latter during World War I and another fluorspar boom occurred during the second World War.

The camp was founded in 1865 and first called Elysian Park. But when residents petitioned for a post office they asked for the name Camp Jimtown. Apparently the post office department didn't think this dignified enough and renamed it Jamestown. Jimtown, however, has remained the popular name of the community.

The town really took hold during the second and third booms (1875 and 1882) and most of the lasting construction was done during these periods. The two top hotels, Evans House and Martin, were built, along with churches and a school, some 30 saloons and numerous dance halls and parlor houses. Gambling halls were busy around the clock. Another money-maker was the toll road from Left Hand Canyon. It was a sociable town. A community hall was built, and dances were held weekly.

Jamestown did not have a disastrous fire as many of the other boom towns did, but a flood roared down Jim Creek in June of 1894, and washed away much of the low-lying area of the city. The flood was caused by a cloudburst on top of the heavy run-off.

TOP MINES: Golden Age, Wano, and many others.

GOLD DUST: Movie idol Douglas Fairbanks Sr. came from here . . . . some gold was found to be so rich here it was sent directly to the Denver Mint . . . . by 1902, the Golden Age, the best mine in the district, had been in continuous operation longer than any other mine in the state. It was located in 1875 by Frank Smith and Indian Jack, and although the ore was assayed as high as 50 per cent gold, they sold the claim for a measly $1,500 . . . . the Buena was found the same year and produced over a million dollars worth of gold. The mine is now called the Wano. The mine was closed by the government in 1940 when the War Production Board began processing fluorspar in the Wano Mill. The mill was still running . . . . the Golden Age Mill can be seen between the town and Left Hand Canyon . . . . Jamestown had good radium springs and could be a great tourist mecca.

*BALARAT* (also spelled Ballarat)

Only a whisper of the once-prosperous city of Balarat remains.

The Smuggler vein was located in 1875. Other important locations were made in the following months. By 1877, the gulch was dotted with cabins, several businesses and a saloon. The same year a stamp mill was built.

But Balarat's trouble was in transportation. Although only three and a half short miles from Jamestown, the road was difficult and slow. It usually took two days for the ore wagons to reach Boulder.

But mining continued off and on through the years. In 1918, eastern

97

interests organized the Smuggler Mine and Milling Company, and worked the area profitably until recent years.

Much of Balarat was destroyed in the flood of 1894. The rest has failed the test of time.

BEST MINES:   Smuggler, Bindago, Eldorado, Careless Boy, Little Eddie, and Waumega.

## CAMP PROVIDENCE (John Jay Camp), CAMP ENTERPRISE, GLENDALE, and GRESHAM

Some of the more important camps that erupted around Jamestown during the 70's and 80's.

Camp Providence, also known as John Jay Camp, got its start in 1875—the same time as the second Jamestown boom—when a Central City party found telluride veins on Overland Hill. The camp was located three miles southwest of Jamestown on Big Jim Creek. The John Jay was the leading mine.

Camp Providence was named by J. J. Van Deren of Boulder who believed Providence led to discovery of the mines.

Camp Enterprise, four and a half miles west of Jamestown, also arose during the second Jamestown boom.

An old post office is all that remains of Gresham, over a difficult and harrowing road.

Glendale had its beginning in the early 80's. It is in Left Hand Canyon, two miles beyond the Jamestown turn-off. Glendale was on a junction of a difficult road connecting Sunshine with Left Hand Canyon. Several cabins mark the site.

## ROWENA (Rockville)

Only the foundations of once huge mills remain at the site of Rowena. Located in the center of one of the richest gold and silver areas in the region, the mills of Rowena processed millions of dollars in minerals in their day.

The mills handled ore from the Prussian, Gold Nugget, Cold Spring and other good mines. The Prussian earned $175,000 in two years running.

Rowena is connected with Gold Hill by Lickskillet Gulch, a short but steep gulch down which the ore wagons used to race in Lickskillet speed.

The Rowena cemetery is located a couple of miles south of the townsite.

## SPRINGDALE

Springdale, in its day, was better known for its mineral springs than for its mines.

The springs, at the top of the gulch, came to be known as Peabody's Hot Springs, and were said to be similar to those of the famous Seltzer Springs in Germany. A resort hotel called the Seltzer House, and several resort cottages, were constructed in the gulch. The water was bottled and sold far and wide.

Miners' cabins also dotted the gulch during the 70's and 80's. More than 300 lived here during the boom. But the mines were not so good as others in the district.

Much of Springdale was caught in the flood which hit Jamestown in 1894. Most of the buildings that were left have burned down since. Now, only a couple of buildings remain.

BEST MINES: Grand Central, King William, Copper Blush, Gladiator, Big Blossom and Rip Van Dam.

## GOLD LAKE

Gold Lake was both a mining and a recreational enterprise. It still has possibilities but the first attempts didn't pan out.

Some "good paying mines" were located near here shortly after the Gold Hill boom. The best properties were the Bonanza, Oro Cash, Ready Cash, Greenback and West Wing. Although apparently paying well for a while, the mines soon played out and Gold Lake was abandoned as a mining area.

But during the mining boom in the early 60's, promoters saw the possibilities of Gold Lake as a resort. They drew up elaborate plans for the site, calling for buildings to surround the lake. Only one building was constructed, and that was used to house the over-ambitious planners.

Nothing remains but the lake.

## CAMP TOLCOTT, QUIGGLEYVILLE and PUZZLER

Three camps east of Ward, growing out of mining activity in the area.

Puzzler was the largest and most active. Located in Puzzler Gulch, once filled with diggings, Puzzler had a school house, post office and a large mill, the Puzzler, above the city.

Puzzler was also a station on the railroad. The ruins of several workings and cabins, and the old school house are still standing.

Camp Tolcott and Quiggleyville were both fathered by Colonel Wesley Brainard of Evanston, Illinois, who had great confidence in the region, and who worked among the hills for more than twenty years. The camps never amounted to much and don't amount to anything at all now.

## WARD

Ward is sitting on a gold mine. Such a wealth of precious metals is believed to still exist beneath the city, it has frequently been suggested that the community be razed and the hill leveled for its minerals.

But the riches surrounding Ward were enough to satisfy most ordinary prospectors. The Ward district was one of the richest in the state. Its mines produced millions in gold, and some lead and other minerals were found here. One mine produced more than two million ounces of silver during its three-year existence.

Calvin Ward, for whom the city was named, located the Miser's Dream in 1860. But the boom didn't take hold until the following year when Cy Deardorff located the Columbia vein. In its day, the vein produced more than five million dollars, with the Utica its top property, producing more than a million.

Another valuable property was the Ni-Wot, but litigation and constant changes of ownership erased much of the profit, said to have been over a million and a quarter.

A man named C. H. Merrill paid $50 for the property and was laughed at for doing so. Merrill did almost nothing to the property and sold it two years later for $15. The new owners, Sam Breath and W. A. Davidson, realized $50,000 from it the first year and, after greatly developing the property, sold it for $300,000. The next owners turned around and sold it for half a million dollars. Much London money, and H. A. W. Tabor, were involved in the many other transactions that followed.

The area flourished all through the 70's, 80's and 90's, with the population varying from 400 to a thousand, and sometimes more. The city was incorporated in 1896. The following year, work began on the railroad from Boulder to Ward. The arrival of the first passenger train in June of 1898 was cause for a wild celebration, lasting for days. A lavish welcome awaited the train carrying Governor Alva Adams and many other Colorado officials and celebrities.

Before the railroad arrived, Ward was connected with the outside world by difficult wagon roads and trails. Much ore had been stored because of the costs of shipping. But after the railroad began making regular runs, the ore was shipped out easily and cheaply, and the mining activity in the region increased greatly. As much as 100 tons of ore was shipped daily. And passenger trains carried an average of 250 persons to and from the booming community each day.

Ward, as most other Colorado mining camps of the day, had its fires. The worst one started in an ashcan behind the McClancy Hotel on January 24, 1901. Before it had run its course, more than 50 buildings were destroyed and close to $90,000 damage had been done. But, as in other thriving mining camps, Ward was rebuilt, and sturdier material was used.

Ward is not a ghost town. Some mining is still carried on in the area, and the minerals still buried in the region indicate the city may boom again one day.

TOP MINES: Ni-Wot, Columbia, Utica, East Columbia, Central Columbia, Baxter, Idaho, Boston, Miser's Dream.

GOLD DUST: The fireplace in the Ward Hotel is constructed of gold ore . . . . *The Ward Miner* was the oldest and most notable of the city's newspapers . . . . to save the schoolhouse and the Congregational Church from the 1901 fire, the residents drenched both buildings with water. Both are still standing . . . . the Colorado and Northwestern railway line to Ward was called the Switzerland Trail and the Whiplash Route because of the Swiss nature of the land it crossed and because of the twisting route needed to negotiate the steep grade and mountains along the way . . . . the Utica Mill, built of stone and one of the oldest in Colorado, still stands beside the road just below Ward. The mill was first run by water power, piped five miles over the hills . . . . the first successful chlorination mill in Colorado was built in Ward . . . . 35 million dollars were taken from the Columbia and three other gold veins here.

## CAMP FRANCIS (Francis)

A busy camp south of Ward.

A large syndicate took over the operation of many of the properties in the gulch during the 90's and developed them into well-paying mines. Much of the ore from the mines was carted through the Adit Tunnel and processed in the Big Five Mill built on the side of the gulch.

Camp Francis was also an important link in the railroad. Work crews were usually busy all winter long keeping the railway open from here through the narrow cut in the mountain to Ward.

A disastrous slide occurred on the run in 1901. A passenger car waited down the line as a double-engine atempted to bully itself through huge drifts. It was uncertain if the train itself caused the slide or if the slide was destined anyhow. But the huge avalanche roared down the mountain onto the engines, killing two firemen, a brakeman and a conductor, and injuring many others, who somehow were able to work themselves free. Several hours later, another engine from Boulder arrived at the scene to carry the passengers to safety, and to carry the bodies of the crewmen back for burial.

The population of Camp Francis remained at around 200 through the 90's, with about half of the residents employed by the Big Five Syndicate.

Some tumble-down cabins can be seen just off the Peak-to-Peak highway, and the ruins of many workings and the giant Big Five Mill can be seen farther up the gulch.

BEST MINES: Adit, Ni-Wot, Dew Drop and Columbia.

## WILLIAMSBURG (Switchville)

Newspaper reports in the very early 70's were booming Williamsburg as a close rival to Caribou. The reports had the silver found at Williamsburg as good as that found at Caribou, and the location—although still isolated— as more ideal than that of the other camp.

But the unceremonious and almost unheralded demise of Williamsburg indicates that the town couldn't compete.

George Williams and Bolus Mitchell were attracted by the specks of silver sulphurets found here in 1871, and began prospecting the region.

They located a rich deposit and staked out a claim. By the following summer, scores of prospectors were in the area and the town of Williamsburg was platted.

A number of "good" strikes were made and work began. The best strike, however, was the Washington Avenue, made by Williams and Mitchell. The original claim was said to have been made on an extensive vein, which was staked in both directions. In fact, the entire area was staked out.

Reports of the strikes were glowing:

"The remarkable thing about the lode (Washington Avenue) is that a body of silver ore so rich, pure and apparently so extensive could be so close to the surface (beginning at ten feet)."

Another newspaper called the Washington Avenue "a mammoth vein carrying from two to five feet of solid galena and zinc ore."

The ore averaged about 260 ounces of silver—or $328—to the ton. Similar blossom rock was found both east and west on the Divide between North Boulder and Four Mile Creeks.

An organization called Welch and Company discovered and began developing the Mayflower Mine, at the head of Pennsylvania Gulch, about a mile and a half from Williamsburg. The ore was said to have been as good as that found in the Washington Avenue.

A large town was laid out in the narrow valley just below the present Peak-to-Peak Valley. Business was booming and hundreds of prospectors were in the area.

Although there was an old trail that pretty much followed the present-day Peak-to-Peak Highway, Williamsburg was all but isolated. The town was about as far from the Caribou Mill in Middle Boulder (Nederland) as was Caribou, but the road was bad, impassable most of the time. There was widespread talk of improving the road, and also of building a road down Pennsylvania Gulch to Boulder. However, it was apparently little more than talk, because the roads had other destinations when they were improved upon or built a few years later.

Apparently the ores at Williamsburg weren't so fabulous after all.

The next time the town was heard from was a few years later as a station on the railroad. And then it was called Switchville, evidently a switching station.

A few old, old cabins, blackened by time, remain of Williamsburg. They can be seen just below the Peak-to-Peak Highway. Drive slowly or you may miss them.

## CAMP ALBION

Nothing is left today of Camp Albion, headquarters of the Snowy Range Mining district.

The district was organized in 1861, and some miners worked the area off and on through the 80's. Most of the best mines were located on Mount Albion, near the Divide.

Peak population of Camp Albion was never more than 200.

*And Then There Were* . . . . EAGLE ROCK (Wheelman) a small camp a short distance north of Magnolia and along Boulder Creek. The camp was called home to miners working in the Eagle Rock, Milan, and Paymaster. There were also some mines along Bummer Gulch, farther north of Eagle Rock . . . *SWITZERLAND PARK*, a combination resort and mining community north of Boulder Creek. There were several mining properties surrounding the community, but none of them paid too well . . . . *GOLD HILL STATION*. The Colorado and Northwestern railroad never quite got to Gold Hill. Instead, it built a station a short distance beyond Mount Alta on the highway between Gold Hill and Ward. Here the stage coaches and supply wagons would load up and rumble the rest of the way into Gold Hill . . . . *JACKSON'S CAMP*, located around some mines a short distance away from Magnolia, and soon overshadowed by the larger camp . . . . *CAMP LYON* and *TELLURIUM*, a couple of small, short-lived camps within a half mile of each other at the head of Sand Gulch, and only a mile from Sunshine. Sunshine soon took over . . . . *BLOOMERVILLE*, an obscure mining camp and railroad stop a short distance south of Camp Francis . . . . *PRIMOS* (not on map), a camp around some mining properties about two miles northeast of Lakewood. The workings weren't very extensive and the camp apparently didn't last long. However, some local residents have located some ruins at what was most likely the site of Primos. The history of the camp may be connected in some way with the huge Primos Mill at Lakewood. . . . *ALLEN'S PARK*, a fairly important town that lasted from 1896 to shortly after the turn of the century. The town was located eight miles north of Ward. The prospects were said to be located on veins running all the way from Ward. A news report in 1897 said there were 30 prospects and the town was filling up fast "with many stores and hotels." it had plans for being one of the largest towns in the state. There were plans for building a mill in 1901, but the town and the mines petered out shortly after that. The top mines were the Snowbank, Tiger, Bland, Black Horse, and Vulcan.

103

# V. GUN BATTLE AT GRAND LAKE

E. P. Weber and John Mills both came to Colorado from Illinois and at about the same time. They settled in Grand County and were important in its development. They had much in common and were good friends. Weber was superintendent of the big Wolverine mine. Mills was the leading attorney at booming Teller City and was called upon to settle disputes throughout the district. Both men were elected county commissioners.

It is believed the first major rift in their friendship came during the Republican Convention in 1882. The two men were among the candidates for delegates to the state convention. After a vicious battle, Mills and another man were elected delegates. But Weber and the county clerk named Cap Dean went to the state convention as contesting delegation and the state convention seated them instead of Mills and the other officially elected delegate.

The Mills-Weber friendship went downhill rapidly after that. The rivalry between Grand Lake and Teller City fanned the flames.

The final blow came on July 3, 1883, when Weber and Barney Day, another commissioner, held a county commissioners meeting, ignoring Mills, who was tied up in court. The meeting was held despite a prior agreement to postpone it for a couple of days.

This was too much for Mills to bear. They say he merely planned a sham lynching party the next day to throw a scare into Weber and Day and Dean. Mills called upon his friends, Sheriff Charley Royer and undersheriff William Redman, who also had grievances against the other men.

Their plans of make-believe first went awry when Weber, Day and Dean, apparently expecting trouble, left the Grand Lake Hotel fully armed.

You can't play-act with loaded guns.

It's not clear who fired the first shot and why. But the first shot was followed by many more. When the gunsmoke settled, Mills, Weber, Day and Dean lay dead or dying along the edge of Grand Lake. Royer and Redman fled the area.

Royer was found dead with a bullet hole in his head in a Georgetown hotel room a few weeks later. They ruled it a suicide, but some say the position of the gun to the body made suicide improbable, and murder more likely.

A man fitting Redman's description was found murdered along a trail in Utah a month after the gun battle. There were those who claimed it wasn't Redman, but many believe it was.

The gun battle—one of the blackest chapters in Colorado history—may seem out of place in the serene setting of Grand Lake. However, early history here is full of violence and tragedy.

104

Shortly before the white man came, a major battle between the Arapahoes and Utes was held over this favorite camping ground. The Utes built hasty barges and rafts, and set their women and children adrift on Grand Lake so they would escape the fighting. But a sudden storm came up, turning the lake into a watery hell, and sending scores of women and children to the bottom.

Another tale of violence, between white men and Indians, involves buried treasure.

Four prospectors, who made their lot in the California gold fields, stopped here to hunt and fish on their way back East. They buried their gold along the banks of Grand Lake and marked the spot by jamming a hunting knife into a nearby tree. Legend has it that an Indian scare forced the men to leave suddenly, without taking time to pick up their gold. Three of the men were killed by Indians. The fourth died shortly after he arrived at his home in the East.

People have been looking for the buried treasure ever since. No one has ever found it. Chances are some one, many years ago, found the knife in the tree, and that was treasure enough for him.

"Texas" Charley did his share in bringing violence to Grand Lake and the surrounding area. He bullied the entire area for quite a spell, beginning about the time of the shooting in 1883.

He was always looking for a barroom to shoot up, and his favorite form of diversion was shooting off the bootstraps of the miners, or shooting between their legs to see them dance. The law meant nothing to Texas Charley. One time in Hot Sulphur Springs he tore a warrant for his arrest into tiny pieces and scattered them along the main street, in full view of all the townspeople. He boasted there wasn't a man good enough to take him in.

He was suspected of rustling, and there were many tales of his shooting down adversaries. No doubt, many of these stories originated with him.

But finally he was too much to take. About fifteen of the leading citizens of Hot Sulphur Springs waited in ambush for him and shot him dead, dead, dead.

Grand Lake outlived its reputation and has been living clean ever since. They have even rid the town of its one-armed bandits in recent years.

*MAP FIVE*

### THE GRAND LAKE AREA

Gaskill (Auburn)
Wolverine and Ruby Mines
Hitchen's Camp

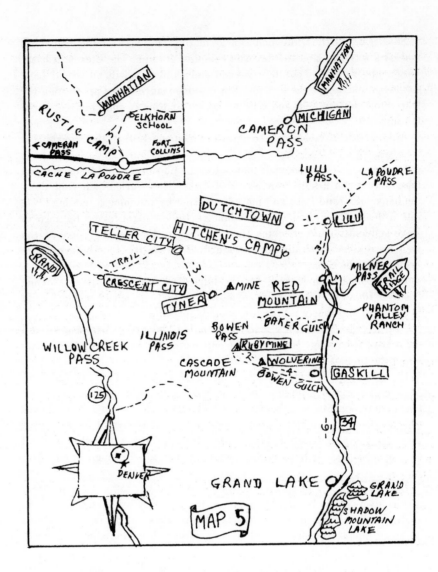

MAP 5

Lulu (Lulu City)
Dutchtown
Teller City
Crescent City
Tyner
Manhattan
Cummings (Cummings City, not on map), Park City (not on map), Michigan City and Mason (not on map)

*GASKILL* (Auburn)

Gaskill promised to be an important metropolis, but destiny and the gods of gold and silver, if there are gods of gold and silver, didn't keep the promise.

Gaskill was located near the north fork of the Colorado River, eight miles north of Grand Lake. It served as headquarters for the Wolverine, Ruby, and other mines up the gulch and the Grand Lake mine nearby. The camp was named for Captain L. D. C. Gaskill, one of the owners of the Wolverine Mine.

The mines were located, and Gaskill was founded, in the early and mid-80's.

The Grand Lake lode, located in 1883, was boomed to be "one of the richest in the state." It wasn't.

But the mines were sufficient to cause the development of a comparatively large community. Gaskill had a large hotel, the Rogerson House, and dozens of other buildings and cabins. The town had regular mail delivery and stage connections from as far away as Georgetown. There was a large wine cellar here, also.

But the boom only lasted three or four years and Gaskill quickly faded, leaving hardly a trace.

## WOLVERINE and RUBY MINES

There is evidence small camps were established around these mines near the head of the gulch running from Gaskill. Gaskill, however, was the center of activity in the gulch.

Three important characters in the mining story of the Grand Lake area were connected with the two mines.

The Ruby Mine was operated for several years by John Barbee, a well-educated and bombastic Kentucky gentleman, who also served as a justice of the peace, superintendent of schools in the area and, for a short while, editor of the *Grand Lake Prospector*.

His foreman of the mine was "Antelope" Jack Warren. Old timers say Barbee and Antelope Jack were as opposite as two men could be and spent much of their time cussing each other out. But they were inseparable and Antelope Jack was a faithful bodyguard to Barbee.

The Wolverine Mine was run by G. P. Weber, a county commissioner and one of the men killed in the notorious Grand Lake shooting.

## HITCHEN'S CAMP

Old Man Hitchen—for he was known only as Old Man Hitchen—was a well-known personality in this area for several years—he and his dog.

Actually, he had three dogs, but one at a time. One dog would stay at his master's heels until the animal died at a ripe old age. Hitchen would grieve strenuously for a few days and then go out and get another dog. Hitchen spent much of his later life alone—alone with his dog. He talked to his dogs as if they were people. He loved them more than he loved people.

He often expressed fear of the hereafter because he knew he would meet all three there, and then they might be jealous of one another and not get along.

There was a small camp at the foot of Red Mountain in Hitchen's Gulch during the boom in the area. However, the ore was not of sufficient quantity nor quality to sustain a camp for very long. Soon, all left—but Hitchen and his dogs. They worked the area for several years.

The camp was kept in fairly good repair until recent years, but it is now deteriorating. Of course, Hitchen and his dogs are gone. The camp can be reached by hiking or by horseback.

## LULU (Lulu City)

When the miners first swarmed to Lulu in 1879, they dug in as if they planned to stay. But when they started leaving three or four years later, they left so fast they left their dishes on the tables and clothes in the closets.

Some historians say Benjamin Franklin Burnett founded Lulu. Others say it was Captain Yankee.

All agree the place was swarming with excited prospectors inside a few short weeks. The city was laid out on an ambitious scale. Nineteen streets, one hundred blocks, were platted. Every sort of building was planned, many were built.

In no time, Lulu had four lumber mills, a fancy hotel, a justice of the peace and a post office. The stage from Fort Collins was routed to here and arrived three times a week. Saturday night Lulu was just about the liveliest place around.

Some good gold, silver and lead was mined, but generally the high costs and low-grade ore were hardly worth the trouble.

The boom actually lasted only one year, when Lulu had a Saturday population of more than 500. The wise ones began to leave after that, and Lulu was virtually empty by 1884.

The community was named for the daughter of Burnett.

A well-known character about Lulu was "Squeaky Bob" Wheeler, nicknamed for his high-pitched voice.

Squeaky Bob got drunk once in a while and shot up a tavern or two. Otherwise he was known as a mild-mannered and likeable fellow, full of yarns and good humor.

Bob worked Lulu for a while and made some money. He liked the country so well he purchased a ranch south of Lulu. It became a well-known stop.

Bob cared for the place himself, insisting on doing all the housework and cooking.

His place, known as the Phantom Valley Ranch, was famed for its cooking and cleanliness. Bob's hospitality and tall tales were attractions also.

Bob sold the ranch in 1926, but it has remained a hospitality spot.

BEST MINES: Carbonate, Friday Nite, Tiger, Southern Cross, Rustic.

## DUTCHTOWN

Dutchtown was a result of a drunken brawl in Lulu.

It seems a couple of Germans got loaded one night and shot up the town. They were run out of Lulu, prospected farther up Red Mountain and hit pay dirt. The resulting camp was named in their honor.

The camp was built near timberline. Winters were severe, transportation haphazard, and the ores weren't any better than they were at Lulu. So, Dutchtown only lasted a couple of years.

Due to its isolated location, some cabins remain. But it takes a good hike or horseback ride to get there, either by way of Lulu or Hitchen's Camp. Hitchen's Camp is less than a mile away.

## TELLER CITY

At one time, Teller City was the most important town in the North Park area. That was some 70 or 80 years ago. Teller City is nothing now.

Reports of rich silver finds in North Park brought prospectors tumbling into the area in the late 70's.

The city was established in 1879 and named for popular Senator Henry M. Teller—teacher, lawyer, major-general of the state militia, Secretary of Interior for President Arthur, and for thirty years a Colorado Senator. He was called the "grand old man of Colorado."

Teller City had a population of about 300 that first year. There were 400 by the following year. And the city reached its peak by 1882 when it boasted a population of 1,200. The city had a lavish hotel, the Yates House, which had forty rooms and a piano. There were a newspaper, two steam saw mills, two doctors and many other businesses, including twenty-seven saloons and numerous parlor houses.

A stage road was built to Laramie, Wyoming, and later a crude road was cut to Georgetown. But transportation was difficult and mining costs were high; eventually this caused an end to Teller City.

The town faded from 1,300 in 1882 to 300 in 1884. Here too, they left the area so hurriedly, they left dirty dishes on the tables and clothes in closets.

Before the city died, however, it collected its share of legend. Two stories stand out.

One concerns the "hundred-foot swindle." An eastern company hired two men to sink a 100-foot shaft. The men dug 50 feet into the ground when they hit water. It was too difficult to bail out the water and keep going, so the men started on another hole. They again hit water at 50 feet. Putting the two holes together, the men figured they had dug 100 feet, sent the company a bill, collected their money and left.

The second story concerns horse-racing, a popular sport among the mining camps. The Teller City area had, or thought it had, a champion in a horse named Sharp. For several months Sharp took on and defeated all comers. The horse was from Wolverine, but ran most of his big races in Teller City.

Well, along came a mysterious challenger named Montgomery, who was figured to give Sharp a close race.

The famous race was run down the main street of Teller City. Almost everyone around participated in the betting, which ran into thousands, much of the money held by Sharp's owners and jockey.

Anyhow, as the story goes, the race was close but Montgomery won by a few feet.

As far as Sharp was concerned, the race wasn't over—not by a long shot. Sharp and his jockey kept right on going into the woods. There, legend says, the jockey picked up a parlor house girl who was waiting for him, and rode off into the sunset, never to be seen again.

The ore around wasn't bad, running from $20 to $3,000 a ton. But the costs prevented Teller City from being better than it was. The best mine was the Endomile, about three miles from town, which produced both gold and silver.

Now, only the ruins of a few cabins, some rusty machinery, and a weed-filled graveyard mark the spot. The site can be reached by pack horse or long, long hike.

### CRESCENT CITY

A small camp southwest of Teller City which pretty much paralleled, on a smaller scale, the life and death of the larger camp.

Crescent City was apparently large enough and lasted long enough to have a post office as it was listed in the postal directory around 1880.

### TYNER

Tyner was another camp which had a lot of promise, but the promise wasn't kept. Its history is more obscure than that of the other camps during the mining craze, and the camp apparently didn't last very long. But it got good press notices at the offset. One newspaper thought it might rival Teller City. A mining journal described Tyner as a place where "silver mines abound."

110

The ores were ruby, sulphuret and silver glance . . . that's what the journal said. The mines were Gas Light, Eldorado and Dolly Varden, all along Jack Creek. The peak population of the community was never more than one hundred.

There was a fellow named Tyner who was mentioned a time or two in reports from this region. Maybe the camp was named after him.

## MANHATTAN

Manhattan, the farthest east of the camps around Rand, was located about four miles northwest of Rustic Camp on the Poudre River.

Manhattan was a bustling community during the 80's when some good ore was found in the neighboring hills. Several cabins and stores were constructed, primarily along one wide thoroughfare which served as the main street.

The ore, however, was not of high quality and the cost of getting it out of the isolated area ate up most of the profits. Most of the residents drifted off after a few months.

Some old ruins are left of the isolated town.

*And Then There Were . . . . MICHIGAN CITY*, a small short-lived camp around the Michigan mine and just north of the summit of Cameron Pass. Its life paralleled the Lulu boom. Michigan City had a post office . . . . *CUMMINGS, PARK CITY* and *MASON* (not on map), small temporary camps that came into existence in the early boom years of the area. It was located on the old stage road from Cameron Pass to Teller City along Michigan Creek. The last remaining building was torn down in 1913 to build a homestead cabin. The community of Gould came into existence a few years later at approximately the same location.

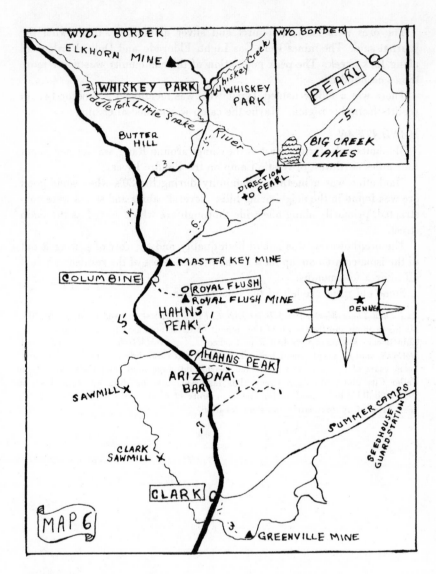

*MAP SIX*

## THE HAHNS PEAK AREA

Hahn's Peak (Poverty Bar)                  Whiskey Park
Bugtown (National City)                    Pearl
National City (International Camp, Bugtown)   Clark and Greenville
Royal Flush                                Slavonia
Columbine

112

# VI. THE HAHNS PEAK AREA

*HAHNS PEAK* (Poverty Bar)

The story of Hahns Peak is well-known to historians and residents of northern Colorado as one of the more tragic tales of Colorado mining.

There are two beginnings to the story. One says Joseph Hahn (which may also be Henn) traveled north from Empire in the early 60's and found traces of gold at the foot of the peak which later bore his name. The following year, Hahn organized a company, headed by himself, William Doyle and Captain George Way.

Another version has Way making the discovery in 1864 and bringing the other two men into it.

Anyway, we have the gold discovered. During the winter of 1865-66, the three men led a party of 50 through deep snow to Hahns Peak. They laid out a town, set up a district, and half the group began building cabins while the other half searched frozen Willow Creek for gold.

The group set up a mining district, electing Hahn its head. Doyle named the peak for Hahn, and the party named the nearby gulches for their native lands or homestates: Germany for the land where Hahn was born; Nova Scotia for Doyle's homeland, and Way named another gulch Virginia for his home state.

All but Hahn, Doyle and Way returned to civilization that first winter. These three did some mining in the hard ground but generally spent their time preparing for an early attack on the mountain in the spring.

In October, Way returned to civilization for supplies and provisions. He never returned. Some historians claim Way's "sell out" of his friends is one of the most disgraceful incidents in Colorado mining history. More lenient folk, however, say it was impossible for Way to return in the heavy snow.

Whichever the case may be, Hahn and Doyle faced the impossible winter with little more than hope of Way's return.

They almost made it through the winter. It wasn't until early spring, the two men, half-dead from cold and starvation, decided they could do nothing else but attempt to make it back to civilization. Hahn was too sick and feeble to travel by himself, and Doyle was forced to carry him much of the way.

Hahn died a few days later. Doyle left his friend in the snow and attempted to carry on. A few days later a search party found Doyle snowblind and stumbling, walking around in circles, more dead than alive.

Hahns Peak was all but forgotten for another two years before more paying quantities of gold were found and two large companies, The Purdy and Hahns Peak, were formed to develop the area.

The two companies settled in camps a short distance apart. One camp was called Bugtown (see Bugtown for derivation of name) or National City. The other camp was originally called Poverty Bar and later Hahns Peak.

The Bugtown property was owned by Farwell, a religious man, who did not allow drinking or gambling. Poverty Bar was wide open. Naturally, it was the larger and more popular of the two camps.

The gold was found in an ancient volcano, similar to that of Cripple Creek. And it was rich ore. Some $100,000 in ore was taken from Poverty Bar its first year. By 1874, production reached five million, despite the fact the long, extreme winters held the top production time down to a few weeks a year, and the costs of getting the ores out were almost prohibitive.

These factors, however, did prevent top development of the area and did bring about an untimely end to mining in the Hahns Peak region.

The end began during the mid 70's and was almost complete by 1880, although there was some mining done here off and on for years. Individual prospectors have been working the streams in the Hahns Peak area in recent times.

The city, however, was active enough to hold down the county seat of Routt County for 30 years, despite repeated efforts to have it moved. The county seat was moved to Steamboat Springs in 1912.

And while it lived, Hahns Peak enjoyed a boisterous and colorful life. Its most noteworthy episode was its daring jail escape and the equally daring recapture of the escapees.

Escaped murderers Harry Tracy and David Lant were being held in the Hahns Peak jail in 1898, awaiting disposition of their cases. They tricked Sheriff Charles Neiman when he brought them their food one night, overpowered him and took away his keys. The two murderers then proceeded to beat the sheriff within an inch of his life, figuring he wouldn't come to for hours and they would have plenty of time to make good their escape.

Lant and Tracy stole some horses and set out for Hot Sulphur Springs. Their progress was slowed, however, by the cold. Not dressed for winter, the two were forced to stop periodically and build a fire to keep from freezing.

And Sheriff Neiman was made of sturdier stuff than they had figured. He came to an hour or two later, organized a posse, and set out in pursuit. Neiman figured the escapees' best bet was the daily stage running from Hahn's Peak to Hot Sulphur Springs and points south. Neiman and a deputy bundled up in heavy coats to keep warm and to disguise themselves, and then boarded the stage a short distance out of Hahns Peak.

Sure enough, just about daybreak, the two escapees hailed the stage from a ranch south of Hot Sulphur Springs. When they opened the door they were looking down the barrels of the sheriff's guns. Said Tracy simply:

"Hello, Neiman. I thought you would just be waking up."

In later years, much of Hahns Peak activity stemmed from its being a supply center for the extensive ranching activity in the region. Like many another area in Colorado and the west, the Hahns Peak region was the battlefield of the bitter range wars between cattlemen and sheepmen.

The ranching continues, but the ranchers get their supplies elsewhere. There is increasing tourist activity here and frequently some prospecting and mining. But Hahns Peak is no more. Only a trace of it remains.

GOLD DUST: Chicago money financed much of the early development of the area . . . . some Hahns Peak ore was valued as high as $15 an ounce . . . the nearest railroad was 110 miles away and the ore had to be carried out on burros or ore wagons over rough, sometimes treacherous roads.

## BUGTOWN (see National City)

Although Bugtown was apparently the predecessor of National City, there are many discrepancies in its history.

The most reliable information indicates Bugtown and Poverty Bar were the first camps in the Hahns Peak area, located two miles apart. Poverty Bar, the more dignified of the two camps, eventually became Hahns Peak, while Bugtown became National City.

One source claims National City came first and was later called Bugtown. Another source says Bugtown was never more than a nickname for National City.

There are also two versions of how the name came about. Both versions are used almost equally by the historians.

One says the name came from the investments made by eastern capitalists, called "Big Bugs" in those days.

The other story claims the name came from the fact the site was actually a favorite rendezvous for bugs, blamed for the typhoid and diphtheria epidemics which all but wiped out the camp during its early days.

## NATIONAL CITY (International Camp, Bugtown)

A camp, twin to Hahns Peak, that grew out of Bugtown.

The camp was located in Way's Gulch, about two miles from Poverty Bar or Hahns Peak.

A fellow by the name of Farwell purchased the property and laid out the town. He was a deeply religious man, permitted no work on Sunday and no saloons any time. He even imported ministers from nearby towns to preach to the men in the camp.

After spending about $150,000 on the site, Farwell sold out for $32,000 in 1879.

National City soon faded along with Hahns Peak when low-grade ores could not pay for the tremendous costs of taking them out.

### ROYAL FLUSH

An obscure little camp which grew around the Royal Flush Mine and Mill, two miles from Columbine.

The camp was a haphazard development in the first years of the mine, but became more organized in the boom of 1904 which brought new activity into the area. The camp faded rapidly during the war and the mill was dismantled and closed down in 1918.

The mill skeleton and several delapidated cabins remain at the site.

### COLUMBINE

A couple of teen-agers have revived a bit of the summer activity at ghost town Columbine. Bob and Peg Lundquist of Denver operate a summer store for sheepherders, loggers and occasional tourists.

It is about the only life in Columbine.

Columbine, about four miles north of Hahns Peak, was established in 1897 when some ore was found nearby. The best mine was the Royal Flush.

Some logging was done here then, and has been carried on since. Sheep men came to the area early, and stayed on after the mining faded.

Other than the summer store, a few unoccupied cabins and buildings remain at the site.

### WHISKEY PARK

At one time—a very short time—Whiskey Park was believed to be the heart of the "richest portion of Colorado." At least one report indicated as much.

Whiskey Park erupted shortly before the turn of the century. No evidence was found on how the name came to be Whiskey Park. 'Tis a pity. It would have been interesting.

In 1897, a mining report said, "Early prospectors claim great lodes of precious metals. These still exist or have been eroded by glaciers."

Although Hahns Peak was primarily a gold area, there was some silver found here. The Elk Horn was the most developed claim. At 40 feet the developers hit "fourteen inches of solid silver." The streak was said to be one-fourth solid silver, valued at $1,000 a ton, plus $30 in gold and two per cent copper.

Another property was mentioned, the Davis mines. Reports from the area at the time said a steady flow of gold seekers were pouring into Whiskey Park.

That was the last time Whiskey Park was heard from.

### PEARL

A relatively obscure mining town located near the Wyoming border.

Little is known about the town except how it got its name—and there is some argument about that.

116

One side says the town was named for a daughter of Benjamin Franklin Burnett, a man well-known in the development of many northern Colorado communities. Lulu was named after another of his daughters.

Another side says the town was named after Pearl Ann Wheeler, postmistrses and wife of Luke Wheeler, brother of "Squeaky" Bob Wheeler, who founded the Phantom Valley Ranch.

After the mining petered out here, the cattle took over and have remained. However, there are a few ramshackle buildings left and the remains of an old wooden sidewalk.

## CLARK and GREENVILLE

Clark was dependent upon the Greenville Mine which produced gold, silver, and copper. A couple of sawmills were built up the gulch. Clark also had a post office.

The community was probably named for Worthington Clark who owned land near Walden and was a co-partner in stagecoach operations in the area.

There may or may not have been a camp at the mine, but a couple of reports from the area refer to Greenville as if it were a town. One such report said "although gold was predominant in the Hahns Peak area, there was plenty of silver at Greenville."

The mine paid pretty well while it paid.

## SLAVONIA

Slavonia was an isolated camp around the Slavonia Mine, east and a tiny bit south of Hahns Peak, at the western foot of the Continental Divide. The camp was located at the confluence of Gilpin and Gold Creeks, a fair hike beyond the Seedhouse Camp Ground area. Due to its remoteness, there is still a ruin or two, hidden among the trees. The scars of the Slavonia Mine can be seen above.

## VII. THE BIG THREE

Fairplay, Alma, Buckskin Joe and their neighbors were many things and many people. But a balky old mule, a snowshoe-wearing traveling salesman for God, and a dancehall girl will always speak for this district as long as history remembers the mining camp. No mining camp in Colorado—or anywhere—could be better represented.

Silver Heels! . . . . What was her real name? Her puckish smile and flashing feet turned many a heart in Fairplay and Buckskin Joe. In the early days she had a name of her own, but then one of her vast number of followers presented her with a pair of silver slippers. She always wore them. How they sparkled as she danced!

In 1861 the smallpox epidemic hit Buckskin Joe—where Silver Heels danced then. They say her lover was one of the victims. But she had many lovers. All the women and children left camp for safety. Many of the men left too. Silver Heels remained. She was everywhere. She cared for the sick as if each one was her lover.

Many died. Eventually the epidemic subsided, but only after the beautiful Silver Heels was pock-marked and ugly.

But to the miners and those who lived there, Silver Heels was more beautiful than ever. To men who know only the constant battle for gold, money was the only expression of appreciation. They collected $5,000 from the rich, and from the grubby prospector who only had a few grains of gold dust—and went to present the gift to Silver Heels.

She was gone! . . . taking the hearts of all the miners with her. They named the mountain for her, because prospectors and miners worship mountains.

Several years later, an elegantly dressed woman, wearing a thick veil, made a pilgrimage to Fairplay and Buckskin Joe. She walked through the old cemetery alone. No tears could be seen through the veil, but oldtimers say they were there. She wore street shoes. But oldtimers are sure she was Silver Heels.

Then she returned no more. Only the mountain remained.

Father John L. Dyer had practical experience in mining and preaching in Wisconsin and Minnesota before he came to Buckskin Joe in 1861. He had little more than the clothes on his back and a prayerbook in his pocket.

He wasted little time with preliminaries. He began preaching immediately . . . the first time he could get a few men together, in a barroom, gambling hall or prospect hole. His audience was usually more interested in gold than God. Some smirked. But they tolerated him.

His "beat" covered most of the camps in the area. He was over fifty years old at the time, but he maintained an arduous schedule. Within two

118

months he had walked more than 500 miles. His collections totaled $43.00. He began carrying the mail to help pay expenses. He bought snowshoes so he could go anywhere, anytime.

One time when his way was blocked by an Indian scare, he drove a stage back and forth to Denver. Another time he lugged heavy bags of gold dust, plus mail, over Mosquito Pass for $18.00 a trip.

Colorado history had many "snowshoe itinerants," who carried God to god-forsaken pockets of the mountains. Father Dyer was one of the first, the most durable and most dedicated. He helped hold off the Devil until the churches were built.

It took a while, but pretty soon they began to listen.

Fairplay was called the Burro Capitol of the World. They have a monument to prove it.

Prunes had many owners. Everyone in Fairplay owned him. He worked hard much of his life. His last years were on the town. He bummed food at most of the back doors of Fairplay. His last owner, Robert Sherwood, died in 1931 and was buried near Prunes.

Prunes died at the age of 63.

Prunes' monument was a memorial to all the burros—or "Rocky Mountain canaries" as they were called.

There were other burros. Shorty, and his faithful dog companion, Bum, were almost as well known in South Park as Prunes. Shorty refused to walk in the street, but would walk on the sidewalk. He and Bum made the rounds of the houses of Fairplay, asking for hand-outs. Shorty was killed by a hit-run auto in 1951. Bum kept guard over Shorty's grave for a few weeks until he, too, died. The two of them were buried together. There is a monument for them, too.

Bosco was another famous burro. He walked from Los Angeles to Denver with his owner. There were also Prunes II and Prunes III. There were thousands of burros in Colorado, and hundreds of heroes among them. They played a vital part in the early history of the west.

The burros helped break the first trails through the wilderness. They carried the supplies. They needed little care and upkeep. They could go where wagons and coaches couldn't go. They could even sniff out the water holes. They frequently kept their masters warm in winter. They also provided the prospector with an outlet for his disgust. It did a man good to cuss out the animal now and again.

There are several stories of burros wandering away from camp during the night only to be found the next day on a rich strike.

It seems only natural. They say the burro was part of the prospector. Often it was impossible to tell where the burro left off and the prospector began.

Fairplay (Fairplay Diggings, South Park City, Platte City)
Montgomery
Quartzville
Hinsdale (not on map)
Dudley (Dudleyville)
Buckskin Joe (Laurette)
Alma
Park City
Mosquito (Musquito, Sterling City, Camp Sterling)
Sacramento
Pearts, Holland and Mullensville
Horseshoe (Doran, East Leadville)
Mudsill
Leavick
Weston
Garo, King (just east of map), Buffalo Springs (just south of map), Hilltop
    Junction, Arthurs, Platte Station, Alma Station (London Junction)
Red Hill (Mayol's)
Como
Tarryall (Whiskey Hole)
Hamilton
Silver Heels
Dyersville

*And Then There Were . . . PUMA CITY* (east of map), *FORTUNE PLACERS,
COTTAGE GROVE* (not on map), *HILLSDALE, HILLTOP* (not on map), and
*NEW LEAVICK.*

*FAIRPLAY* (South Park City, Platte City, Fairplay Diggings)

Fairplay, one of the oldest cities in the state, has a new suburb, perhaps one of the strangest suburbs of any city in the world.

The new suburb, called South Park City, is composed of old cabins and frame houses, some nearly 100 years old. The buildings are actual cabins and business houses used during the early days of South Park. Each building has been restored and refurnished as authentically as possible to match the original. Although the cabins were moved from Buckskin Joe, Horseshoe, Leavick and other sites, and represent the last marker of those historic cities, the buildings will be protected here from the ravages of time and vandals.

Fairplay is the perfect location for such a project. It is, and always has been, the hub of activity in South Park—perhaps the most historical section in all Colorado.

For centuries before the white man entered South Park, it was a favorite campground for Indian tribes. The Kiowas, Arapahoes, Apaches and Utes

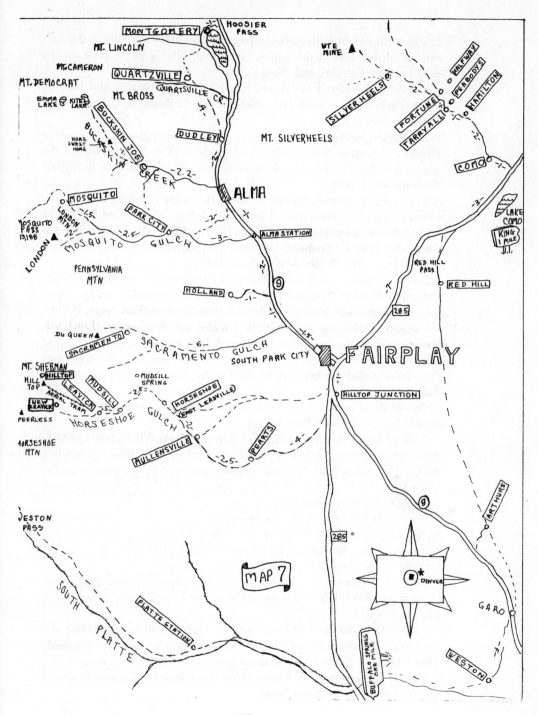

MONTGOMERY
HOOSIER PASS
MT. LINCOLN
UTE MINE
MT. CAMERON
HALFWAY
MT. DEMOCRAT
QUARTZVILLE
PEABODY'S
HAMILTON
QUARTZVILLE CR.
SILVER HEELS
FORTUNE
EMMA LAKE
KITE LAKE
MT. BROSS
TARRYALL
BUCKSKIN JOE
HOME SWEET HOME
DUDLEY
MT. SILVERHEELS
COMO
BUCKSKIN CREEK
2.2
ALMA
LAKE COMO
MOSQUITO
2
KING 1 MILE
J.T.
MOSQUITO PASS 13,188
LONDON MTN
PARK CITY
1.5
ALMA STATION
2
LONDON
2.5
MOSQUITO GULCH
3
RED HILL PASS
RED HILL
PENNSYLVANIA MTN
7
HOLLAND
1
9
285
1.5
DU QUEEN
SACRAMENTO
6
SACRAMENTO GULCH
FAIRPLAY
MT. SHERMAN
HILLTOP
SOUTH PARK CITY
HILL TOP
LEAVICK
MUDSILL
MUDSILL SPRING
NEW LEAVICK
AERIAL TRAM
2.5
HORSESHOE
HILLTOP JUNCTION
PEERLESS
HORSESHOE GULCH
EAST LEAVILLE
2
HORSESHOE MTN
MULLENSVILLE
PEARTS
4
2.5
ARTHUR
WESTON PASS
9
MAP 7
285
DENVER
GARO
SOUTH PLATTE
PLATTE STATION
WESTON
BUFFALO SPRINGS ONE MILE

121

fought for the right to live here. Eventually, the Utes won title to the land and established one of the largest permanent villages in the state on the delta between Fairplay and Alma.

The Spanish entered the region in the eighteenth century and built in South Park the first gold and silver mining facilities in Colorado (see Buckskin Joe).

Despite the Indians, South Park was a favorite campground and meeting place for the early white hunters and trappers. The Spanish labeled the site "Bayou Salado" for the salt marshes here. Other mountain men liked the name and kept it.

The explorers passed through South Park. Some reported the first discoveries of gold by the whites. Pike reported that a man named Pursley or Purcell discovered gold here as early as 1806 or 1807. The west's incredible pathfinder, John C. Fremont, reported the discovery of gold by mountain man "Parson" Bill Williams as early as 1849.

About the same time, Thomas Jefferson Farnham traveled through South Park, over Hoosier Pass and down into northern Colorado, cutting one of the first north-south trails through the Colorado mountains.

Fairplay, itself, was another city founded by disgruntled prospectors turned away by the possessive attitude of the Tarrayall settlers. The first cabin was built here in 1859. The settlement was named for the treatment the miners would get here, as opposed to the treatment they received in Tarryall.

One of those early leaders who proposed the name was Jim Reynolds, soon to become a South Park legend.

A short time after the founding of Fairplay, Reynolds turned highwayman. His gang was as effective as any in Colorado at the time. Then when the Civil War broke out, Reynolds headed south to lend his services to the Confederate cause. But his talent and knowledge of Colorado were more valuable to the South than his presence.

With eight hand-picked Rebels, Reynolds returned to Colorado intent on highjacking as much of the territory's gold as he could to help finance the Southern cause. But what could have been one of the most historic adventures of the Civil War turned out to be a farce.

They say Colorado was tipped off that Reynolds was returning. More likely it was Reynold's own over-confidence and gentlemanly manner that was his downfall.

According to the most authentic sources available, Reynolds robbed one stage near the present site of Como. Although some legends have Reynolds a black villian with the blood of many men on his hands, there is no record of his ever killing a man. The stage driver was released unharmed, to spread the word that Reynolds was back.

To top this off, Reynolds and his gang stopped at all the best stage stops, and took their merry time enroute to Denver, where they planned to take over the gold of the state treasury. Reynolds wasn't one to do things in secret.

By the time he was slightly more than halfway to Denver from Fairplay, everyone—even those that weren't interested—knew Reynolds was back, where he was headed, and what he was up to.

The large posse formed in Fairplay could easily have caught up with the gang. But it was inept. Reynolds outfoxed it. However, a larger, more efficient posse was bearing down on the gang from Denver.

They say Reynolds, who knew the region as well, if not better, than anyone else, could easily have eluded the Denver posse. But poor judgment led to his downfall and the end of his adventure.

The first gang member was captured and decapitated. His head went on display. Five more were captured and shot down by a firing squad near Denver. The last three, including John Reynolds, fled to New Mexico.

The true story of this fiasco has been clouded by legend, which seems to compound as the years go by. There is still no record of Reynolds ever killing a man. He was a gentleman at all times, and treated his hostages well. They say he buried his loot somewhere in the vast expanse between Fairplay and Denver. Stories of buried treasure are always popular. But more industrious students claim the "loot" was not of treasure proportions in the first place—a few hundred dollars at most. (The treasure in legend has now reached as much as $100,000.) The sum was certainly not enough to force Reynolds to bury it to lighten his load for escape purposes. Some gold was recovered from captured gang members. The treasure, if there was any treasure, certainly isn't worth looking for.

So much for Reynolds. His story could have been an epic story of the Civil War.

Fairplay had other colorful characters.

Silver Heels; Prunes and other noble burros; a few outstanding murderers; Father Dyer and other famous men of the cloth, such as Sheldon Jackson and Father Macheboeuf, all paraded across the Fairplay stage, and had speaking parts.

An important stage prop in the Fairplay drama was the courthouse, built in 1874 and the oldest permanent courthouse in Colorado.

The court has been called "the hanging court" and the "court that never adjourned." Both nicknames stem from the same incident.

John J. Hooper, said to be a distant kin of H. A. W. Tabor, killed a man named Bennett in 1880 in an argument over a drainage ditch. The judge sentenced Hooper to eight years in prison. The citizens, thinking the sentence too light, broke into the jail that night and hung Hooper from the second story window.

Another killer was scheduled to be tried the next day, so as a reminder to the judge and prosecuting attorney, the citizens committee left the noose on the judge's desk. The judge and attorney soon disappeared without bothering to adjourn the court.

Hence, both nicknames.

An aftermath of the incident occurred in 1953. Workmen repairing the courthouse found a noose under the floorboards with other evidence against the vigilantes committee. Historians believe the rope was the same one used to hang Hooper, and that the judge had hidden it to save as evidence in future prosecution against the lynching committee.

The man scheduled to be tried for murder the day after the Hooper trial was Cicero Simms, a youthful, swaggering trouble-maker who shot down his best friend on the main street of Alma. It seemed to be the end of the line for the slight, 19-year-old Tennessean, who bragged of killing several men on his cross-country trip to join his two older brothers in Fairplay.

After the Hooper incident, there was no doubt about the outcome of the Simms trial. He was sentenced to be hanged. Here the legend (or was it legend?) begins.

Young Simms boasted he was too light to be hanged. This added to the color of the incident and thousands gathered to watch the public execution. It came off as expected although there was no evidence on the body that the rope had broken Simms' neck. He was pronouced dead, however, and most of the town paraded by the coffin to view the body.

After the execution, Simms' brothers, who had been locked up during the trial and execution to avert possible trouble, were released from jail.

That night, a stage driver named McCarthy said he was hailed by two men with an "injured" youth outside of Fairplay and forced at gunpoint to take the three to Leadville.

McCarthy identified the "injured" youth as Cicero Simms. The remainder of the story is clouded by rumors, and although nothing official was ever heard of the three again, some oldtimers swear Cicero lived long after his "execution."

The same year (1880) Sam Porter, another swarthy drunk-about-town, threatened, during his final binge, to shoot the first man he saw. He did.

So the lynching party called another meeting. They carted old Sam off, placed the noose around his neck and asked if he had any last requests.

"Yes," said Sam. "Pull."

A fiddler and another prisoner escaped from the courthouse jail one day. It seems the fiddler fiddled to cover up the sound of his cohort's filing away at the bars of their cell. Right after the escape, however, the fiddler reported the escape to the authorities, and later testified against his ex-companion.

The courthouse was also used to house the women and children of Fairplay during an Indian scare in 1879.

Fairplay was the original name of the city. Then it was called Fairplay Diggings. In 1861 it was named Platte City, then South Park City in 1869. The territorial legislature officially changed the name back to Fairplay in 1874.

The town soon became the supply and "Saturday night" center for all the rich mining camps around. Population during its heyday has been estimated as high as 8,000. When many of the camps faded a few short years later, Fairplay continued as a main point for dredge mining operations. The silver rush of Leadville also hit the Fairplay region and bolstered the city that was, even then, becoming a center of the rich ranching and farming operations in South Park. And tourist trade, stimulated by the rich historical value of Fairplay, is increasing yearly.

GOLD DUST: The Sheldon Jackson Memorial Chapel, built in 1872 by the great missionary, is still in use. Father Dyer's original church-cabin is now contained in South Park City, Fairplay's historical suburb . . . . the grave of the burro, Shorty, and his faithful dog companion, Bum, is located in Fairplay's interesting cemetery behind the town . . . . during Fairplay's heyday, it contained two top hotels, the Berge and Fairplay, a newspaper, *The Fairplay Flume*, scores of business houses, several churches and schools, and an even dozen parlor houses . . . . a fire in 1873 destroyed much of the business section, but it was rebuilt, largely of brick and stone . . . . the annual burro race over Mosquito Pass from Leadville to Fairplay began in 1949, and follows the same route taken by thousands of travelers during the early days of the area . . . . the Chinese played a prominent part in early Fairplay. "China Mary," a hard-working laundrywoman, was a favorite figure in the early years of the camp. Her house is still used as a private home . . . . before the dredges began work on the Platte and other nearby streams, Chinese used to work the gravel by hand, paying the claim owners a dollar a day, whether operations that day were profitable or not . . . . dredge operations in the Platte were carried on from 1922-24 . . . . one of the recent crazes in the area is gem-hunting. Several kinds of valuable stones—amethyst, topaz, tourmatine, turquoise, etc.—have been found on high mountain ridges, slide rocks, streambeds, and old placer dumps, some bringing as much as $1,000 . . . . the hospital was once the headquarters for the Ku Klux Klan in Leadville.

## MONTGOMERY

The city of Montgomery, whose explosive growth once rivaled that of any Colorado mining town and earned the city the distinction of being considered the state capitol, is no more.

Waters behind the Montgomery Dam, part of the Colorado Springs water system, cover the mountain pocket beneath the southern half of Hoosier Pass, where Montgomery once stood. A trace of the mining activity that made Montgomery famous can be seen on a ledge behind the reservoir. But, alas, it may soon be gone also.

The site, at the extreme headwaters of the South Platte, erupted with activity in 1859, when good gold strikes were made in the mountains. Within weeks, thousands of fortune seekers were in the area. Montgomery's population threatened to top that of Denver. The early residents were boosting Montgomery for state capitol. But before long, Montgomery's growth leveled off, Denver's continued, and Montgomery was no longer in the running.

The first boom hit its peak in 1861. At the time, Montgomery was the largest city in the region, even larger than Buckskin Joe and Fairplay. There were dozens of prosperous businesses, including two large hotels, and a big showplace which doubled as a theatre and dance hall, the largest in the region.

New strikes were made all the time. Within a two-week period in 1861, between fifteen and twenty rich strikes were made. The Pendleton was the best.

Montgomery was a favorite spot of Schuyler Colfax, a member of President Lincoln's cabinet.

In those days, mountain climbing was one of the most popular sports, and Mount Lincoln was one of the more ambitious goals for the outdoorsmen.

A mass meeting was held in 1861 in Montgomery to name the nearby mountains. (Mountain-naming was another popular pastime among early residents.) Thinking "their" mountain was the highest in Colorado, Montgomery residents named the peak Mount Lincoln for the president. The miners consummated the ceremonies by sending the president solid gold bar made from the ore in the region.

In one of his last acts before his assassination, President Lincoln dispatched Colfax to Colorado to thank the miners personally.

Colfax climbed the mountain himself. It is said he proposed to his future wife on the summit of the peak. And she is said to have been the first woman to reach the summit.

Meanwhile, the Montgomery boom was dying on its feet. The area faded almost as rapidly as it had soared into existence. The site was all but deserted by 1868. The ore was good but not plentiful.

Then came Leadville, and the mountains far and wide were probed once again for the new god, silver. Some was found in the Montgomery region and the city stirred with life once again. Even then, however, many of the miners chose to live in the nearby boomtowns. of Quartzville, over the mountains, or Alma, down in the valley. Many Montgomery citizens took their cabins with them when they moved.

There was another flurry of activity around Montgomery near the turn of the century when new discoveries were made. But for all intents and purposes, Montgomery was dead. Now she sleeps in her watery grave.

TOP MINES: Magnolia, Montgomery, Pendleton.

## *QUARTZVILLE*

A few rotting cabins remain of the city of Quartzville, in a pocket of towering Mount Bross a few miles beyond the site of Montgomery. A hike is necessary to get there, although some jeepsters claim they have driven it.

Quartzville got its start during the early 70's, in a lull of the activity at Montgomery. When Montgomery experienced its second boom, Quartzville was still going strong and won many of Montgomery's residents.

Quartzville thrived throughout the 70's and 80's, had a peak population of some 2,000, had a post office, a bank, and several other businesses.

Quartzville had six top mines, five silver and one gold, the Hoil group being the most prominent.

The Moose mine was by far the best here and was one of the first good silver mines in the state. It opened at a point close to 14,000 feet up Mount Bross. Some three million dollars was taken from the mine from 1871 to 1876, and it produced off and on until the crash in '93. An expensive tunnel was built in 1884 in an effort to give the mine new life, but you can't bribe an old bore.

Another good mine was the Russia.

## *HINSDALE* (Not on map)

An important although small and short-lived lumber camp near Quartzville.

Records show the camp supplied much of the lumber for the mines and mining towns in the region from about 1870 to 1875. There is no record of activity here after 1875.

The camp was located at 11,000 feet on the west side of the South Platte River north of the mouth of Quartzville Gulch. You can look for it, but you won't find it.

## *DUDLEY* (Dudleyville)

Dudley grew around the mill built in the early seventies to handle the ore from the Moose mine. The town was located two miles north of Alma and four miles from Quartzville, at the foot of Mount Bross.

The Moose mine was the primary *raison d'etre* for all three communities. It produced three million dollars from 1871-1876, and was worked until the panic of 1893 tumbled the price of metals.

Dudley, or Dudleyville, was named for Judson H. Dudley, one of the developers of the Moose mine. Population of the town never got over 200 and faded quickly when the mill was closed down in 1893.

## BUCKSKIN JOE (Laurette)

Buckskin Joe was perhaps the most colorful camp in the area during its day—as much for the events and people that marked its short history as for its name.

The camp was named for Joe Higgenbottom, nicknamed "Buckskin" for the leather clothing he wore. Legend says Buckskin Joe made the original strike here but records show a man named Harris turned the trick, and Joe was just an early-comer after the strike was made.

Both legend and fact agree on the way the rich Phillips strike was made. Harris was hunting in 1860 when he spotted a deer. He took aim and fired. He was sure the bullet hit the mark but the deer scampered off.

In looking for traces of blood, Harris found where the bullet had pierced the ground. And here was rich placer gold.

How the claim was named the Phillips is another interesting story, cloaked in legend. It seems a man by the name of Phillips arrived here the year before and staked his claim. But he left as winter approached and was never heard from again. Some believe he was murdered.

The Phillips paid off from the first. Harris worked the place by himself and attempted to keep his activity a secret. He hid the ore in everything he had—boots, pans, and the like—and stuffed it all under the floor of the crude cabin he had constructed.

But his secret leaked out. The following year hundreds of gold hunters were here, and the city of Buckskin Joe roared into existence.

Here, during 1861 and 1862, came more than 5,000 people, including H. A. W. Tabor, who opened a store and, as was his wont, attempted a little prospecting . . . (as usual, he was unsuccessful) ; Father Dyer and other itinerant preachers who made Buckskin Joe their headquarters; Silver Heels, who soon captured the hearts of the miners and prospectors; and the other camp followers, the gamblers, scarlet ladies, barkeeps and hangers-on.

Buckskin Joe, the man, was already here. He staked his claim in 1860, not far from the Phillips lode. He was an eccentric, but a popular one. And there was no doubt about the name of the town from the first. Old man Dodge, a pretty influential man-about-town, tried to get the town named Laurette for his wife and daughter (Laura and Jeannette) and the post office was named this for a while, but Buckskin Joe it was and will ever be.

Tabor was instrumental in the construction of a courthouse, and the city

128

was the county seat from 1862-66, when another election was held and Fairplay took over. The courthouse was moved to the new county seat.

Buckskin Joe, during its brief existence, had a newspaper, two banks, post office, several dance halls (three set up by Harris and his partner, who also built a theater), plenty of saloons and parlor houses, a dozen other respectable businesses and a brass band that played on the street corner every night.

The band played on as long as the Phillips lode, known as "the Diggins," paid off. It produced a half-million during the first two years, and a total of more than three million by 1864, when it seemed to pinch out. Within hours Buckskin Joe was all but deserted.

Among the few to remain was H. A. W. Tabor, who was either temporarily winded from his helter-skelter chase after fortune, or temporarily smitten by the place where he had come closest to success. They say Tabor was mayor of Buckskin Joe, but reports vary as to when—during the boom or after the boom when there were few people around to vote. But, eventually he too wandered over the hill to Oro City and fame.

Another stay-behind was J. P. Stancell, a theater usher in Oro City who came to Buckskin Joe late and remained to work the Phillips by himself. Within a year he had accumulated a fortune just by going through the leavings of the fabulous mine.

Eventually, however, they all left and Buckskin Joe was just a memory. A few years later the site became ranchland and the few remaining relics of the fabulous camp were fenced off. Later still, the two remaining buildings —said to be Tabor's store and a dance hall—were carted off to Fairplay for the reconstruction of the early historical buildings in South Park.

GOLD DUST: 2.7 miles up Buckskin Gulch from Alma are three of the seven arastras (see Arastra) built by the Spanish in the 18th century to work the gold here. Many legends of Spanish gold concern the Spanish Caves facing the gulch . . . . the Phillips lode paid from the ground down and was worked in layers as a quarry . . . . several stamp mills and a dancing school were here . . . . a Negro minstrel group played continuously at the Harris theatre and was a great favorite in the town . . . . as with most boom towns in Colorado, Buckskin Joe had its share of shootings, robberies and kidnappings, many of them took place in the Red Light district . . . . legend says Buckskin Joe traded off his claim here for a revolver, pony and other small items, and he gave up his water rights in payment of a whiskey bill.

## ALMA

Alma deserves a longer story. Although it came later than most of the colorful cities around, its history parallels that of the other towns, and the same characters—Silver Heels, Father Dyer, Prunes, and the rest—were a part of Alma also.

A smelter built here the same year the smelting process was invented worked the ores from the other cities and helped make them prosperous.

An early Indian village was situated not far from the present site of Alma. Pike, Fremont and other explorers camped near here.

Alma, perhaps, had more truck with "The Bloody Espinosas" than the other towns around. In fact, the Espinosa Brothers were said to have killed six of their estimated thirty-two victims in and around Alma.

There have been many reasons given for the Espinosas' hatred for Anglos. Some claim the whites killed their parents, others say the whites kicked the Espinosas off their land. The most-heard story is of a vision the brothers had of the Virgin Mary, who ordered the brothers to kill all Americanos.

Their private crusade not only claimed the lives of thirty-two innocent victims, but terrorized much of southern and central Colorado during the mid-60's. A large bounty was placed on their heads, but the brothers managed to elude even the most efficient posse, although a posse of miners from California Gulch was said to have captured and killed one of the brothers on nearby Espinosa Peak.

Finally, Tom Tobin, famed scout, Indian fighter and mountain man, leading a posse of miners, surrounded the brothers and their cohorts near the southern Colorado border, and killed them all. Tobin brought back to Fort Garland a head of one of the Espinosas as a trophy, and as proof he had done his job.

Although there was some activity here previously, Alma got rolling with the silver craze in 1879 and 1880. That was about the time of the Meeker Massacre, which sent a scare throughout the state. Alma got more of a jolt than most towns, however, when one of its citizens shot holes in his own coat and ran through the streets shouting "The Indians are coming!" while indicating his close call by showing the bullet holes in his coat.

Alma had quite a few rich mines around and also came to be an important smelting center. As the transportation facilities in the area got better, many miners from nearby camps moved to Alma.

There are four theories on how the city was named: for Alma Jones, wife of the first merchant; for Alma Graves, wife of a mine owner; for Alma Jaynes, wife of a townleader who wanted the town to be called Jaynesville; and for all the Almas here.

Alma has had its ups and downs, but has never been deserted. It is very much alive today. Much lode mining is still carried out in the nearby mines. The city was almost destroyed by fire in 1937, but most of it has been rebuilt.

## PARK CITY

There was another Park City three miles west of Alma and near the foot of Mosquito Pass.

The city had an early population said to be about 300 and had a large stage coach hotel for the stages bound for Leadville. It was also a railroad terminus.

Many cabins of this all-but-unknown city remain.

## MOSQUITO (Sterling City, Camp Sterling, Musquito)

Shortly after the founding of Montgomery, gold was discovered high in the mountains between Oro City and South Park. The resulting rush to the spot gave birth to Mosquito.

The story of its name is an interesting bit of history.

It seems the first settlers, about 250 of them, found it difficult to agree on a name. A meeting was held, several names were suggested, but no agreement was reached. Another get-together was scheduled.

At the next meeting, the group secretary turned to the minutes of the last meeting and found a mosquito had been crushed between the pages. The group decided upon the name then and there. It is said, however, the man who recorded the historical event couldn't spell, and until a more erudite man came along, the name was spelled "Musquito." Records further show, at one time or another, the city tried on "Camp Sterling" and "Sterling City" for size. But these names didn't wear well, and Mosquito it was.

The camp was organized in June of 1861. The first settlers were enthusiastic about the future of the camp. An elaborate city was planned and much of it was built. There were several good placer mines here. About 50 claims were working during the 60's. The most important were the Sterling and Newland.

Despite the rugged life of the early settlers, Mosquito was one of the most law-abiding communities in the state. The better element seemed to be in complete control at all times, and there is no record of a murder or a lynching in the town.

The Civil War helped deplete the population. Also, the camp was overplanned and the mines were overworked. It soon began to fade, and as other more important discoveries were made in the neighborhood, this fading gained momentum.

Before the site died completely, however, Mosquito Pass was cut over the hill and down into Leadville country. And Mosquito entered into another phase of its history: that of a stage and wagon stop.

During its years of use, Mosquito Pass was one of the most important passes in the state. It was the key route to the Leadville boom area. During this time, and before railroads were built to the new carbonate center,

131

Mosquito Pass was the busiest small stretch of road west of the Mississippi.

The pass was nicknamed the "Highway of Frozen Death." During the stampede to Leadville, hundreds of ill-clothed and ill-advised travelers perished along the short, but treacherous, route. During the winter the 13,182-foot pass was continually blocked by blizzards and cold. But hundreds couldn't wait until spring.

The pass gradually fell into disuse and was completely closed by 1910. Some improvements have been in recent years, and jeeps can generally make it in the summer months. The annual Leadville-to-Fairplay Burro Race takes the same route over Mosquito Pass that thousands of burros took in the past.

Nothing is left of Mosquito but the mute evidence of past mining in the nearby hills. Ruins of an old storehouse just over the pass are still visible. The storehouse was built by French prospectors who struck it rich, but were said to have been murdered when they tried to take their riches out.

A short distance south of the route to Mosquito is the site of the London mine (also called New London mine), one of the richest in the state. The mine was worked profitably for more than 50 years. It produced some four million dollars worth of precious metals in the middle 1930's. Ruins of the mine offices and houses of one of the mine's many owners can be seen via a cutoff just north of the jeep run south of Alma.

An Illinois and Colorado group is planning to turn the cabins and building site into a tourist area.

### SACRAMENTO

This short-lived camp west of Fairplay was founded by chance by men returning from the silver fields on the other side of the mountains.

During its existence from about 1878 to the early eighties there were about one hundred residents at the most. The inaccessibility of the camp coupled with the average grade of the ore soon spelled its end.

The crude road built to the site was obscured by time, blocking vandals from the site. Consequently more than half of the original twenty buildings are still standing, but one must hike there.

BEST MINES: Toby, LeDuc and Dwell.

### PEARTS, HOLLAND and MULLENSVILLE

Three obscure camps in the Fairplay area. Little is known about them, although there is some information on which to base guesswork as far as Pearts and Holland are concerned.

A John Pearts was a well-known figure in the Fairplay area. One source lists him as a South Park pioneer. He operated the Crusader, a small mine on Horseshoe Mountain. Since early maps show Pearts, the place, to be on

Horseshoe Mountain, it may have been the camp at the mine. The report said, however, only a handful of men worked the mine, so it couldn't have a very large camp.

There was a little mining at Mullensville, a short distance west of Pearts, but the town was primarily a post office and ranching community.

The ruins of a couple of once-grand houses and several cabins remain at the site of Holland. Some residents in the area claim the houses were built by former owners of the London mine. However, the site seems somewhat inconvenient for easy access to the mine. Holland may have been a camp around the Holland Reduction Works that enjoyed a brief existence in the middle-seventies. The mill was as modern as possible and was built in 1874 at considerable expense. Nonetheless, it was little used and was sold at a sheriff's sale in 1875.

Some Illinois and Denver people who own summer cabins at the site are considering turning the area into a resort.

## HORSESHOE (Doran, East Leadville)

The first silver strike in the valley was made at Horseshoe, named for the famed Horseshoe Cirque, a classical example of a glacial mountain crater.

The town was founded in 1879, after the silver find. It soon had a population of 300. The peak population in the following years was 800. There were two hotels, two smelters, two saw mills and several stores, saloons and other businesses.

There were plans made to build a railroad to the town during those boom days, but these early plans were abandoned in the late 80's.

Because of the silver find, and partially because Horseshoe was almost as close—as the crow flies—to Leadville as it was to Fairplay, Horseshoe was also called East Leadville. Eventually, however, the residents settled for Horseshoe.

Horseshoe began fading in the late 80's and early 90's. The death of the town was complete with the silver crash of 1893.

There was a revival in 1896 when the Denver and South Park and Hilltop Railroad went up the gulch to serve the Hilltop and Last Chance mines. Horseshoe served as a rail head and there was a new spurt of mining here, too. But eventually, the railroad was continued up the gulch to Leavick, nearer the mines. Horseshoe faded again.

The post office name was changed to Doran in 1902, but residents kept the name of Horseshoe. The site was virtually empty by 1907, when two mines were reopened. But they were closed again two years later. There was an even shorter revival in 1920.

About all the later revivals succeeded in doing was destroying many of the unused and unneeded buildings in the old town. Vandals, in recent years, almost completed the job.

The last two cabins were rescued, restored and established in Fairplay's new South Park City.

## MUDSILL

A rather small camp in existence for three or four years at the Mudsill Mine southwest of Fairplay.

The mine was located in the late seventies by S. A. McLean and others. By 1879, the mine had 1,600 feet of tunnels, drifts and inclines. The ore bodies ranged from 30 to 50,000 tons, but most of it was low grade.

The owners planned to ship out 30 to 40 tons a day and figured there was enough ore to last about three years. Little work was done in 1878 and 1879 while the owners waited for a planned mill to be built at the end of the gulch. The ore didn't last three years, however, and what was shipped out wasn't as good as expected.

A story is told that after the ores ran out, one of the owners salted the mine with silver dust and sold it to the Lord Mayor of London for $190,000. It may just be a story.

## LEAVICK

The three remaining buildings of Leavick have been moved to Fairplay as part of the historical project to preserve the memory of yesterday's ghost towns.

The Last Chance lode was located in 1873 on a 12,600 foot saddle between Mount Sherman and Mount Sheridan. The Hilltop mine was located nearby a short time later. Eventually a mill was built at the base of the range, and Leavick grew around the mill. The city was named for Felix Leavick, an early prospector in the region. The ore was shipped down to the mill via a 13,000 foot-long aerial cable, still visible running up the mountain.

The community had several business houses, two saloons, a parlor house, a barber shop, dentist, and, in later years, a baseball team. Several hundred persons lived here, but most of them left after the panic of '93. The city recovered slightly three years later when the Denver and South Park constructed a branch here, but activity slowly trailed off.

Operations resumed at the Last Chance-Hilltop properties in the early 20's, and for the next dozen years or so mining continued, with zinc as the primary metal.

During the years before 1920, the town of Leavick was well preserved. When mining operations resumed, the company promoted a road to the site to take the ore out. This also let the vandals in, and hastened the destruction of the old town. The South Park Historical Society saved the last buildings of Leavick from a similar fate.

The site of Leavick is actually closer to Leadville—seven miles as the crow flies—but on the opposite side of the Mosquito Range. The site can be reached easily from Fairplay, but there's not much to see.

## WESTON

For a short period of time during the Leadville boom, Weston Pass was one of the busiest stretches of road of similar length in the west.

Weston was the shipping point at the eastern end of the pass. During the boom, the flatlands around Weston were piled high with freight waiting its turn to go over the pass. And the dust from the steady stream of wagons left a cloud over the city.

The rush to Leaville and the desperate need for supplies could well have caused chaos in Weston were it not for the organizational genius of Colonel Robert J. Spotswood. Spotswood controlled the flow of traffic over the pass and kept it rolling smoothly. He supervised the disposition of the freight and made sure none was left behind. Three large forwarding and commission houses had a monopoly on all wagons, horses and burros going over the pass.

As long as Weston remained an important shipping point, her businesses thrived. There were eleven restaurants, and Weston's many saloons and gambling halls were running night and day. Water sold for 35 cents a barrel.

The pass was an original Ute trail which crossed the divide at 12,109 feet. It followed the Platte into the mountains. As with Mosquito, Webster and other passes, Weston Pass had its share of wind and weather. But although there were some robberies along the trail, Weston Pass was generally too busy for road agents.

The South Park Railroad reached here in 1879, stimulating Weston's activity as a loading station. Eventually the railroad pushed on to Buena Vista and then on to Leadville. And Weston was suddenly forgotten.

Nothing remains of the site today. But evidence of the gigantic movement to Leadville has been found all along Weston Pass. The pass has been improved in recent years, and can be negotiated in jeeps and even standard autos much of the time.

## GARO, KING (just east of map), BUFFALO SPRINGS, HILLTOP JUNCTION, ARTHURS, PLATTE STATION, ALMA STATION (London Junction)

Towns east of Fairplay with various occupations.

Garo, still in existence, was founded in 1863 by Adolph Guiraud, one of the first sheepmen in Colorado. Guiraud was born in France in 1823, came to the United States in 1850, and to Colorado about ten years later. Garo, (the phonetic spelling of his name), is still an important sheep center.

King was once a busy coal mining town and was a stop on the railroad. It was named after C. W. King, a bookkeeper for the coal company.

Hilltop Junction, just outside Fairplay, and Arthurs were railroad stations.

Alma Station was a travel junction south of Alma, at the cut-off going up to Buckskin Joe. Platte Station was a stage stop on Weston Pass. Buffalo Springs was a post office town near Fairplay.

## RED HILL (Mayol's)

Red Hill, four miles northeast of Fairplay, was once a important station and loading point on the narrow gauge South Park line.

Other than the station, there were a few cabins and a couple of businesses in the town.

In August of 1880, a fire broke out in the station and exploded a half ton of powder. The entire city was destroyed. (Human casualties were overlooked in historical reports. Life was cheap then). Only the station was rebuilt. It was used for a while longer, then it too was forgotten. Ruins of the old station can still be seen.

The village was named for the rusty color of the soil.

## COMO

Como was primarily a railroad town, although there was some mining done here—coal mining.

When the Denver and South Park Railroad, rapidly treading its way to Leadville, reached this point in 1879, a city grew overnight. It was an ideal location, because, other than being handy to the South Park cities, it was at the foot of Boreas Pass into Breckenridge. Stages would load up here for the trip over the pass, and later a branch of the railroad was extended to Breckenridge.

Some coal mining had been done before and the mining activity increased when the railroad came. The miners were predominately Italian. They named the nearby Lake Como for the lake back home, and they named the town Como for the lake.

In 1879, the mine owners imported some Chinese miners from Fairplay to work in the coal mines. The Italians beat up the man who hired the Chinese and ran the latter out of the camp.

An explosion in the King Cole, largest mine in the district, killed sixteen miners.

The railroad brought a more cosmopolitan atmosphere to Como. There

136

were several wide-open saloons and gambling houses. Two newspapers were published during the 80's. The railroad shops and roundhouses were established here.

The permanent residents of the city during the 80's remained at about 500, while thousands upon thousands of travelers paraded through the city bound for the gold and silver fields to the north and west.

But, as activity slowly decreased over the years, so did the importance of Como.

Most of the railroad shops were burned down in 1909 and never rebuilt. Two years later, the rest of the shops were closed. The junking of the Denver and South Park in 1937 ended an era for Como.

A few people, mostly miners, still live in the cabins of Como, a short distance off the main highway, but they too may soon be gone. And Como will join the ranks of the hundreds of ghost towns in Colorado.

## TARRYALL (Whiskey Hole)

When the prospectors arrived here in 1859 they found the ruins of a few log cabins, believed to have been those of miners killed by the Indians as much as ten years before.

This may have been the sight described by John Fremont where "Parson" Bill Williams, beaver trapper and guide, made a gold discovery in 1849, one of the first such discoveries by a Yankee in Colorado.

The '59ers, perhaps drawn by the old cabins, panned gold "as big as watermelon seeds" in the creek here. Impressed with their find and feeling magnanimous about it all, they said "let us tarry all and share the wealth of the area."

Their invitation was carried far and wide. Before long fortune hunters were flocking here by the hundreds. But instead of the hospitality they expected, they found all the best sites staked out and the welcome a cold one, indeed.

In disgust, they named the camp "Grab all" and rushed on to locate their own camps and claims. The names of the camps they founded include Fairplay, Hamilton and Jefferson.

Enough managed to stay on at Tarryall to found a city, laid out in 1861. Several hundred persons were here, and Tarryall became the county seat of Park County for a short while. John Parsons set up a private mint and turned out $2.50 and $5.00 gold pieces.

However, the "watermelon seeds" soon gave out. Many residents left. The town was all but deserted when some new strikes were made, keeping the town alive for a few more months.

Most of the miners moved to the cities that grew as a reaction to the treatment received during the first months of Tarryall. Others moved to

137

Como, an important station on the newly-constructed railroad. Tarryall was deserted by 1875.

"Whiskey Hole" is about all that remains of the site of Tarryall. Whiskey Hole was a placer claim open to miners low on funds. During the boom days, the claim was set aside by 150 miners. When anyone desired a drink and had no funds with which to quench his thirst, he could pan enough gold out of the hole to pay for the liquor.

## HAMILTON

Hamilton was just across the creek from Tarryall and a few yards upstream, but because of the treatment the early settlers received at Tarryall, they refused to merge, and for the most part would have nothing to do with the adjacent city.

Hamilton had a right to be this way. Although founded a few weeks later than Tarryall, Hamilton soon surpassed the other camp and was a much greater place in its day.

Within weeks after the site was located in 1859, some 3,000 miners and prospectors were here. The following year the number was doubled.

Hamilton was also more cosmopolitan. It was a wide open town, with plenty of saloons and gambling houses. It had a newspaper, *The Miner's Record*, published by the *Rocky Mountain News* in Denver and circulated here. Later, it had its own theater, and many of the top acts in Colorado played here. Governor Gilpin visited both camps in 1861. Hamilton outdid itself in welcoming the state executive.

The city was named for Earl Hamilton, one of the founders of Tarryall.

Hamilton was situated at an important junction in the old road that ran to Fairplay. One road went to Fairplay and the other went over Boreas Pass.

Oldtimers say bands of Utes and Arapahoes used to camp nearby just to watch white men dig for gold. Although the two tribes were constantly at each other's throats, they caused the white men little harm other than a few midnight "shopping" sprees.

Hamilton died about the same time as Tarryall, in the early 70's. The dredges moved through here in later years, but the workers headquartered a few miles upstream.

Nothing remains of Hamilton except the scar tissue of past mining operations.

## SILVER HEELS

Silver Heels, the camp, started out to be as illustrious as its namesake. It received glowing reports its first few months. The camp grew rapidly, the mines and the town were well on their way toward fame. Then Silver Heels,

138

the camp, quietly died and was never heard from again until this book was published. It was located on Silver Heels Mountain, southeast of Breckenridge and six miles from Como in the Tarryall district. It was named for the mountain which was named for the dancing-girl heroine of the smallpox epidemic in Buckskin Joe. (see Buckskin Joe.)

*The Mining and Industrial Reporter* in 1897 said: "no new gold camp in the state has brighter prospects than Silver Heels." What seemed to be good gold strikes were located on the mountain in late 1896. The stampede began when the snows melted the following year. Within a few weeks 25 families were here and 150 men were at work in the mines. Cabins and frame houses were going up, a hotel was under construction. There were plans for a store, an assay office, a blacksmith shop and a saloon. The residents had petitioned for a post office and daily mail service.

The ores in the many diggings were said to have been very rich in gold and tellurium, with enough iron found in the ore to pay for smelting and freight.

The most developed property was the Iron Mine, which the *Mining and Industrial Reporter* called "one of the largest mines in the state." The mine was operated by Peter Breene. Its vein of "solid ore" was said to be fifteen to twenty feet wide, and so pure it "goes without sorting." Breene planned to ship fifteen to twenty carloads a day.

The Stonewall Mine hit a similar vein fifteen feet wide. Another property boasted a ledge eighty feet wide, with one specimen half native gold and half tellurium.

No less than four tunnels were built or under construction that first year. The Silver Heels Tunnel, financed by businessmen from Lincoln, Nebraska, uncovered and shipped "high grade ore" from three or four lodes cut by the tunnel. Denver financiers built the Mineral Hill Tunnel. The Fowler Tunnel went 400 feet, and there was also the King Solomon Tunnel.

The newly-formed Tarryall Tunnel Company planned to cut a tunnel 3,000 feet into the hill, six feet wide and six and a half feet tall. The company expected to cut no less than ten veins.

There were other properties. There were the Golden Ledge, Eureka, Little Nell, Astick, North Star, Queeen of Sheba, King Solomon, Old Reliable and Lena—all on Silver Heels Mountain. On Mineral Ranch Hill there were the Little Mattie, Dorothy, Mineral Ranch, One and Two, Helen and Lucy Marlin. The Iron Mines, Numbers One, Two and Three were on Mineral Hill.

It seems incredible that a mining area, seemingly so well begun, and a town, so well established, could vanish so quickly and quietly. But apparently that's what happened. There was only vague mention of the town in the ensuing months. Then, nothing at all.

What a pity! Colorado could do with a town—and a rich mining town—called Silver Heels.

## DYERSVILLE

One of Colorado's many erstwhile history snoopers, Caroline Bancroft, recently discovered a ghost town. It was named for another of Colorado's illustrious characters, although of a different calling than Silver Heels. The Warriors Mark mine was said to be one of the discoveries Father Dyer made in his expeditions to carry the gospel to forgotten pockets of the area.

Thinking the mine might help finance his mission in life, the good Father built a cabin a short distance from the claim and set out to develop it. His interest spurred others to come and try their luck. And in the early eighties, several cabins were thrown up in the town. A mill was erected in 1883 and the Flanders spur on the Denver, South Park and Pacific railroad was run in to haul out the ore.

A year or two after his discovery, Father Dyer sold out his claim for $2,000 and returned to his more spiritual enterprises. The town "flourished" from about 1880 to 1885, according to Miss Bancroft. She points out, however, that although the mine was worked on until 1908, it never amounted to much and the town never amounted to much.

Miss Bancroft says there are still about ten or twelve cabins left in the town, none of which match the description of Father Dyer's original cabin. She says the site is relatively easy to reach, too. According to her directions, it is near the head of Indiana Gulch, about two miles northwest of the top of Boreas Pass. The last half mile of the journey is better suited to jeeps, she says, "but the foolhardy drive their cars the whole way." The Flanders Spur has been converted to an automobile road, and there is a U.S. Forest Service sign reading "Indiana Creek, Pennsylvania Creek," and pointing down into the gulch. This leads to Dyersville.

*And Then There Were . . . . FORTUNE PLACERS*, four miles above Como, and still visible. The hydraulic operations began here in 1911 and continued for many years . . . . *PUMA CITY* (east of map), a latter day camp that erupted in the nineties with this discovery of rich minerals. The camp hit its peak in 1897 when five mines were shipping and the population was better than a thousand. The city had three hotels, two sawmills, a newspaper, *The Puma Ledger*, five saloons and several other stores and businesses. A daily mail and stage line arrived in Puma City from Lake George. The best mines were the Boomer, Red Skin, Climax and Colonel Settars. When they faded, so did Puma City . . . . *COTTAGE GROVE* and *HILLSDALE* (not on map), two small camps in the Alma area which were apparently large enough to have post offices (in the early eighties) but not large enough to leave any lasting imprint on the history of the area . . . . *HILLTOP*, there are a few old cabins just over the crest of the hill north of the Hilltop Mine above Leavick. The cabins were used by miners from the mine who didn't care to go all the way down to Leavick each night. The small ghost community is not visible from below, but it's there . . . . *NEW LEAVICK*, there are a few newer-type cabins and buildings a mile or so above the ruins of Leavick. The buildings are still being used now and again. The primary metals mined are lead and zinc.

## VIII. THE COLORADO NAVY

One of the most bizaare events in Colorado's early history was the story of the state's first—and last—navy.

During those early years, a direct water route from Colorado to California was still considered a possibility. The quest for such a route was nearly as important a pursuit for pathfinders as feasible railroad routes were later.

In 1869, Sam Adams, part-time water expert and full-time promoter, thought he had figured out a water route to California.

Not one to keep secret about such things, Captain Sam trumpeted his discovery. He found enthusiastic support in Breckenridge. Several of the boom city's leading citizens aided Captain Sam in building four durable boats. They donated equipment and supplies. The ladies of Breckenridge made a fancy banner which read: "Western Colorado to California— Greetings."

By mid-July, the fleet was ready to set sail. In perhaps one of the most formal ceremonies the Colorado Rockies had even seen, the Colorado Navy was launched.

In the flagship was Captain Sam, feeling no doubt a little like Columbus. The rest of the complement included ten able seamen and one dog.

In the run down the Blue River, and before the fleet had even entered into the Colorado, half of the crew, including the dog, had jumped ship. But Captain Sam and his more hardy followers sailed on, and on.

By August ninth they hit the rapids in the canyons of the North Park. Within hours all the boats were splintered and the crew was soaking wet. But they were still determined.

They built a raft and set off once again. The raft tore apart four days later. The boys decided they had had enough.

But old Captain Sam wasn't through yet—now that he had had actual sea experience.

A few months later he almost wangled a large sum of money from Congress as "the man who established a water-way to California."

The true fact came out just in time, however, and the United States was spared the expense and the embarrassment.

*MAP EIGHT*

## BRECKENRIDGE and MONTEZUMA

Breckenridge (Fort Meribeh, Breckinridge)
Conger (Conger's Camp)
Lincoln City (Paige City)
Wapiti, Rexford, Nigger Gulch, and Preston
Delaware Flats (Delaware City, Braddock, Preston)
Swan City
Tiger
Spencerville
Parkville (Park City)
Montezuma
Sts. Johns (Coleyville, St. Johns)
Adrain
Franklin (Franklyn)
Filger City
Chihuahua
Mitchell Cabins
Peru
Argentine (Rathbone, Decatur)
Haywood
Keystone
Geneva (Geneva Gulch)
Hall Valley (Hallville, Hall City) and Handcart Gulch
Jefferson
Webster
Peabody's, Halfway, Boreas, Farnham (Farnham Spur), Baker's Tank,
    and Bacon
*And Then There Were . . . . SWANDYKE, SWANVILLE* (Swan Camp), *WARREN'S
STATION, KENOSHA, HOOSIER, DICKEY, VALDORO, LAURIUM, QUANDRY
or QUANDARY CITY and MAYFLOWER*

## BRECKENRIDGE (Breckinridge, Fort Meribeh)

They've taken precious metals out of the Breckenridge area in every way possible. They're still taking it out. Experts say there's still plenty left.

Here they panned the gold, placer mined it, dug for it, washed it out of mountains with giant hoses, and before the dredges began cutting their way through the valley, scores of Chinese miners went through the gravel and picked out the gold-bearing stones by hand.

The Breckenridge area was called the "shirt-tail" mining area after a drawing of suspenderless miners panning gold received wide circulation back east.

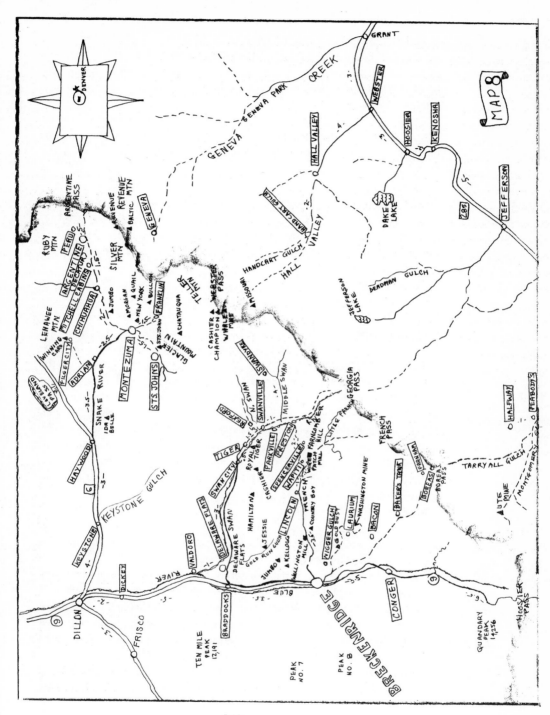

143

The first prospectors entered the area in 1859 and, to protect themselves against the Indians, built a fort a short distance away from the present site of Breckenridge. Gold was discovered in good quantity, and as the number of miners and prospectors increased, the fort was abandoned and a city was built.

To win government interest, the residents named the soaring city Breckinridge, for John C. Breckinridge, Lincoln's vice president. A few months later, when John C. expressed sympathy for the southern cause in the Civil War, the residents, overwhelmingly Yankees, changed the first "i" to "e" just to show John C. how they felt.

Rich placer and lode locations were made all around Breckenridge, and within months some 8,000 persons were here. During the 60's the Breckenridge area boasted one of the richest placer areas in the state. And before the placer locations gave out, lode mines were discovered and the miners began digging for gold.

Breckenridge jumped on the silver bandwagon of the late 70's and early 80's quite by accident. The story goes that a gold miner was getting a haircut in a Breckenridge tonsorial parlor and he and the boys in the barber shop were discussing the fabulous rush to Leadville, when the barber noticed, and mentioned the fact, that the miner had silver dust in his hair.

Despite the isolation of the city, Breckenridge suffered little from the transportation problem. Hoosier Pass to Montgomery and Fairplay was completed as early as 1860, and named by some early prospectors from Indiana. In the following years, prospectors and visitors reached Breckenridge via Argentine, Webster and even Loveland Passes. But the most important pass in Breckenridge's early history, and one of the more fantastic in Colorado, was Boreas Pass, running from Como to Breckenridge.

Before the huge dredges came here in the early years of this century, giant hoses with a powerful 250-foot spray washed into the mountains, filtering out the rich minerals.

Evidence of the dredges, for which Dredge County is named, is everywhere here, from above Breckendridge down to Fairplay and off into the gulches all along the way.

The dredges would cut a path sometimes as much as one hundred yards wide and eighty feet deep, and through a unique system of filtering, the rich gold dust would gather on the large pontoon boats behind the dredges. This system earned as much as $20,000 per week. The dredging continued for many years, but finally, after all the streams had been scooped out, the dredges and boats were carted away in a World War II scrap drive.

Despite all its colorful history and the millions of dollars in precious metals, the Breckenridge district has produced, it was not officially a part of the United States until 1936. At that time, a Breckenridge women's club discovered that in all the ancient purchases of land by the nation, a 1,300 square mile area from Breckenridge north to Grand Lake had been neglected and was not officially a part of Colorado, or the United States.

So Colorado's energetic Governor Ed Johnson, amid much fanfare, took matters into his own hands, raising the U. S. flag over the "foreign" territory and welcoming it into the union.

GOLD DUST: Fort Maribeh was named for Mary B., the only girl in the fort . . . . it is said the first Breckenridge prospectors returning to the eastern plains for the winter of 1859-60, settled at the foot of Pikes Peak, and were the first residents of what was to be Colorado Springs . . . . the first stagecoach entered Breckenridge in 1860. The city was also on the Pony Express route . . . . there is a story of a large cattle drive heading for Breckenridge during the first years. The drive started too late and was caught in a blizzard and most of the cattle died . . . . another story concerns a duel between two men who weren't used to that sort of thing. With most of the town looking on, the two men stepped off 15 paces, and then started running. They were never seen again . . . . a false rumor that the Indians had attacked Breckenridge, burned the city and slaughtered the resident, was cause of a major Indian scare in 1879 . . . . a $200,000 lump of almost pure gold was dug up on Nigger Hill near where the Club House now stands . . . . the Silverthone Hotel, for years the center of Breckenridge's social activity, is still standing although it has been vacant for years. It was run by the wife of Judge Silverthone, a civic leader in the Breckenridge area . . . . Breckenridge is the only survivor of the many cities and camps that once flourished in the area, and although many of its houses and buildings are empty and the population has dwindled to 500, Breckenridge is far from dead. Other than the profitable mining activities still carried on, the city is now the center of increased tourist activities . . . . General Fremont crossed the pass in 1844 and witnessed an Indian battle here . . . . The following appeared in the *Breckenridge Journal* in July of 1880: "A Tenderfoot from the states who had been drunk from the time he left Chicago until his arrival in this city, sobered up when seeing snow on the hilltops, blurted out: 'The longest drunk I ever took from Fourth of July till winter; gimme another drink, may as well keep it up till spring'."

## CONGER (Conger's Camp)

An important, although previously little-known camp, near Breckenridge during the early 80's. Like many another camp, its prospects were glowing and early strikes lent credence to the glowing promise. But the rich lodes were not as extensive as they seemed to be and the site was soon forgotten.

The first strike was made here in the spring of 1879. By the end of the summer Conger's Camp was a "vigorous" community. It was named for Colonel S. P. Conger, a veteran prospector who discovered the Caribou Mine and later was instrumental in starting the tungsten boom in the Nederland area. Conger came here and located the Dianthe, a rich fissure mine which was reported to run from 1,000 to 2,000 ounces per ton.

By 1880, some 30 to 40 houses had been built. There were a post office, a saw mill, and several stores. A fifteen-stamp mill was built, and a smelter was planned. The surrounding hills were covered with claims, but only a few properties were developed to any extent. They were placer lodes, said to be rich in ruby, brittle silver and copper, running all the way from $200 to $22,000 a ton. (The latter figure would make it some of the richest ore found in Colorado).

One report said the "Carbonates were similar to those found at Leadville, galena as fine as any around Georgetown, quartz will run 50 to 250 ounces."

The richest mine at that time was the Case. Its shaft was down 100 feet by 1880 and its best ore was running from 600 to 1,000 ounces per ton. A gray copper fissure was found in the Warrior Mark on Baldy Hill which was found to be 6,000 ounces per ton. The Daisey, at only eight feet, showed 200 ounces of silver and one ounce gold.

Other good properties were the High Line, Newark City, Greenwood, Young America, Franklin, Great Republic and Gray Horse.

Properties changed hands frequently. The Brown brothers sold a prospect on Baldy Hill for $20,000; and another claim sold for $30,000 before its shaft had gone down 30 feet. The Daisy sold for $5,000.

The first problem encountered by the camp was the miner supply. There were too many prospectors and not enough miners—too many chiefs and not enough Indians. Early Conger entrepreneurs also attempted to attract working capital with which to develop the mines, but reports indicated there was not enough outside investment—although there was some. And then, the veins apparently just weren't as extensive as they appeared. What there was must have been spread pretty thin.

Conger also served as a lumber camp, and that helped keep it alive a little longer. There was some mining here, on a small scale, for several years. In fact, there is a little mining carried on in the general vicinity of Conger even today, but Conger, as a boom town, died in two or three years.

EDITOR'S TANGENT: The following quote appeared in a description of Conger Camp in the Denver *Rocky Mountain News* shortly before the general election of 1880. It's got nothing to do with Conger Camp but it gives a good picture of how high-strung newspapers were in those days. The parentheses are mine (P.E.)

"Hancock and English (political candidates) are the Penants of Conger Camp. The apostle of fraud, perjury, salary grabs and the rhetorician (that's what the man said) who made his fame by the 'cheap and nasty' silver epigram has not a corporal's guard here to fire a salute on the second of November (election day) over his grave, where he, the Republican Party and the bloody shirt, will be laid away in oblivion."

## LINCOLN CITY (Paige City)

Lincoln City on French Gulch east of Breckenridge had a little Civil War of its own during its early days, and it greatly hindered the development of the rich area.

Twisted wire gold of unusual quality was found here during the early

146

60's. The first man to find the gold was Harry Farncomb. While most of the other prospectors were off working the known mineral fields in the area, Harry had French Gulch pretty much to himself. As he worked it he continued to purchase more land until he had several acres. Nobody cared until Harry journeyed to Denver and plunked down a sack of almost pure gold in a Denver bank. Interest grew rapidly in the "Wire Patch," so named because of the wire gold found here.

The acreage Farncomb had purchased was not in line with accepted mining procedures. A group, supported by Denver capitalists, attempted to wrest the land away from Farncomb, precipitating what was know as the "Ten Years War." The first phase of the war was a legal one which cost hundreds of thousands of dollars, and tied up the top mining lawyers in Colorado for months. The Denver bank went busted.

When it seemed nothing could be settled through legal means, the Denver group attempted to take away the land by force, and firing broke out in French Gulch. Dozens of men participated in the battle that ranged up and down the gulch for the better part of a day. When the smoke cleared away, many were wounded, three were dead, and nothing was accomplished.

Eventually a third party purchased the land and French Gulch, after a slow and costly start, came into its own. But Farncomb was already rich.

Population grew from about 300 in the late 70's to more than 1,500 in the 80's. Two hotels, the Wheeler and the Perkins, a sawmill, three stamp furnaces, a stamp mill, several businesses and cabins marked the site.

One of the early miners here was perhaps the only man tattooed with solid gold.

During the early years of Lincoln City, the miners used to take turns walking into Breckenridge for the mail. One day, the postmistress had some wire gold drying in the oven when the miner came for the mail. While her back was turned, the miner slipped the gold into his shirt. Before he could get the gold out, the miner had burned a reminder into his skin that crime does not pay.

French Gulch is another Colorado area which claims title to the world's largest solid gold nugget. A miner in 1869 picked the nugget off the ground —it weighed nine and one-half ounces.

Lincoln City was hard hit by the crash of '93, and although some mining has been done here off and on since, including the dredging operations of later years, Lincoln City became but a memory.

A few ramshackle cabins at the foot of Farncomb Hill are all that remain. TOP MINES: Willington, Minnie, Country Boy, Cincinnati, American Union, Elephant, Governor King, Queen of the Forest and Bismarck.

147

## WAPITI, REXFORD, NIGGER GULCH and PRESTON

Mining camps located near Breckenridge.

Nigger Gulch, located one mile east of Breckenridge on French Gulch, was described as "a busy camp of several hundred miners in early placer days." The camp was deserted, however, when the hydraulic dredges came through in 1881.

Rexford was apparently a small company town at a mining property operated by the Rexford Mining Corporation. The corporation was organized in 1881 with a capital stock of $100,000. The company operated around the state, but primarily in this area.

Wapiti was a small camp, four miles east of Breckenridge. The name means "elk" to Indians.

Preston was a small camp around a mine on the lower Swan. It is also shown on early maps as a junction point where the road from Beckenridge via Lincoln runs into the road over Georgia Pass. Preston was listed as one of the earlier post offices in the area. It was all gone by 1900.

## DELAWARE FLATS (Delaware City, Preston, Braddock)

Delaware Flats was only the first of the many names given this camp, but no matter how many names it had, it will always be remembered as Delaware Flats.

Miners and historians love names like that.

Delaware Flats was laid out on Silver Creek, near the junction of that stream with the Blue River, during the winter of 1859-60. By the following year the camp had a post office and a few hundred residents. The post office, under the able guidance of Postmaster George Anderson, was discontinued two years later, but re-established later the same year. The name was changed to Preston in 1875, and to Braddock—later-day postmaster and donor of the townsite—in 1884. The post office was discontinued for good in 1890.

Other than the city's usually having a post office, little else is known of Delaware Flats-Delaware City-Preston-and-Braddock.

The mines, however, produced gold, silver, lead and copper. The best properties were the Discovery Belt, Intermediate, Adelia, Timothy, Inferno and Surles.

## SWAN CITY

Swan City was laid out about the time Parkville died, in 1880. By 1883, the city had a hotel, post office, a general store, a couple of saloons and about 300 residents. Mail delivery was made three times a week.

The population wavered between 200 and 300 all during the 80's, but began to dwindle rapidly in the 90's.

Placer mining and quartz mining were done here and some ore assayed as high as $800 a ton. There was some activity here during this century when the dredges passed by.

Nothing is left of the site.

## TIGER

Tiger was the most recent city in the Swan River area, and is therefore the best preserved. In fact, most of the cabins still standing in Tiger are used by tourists and outdoorsmen during the summer.

The summer cabins were once miners' bunkhouses, a general store and employees' cabins left over from the day the city depended upon the Tiger mine, later known as the Royal Tiger Mines.

As other camps faded in the area, the miners and prospectors drifted here. Some minerals were found. Much money was spent in an attempt to develop Tiger into a top producing area. The plan didn't work. The city was snowed in much of the year, and the ore had to be shipped out in sleds.

The dredges plowed by here in later years.

## SPENCERVILLE

A temporary camp located near Georgia Gulch in the winter of 1860.

It was named for W. W. Spencer, who was among the first group which discovered rich placer gold here.

The camp saw some activity for a few short years and then lost out to the other camps around.

## PARKVILLE (Park City)

Parkville, on the south fork of the Swan River, is believed to be the only town in Colorado to have been buried by its own industriousness.

Parkville was *the* mining camp of Summit County during the early 60's, and as many as 10,000 persons lived in the narrow gulch. But in a few short years the mines had been worked out and the tailings of the mines had completely buried the city by the early 1880's.

But Parkville-ites crowded a lot of living into those few short years.

The first strike was made in 1859, and by the time the election of 1860 rolled around, some 1800 voters were here. Parkville was made county seat. An estimated three million dollars in gold was produced here during the first two years. J. J. Conway and Company established a mint and turned out $2.50, $5.00 and $10.00 gold pieces.

As well as being the supply center for the entire Georgia Gulch area, Parkville was also the social center. The top entertainers and troupers of the day in Colorado passed through the town. Langrishe and Daugherty of Central City fame (see Central City) opened a large theatre here and produced many shows, always to an overflow crowd.

After the placer gold was gone, lode mining was the thing. When that pinched out, hydraulics were used to chisel out the golden gravels . . . and bury the city.

Then, the buried city of Parkville, one of the largest of its day, died as abruptly as it was born.

## MONTEZUMA

Montezuma, this once proud silver camp, is doggedly fighting extinction . . . but the deck is stacked against it.

A telling blow in the town's battle for survival was delivered a week before Christmas in 1958 when a flash fire swept through the town, completely destroying a hotel, the town hall, two houses and six garages, and damaging several other buildings. The fire started in the Summit House hotel, which housed five families. Most of the menfolk were off working, but the women and what was left of the men heroically prevented loss of life and greater damage by the flames. Almost half of the town of 75 residents were made homeless.

Donations of food, clothing and Christmas presents came from throughout the state, but it was a bleak holiday season nonetheless.

The fire came at a time when Montezuma was experiencing a mild upturn. Montezuma was not a ghost town but it was hovering on the brink in 1956 when only about a dozen people lived here. Then the Roberts Tunnel, a part of the Denver water system, went under construction a short distance away. Montezuma was the most convenient place for the construction workers to live.

After the fire, the homeless were taken in by their more fortunate neighbors. Some other living quarters were being prepared, almost before the last embers had died.

Montezuma isn't dead yet . . . . but it has lost a lot of its confidence.

The story goes that H. M. Teller was the first to strike gold here. The story probably goes that way because Teller later became a senator in Colorado and was important in the state's history. Reports show, however, that Teller was merely among the first to prospect in the region, and he and others, including D. C. Collier, made their strikes at just about the same time.

Collier was perhaps more important to Montezuma than Teller. He (Collier) was the guiding force in laying out the city. He suggested the name Montezuma for the late Aztec ruler of Mexico. Collier Mountain, on which many of Montezuma's best strikes were located, is just above the town.

The strikes were made in the 60's, but because largely of the transportation problem, the camp grew slowly, having a population of but 200 in the early 70's. With the development of Webster and Argentine Passes and other routes in and out of the district, Montezuma picked up speed, hitting its peak about 1880, when more than 800 persons lived here. By this time Montezuma had a post office, three hotels, a schoolhouse, steam sawmill, smelting furnace and concentration works. The city was incorporated in 1881. The following year, a newspaper, *The Montezuma Millrun*, began publication. A second newspaper followed.

The first school was built in 1876, about midway between Montezuma and Sts. Johns and was named, oddly enough, Halfway Schoolhouse. The second school was built in Montezuma in 1880, although it still served both communities. Within three years, this school proved inadequate and the third, larger school was constructed in Montezuma in 1884. The school is still standing. The 1880 school is now a private residence.

The first hotel was built in 1868. The larger Preston House Hotel was completed the following year and the Rocky Mountain House went into operation in the late 70's.

A story is told of Montezuma justice—an almost identical story is told around Geneva Gulch. They may have come from the same incident.

The story concerns two prospectors in love with the same girl back in Missouri. The two worked around several of the boom areas, saving their money for the day their fortunes would be made and they could return home to claim their lady love. They believed, perhaps separately, that the first one to gain a fortune would be the one to win the lady's hand.

Enroute to Montezuma one night, around their campfire, the two began boasting of how much they had saved and how near they were to their fortunes. Suddenly, one of them got the bright idea of doubling his fortune by doing away with the other. In this way, he would have enough money to return home and get married.

The murder was accomplished, but the deed was discovered by the time he reached Missouri and he was brought back. On the way back, the miner decided he could spend his money more wisely by hiring a good lawyer. He did so in Denver.

Meanwhile, back in Montezuma, the justice of the peace was preparing a royal welcome. By the time the murderer and his lawyer returned to Montezuma, the scaffold was all built and ready, and the execution papers were all signed.

The lawyer wasted no time in explaining to the eager justice of the peace that one just doesn't carry out the law in this manner. While the lawyer

151

was explaining the finer points of the law to the justice of the peace, the murderer escaped and was never heard from again.

Montezuma and its satellite camps were known for their hospitality and social activities. There was much friendly rivalry between the camps, including sports competition and exchange dances.

Montezuma was famous for its poker playing. They say the early settlers had a game going constantly night and day. When somebody dropped out, somebody else would be ready to fill the vacancy. They took the game seriously, but played it honestly. Lord help the man who dealt from the bottom!

However, there is a story told of a professional gambler's ambling into town one day. He gave the appearance of a rube, although he let it be known he wasn't so prudish as to be averse to a little gambling. The game got underway between the stranger and Montezuma's best poker players. One by one, over the hours the Montezuma-ites dropped out, cleaned out, until finally the pride of Montezuma depended upon one man. The game dragged on through the night, until, eventually, the stranger got up and said he had to go. He had to walk out of town because he didn't have the fare for a coach.

Montezuma was threatened by the forest fire in 1889 which did heavy damage to many of the other camps in the area. But through hard work by the miners and a favorable wind, the city was spared any major damage. However, Montezuma was cut off from the outside world for several days because of burning logs falling across the routes out of town.

Montezuma was hit hard by the panic of '93, but was able to hold on until the camp came into better days. The city was never deserted and some mining is still being done here, although most of the residents are workers on the Roberts tunnel.

Montezuma's proud mining days are over.

GOLD DUST: Father Dyer was said to have located a mine on Webster Pass above Montezuma during one of the "snowshoe itinerant's" many trips into the area . . . . an old mine shaft can be seen about 400 feet above the city on Collier Mountain . . . . Governor Evans visited here in 1868 . . . . silver ore from the mines here was valued up to $6,000 a ton . . . . in its heyday, Montezuma had visitors from foreign nations and several eastern states. One time an entire class of mining engineers from Missouri lived in Montezuma to study its operations.

## STS. JOHNS (Coleyville, St. Johns)

There are two stories of the finding of gold here. One tells of hunters running out of bullets while on a hunting expedition in 1861, and using rocks as shells. Two years later, one of the hunters saw some high grade ore in Nevada and noticed the similarity to the stones used as bullets. He notified John Coley who located the ore.

152

The other, less colorful, story tells of Coley, a Georgetown prospector, coming here frequently in search for gold, and locating a strike after several months of prospecting.

Anyway, Sts. Johns was founded and Coley was the big man in finding it. In fact, the city at the site of his strike was first called Coleyville, but some Freemasons exerted their influence and gave the city the biblical name. In later years, Sts. Johns was simplified to St. Johns.

There is another interesting story of a big strike made here by Bob Epsey. It seems Bob was hungover one day and instead of prospecting for gold he found a good shade tree and lay down to take a nap. He was still a little shaky on awakening and needed to grab onto a rock to steady himself. Well sir, part of the rock broke off and there was solid ore . . . big as life.

These strikes and more, mostly made during the 60's, eventually fell into the hands of eastern capitalists, and Sts. Johns became, for the most part, a company town.

The Boston Silver Mining Association took over operation of many of the workings in 1872 and, at great expense, built the most complete and up-to-date milling and smelting works possible at the time. The bricks were imported from Europe. In 1875, the Boston Silver Company took over, and three years later the Boston Mining Company was formed, and it continued to develop the area into one of the most complete company towns in Colorado.

The company had a two-and-one-half story boarding house, guest house for visitors, private houses for company officials and for employees with families, a dining hall, company store and an assay office.

The most beautiful house here and just about any place else in Colorado was erected for the superintendent. The furnishings were brought all the way from the east and even Europe. The house served as a showplace for many years and all the important visitors were entertained here. When the company ended operations, the superintendent at the time packed his bag and walked out of the house, leaving it just as it was. The house is still standing, but the beautiful furnishings disappeared one by one through the years.

Sts. Johns was unique in another respect. It boasted of being one of the few Colorado mining towns of any size that didn't have a saloon. But it did have a library. The 300-volume library was donated by Bostonites, and eastern newspapers and many European newspapers were sent here regularly.

As with most other mining camps, transportation and winter were the two main problems. The Argentine and Webster Passes were frequently closed by snow and rock slides. Several persons were said to have been killed in snowslides near here. One early resident counted ten snowslides in one morning in 1898, one of Colorado's worst winters.

The camp dwindled slowly during the 80's and died during the 90's, although some mining has been carried on here off and on since. For the most part, however, the miners live in Montezuma, two miles away.

GOLD DUST: John Coley, who made the first strike here, was blinded a few years later in an accident . . . . Georgetown was booming when the first strike was made here in 1864, so little interest was shown in the new area. Interest increased rapidly the following year with the finding of the Comstock lode of Sts. Johns mine. Several other rich strikes were made shortly thereafter . . . . several buildings marks the site of Sts. John, including the superintendent's house and the 2½-story miners' boarding house . . . . the road to Sts. Johns from Montezuma is difficult but passable much of the year . . . . the ruins of Coley's first furnace are still visible about a quarter-mile from his original strike. It is said to be the first silver smelting furnace in Colorado . . . . a small smelter built here in 1872 was also said to be one of the first successful smelters of this sort built in Colorado . . . . the city's first hotel, also housing a post office, was called the Summit House . . . . many of the best workings here were on Glacier Mountain just behind the city.

BEST MINES: Sts. Johns, Comstock, Potosi, Herman, Silver Wing, Napoleon, Sukey, Bell Chatauqua.

## ADRIAN

A Dr. McKenney of Illinois planned to make Adrian a resort area, and a base for pleasure excursions up and down the Snake River. But only a few cabins were built before Dr. McKenney died and the project was abandoned. Other settlers in the area tore down the cabins and rebuilt them in more convenient locations.

Nothing remains of the elaborately-planned city, 2.5 miles north of Montezuma.

## FRANKLIN (Franklyn)

The Montezuma Silver Mining Company selected a site a short distance away from the workaday mining camps for construction of an elite headquarters community, to house company officials and entertain important visitors. The site selected was on the north bank of the Snake River near its junction with Deer Creek, and about a mile and one-half south of Montezuma.

A large two-story residence, the Franklin House, a boarding house and sawmill were all that was ever built. But although the remainder of the plans never saw daylight, the two-story superintendent's home did become a showplace and social center for a while.

Only the foundation of the Franklin House remains of the site today.

## FILGER CITY

Another elaborately-planned city that never got much further than the planning stage. It was founded in the early 80's shortly after Isaac Filger located the Winning Card mine on Lenawee Mountain. The mine looked promising and soon employed a large work crew, and the elaborate city was planned.

But only a few cabins were built before the rich ore played out and all dreams were forgotten.

## CHIHUAHUA

During its boom, Chihuahua rivaled the top camps in the district, and had just about everything but a doctor and a priest.

The residents boasted the medical and the clergy weren't needed because there was no sickness nor sin in Chihuahua.

The city was founded in 1880, shortly after rich strikes were made on the surrounding mountains. By the following year the population topped 200 and some 50 buildings marked the site, including two hotels—the Chihuahua and Snively—a sawmill, reduction works, three restaurants and three saloons.

The city was believed named for a state in Mexico, although some old-timers claim it was named for an old Indian Chief called Shu-wa-wa.

Despite the boast of sinlessness, Chihuahua's short history is colored with a triple-lynching. It seems three road agents waylaid two Chihuahua prospectors a short distance out of town, robbed them and killed them. Chihuahua residents heard of this within minutes and the whole town took off after the killers. Three of the suspects were caught near the top of Ruby Mountain, and without benefit of a trial or clergy, the three were hanged on the spot.

All five bodies were taken back to town and buried in two separate graves.

The city began fading with the ores during the 80's and when a forest fire hit the town in 1889, destroying virtually all of the business section, nobody bothered to rebuild it.

The ruins of one old cabin and several foundations mark the spot.

## MITCHELL CABINS

About halfway between Chihuahua and Decatur (Argentine) were some cabins built by an old couple who worked their small claim, mostly by themselves. They were said to be very industrious and almost hermit-like. Mrs. Mitchell was the harder worker of the two. When not digging into the mountain she wrote and sold short stories to help finance their mining experiment. Mr. Mitchell carried the mail to help buy the beans.

They were also known to be rather miserly. At one time, they boarded a miner to help them work their claim. Come payday, his wages were equal to the board bill with which he was presented. The miner didn't stay for another payday.

## PERU

Peru was never an official town, merely a convenient title given the boarding house and miners' cabins around the Peruvian mine a short distance north of Decatur (Argentine).

The Peruvian was located in 1874, several years after the Paymaster, the first claim in the basin, was located. These were the two top mines here and even they didn't produce too steadily.

But the place known as Peru did live long enough to record two outstanding events. One was a visit by Governor Evans and the other was a clever swindle.

It seems some absentee mine owners hired a work crew, headed by a man called Gassy Thompson, to dig a 100-foot tunnel into the mountain. But instead of digging into the mountain, Gassy and his crew began building snowsheds out from the mountain. They kept building as the snow fell. When the snow sheds measured 100 feet, Gassy roused the owners and said the work was completed.

The owners inspected the project, complimented Gassy on his work and paid up in full. Before the snow melted, Gassy and his gang were gone.

## ARGENTINE (Rathbone, Decatur)

This camp is known now as Argentine but is better known to the old-timers as Decatur. It seems the site underwent periodic revivals, and every time it was re-born under a different name.

It was originally named Decatur for "Commodore" Stephen Decatur, but activity here died out and the site was deserted. It was revived around 1893 and named Rathbone. Shortly after the turn of the century, work was taken up again and this time the site came to be known as Argentine, taking the same title as the mining district which was apparently named several years before for Argentine Pass.

The site experienced its greatest boom under the name of Decatur.

Some prospecting was done here during the middle 60's and some silver was found. The town was laid out in 1868 by Decatur. But because of the almost prohibitive costs of carting out the mediocre ore, the town's growth was slow until the Pennsylvania was located in 1879 by J. M. Hall.

Within a short time, nearly a thousand persons were here and Decatur became an important camp. Other strikes were made in 1880 and eastern capital was invested in the mines.

Decatur, although a man of mystery, was an important figure in early

Colorado history. Many oldtimers believed him to be a descendant of the commodore of "our country right or wrong" fame who was killed in a duel in 1820. Colorado's Commodore Decatur apparently didn't work too hard dispelling all the rumors about him.

It is believed his name was actually Stephen Decatur Bross, but he dropped the Bross on coming to Colorado in 1859. He was thought to be the long-lost elder brother of Illinois' Governor Bross. Much fanfare was given the relationship at the time, and the Illinois governor personally came to Colorado to investigate. He identified Stephen as his brother, but Stephen denied the relationship and would have nothing to do with the Illinois official. Reports say Stephen Decatur actually admitted the relationship many years later in confidence, but the entire situation remains a source of speculation to this day.

Stephen Decatur Bross was a professor of a school near Poughkeepsie, New York, when he disappeared in the early 1840s, leaving a wife and two children behind.

Colorado's Stephen Decatur was a prominent figure in the early years of Georgetown. He came to Decatur in the late 60's to found the city which bore his name. He was a successful Indian fighter, mining man, city builder, and later Colorado senator, before he died penniless in Rosita.

The Pennsylvania mine was far and away the best property here. In its day it produced more than three million dollars in ore. It was one of the few silver mines to survive the silver crash of '93. The mine set the pace of activity. It had its ups and downs but was worked almost continuously for more than 20 years and has been worked off and on until recent years.

A giant snowslide roared down Gray's Peak in 1898 and carried off much of the site, perched on a rugged ridge of the mountain. Little was rebuilt and only the ruins of a few cabins mark the site of Decatur-Rathbone-Argentine.

## HAYWOOD

A few hundred feet northwest of the junction of U. S. 6 and Colorado 294 can be seen the ruins of Haywood, a once-busy stage station between Georgetown and Kokomo.

In 1880, the station contained a single log building which housed a hotel, restaurant and post office. Later some cabins were built around the building.

The station was named for Kate Haywood, postmistress and wife of the operator.

Thousands of miners and tourists traveling over Argentine, Webster and, for a short while, Loveland passes, stopped at Haywood to reinforce themselves for the perilous trip ahead, or calm their nerves after the trip had been made. The passes were frequently closed by weather, and the travelers were forced to "wait it out" at Haywood.

Later, as the routes were improved and the railroad was extended to many farther points, Haywood gradually faded away. It was dead by about 1890.

## KEYSTONE

Keystone was a loading station for the Colorado and Southern narrow gauge railway and was named by the railroad. Much lumber was shipped from here for construction of many of the towns around, and much ore from the nearby boom towns was shipped out from here. There was a little mining nearby.

The site is just a stop on the road today.

## GENEVA (Geneva Gulch)

A dagger carved on a tree in Geneva Gulch marks the site where the notorious Reynolds gang (see Fairplay) was said to have buried from $50,000 to $100,000 in loot from their nefarious enterprises. Some historians dispute the claim, however.

Geneva was a two-story boarding house, a general store and a few cabins, used by employees of mines in Geneva Gulch. The mines and much of the settlement were above timberline.

## HALL VALLEY (Hallville, Hall City) and HANDCART GULCH

Hall Valley is located in Handcart Gulch on the route to the old Webster Pass. A smaller camp named Handcart Gulch was a short distance beyond Hall Valley.

The gulch was named for the handcarts used by the miners to pull outfits up the steep walls of the valley. Hall Valley was named for Colonel J. W. Hall.

Stories disagree on Hall's place in the scheme of things in Hall Valley. There is disagreement over the cause of the downfall of the area.

One story said the claims made here were sold to Colonel Hall in 1866. The story says the best claim was the Whale mine, which made Hall rich. Another story says Hall merely managed the mine, and through his incompetence the mine failed. Yet another says the failure of the area was due to the incompetence of appointed officials of an English company, who took over the workings and spent money so lavishly it ate up the profits.

At least we know the place wasn't run right.

It is known for sure, however, that Handcart Gulch was a rowdy area as long as it lasted. It reached its peak in 1876-77 when there were several hundred miners here. Gambling and drinking went on night and day. Two mine foremen were bullies, so the miners took them out and lynched them.

A tumbledown cabin and the ruins of an old mill mark the spot.

## JEFFERSON

Long before Colorado became a state in 1876, there was talk of establishing the Pikes Peak region as the State of Jefferson. This city was founded while the Jefferson craze was going on, and the city was named in the hope it might become the capitol of the new state.

Prospectors, disgusted by the treatment they received at Tarryall, washed out some gold here and set up a shop of their own. As a gold camp, however, Jefferson didn't last long.

But when the Colorado and Southern Railroad extended its line into South Park in 1879, Jefferson became a side track and shipping station. At first it was a supply depot and shipping point for ore from other camps. In later years it served as a shipping point for cattle and timber.

The station still stands, but the tracks were torn up in the 1930's.

## WEBSTER

Webster was a shipping station at the foot of another pass, important in the development of the South Park and Breckenridge area.

The pass was built in 1878 by William Emerson Webster, in partnership with the Montezuma Silver Mining Company, and ran from Webster to Hall Valley through Handcart Gulch to Montezuma. For several years it was the chief freight route from Denver to the Snake River Mining District.

The pass was covered by snow much of the year and had its share of highwaymen and death (see Montezuma). Father Dyer traveled over the pass frequently on his rounds of the silver camps in the area, to carry mail, and the word of God.

As other passes were developed, Webster Pass lost its importance. Today, it and Webster, on the highway to Kenosha Pass, are no more.

## PEABODY'S, HALFWAY, BOREAS, FARNHAM (Farnham Spur), BAKER'S TANK and BACON

The more important stations on Boreas Pass, running from Como to Breckenridge.

The pass was named for the Greek God of the North Wind. A more appropriate godfather couldn't be found. The 11,498-foot trail was one of the most feared of all the early and perilous passes in the state. The steep inclines, sharp curves and ledge roads which, as one poet put it, "clung to the edge of eternity," were constantly swept by storms and bleak, howling winds.

Despite its fearsome features, however, the pass was in constant use, and vital to the activity in Breckenridge. Stages whipped over the route in a

159

constant stream, meeting ore wagons grinding their way to market. Later a branch of the South Park Railroad was built over the pass, making it, for a time, the highest railroad run in the nation.

The pass had eleven snow sheds and grades up to 4½ percent, so steep engines could pull no more than three cars at once.

Many tales are told of the trip over the pass, before and after the railroad was built. Perhaps the most colorful stories concerned the time Barnum's Circus Train was heading for Breckenridge. It seems the heavy train almost stalled on the steep incline and it was feared the cars wouldn't make it to the top. So the elephants were taken out of their cars and made to push the train up three miles of the steepest grade.

The European Alps had its Hannibal and his elephants. Colorado had its Barnum and his elephants on Boreas Pass.

In recent years, the Army Corps of Engineers cleared the old railroad grade for automobile travel, opening up one of the most scenic and interesting trips in Colorado. Many relics of the past can be found along the way. A tall ore tipple skeleton and two buildings remain at Farnham spur. Ore from the 710 Mine tunnel up the slopes was carried to the tipple by aerial cable tram. Ore was also brought here from the Warrior's Mark Mine at Dyersville on Indiana Creek just below (see page 140). A timeless log section house still stands at the site of Boreas, atop the Continental Divide. At one time there was a stone engine house, a station, a 950-foot-long snowshed, and the highest post office in the United States here. Boreas station burned to the ground in 1934, three years before the D.S.P.&P. finally discontinued the line.

*And Then There Were . . . . SWANDYKE* and *SWANVILLE* (Swan Camp), two camps that enjoyed a short existence on the lower Swan. Since Swandyke is one of the most inaccessible, several old buildings remain, half hidden by the trees . . . . *WARREN'S STATION* (not on map) another stage stop on the western side of Loveland Pass. One large cabin hotel-restaurant-saloon was built by Chauncey Warren about 1880. After about two or three years, Loveland Pass, considered too steep and treacherous for practical use, lost much of its business to the other passes around, and the Warren family packed up its bags and moved to Frisco . . . . *KENOSHA* and *HOOSIER*, two railroad stops on Kenosha Pass. Both towns had post offices. Kenosha is believed to be a tribe of Chippewa Indians. The town of Kenosha was at the summit of the pass . . . . *DICKEY* was shown on some early maps as north of Breckenridge. It was a big coaling and switching station on the Denver and South Park line. There was a roundhouse and large coaling station here . . . . *VALDORO*, a fairly large community at one time although not too much is known about it. There was some mining here but it appears to have been more important as a railroad town. It was on the Colorado and Southern narrow gauge line and there was a side track here . . . . *LAURIM*, a camp at some mining properties a short distance southeast of Breckenridge. The largest mine was the Laurim. There was another large mine just south of Laurim, the Washington. It also had a small settlement near the mine but the camp apparently didn't have a name unless it was called Washington . . . . *QUANDRY or QUANDRY CITY* (not on map) an obscure camp on the Hoosier Pass. The town was said to have had a hotel and a smelter. The mountain was named by early prospectors who reportedly were in a quandary as to the kind of ore they found on the mountain . . . . *MAYFLOWER*

was a cluster of cabins around the Mayflower and other mines high above Breckenridge. The Mayflower dated from August 1, 1887. Other claims included the Garrison,
Bronson and others operated by Glen Mohawk Mining Company. A hermit named
Tom Davidson lived alone in the town for many years. He was found dead in a cabin
about fifty years ago. His cat was found frozen stiff in the window.

An old dredge near Breckenridge. This and later model dredges filtered
millions of dollars worth of gold out of the creeks and streams in South
Park and the Breckenridge area. *Photo courtesy Glenn L. Gebhardt.*

Hall Valley, showing the Whale Mine in the center. Picture looks southeast down the valley. *U. S. Geological Survey photo.*

Holy Cross City, in the shadow of the famous mountain for which it is named. *State Historical Society of Colorado photo.*

Old buildings at Fulford. *Picture by Jim Ward.*

Modern cliff dwellers in the still-going town of Gilman, one of the few towns in Colorado where much of the mining was done below the town. Recently built houses are to the right of the picture. *Colorado Publicity Department photo.*

W. H. Jackson packed his photo crew supply wagon on mules when the trails gave out. *Colorado State Highway Department.*

The mountain of molybdenum at Climax. The American Metals mine is in the foreground. *U. S. Bureau of Mines photo.*

The second Oro City in California Gulch. Picture was taken by William H. Jackson in 1873 just a few years before the great Leadville boom. Oro City moved up the gulch to be near the Printer Boy Mine, barely visible near top of center hill and a little to the right. *U. S. Geological Survey photo.*

Leadville from Carbonate Hill, 1882. *U. S. Geological Survey photo.*

The Leadville Ice Palace, built in 1895. The palace covered five acres and was built completely of ice blocks eight feet thick. Ore samples were frozen into the wall and numerous ice statues melted away inside. *State Historical Society of Colorado photo.*

Ashcroft now. *Colorado Publicity Department photo.*

Old rotary type snowplow on Hagerman Pass. This line was the first standard gauge railway into the heart of the Rockies. The Colorado and Midland spent millions keeping the line open in the winter. *State Historical
Society of Colorado photo.*

Aspen about 1892. Clarendon Hotel at Left of Mill Street. *Jake Wurtz.*
Reprinted by permission from Len Shoemaker, *Roaring Fork Valley*, copyright 1958.

167

Aspen, the ski town, where the ski runs meander down the hill, amid the mills and mine shafts which remain from the day when Aspen was the greatest silver camp in the world. Note mine and mill properties near foot of mountain. Ski run to left is Spar Gulch and Ruthie's Run is at right. *Photo courtesy Aspen Chamber of Commerce.*

The up and down camp of Lenado, near Aspen. *U. S. Geological Survey photo.*

# IX. BUCK ROGERS' LOST FORTUNE

The Camp Fulford-Glenwood Springs area holds the secret to one of Colorado's most lavish, and perhaps most authentic, buried treasures.

It seems a fellow by the name of Buck Rogers led a party of Illinois prospectors through this area in 1849, enroute to the California gold fields. But, somewhere in this region, they found good gold. Some of the party continued on its way, but Rogers and five others remained.

They established what may well have been Colorado's first gold camp. They dug in for the winter, meanwhile amassing and storing from $60,000 to $100,000 in gold.

When provisions ran low, Rogers took $500 from the kitty and set out for supplies. This was in the early winter or late fall. However, Rogers wasn't true to his trust. On reaching civilization, rather than face the cold, perilous trip back into the mountains, he chose the warm light and hot whiskey of the barroom, spending a large part of the provision funds for hooch.

After a few weeks of this, his conscience began to gnaw on him, and he finally headed back to camp. When he arrived at the scene, he discovered a huge snow and dirt slide had completely buried the camp—the men, gold and all.

Rogers never recovered from the incident. He became a broken, babbling drunk, wandering from barroom to barroom telling of his lost friends and the lost fortune. In his ramblings, Rogers told of the general area of the treasure and Slate Mountain, but no one could get any specific location from him.

During the ensuing years, no doubt, hundreds of men searched for Slate Mountain. If anyone found it, no one knew.

The legend grew.

Forty years later, an old miner stumbled into the stage station run by Arthur H. Fulford, who also served as marshal of Redcliff. The miner said he had found Slate Mountain and had ore samples to prove it. The miner took Fulford on as partner and the two of them began to prepare for an expedition to the mountain.

But before the trip got underway, the miner was shot and killed in a drunken brawl. Fulford searched the miner's cabin and found some evidence of where Slate Mountain was located. He set out for the mountain by himself. He was reportedly killed in a snowslide on New Year's Day, 1892. His body was never found.

Many another story stems from the quest of Slate Mountain.

One tells of a miner clumping into a Denver saloon in 1881, ordering drinks for the house and paying the tab in gold dust. His tongue worked faster with each drink, and eventually he confided to the bartender that he, the miner, had located Slate Mountain. He babbled that he had murdered his partner in self defense in an argument over dividing the treasure. The miner said his partner's body was buried at the head of Brush Creek and he gave the bartender the location of Slate Mountain. Then the miner disappeared.

The bartender became ill before he could check out the location of the mountain. And, in payment of the doctor bill, he told the doctor where the mountain was located.

The doctor attempted to locate the mountain time and time again, but could find no trace of it.

Perhaps the miner or the bartender falsified the directions. But they are public domain now. If you care to try your luck, here are the directions: "Go along Eagle River to mouth of Brush Creek. Follow creek 5 miles to the forks. Take east branch about 5 miles until you come to a shift of rocks coming almost at water's edge. Follow dry gulch running north until you come to 4 large trees standing close together with the bark all taken off. About 2 feet around it, turn due east and go directly up the hill until you come to a small hole dug in the ground. Continue on until you come to another hole, and so on, until you come to a third hole. This line is also marked by blazed trees on both sides. From the third hole turn due north and about 200 feet from the last blazed tree you will see 3 tall trees standing in a triangle. The trees have their tops broken off about 30 feet up. This is about 300 feet from timberline, and the vein runs north and south on the place described."

## EAGLE RIVER COUNTRY

Frisco
Kokomo and Recan
Junction City and Clinton City
Ten Mile City, Summit City, Robinson's Camp and Sheldon City (Sheddon City)
Robinson
Carbonateville
Mitchell (Roundebush, Eagle City)
Gold Park
Holy Cross City
Camp Fancy and Missouri Camp
Pando
Redcliff
Cleveland (Bell's Camp)
Gilman (Clinton, Battle Mountain, Rock Creek)
Belden
Astor City
Eagle, Minturn, Wolcott, Avon, Allenton (Wilmore), Edwards (Berry's Ranch), Ortega, and Wheeler
Tracy's Hideout
Fort Defiance and Blake City
Glenwood Springs (Defiance City)
Carbonate (Carbonate City, Carbonate Camp)
Fulford (Nolan's Creek Camp, Camp Fulford)
New York Cabins and Adelaide Park
Whiskey Springs
Mill Pond (Treasure Vault)

## FRISCO

An old Indian scout named Captain Leonard built a cabin here shortly before the boom. Above his door he wrote out "Frisco City." It is believed the old boy was infatuated with San Francisco, but nobody seems to know for sure.

Anyhow, the name stuck and the community which grew near Captain Leonard's cabin took on the name of Frisco.

Frisco has had many ups and downs. It was one of the liveliest camps in the area around 1880, boasting of two hotels, several businesses and scores of cabins. But when the gold, silver and lead seemed to pinch out a few years later, Frisco all but died.

171

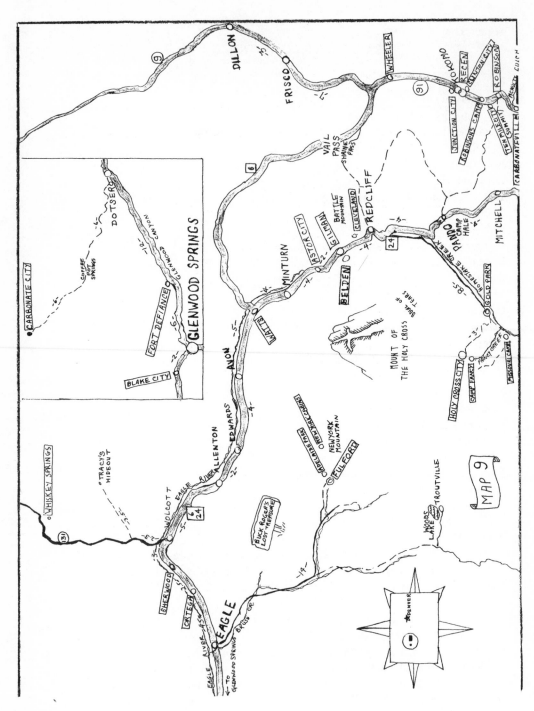

MAP 9

New strikes caused the first revival in the late 90's. Activity fluctuated after that until the increase in gold and silver prices in 1932 caused a rebirth which resulted in the sprucing up of the whole town.

Frisco all but died again just before, and during, World War II, but has been growing since the war, largely because of the tourist business.

## KOKOMO and RECEN

Kokomo and Recen were adjacent camps. They traded names and even sites. And when they became a single town, one name was used for a post office and the other name was retained for the town. Even today, one map may designate the near-ghost town Kokomo and another map may say Recen.

One just can't separate them.

There were other camps involved in the haphazard history of the site. Robinson, Ten Mile City, Edmundville, Carbonateville, Summit City, Junction City, Sheldon City and Kokomo were all within a four-mile radius of one another during the boom in 1881, when some 10,000 miners scrambled into the area. Most of the camps were soon overshadowed by Kokomo. Recen was a twin city in the valley just below Kokomo.

When most of Kokomo was destroyed by fire in the winter of 1881-82, what remained of Kokomo merged with Recen, although oldtimers referred to the whole shebang as Kokomo.

Some placer ore was found here in 1860, but little mining was done until the Leadville boom, when several rich strikes were made on White Quail and Elk Mountain. It is said the Dead Man claim was located when a miner dug a grave to bury a friend.

There was much lumbering done here also.

The site began fading rapidly in the 80's but has never completely died out, although the town has wavered on the brink of emptiness for several years of this century.

It has seen a rebirth in recent years, primarily as a residential area for Climax Molybdenum employees. As many as 100 to 200 persons live in the town, and a school operates through the winter.

A former teacher here was Magnus Bucher, internationally-known skier, who got in much of his practice by skiing to school. The new teacher, Emma Sawyer, has taken up skiing only in recent years. Virtually all of the students ski to class in the winter.

Kokomo was named after the city in Indiana, birthplace of some of the early settlers. Recen was named for the Recen brothers, prominent in the early history of the area.

## JUNCTION CITY, CLINTON CITY

Two "cities" around Kokomo.

Junction City was little more than a tent city just north of Kokomo. Only a cabin and a stable were built before much of the settlement and all of the inhabitants were absorbed by Kokomo.

Clinton City became the southern addition of Kokomo. Big plans were made for the "city," but before they could be carried out, Clinton City found itself a part of Kokomo.

## TEN MILE CITY, SUMMIT CITY, ROBINSON'S CAMP and SHELDON CITY (Sheddon City)

Some of the many camps along Ten Mile Gulch and near Kokomo. Most of the camps ran together. Their history is obscure, and they may have been interchangeable.

Ten Mile City, Robinson's Camp and Summit City apparently ran together and may have been different names for the same camp.

However, all of the camps were eventually overshadowed by Kokomo.

Ten Mile City was founded about 1879 or 1880, and for a short time had dozens of cabin and tent dwellings, plus four sawmills.

Summit City was described as a camp of about 300 miners, southwest of, but similar to, Robinson's Camp. Summit City received its name from the fact it was highest of all the camps.

Most of the camps were near timberline.

Sheldon City erupted about the same time as the others in the Ten Mile district. It may really have been called Sheddon City for Jack Sheddon, who prospected the region in the late 70's and found some silver here.

## ROBINSON

Robinson, now covered by the Climax Company tailing ponds, was the largest camp in the Ten Mile district and rivaled Leadville for a short while around 1880.

There was some placer mining near here in the early 60's, but the placers soon played out and the area was forgotten for 20 years. During the first months of the Leadville excitement, George B. Robinson grubstaked a couple of prospectors. The two men located several good claims in the Ten Mile region, and the rush was on.

Some 2,000 men were here in 1880 and 1881. The first residents thought they had another Leadville going so they laid out a city they could be proud of. Before long, Robinson had a hotel, newspaper, smelter, Catholic Church, band and several other businesses. The Denver and Rio Grande Railroad reached here in 1880.

Robinson, the man, became rich off of his properties, and as with many another carbonate king, turned to politics. He was elected lieutenant governor in 1880.

About this time, a dispute arose over his Smuggler mine and he hired some armed guards to protect it. At the height of the dispute, when Robinson feared that armed thugs might attempt to take over the mine by force, Robinson made a surprise inspection tour of his guards. The guards, expecting trouble at any minute and not expecting their boss, shot and killed Robinson before he had a chance to identify himself.

A fire in 1882 destroyed some mine buildings and part of the city. But the city was already beginning to fade and little was rebuilt.

Virtually all the mines pinched out during the 80's and Robinson was practically a ghost by 1890.

## CARBONATEVILLE

Another brief but busy camp that grew out of the mining excitement around Ten Mile Creek.

Carbonateville, the first camp north of Fremont Pass, was born in the winter of 1878 when ore was found nearby. It thrived in 1879 when several hundred miners were here; began to fade rapidly in 1880, and was a ghost town by 1881.

Most of the miners drifted off to the booming town of Kokomo.

## MITCHELL (Roudebush, Eagle City)

A fellow named Roudebush built a cabin here in 1878. A couple of other cabins went up and the place, for a short time, was called Roudebush.

About 1879 or 1880, some placer gold was discovered nearby. There was a small stampede, and the camp was named Eagle City.

However, the gold soon gave out, and most of the inhabitants moved away. The few who remained worked in the wood-burning kilns in Eagle Park. George Mitchell, one of the discoverers of placer gold here, rearranged the town to center around his cabin, built a hotel and became postmaster. It was an easy thing for him to name the town after himself.

## GOLD PARK

Although never achieving the prominence of Holy Cross City, Gold Park, during its short lifetime, was the larger camp of the two.

It started about 1880 and soon had a population of 400, two hotels, a post office, a lumber and transfer company and several other businesses and stores. Later, a stage rambled in from Redcliff every day.

The big outfit was the Gold Park Mining Company, which owned many claims here and at Holy Cross City. The company also constructed and operated a fairly large mill. The company's mills in the two towns were connected by a two and one-half mile flume.

175

But Gold Park was destined to die almost overnight. The camp was all but deserted by the end of 1883.

Several cabins and a large community house still stand on the site.

## HOLY CROSS CITY

The legend of the "Cross of Snow" was a big deal in the early history of Colorado. Indian scouts and mountain men told of seeing the giant cross. Indian scouts and mountain men were always telling whoppers. The Cross of Snow became just another of the fantastic legends of the unknown Rockies.

Then, as more and more prospectors journeyed through the Rockies, the legend took on more realistic proportions. But, although more prospectors saw the cross every year, its exact location became legendary. Contradictory locations hampered its official discovery. Some prospectors even told of a jinx connected with the fabulous mountain, that all fellow prospectors who attempted to mine there met with tragedy. The legend grew. Some still believe it.

Finally, F. V. Hayden set out to chart the area in 1873. One of the goals of his expedition was to chart the mountain with the fabulous Cross of Snow. With Hayden was William H. Jackson, the Rockies' first and greatest photographer. It was Jackson's ambition to photograph the cross—to show those doubting Thomases back east.

As the expedition progressed, the quest of the snowy cross became virtually the only goal of Hayden's party. Questioning everyone they met, the party came closer and closer to pin-pointing the location of the mountain. Finally, as the story goes, the party met with a band of Utes. Fortunately, for Hayden and his crew, the Indian band was headed by Chief Ouray. Sure, he knew where the cross was. Sure, he would take the white men there—although he couldn't see what all the excitement was.

Jackson got his picture and it became the most publicized picture of its day. It is still one of the most famous photographs of Mount of the Holy Cross. The photograph encouraged many of the nation's outstanding artists to journey to Colorado to paint the mountain.

Henry Wadsworth Longfellow honored the peak in a poem written to the memory of his wife which was published after his death. The poem, entitled *The Cross of Snow* concludes:

> There is a mountain in the distant West
>   That, sun-defying, in its deep ravines
>   Displays a cross of snow upon its side.
> Such is the cross I wear upon my breast
>   These eighteen years, through all the changing scenes
>   And season, changeless since the day she died.

Mount Holy Cross was designated a National Monument in 1929. It is still one of Colorado's best-known spectacles. The Cross is formed by snow and ice in a cross-shaped crevice 50 to 80 feet deep. The bars of the cross are 450 feet across and 1,400 feet vertically.

In sight of the fabulous mountain is Holy Cross City. It can be found over a four-mile road from Gold Park, a road to challenge the best jeepsters.

Holy Cross City began about the same time as Gold Park. The story goes that an old Frenchman, who lived here long before the boom, babbled one day about some gold float he had found. And the rush started.

As with Gold Park, the Gold Park Mining Company was the big producer here. The flume between the company's mills was active, and wagons rolled up and down the perilous cliff road almost constantly.

As many as 300 people lived in the town. There were a school here and the Timberline Hotel, as well as several other stores and cabins.

But Holy Cross City faded even faster than Gold Park. It was deserted by 1883.

## CAMP FANCY and MISSOURI CAMP

Two of the larger camps in the Holy Cross district.

Camp Fancy was situated up Fancy Creek near Holy Cross City. It tried hard to make something of itself in the early 80's, but soon gave up the ghost. Most of the inhabitants moved to Holy Cross City.

Missouri Camp was located about six miles from Holy Cross City and had much the same history as Camp Fancy.

The life and death span for both camps generally was between 1880 and 1884. Both camps found little ore worth the trouble of mining.

## PANDO

There was some mining in the Pando area, but the site is best known for nearby Camp Hale, where the nation's first ski troops were trained during World War II.

Pando was a construction camp for workers who built the unique army camp. Some of the best skiers of the allied nations were instructors at the camp and the effectiveness of Colorado as a ski training area did much to focus attention on the state as a winter sports paradise.

Pando is Spanish for "Pond."

## REDCLIFF

Redcliff is another town that got its start at the time of the Leadville boom. Prospectors, crowded out of the Leadville region, began probing the hills in all directions from the carbonate camp. And good ore was found on Battle and Horn Mountains.

Redcliff became the largest of the many camps in the area, which was now populated enough to be a county. Redcliff became county seat of the newly-formed Eagle County.

The Meeker Massacre occurred about the same time Redcliff was beginning. The Massacre sent shock waves throughout the state. Like many other mining camps, Redcliff girded itself for possible Indian attacks. A blockhouse was hastily constructed, in which the women and children huddled while the men took turns being guards.

But the Indians never came.

The camp was snowbound during the winter of 1883-84. Supplies were short. The newspaper, *Redcliff Comet*, soon ran out of paper stock. So, the editor printed several issues on wall paper.

Redcliff was a regal town with many thriving businesses. Besides the newspaper, there were five hotels, post office, school and numerous shops and saloons. The city was also noted for its opera house and brass band.

A story is told about the cemetery they established. Shortly after the cemetery was set up, the bodies of two men who had killed each other in a gunfight were brought into town for burial. Redcliff refused to give their new cemetery a bad name by numbering murderers among its first customers. So the two men were buried alongside the road.

Redcliff remained the center of a rich mining area for several years, and much mining is still carried out in this region. Redcliff is also developing into a resort center.

### CLEVELAND (Bell's Camp)

This camp, situated halfway up Battle Mountain, between Redcliff and Gilman, was known as both Bell's Camp and Cleveland.

Cleveland existed both as a mining camp and lumber camp. Much of the lumber used in the construction of nearby communities came from the mills here.

The post office was maintained at Redcliff and the mail was taken to Cleveland twice a week, fair weather or foul.

The name Bell's Camp was in honor of a Dr. Bell, one of the first settlers here when the camp was founded in 1880.

### GILMAN (Clinton, Battle Mountain and Rock Creek)

Gilman, perched precariously on the side of Battle Mountain, was once the most important city in the region.

One of the many camps born of the overflow of Leadville, Gilman was founded in 1886. It went through other names before it became Gilman, in honor of Henry M. Gilman, prominent mining man.

Although there were several good strikes made here, the "Iron Mask" was by far the best and became the pulse of activity.

The city had as many as 2,000 residents during its early boom years, but the population settled down to a few hundred after the first stampede. It was a bustling, prosperous place with plenty of drinking and gambling. The town had a drama club, and a newspaper, *The Gilman Enterprise*. There were several hotels, boarding houses, and thriving businesses.

Most of the cabins were built on the side of the steep hill, and steps were constructed up the cliff to get to the mines.

One of Gilman's more prominent citizens was Obediah M. Warner, who was elected to the state legislature in 1890. Shortly after his election he was accused of obtaining $500 under false pretenses. The sheriff went to Denver to bring Warner back, and being friends, the sheriff neglected to handcuff his prisoner on the train ride back to Gilman. Warner escaped during the night and was not heard from again. There was some talk about Warner's planning to run off from his wife, anyway.

Half of Gilman was destroyed by fire in 1899, including the Iron Mask Hotel, the schoolhouse, and most of the business section.

Although Gilman has lost some of its residents to Redcliff, much mining is still being carried out here. In fact the Battle Mountain and Eagle district has been one of the ranking producers of gold, silver, copper, lead and zinc in the state. In 1950, total production was nearly 13 million dollars and was well above five million in 1953.

GOLD DUST: Battle Mountain was named for a historic battle between the Utes and Arapahoes in 1849 . . . . much of the ores from the mines were brought down by aerial cables . . . . the long-established zinc industry here picks up enough gold from its ore each year to pay operation expenses . . . . a conspicuous ore vein can be seen from Battle Mountain on the opposite canyon wall. The ores were deposited there when the surrounding rock, in molten form, was shoved up between the other formation . . . . Gilman was still the principal town in the area as late as 1918, and still is far from being a ghost.

## BELDEN

Belden, near Gilman, was an impossible camp, one of the rare ones where the miners' cabins were situated above the mines.

The camp was the white man's answer to the Indian cliff dwellings, as most of the camp was situated on or near the top of the cliffs of Eagle Canyon, and the mining was carried out within the cliffs below. In fact, the entire operations of the Empire Zinc Company concentration mill were inside the mountains.

The camp was named for Judge D. D. Belden, who discovered the Belden Mine here in 1879, and built a smelter a year later.

The Denver and Rio Grande reached here in 1881.

179

## ASTOR CITY

Astor City, or the site thereof, was important before the mining excitement in the area. Long before the mining men ventured into the region the Astor Fur Trading Company constructed a trading post as a meeting place and center for the trappers.

The mountain men would bring their pelts to the old trading post, barter their catch for more provisions, some money, and some booze, and carouse a little with other mountain men, then head back into the mountains.

Years later, during the mining excitement, a few locations were made near here and a small camp was established near the site of the old trading post. Although much of the camp consisted of tents and bough huts, several cabins were built, as well as a store and a saloon. The saloon was called "Saint's Rest" for some reason.

## EAGLE, MINTURN, WOLCOTT, AVON, ALLENTON (Wilmore), EDWARDS (Berry's Ranch), ORTEGA, and WHEELER

Communities of various occupations which had little or nothing to do with the mining boom in the area.

Eagle is the county seat of Eagle County. It is a ranching and agricultural town and is developing into a summer recreational center. Hay and potatoes are the principal crops.

Minturn is a railroad and lumbering town. Avon is a grain and cattle-raising town.

Wolcott, now a ranch center, was once an important stage and mail stop in the 1880's and 90's. The town was named for Senator Edward O. Wolcott.

Edwards, formerly known as Berry's Ranch, was made a Denver and Rio Grande siding and named after Melvin Edwards, former postmaster at Redcliff, who was elected secretary of state in Colorado in 1883.

Allenton, Ortega, and Wheeler were also stops on the D & RG. Allenton, formerly called Wilmore, is still alive but its post office is at Edwards.

There was a little mining in and around Wheeler. The town was also a farm and ranch trading center. Top population was never more than 200.

## TRACY'S HIDEOUT

An old ranch house which once served as a hideout for a notorious gunman and escape artist.

Harry Tracy and a man named Lant escaped from the Utah state penitentiary and made their way to Colorado. Posses from Utah, Wyoming and Colorado converged on the men in the Brown's hole area in northwestern Colorado. The two men were captured after a long siege and after one of the law officers had been killed.

180

The two prisoners were taken to the Hahns Peak jail where they made another daring escape (see Hahns Peak). They were recaptured and taken back to the Hahns Peak jail. Unable to escape again, the two devised another plan which they thought would give them freedom—or at least express their bitterness toward the world. They slept days so that they could spend their nights hooting, hollering, kicking their cell walls, and just generally making a din. It took only a few nights for the sleepless townspeople to be up in arms. To give the townspeople a rest and possibly to prevent their being lynched, the prisoners were transferred to the Pitkin County jail in Aspen.

Shortly after their transfer—in 1898—the two men escaped again after almost beating the jailer to death.

Lant disappeared. Tracy blazed a trail of terror throughout the northwestern states. He was arrested and put in jail in Oregon. He escaped again, and became the object of one of the greatest manhunts in the history of the west. In his final, desperate flight for freedom, Tracy shot down eight law officers—some sort of record.

The circumstances of his own death in Wyoming are still subject to debate. Some say he took his own life rather than being taken alive. Some say he was shot down in a gun battle. Then there are those who claim he shot himself by accident. This doesn't seem plausible . . . . since we know Tracy knew how to use a gun.

The area around Tracy's Hideout is known for one other thing. An almost perfectly preserved fossil of a prehistoric three-toed horse was found near the cabin site in 1934. It is now on exhibit at the Denver Museum of Natural History.

## FORT DEFIANCE and BLAKE CITY

A block house was built here by eager miners who beat the rush to the area despite the constant threat of Indians.

Two Leadville prospectors, who probed the section the year before, called attention to the riches to be found here. When they returned the following year several other men came with them. The Indian threat hampered the prospecting and most of the prospectors returned to civilization in short order.

A couple of years later Glenwood Springs claimed the few prospectors that stuck it out at the fort.

Fort Defiance was located about six miles northwest of the site of Glenwood Springs and about twelve miles south of Carbonate.

Blake City was a short-lived camp two miles below the mouth of the Eagle River and took in both sides of the Grand (Colorado) River.

Harry Blake and W. M. Bell operated a ferry across the river. One of the first camps in the region, Blake City came to a speedy demise because of the Indian scare and other lesser problems.

## GLENWOOD SPRINGS (Defiance City)

Glenwood Springs is an outgrowth of Fort Defiance and was one of the first permanent settlements in Ute territory.

The town was founded in 1883 by a group of Leadville settlers. The party platted an elaborate townsite on 640 acres of land and offered free homesites to anyone willing to settle here.

The Indian scare was still too much for most and few people accepted the offer. Within a few months, however, the Indians were driven off and the settlers started coming.

The city has been going strong ever since. It is now a resort capital as well as an important supply center for the fertile farm and ranch land about.

## CARBONATE (Carbonate City, Carbonate Camp)

Carbonate, located about a dozen miles north of Glenwood Springs, had a short but sweet existence during which it was county seat and boasted a population of between 2,000 and 3,000.

But in a few short months, only one man remained, and the postman gave him $100 to get out of town so the mailman could erase the city from his route.

The quality of the ores located here in 1880 was greatly exaggerated, luring more than 2,000 prospectors to the region. Tents and huts were thrown up all over the place. But most of the prospectors became discouraged during the next year or two.

By 1883, only about 300 or 400 remained. They established a camp and named it for the type of ore found here.

The camp was made county seat of the newly-formed Garfield County. The Carbonate Town Company, purchasers of the 160-acre townsite, drew up lavish plans for the city. But by the end of the year, the miners realized they couldn't make anything out of the ores, and stopped trying.

The county seat was moved to the growing community of Glenwood Springs, and so were most of the miners.

The camp was deserted so quickly that by the time the government got around to giving a contract to E. E. Winslow to carry the mail to Carbonate, only one person remained in town. Since the contract stated the route included Carbonate as long as anyone remained there, Winslow made one tortuous 40-mile trip to the camp, bought off the last inhabitant, and crossed Carbonate off his route.

182

*FULFORD* (Nolan's Creek Camp, Camp Fulford)

Camp Fulford was actually two adjacent camps, one making up the lower town and the other the upper town. Both camps started around 1890. The upper town was smaller but contained more business houses. It had a log hotel, some boarding houses, several saloons and stores.

The site was originally called Nolan's Creek Camp for an early prospector who, with another man, located paydirt here in 1887. Many rich strikes were made in the next few months and Camp Fulford became a thriving settlement of several hundred people. Of the 500 claims made, however, only a few were worth developing. The best was Polar Star on New York Mountain.

Some of the mines opened into natural cliffs. Miners gained entrance into the caves by being lowered from the top of the cliff. The Fulford cave remains a tourist attraction.

The camp flourished through the 90's and early years of this century. All but dead by 1912, new silver strikes were made and another boom lasted until about 1918.

The camp faded rapidly after that. The log hotel in upper town and other buildings were torn down and the lumber was used in the mines. Weather and time have also taken their toll.

Today only a few cabins remain.

GOLD DUST: Nolan, the founder, bled to death when he accidentally shot himself while crossing the creek which now bears his name . . . . the camp was named for Arthur H. Fulford, a prominent man in the area, who lost his life in a snowslide on New York Mountain when searching for Slate Mountain (see above) . . . . a 25-stamp amalgamating and concentrating mill was built during the boom years at the turn of the century to handle the ore for many of the mines . . . . Eagle, 20 miles away, was the nearest railroad stop . . . . Fulford, despite its stormy history, was a sociable town and many dances were held here.

## NEW YORK CABINS, ADELAIDE PARK

New York Cabins and Adelaide Park were two of the camps that took shape about Fulford during the mining excitement in that area.

New York Cabins grew around the mining activity on New York Mountain east of Fulford. There were three or four mines near here. Perhaps the largest was the Polar Star high on the mountain. One mine was so inaccessible the miners had to climb up a cable to reach it. The ruins of some of the cabins are still visible.

Adelaide Park was just east of the upper town of Fulford, and it eventually was absorbed by the larger camp. Some cabins remain.

## WHISKEY SPRINGS

This wasn't a still—they brought the whiskey in, leaving the empty bottles around the springs here. Thus, the stage station received its name. The old-timers say travelers needed the whiskey to endure the hazardous roads. But long before the stage was routed through here, it was a favorite camping spot for trappers and hunters. They drank, too!

## MILL POND (Treasure Vault)

One of the most picturesque ghost mining camps in Colorado is locked to all but the most intrepid ghost-towners.

Mill Pond, or Treasure Vault, is located west and a little north of Holy Cross City, which is a fair to middling challenge for jeeps in itself. From Holy Cross City one hikes the two miles to Fancy Pass (one can attempt to jeep it but one must be on constant guard for "bottomless" bogs). From the summit of Fancy Pass it is another rugged one and one-half to two-mile hike to the ghost community, bearing west and a little north until one reaches Cross Creek.

Of course, one could hike in the seventeen miles from Minturn if one can sort out the right fishing trails along the creek.

The old town is about a mile and a half below Treasure Vault Lake and the mine which was the main reason for being of the town. Natives of the area call the site Mill Pond for the colorful pond near which the mill, now a skeleton, was built. Some early maps, however, merely call the site Treasure Vault for the big mine here. Another digging here was the Gold Bug. There were other workings close to Missouri Pass, a short hike away, and for about five miles along Cross Creek toward Minturn.

The old mill here was kept busy processing the ore, which was then carted out in wagons over Fancy Pass and through Holy Cross City. The activity here was an outgrowth of that in Holy Cross City, reaching its peak in the 1890's. The last evidence of work here was in the 1920's. The big old mill has since fallen to ruin, a couple of the remaining cabins are crumbling. There is vague evidence of the many other cabins that once graced the area and there are some rusted machinery and scars left from the mining. Otherwise, Mill Pond is most secretive about its past.

# X.  THE DREAM
#    AND THE DISENCHANTED

His story has been told many times. But no story of Colorado is complete without it.

H. A. W. Tabor is the story of Leadville. The story of his boom and bust, embodying all its gross and lavish qualities, was a model of the boom and bust of many a mining town in Colorado.

Tabor, a Vermont stonecutter, journeyed across the plains with his wife and son in the first Pikes Peak Gold Rush of 1859. It was a difficult trek, the couple's son almost died. Without Augusta Tabor's perseverance the trip could well have been disastrous.

She persevered in Colorado, too. Lacking funds, she took in washing and sewing, cooked, and maintained a boarding house to keep the family alive and her husband in prospecting money.

Tabor knew little of prospecting. He tried the Central City area without any luck at all. He went to other camps. He went to Oro City, set up shop for his wife, and headed for the hills. He dug from 12,000 to 15,000 dollars in gold, tried other places, lost the money he had made. He tried Georgia Gulch, the Granite area, one by one as those areas boomed. No luck.

Finally, he took his family to Buckskin Joe. His wife worked and he prospected. Then they opened a store. Tabor became mayor of the town. But he didn't find any gold.

Buckskin Joe faded and died. Where to go?

They finally decided to go back to Oro City. There was still some activity there. Not much, but some.

He felt his luck had run out, prospecting. He spent a little time at it, but what's the use, he told himself. He opened a store. It did all right, nothing spectacular, but enough to keep the family going.

Then, silver was discovered in large quantities up the gulch. A stampede reminiscent of the early Oro City days began. Tabor may have wanted to join the rush, but the store was too busy now. It was making money. And his luck had run out, prospecting.

One day, two German shoemakers, George Hook and Auguste Rische, came into the store. They had never done a day of prospecting in their lives but they wanted Tabor to grubstake them. Tabor refused. The shoemakers hounded him. Tabor was too busy to be bothered. Finally, he gave them the food and provisions they needed—more to get rid of them than anything else.

Before leaving the store and while Tabor wasn't looking, the two men stole a jug. Then they headed for the hills. Most of the strikes had been made farther up the gulch. But that was too far. The two shoemakers climbed a hill within a mile of the camp. They climbed to the first shaded area. It was too hot in the sun. One man dug while the other sat in the shade and sucked on the jug.

They hit the silver vein within six feet of the surface. Nothing unusual about it—except the vein went straight down. If they had dug a few feet in either direction or anywhere else on the hill, they would have had to dig at least 100 feet to hit it.

The claim paid off big. It came to be known as the Little Pittsburg. Tabor, for staking the two shoemakers to $64.75 worth of food and supplies, became a third owner of the mine. He made a half million dollars out of it and then sold it for a million dollars.

Meanwhile, on Fryer Hill across the gulch, a fellow known as "Chicken Bill" staked a claim and started digging. Maybe Chicken Bill is more a legend than a man. He seemed to turn up at just about all the major boom towns around. At many of the towns they managed to pin a swindle or a hoax on him. He is credited with starting one of the Cripple Creek hoaxes.

Anyhow, there is no record Chicken Bill ever hit it rich. His luck didn't change at Leadville. He dug a few feet into the ground and hit water. It wasn't worth bothering with. So what did Chicken Bill do? He got some silver dust, loaded it into a shot gun and peppered his hole with the stuff. Then, he located Tabor and told him he had a rich claim but didn't have the money to drain out the water and work it. Tabor bought the claim from him. Everyone laughed when they heard of the swindle. Everyone but Tabor. Maybe the story never got back to him. Most likely, by this time, he thought he was too lucky to be swindled. At any rate, he hired some men to continue work on the claim. In just a few days, the men hit the fabulous Chrysolite lode, one of the richest in the region.

That was just the start of Tabor's meteoric rise to fame and fortune. He bought the Matchless for $117,000. Within weeks he was getting back the original investment—just about every month.

Everything he touched turned to precious metal. He invested in several mines. Then he branched out. People were dying all over the place in Leadville. Many businesses were wrecked by rowdyism. Tabor saw the need for insurance. So he started an insurance firm. A lot of people were making money in Leadville, but were being robbed because they didn't have any place to put the money. Tabor opened a bank.

He bought property. Started building, had a commercial police and fire fighting force. Invested in transportation, lumber, water, coal. There's

186

not much he didn't have his golden hand in. He even invested in culture. He built the Tabor Grand Opera House in Leadville.

He was rich now. He owned the world. He didn't need Augusta any more. Anyhow, Augusta, suspicious of the sudden wealth, still had simple tastes and was cautious about spending. She insisted on living in their simple five-room house. Tabor was thinking more in terms of palaces. He spent more time at the club, playing poker, or in his fancy offices at the Opera House.

He also had met a comely young lass known as Baby Doe. Tabor spent some time with her.

Leadville was getting too small for Tabor.

Denver and even Washington were more in keeping with his lavish tastes. With his knapsack and ten million dollars, he headed for Denver. Of course, he took his family, Baby Doe, and a few members of his camp with him.

He invested some more. Eventually he had holdings throughout Colorado, the southwest and even in South America. But now he was primarily interested in politics. Paying huge sums into the Republican fund and a few discreet dollars into a few well-chosen hands, he "worked" his way to the top, or near the top, of the GOP party in Colorado. He was elected lieutenant governor. But that was just to tide him over until the Senate election. Tabor wanted to be senator.

Never did a man spend so much to be elected to a public office in Colorado. But his scheming and spending failed. After a bitter battle with Tom Bowen (see Summitville), the latter won out. Tabor was awarded the consolation prize, a year in the Senate to fill an unexpired term.

Losing the regular election to the Senate was Tabor's first major setback. There were to be many more. But now Tabor took the good with the bad.

He embarked upon his short Senate career with all the pomp and ceremony of a king taking the throne. However, here he met another setback. He had filed secret divorce papers against his wife in Durango, and had married Baby Doe.

A short time later, his divorce was found to be worthless.

Bigamy, by senators, is frowned upon.

With all the scheming and coercion a few million dollars could command, Tabor set things a-right. At least, he thought he did. He acted as if he had. (Lawyers and historians have been arguing the legal aspects of the situation ever since.)

And he married Baby Doe again in Washington in a ceremony that little town hadn't seen the likes of in years. President Arthur attended.

But the tide had turned. And once Tabor began to fall, he fell as fast as he had risen. The big blow was the Silver Crash.

That wasn't all. As, at first, when everything he touched turned to precious metal, now his touch turned things to dust. He had over-invested. What may have been seemingly wise investments before were now not so wise. He had spent a lot of money—an estimated twelve million dollars cash—on "incidentals."

The bottom crumbled in his empire, and the tower plummeted into the hole.

Tabor, back in Denver, found he was destitute, with only a few holdings left that didn't seem to be worth the paper on which they were written. He even journeyed up to the Gold Hill area behind Boulder and attempted to dig out some riches from a mine he owned. It was the first time in several years he had had a shovel in his hand. He found nothing.

He borrowed money to keep going, to try to reclaim his fortune, as he put it. For Tabor was sure his second fortune was just around the corner—easy come and easy go—and easy come again. But he couldn't hope to pay the money back, and the lenders looked upon it more as charity than a business deal. Tabor couldn't even find a job. Still thinking big, he had some fantastic schemes and sought some top positions.

Finally, he was appointed postmaster of Denver. More charity.

It was as postmaster of Leadville that he began his colossal rise to riches. It was as postmaster of Denver, less than thirty years later, that he died, on April 10, 1899.

On his death bed he told Baby Doe, "Hang on to the Matchless."

She did. She lived as a recluse in a small cabin beside the Matchless for several years. She was found frozen to death in the cabin in March of 1935.

A surviving child of the union, named by Tabor "Silver Dollar," had earlier moved to Chicago, in an effort to escape the family misfortune. She found things no better in Chicago. She wrote a few stories for pulp magazines, but otherwise lived a harsh and decadent life. She died from burns received in a tenement fire in 1925. Some say it was suicide.

Augusta died in 1895. She remained frugal and cautious to the end and made the money last which she gained in her settlement with Tabor.

Nothing remains of the Tabor name but an old theatre building in lower downtown Denver. The Tabor empire is dust. Tabor, the man, was so quickly forgotten after his death, it wasn't known for several years where he was buried. Nobody cared. His grave was finally located in the 1930's in a neglected cemetery that used to be east of Cheesman Park in Denver.

A few bones and a handful of dust was all that remained of H. A. W. Tabor, a crude, lavish, selfish yet generous man who accumulated one of Colorado's greatest fortunes. He didn't take it with him. He didn't even have it when he left.

## LEADVILLE

Oro City (Slabtown) and California Gulch
Boughtown
Leadville (Oro City, Boughtown, Poverty Flats, Agassiz, Kelly's Diggings)
Tintown, Jacktown, Stringtown, Bucktown, Little Chicago
Malta (Swilltown)
Adelaide (Adelaide City)
Stumpftown (Stumptown)
Finntown
South Evans
Evansville
Ibex (Ibex City, Ibex Camp)
Howland
Birdseye
Tabor (Tabor City, Taylor City, Halfway House, Chalk Creek Ranch)
Alicante (Summit)
Climax (Fremont Pass)
Lake City and Homestake (not on map)
Camp Harrington and Tennessee Pass (Cooper)
Tennessee Park and Swede's Gulch
St. Kevins and Amity
Gleason Gulch
Clifton
Soda Springs
Evergreen Lakes

*And Then There Were . . . . HENRY* (not on map), *ALEXANDER, WORTMAN, JUNCTION CITY* (not on map), *PARK CITY* (not on map), *ARKANSAS and LEADVILLE JUNCTIONS.*

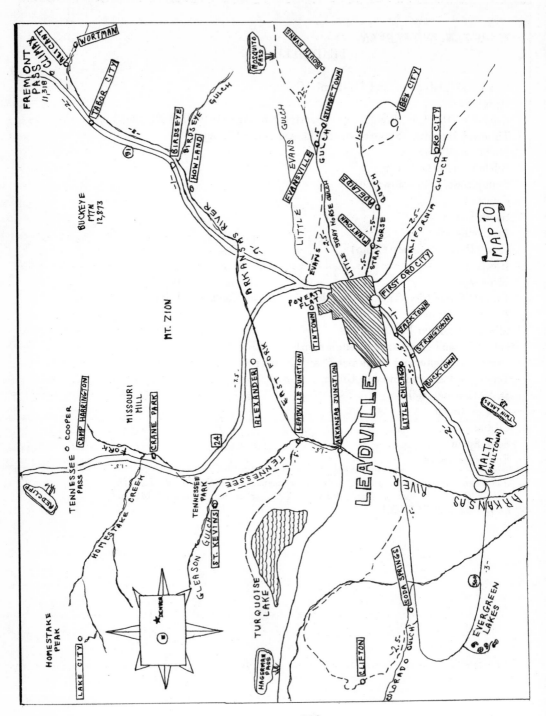

MAP 10

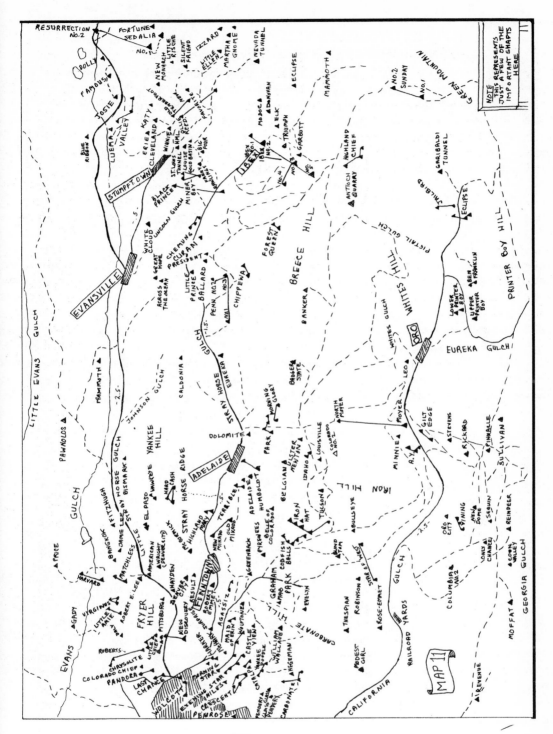

MAP 11

## ORO CITY (Slabtown) *and CALIFORNIA GULCH*

California Gulch was almost as important during the first boom in the early 1860's as it was during the Leadville epic some 15 to 20 years later.

Some 10,000 gold-greedy prospectors stampeded into the gulch in 1860, shortly after Abe Lee panned gold, and exclaimed: "Boys, I've got all California in this pan."

A steady stream of wagons and tents filled the gulch from the site of the second Oro City to the site of Malta.

It was a helter-skelter, boisterous, divergent community. Men slept wherever they could, in tents, wagons, on the ground. At night the gulch was lit by hundreds of campfires. Drunken oaths and singing echoed in the night.

Fancy-dressed gamblers roamed up and down the gulch, promoting games wherever they could. Prostitutes, the first and for a long time the only women in the gulch, worked out of wagons and tents, as the miners lined up outside.

Sharpsters and embezzlers roamed the gulch looking for suckers. Fights and shootings were frequent and easily overlooked. The only law was the law of survival.

Then came the men of God. Wandering through the gulch, along with the gamblers, looking for any old place to hold a meeting. Often, the gamblers and the preachers "worked" the same gathering at the same time.

The first businesses and saloons were tents or wagons. Overhead was practically nil, and a merchant selling supplies out of his wagon made a fortune.

An enterprising businessman put up a circus tent and sold sleeping accommodations for a dollar a throw. He made $1,000 most nights.

And the gulch gave forth its gold. The prospectors dug in to stay. Slowly cabins and frame buildings began to appear.

A number of camps took shape. The greatest concentration of camps arose on the site which became Leadville in later years. Here were Boughtown, Sacramento City, Oro City and a few others.

Oro City, situated at the southern edge of what is now Leadville, soon emerged as the top camp, eventually absorbing the others. The population was upwards of 8,000.

But slowly the workings, hampered by a heavy black sand, began to give out. The disillusioned fortune hunters began to move away.

By 1868, the gulch was a shadow of its former activity. Then, another rich lode was found in the Printer Boy mine, down the gulch. Another lode was located in Five-Thirty. A new boom was started.

All the activity was at the upper end of the gulch. So the remaining residents of Oro City pulled up their cabins, stores and hotels, and established another Oro City about two and one-half miles down the gulch.

The city accommodated hundreds of prospectors for two or three years, until eventually the Printer Boy and other mines began to play out.

The second Oro City was all but deserted, and California Gulch was empty except for William Stevens and Alvinus Woods, who were curious about the black sands along the gulch that had hampered the mining activity.

GOLD DUST: H. A. W. Tabor was one of the early prospectors here. His wife, Augusta, was said to have been the first "family-type" woman in the gulch. She ran a boarding house while her husband was off prospecting. Some historians say H. A. W. accumulated several thousand dollars prospecting in the gulch, but lost it all in later mining ventures . . . . Father Macheboeuf was the first itinerant preacher in the gulch. He conducted his first sermon in a blacksmith shop in the early summer of 1860 . . . . The Boston and Philadelphia Gold and Silver Mining Company built a 25-stamp mill in 1868 . . . . a solid gold nugget weighing 28 ounces was found here . . . . the gulch played an equally important part in the later Leadville silver boom . . . . nothing is left of either Oro City. A considerable amount of machinery and equipment was collected during a World War II scrap drive.

## BOUGHTOWN

Boughtown was an earlier camp on the present site of Leadville. The camp was named for the boughs on the many trees that covered the area in those days. The camp was virtually adjacent to Oro City and rivaled the latter during 1860, before bowing to the phenomenal growth of Oro.

It has been estimated as many as 5,000 people lived in Boughtown during its boom.

The Boughtown-Oro City area was virtually deserted by 1870.

The last miners to leave what had been Boughtown tore down a log gambling house and panned thousands of dollars out of the ground floor and walls.

## LEADVILLE (Agassiz, California Gulch, Kelly's Diggings, Oro City, Boughtown, Poverty Flats, etc.)

Alaska has its Klondyke, Nevada and Montana have their Virginia Cities, California has its Sacramento City. Colorado has its Leadville— as rich and riotous a boom town as was found anywhere in the world.

The Colorado Klondyke has already experienced five eras in its 100 years.

First came the placer gold mining era of Oro City and California Gulch in the early 60's . . . a fabulous time and place that would be better remembered were it not dimmed by the silver boom, the next era.

When the value of silver plummeted in the crash of '93, the Leadville "Gold Belt" was opened and the city entered another era.

Around the turn of the century, a composite mining era began in which millions of dollars worth of lead, zinc, copper, iron and bismuth was mined in addition to silver and gold.

This phase has carried on up to the present time to a varying degree. But, in the 30's, the fabulous molybdenum mountain at Climax became the major source of Leadville's livelihood. Add to this last phase, increasing tourist activity which may become an era in itself.

Leadville may well have other lives in the future, but none could surpass its second life—the silver boom.

The early gold activity in California Gulch was hampered by a heavy black sand which made it difficult to isolate the gold-bearing ore. The sand aided the downfall of the first gold era.

California Gulch was deserted again, or almost deserted. A man by the name of William Stevens continued to probe the hills, believing there were still riches here. He was soon joined by Alvinus Woods, a metallurgist. The two worked alone and all but unnoticed, considered "crackpots" by the others in the neighborhood.

Stevens and Woods became interested in the heavy sand. They sent some off to be assayed. This "sand" turned out to be rich in carbonate, the best source of silver. The two kept hunting for the source. Eventually they located the only place in the gulch where the metal touches the surface.

Stevens and Woods staked a claim and hired some men to work the property. The men weren't too happy about working for crackpots in the first place, but when their job entailed mining sand they talked about quitting. To keep the men on the job Stevens and Woods confided in one worker. The plan backfired. The miner scampered off to stake his own claim. His colleagues were close behind.

This was in 1878. The news got out and the return to Leadville began. As new rich claims were made, the rush developed into a giant unruly stampede.

By the following year, the Leadville area, California Gulch and other nearby gulches were a jungle of teeming, hungry miners—grabbing, scheming, killing and even working for the new king metal, silver. Prospect holes covered the hills and valleys and sold for thousands of dollars. Claims changed hands many times a day.

It was the most ruthless time and place Colorado had ever known.

Hundreds died in the frenzied rush to the new Eldorado. The area couldn't hold them all. An enterprising man put up a huge circus tent full of three-tier bunks and sold sleeping place for a dollar and up. He cleared $1,000 a night.

Exorbitant prices were charged for sleeping places in stables. The floors of every saloon in town were covered with sleeping miners who couldn't find any place else. Still others couldn't find room in the saloons. Hundreds died of exposure . . . and starvation.

Life was cheap. Shootings over a prospect hole, a home site, a gambling debt and anything else were a dime a dozen. Highwaymen had a field day. Hastily organized vigilante committees only added to the confusion and the violence.

Attempts at organizing law enforcement agencies backfired. Some of the new law groups were organized and owned by the newly-made carbonate kings. But the first "cops" were no good, ineffectual—or just downright crooked. The good cops were killed. Marshall O'Connor was shot to death by another officer.

Eventually Mart Duggan took over as marshal. He was a bullying gunslinger, but he wasn't afraid of anybody. He didn't necessarily bring law and order to Leadville, but he did keep the killing to a minimum, doing much of it himself. Duggan reigned until 1888, when he too met his match outside the Texas House Gambling Hall.

Leadville was now a roaring city of some 25 or 30 thousand people. It started with the second Oro City, more commonly known as "Slabtown." There were other camps around. There were Poverty Flats, Agassiz, Kelly's Diggings, and Boughtown, named because of the many trees around. Soon, one large camp encompassed the entire area, all the little camps. Some citizens got together to name the new city. Several names were considered, including Oro, Boughtown, Carbonate and the like. Some say it was named Agassiz, for a Harvard geologist, for awhile. But they eventually selected Leadville.

And there was no longer a lot of trees. The trees on all the hills around were chopped down fast to build the city and the mine shafts, and were used for firewood. Coke and coal cost upwards of $55 a ton.

The hills of Leadville, where once great forests grew, were now as bald and barren as a baby's bottom.

The streets, day and night, were overflowing with all kinds of people, swaggering drunks, starving miners down on their luck, the "holy rollers" trying to talk above the din, the pickpockets, panhandlers and pimps. A half dozen brass bands played on the street corners every night, all night.

Harrison Avenue and Chestnut Street were the business streets, at least the main ones. That's where the hotels, banks, restaurants, and other legitimate businesses were. Tabor built his Grand Opera House on Harrison Avenue.

Harrison Avenue ran into State Street (now 2nd Street), and there was *the* street! It was lined with saloons, gambling halls, and parlor houses.

195

Here the most notorious and colorful gamblers, con men, and shady ladies of the west congregated.

Along State Street were Tiger Alley, Still Born Alley, French and Coon Rows. The Pioneer and Bucket of Blood were the most notorious "hells." Several bullet holes in their walls attest to the fact. Other dance halls and gambling houses were the Bon Ton, Odeon, Little Casino, and the most respectable one of the lot, named, curiously enough, Red Light Hall.

The top madams were Minnie Purdy, Mollie Price, Frankie Page, Sallie Purple and Mollie May. Mollie May and Sallie Purple were deadly rivals and once barricaded their houses and took a few harmless shots at each other. Denver's famous shady lady, Mattie Silks, worked Leadville for awhile.

One of the most popular parlor house girls was lithe, lovely "Red Stockings," who made $100,000 in a few months and then moved to Nevada to live a life of respectability.

The west's top gamblers came to Leadville and either made their fortune and moved on, or were shot down. The queen of the lady gamblers was Madame Vestal, who also ran a dance hall on State Street. She was known earlier as Belle Siddons, former queen of St. Louis society and noted southern spy during the Civil War.

"Soapy" Smith was here. Of course, he was just a two-bit swindler then. He went on to greater things in Denver, Creede and the Yukon (see Creede).

A respectable place was the Carbonate Concert Hall, which advertised: "Wine, women and song: These three are supposed to make life palatial, and while nothing of an improper character is permitted, we can furnish all three any night."

A popular singer here was Stephanie, Baroness di Gallotti. Stephanie was a member of one of Europe's noble families. Her husband, Don Carlos, died while the couple was in Denver. Stephanie married a bartender, Charles Tanner, and the couple came to Leadville. She sang while he tended bar.

Another respectable, but popular, place was the Wyman Saloon, now a boarding house on Harrison Avenue. The place was run by "Pop" Wyman. He didn't allow swearing or boisterous talking in his saloon. Drunks were thrown out. Pop treated his patrons as sons, and he was strict with them. He didn't allow fathers to gamble at his tables and sent married men home at respectable hours.

Some say it was Pop Wyman's place that the celebrated English poet and author, Oscar Wilde, drank six miners under the table. But most reports say the historic event took place in a mine shaft.

Wilde came to Leadville in 1882 on a speaking engagement. Wilde was a controversial character even then, and he carried himself differently from the average Leadvillite. The miners, all top drinking men, schemed to have a drinking bout with Oscar to test his mettle. They say all six passed out while Oscar was still going strong. Wilde lectured at Tabor's Grand Opera House on some erudite subject concerning art or interior decoration. Nobody understood a word he said, but they all listened and gave him a standing ovation when he finished. Leadville liked Oscar. And they say Oscar liked Leadville.

There were other characters in Leadville's past.

Tom Walsh, who made some money up around St. Kevins, ran the Grand Hotel. But he wasn't to become rich and famous until years later. (See Camp Bird.)

A well-known Leadville character was a man known as Professor Joseph Ives, who claimed he had once been a professor at Oxford. He would wander from bar to bar, and the miners would buy him drinks just to hear him talk. He eventually dropped dead in a Stringtown dive.

There was "Broken Nose" Scotty, a good prospector, but hard drinker. They say he sold his claim for $30,000 while in jail.

Perhaps the top newsman was Orth Stein, creator of many of Leadville's legends and tall tales while writing for the *Chronicle*, one of the city's numerous newspapers.

The clergy shouldn't be forgotten either. Father Robinson and Reverend T. A. Uzzel were perhaps the most famous of Leadville's many men of the cloth.

There were hundreds of buildings up in Leadville before anyone thought of erecting a church. The parsons and priests would walk the street, competing for attention and small change. Reverend Uzzel, called "the fighting parson," was the best competitor and took up some of his best collections in saloons and gambling halls. The Reverend could stand up to any man in Leadville, and he often had to. He was well liked and respected. He finally got enough money together to build a church. Then he had to lick three men who attempted to jump the church site. A lot of tales are told about Reverend Uzzel.

Of course, the most dominant, although not necessarily the most colorful characters in Leadville, were the Carbonate Kings.

Some of these were just as colorful as Tabor, although, perhaps, not typical and certainly not well remembered. Tabor, even in his lifetime, became a symbol of something or other.

The most fabled was John Morrissey, an illiterate, but one of the richest men in the camp. Many tales have been told of his frequent displays of ignorance. (For the most classic, see Twin Lakes.) Morrissey toured Europe, squandered his fortune, and died in a Denver poor-house.

Another colorful character was Auguste Rische, who, along with George Hook, discovered the Little Pittsburg on a $64.75 grubstake by Tabor, making all three rich.

Rische spent much of his fortune building a church in Leadville. When a member of the congregation suggested purchasing a chandelier, Rische blasted the extravagance, and said: "Besides, none of us knows how to play on it, anyhow."

George Fryer, who made the first good silver discovery in 1878 on Fryer's Hill, spent a half million dollars as fast as he could, and then committed suicide.

Pat Gallagher, an Irish roustabout, hit it lucky in mining. He spent the next few months walking the streets of Leadville, looking up old friends, buying each an expensive suit of clothes and treating them to gala times of wine, women and song.

Jack McCombe made a fortune on the Maid of Erin mine, and spent most of it buying bountiful presents for everyone in County Antrim, his home in Ireland.

Pete Breene made a fortune on The Crown Point, founded a bank and entered into politics, becoming lieutenant governor and state treasurer.

Alva Adams got his fortune from the Blind Tour. He also entered politics, became a governor and father of a governor.

Samuel Newhouse took his fortune and became a mainstay in English royal society.

John F. Campion became rich in a later Leadville revival and went on to become a leader in the development of the sugar industry in Colorado.

Banker George Robinson came to Leadville after going bankrupt in Michigan. He spent his last few dollars grubstaking a prospector who discovered the Wheel of Fortune. Robinson made millions.

"Judge" Pedery ambled into Leadville with $2.19 in his pocket, and soon became one of the richest men in the area.

They say the Guggenheim fortune was founded here. A lot of people got rich. A lot more didn't.

Before we leave the characters of Leadville, we can't forget "the unsinkable Mrs. Brown."

Her husband made a fortune in mining here, and the couple moved to Denver. Mrs. Brown, despite widespread charity work, was snubbed by Denver society, which wasn't so hot anyway. So Mrs. Brown skipped through Denver and went right to the top of the ladder, becoming the cream of New York and European elite.

But she is most noted for her heroism in the sinking of the Titanic.

Usually, when they got rich in Leadville, they moved on, leaving the fabulous city to the little wheels and the petty characters.

And there were a slew of characters. Leadville deserves a few books on its past.

But we must move on, ignoring Leadville's fires and labor wars, which involve the "Molly MacGuires."

Before we go, however, we must mention the Ice Palace.

The Ice Palace was built in 1895. It covered five acres, was 50 feet high and built of blocks of ice eight feet thick. Ore samples were frozen into the walls, and ice statues filled the inside.

The unusual palace received world-wide attention before it began to melt and was closed down in July of the same year.

Through the years, much of what was Leadville was torn down for firewood. Much of the old city still remains, however, and should remain for years to come. The city still has four lives to lead.

*Places to see:*

*Elks Opera House* (308 Harrison Avenue), formerly the Tabor Grand Opera House, which saw some of the greatest plays and players of its day. Tabor had offices here.

Next door is the site of the once famous *Clarendon Hotel*, where the Carbonate Kings used to meet, drink, and play poker. Some of the greatest figures of the day, including Generals Grant and Sherman, Commodore Vanderbilt, Jay Gould and the Duke of Cumberland, were visitors here. The hotel was one of the first hotels in Leadville. It was torn down in 1939.

*Tabor House* (116 East 5th Street), a five-room frame house in which Augusta Tabor and H. A. W. lived—when he wasn't traipsing after Baby Doe—during their last years in Leadville. Tabor wanted to build a palatial mansion but Augusta, distrustful of the family's sudden wealth, insisted on keeping the small house.

*Hotel Vendome* (701 Harrison Avenue), originally the Tabor Grand Hotel. A four-story hotel with ornate furnishings which was opened in 1885. It boasted the best-stocked bar in the state. The hotel was renamed in 1894.

*Healy House* (northeast corner of Harrison Avenue). A typical house of the 1880's, restored by the National Youth Administration and maintained by the State Historical Society.

*Dexter Cabin* (110 West 3rd Street) one of the first cabins built in the Leadville boom in 1878-79. The cabin has been restored and is now maintained as a museum.

*Pioneer Club* (118 West 2nd State Street) the sole survivor of the many drinking and gambling dens of early Leadville. The first Wurlitzer in the club was brought over from Germany. The many bullet holes in the club attest to its unruly youth.

The site of the notorious *Texas House* can be seen on the southwest corner of Harrison Avenue and 2nd (State) Street. Said to be one of the largest and most prosperous gambling halls in the west. During its heyday, the Texas House made more money than the banks. But the house also lost $30,000 in a day, a record for that time. It was in, or just outside, the Texas House, that City Marshal Mort Duggan was gunned down by a gambler in 1888.

*Matchless Mine* (on Fryer Hill), purchased by Tabor in 1881 for $117,000 and earning him ten million dollars. The Matchless was Tabor's favorite, and he kept it after selling all his other holdings. On his deathbed he told Baby Doe to "hold on to the Matchless." She did. She lived in the cabins just south of the shafthouse. It was in this cabin she was found on March 7, 1935, frozen to death. Some accounts say it was in a shaft of the Matchless that Oscar Wilde drank six miners under the table (if they had a table in the Matchless Shaft). It could be Oscar had more than one drinking bout with Leadville miners. We know he wasn't above it.

The *Robert E. Lee Mine* is south of the Matchless on Fryer Hill. It is said to have been one of the richest yet one of the most undeveloped claims in the area. The mine produced a record $118,500 in one day. The story goes that James Baxter bought the claim in 1879, but sold it for $30,000 after failing to find any silver in the first 100 feet. The new owner used one shot to uncover a vein of almost pure silver. A half million dollars in silver was taken out in three months. The vein was so rich a man offered the owner $10,000 just to work it for one hour. He was refused.

There are many other mines in the area. Some are open for inspection, some are dangerous, some are still being worked.

SILVER DUST: They say Jesse James and his gang resided awhile in California Gulch. Some say he lived a peaceable-enough life, but when stage robberies got out of hand, a few citizens got suspicious, and old Jesse moved on . . . . Leadville is the highest incorporated city in the world at an elevation of 10,200 feet . . . . the ground is frozen tight most of the year, and this was a big problem in mining. They even had to use dynamite to blast holes for graves . . . . some early strikes were made while digging graves, by the way . . . . up until 1953, Leadville and its Lake County neighbors produced $195,413,951 in silver; $107,721,121 in lead; $115,140,701 in zinc; $66,144,179 in gold; and $15,162,107 in copper, plus millions more in iron, bismuth and other minerals. It ranks first in the state in silver, lead and zinc production, second in copper and fourth in gold . . . . Climax, 13 miles away, has produced millions in molybdenum and is the world's largest underground mine . . . . the silver mines produced more than 11 millions in 1881, and maintained a ten-million dollar average for several years . . . . the Leadville area produced a total of more than 14 million dollars in gold, silver, lead, zinc and copper in 1903 . . . . separating the zinc composites was a major problem for several years before they were separated successfully near the turn of the century . . . . Tabor was made mayor of the new boom area in 1879, the same year he struck it rich on the Little Pittsburgh . . . . the population of Leadville during its peak in the early 80's has been estimated as high as 60,000. We do know for sure that it was the city second in population to Denver for several years . . . . another problem in the early days was supplies, especially in winter. Storekeepers made fortunes with their scalpers' prices. Water was even 50c a barrel. Whiskey was even more dear. Two barrels of the stuff brought $2,700. Hay was all the way from $60 to $120 a ton . . . . the Tontine was the most fashionable restaurant. It featured a delicious French cuisine . . . . Father Robinson brought in the first bricks to build his church. Irish miners built the church in their spare time. The railroad donated the bell which is still used . . . . while the First Avenue Presbyterian Church was being built, armed guards surrounded the site to fight off possible claim jumpers . . . . they built everything else first, but by 1882 Leadville had seven churches . . . . the first school was built in 1879. But Leadvillites didn't like it. Besides it wasn't big enough, so another one was built almost immediately . . . . in addition, Leadville had 3 breweries, 13 liquor stores, 10 lumber yards, 6 jewelry stores, 3 busy undertakers, and 19 hotels . . . .

Leadville attempted many tax systems in trying to raise money, but none of them was very effective . . . . the first person judged insane enough to lock up was a man charged with spending all of his time in prayer . . . . a Negro gambler was sold into slavery to pay court costs. The highest bidder got his services for three months for two dollars . . . . too many of the first residents were prospectors and miners were hard to come by, so many were imported, bringing in many foreign elements . . . . the foreign miners were part of the labor wars . . . . the greatest prejudice, however, was shown against the Chinese and Indians. Three Chinese laundrymen were lynched, shot to pieces and thrown down an empty prospect hole . . . . the opening of the Tabor Grand Opera House on November 21, 1879, was not nearly as festive an occasion as was anticipated, or as big as Tabor wanted it to be. For one thing, the weather was terrible. For another, two men hanged by the vigilantes two nights before, were still dangling from the rafters of the jail house, a few steps down the street . . . . there were 28 miles of streets in Leadville by 1880 . . . . profits of some of the best mines were wasted by over-exploitation and squandering . . . . there were many law suits. Seven of the first eleven million dollars in profits from the Iron Silver Mine were spent in legal fees . . . . the Leadville Blues was one of the top baseball teams in Colorado for many years, its closest rival being the Denver Browns. They talked about the 1883 game for several years. The Blue had a substantial 22 to 9 lead going into the eighth, when the Browns rallied and finally won 25 to 24. One newspaper called the game a "slugging match."

## LEADVILLE SUBURBS
### TINTOWN
Tintown was adjacent to the northern limits of Leadville. There were several mills nearby, the largest of which was the Elgin. There were some large railroad yards nearby also.

### JACKTOWN
Jacktown was the first town enroute to Malta on what was called "Smelter Valley." Jacktown was one of the larger "suburbs." It had 45 cabins and houses, several businesses, including a number of saloons, and a bowling alley.

### STRINGTOWN
Another large suburb between Jacktown and Bucktown. The giant Arkansas Valley plant, which was also the main source of prosperity- of Little Chicago and Bucktown, was virtually adjacent Stringtown.

The Great Northern Hotel was located here. There were several cabins, houses and tenements to accommodate the residents. There were several businesses and saloons, and a cobbler.

### BUCKTOWN
Located at the other end of the Arkansas Valley Plant from Stringtown. It was named for a buck deer seen near here. Bucktown was a cabin site in 1879 and was still going at the turn of the century.

### LITTLE CHICAGO
A short distance north of Stringtown and across the river. As with

Stringtown, the residents of Little Chicago worked at the Arkansas Valley
Plant, located between the towns.

## MALTA (Swilltown)

Malta was important to the Leadville story for two reasons: it had the
area's first smelter, and it had a race track. The two really got their start
with the construction, in 1875, of the smelter, built to handle the ores of the
Homestake region. Soon the smelter took on the ores of other mines, and
the city prospered.

By 1878, Malta had two hotels, fifty cabins and houses, a post office and
sampling works. Additional smelters were built here, and by 1881, Malta
had four hotels, a brewery, several saloons and a population of more than
300.

The race track was built in 1879 and cost $5,000. It became a showplace
for horses belonging to the carbonate kings of Leadville, and a popular
racing center.

By 1884, Malta was little more than a junction for the Denver and Rio
Grande Railroad. The smelters were never too successful and as larger,
more modern smelters were built in and around Leadville, Malta couldn't
compete.

Malta never quite became a ghost town, but has lingered on the edge of
it through the years. Nearby is one of the largest and most modern fish
hatcheries in the United States.

Malta is located at the mouth of California Gulch, where the early boom
in the area took place. There was a lot of prospecting done here, and it is
believed Tabor tried his luck around the site of the later city.

## ADELAIDE (Adelaide City)

Adelaide grew around the Adelaide mine, one of the first and richest
mines in Stray Horse Gulch. There was a large smelter here, too. Although usually considered a suburb of Leadville, the city was never included within the corporate limits of the boom town, and Adelaide had a
bustling life of its own.

The mine was located in 1876. A neat little town was built in a small
park near the mine. The town had 36 cabins, 28 business buildings, including 4 saloons, a mining engineer, smelter, lawyer, post office and stores.
It was a wild town with plenty of gambling and brawling.

The city was in the midst of several fairly valuable mines, and was busy
through the silver boom and revived for a short time with some gold excitement around the turn of the century.

The post office was discontinued in 1880, and by 1887 only forty-four

202

people remained. They drifted off eventually. As with most of the Leadville "suburbs," nothing remains of Adelaide.

### STUMPFTOWN (Stumptown)

Stumpftown was located a half-mile above Evansville in South Evans Gulch. It was named Stumpftown after Joseph Stumpf, one of the first settlers, but most of the residents simplified the name to Stumptown.

There were several good mines nearby, the best of which were the Boulder, St. Louis, Louise, South Winnie, and Little Bob. There were about 20 homes and six saloons—but the town got its personality from the pool room.

### FINNTOWN

Finntown was so named because of the many Finns who lived here and helped build the city. The town was located up Stray Horse Gulch, this side of Ibex. It had a public hall, club room, several saloons and stores.

The Finntown climate gave the residents plenty of opportunity for "sauna," the art of jumping into a snowbank after a sweat shower.

### SOUTH EVANS

South Evans was located in Evans Gulch near Snowy Range, about six miles from Leadville. Not much is known about the town, but there were some good mines in this vicinity, including the Little Rische, Resurrection, Fortune, Silent Friend and Favorite.

### EVANSVILLE

Evansville was located near a couple of good fissure mines about three miles east of Leadville near the head of Big Evans Gulch. The town was established in 1879 and soon had a population of 400 residents, and boasted several prosperous businesses. A schoolhouse was built within the next year or two, and had a student body of about twenty-five, who attended classes ten months of the year.

The region was said to have produced about three million dollars in gold in the early days, and some good silver properties were found during the silver rush days of Leadville.

Evansville died slowly. In 1898, only two families lived here. Now, nothing is left of the city.

### IBEX (Ibex City; Ibex Camp)

The famous Little Jonny mine was the sustaining power of Ibex. The Little Jonny (often called Little Johnny) was owned by the Ibex Mining Company and the mine was even called the Ibex for a time.

The town was located about four miles up Stray Horse Gulch on Breece Hill. The city was located at timberline. Winters here weren't ideal. Nonetheless, the city thrived. In its heyday, there were two hotels, fifty cabins and frame houses, and several businesses including two assay offices, two laundries, a shoemaker and even a cigar store. A school was built here, and kids from Adelaide journeyed up the gulch to attend classes, in good weather and bad.

The Little Jonny was quite a mine. It had many owners. In many cases, the owners sunk more into the mine than they got out of it. Still, the mine produced some 13 million dollars in gold, nearly one-third of all the gold production of the entire Leadville region during the years 1893 to 1923. Quicksand within the mine was perhaps the most difficult problem for the Little Jonny owners to overcome. The sinking of the original shaft was one of the most delicate tasks in Colorado mining history.

Since the Little Jonny produced mainly gold, it survived the panic of 1893 which caused such chaos among most of the other mines in Leadville. This was about the most prosperous time for Ibex. By 1897, the output of the Ibex area was as much as $250,000 a month.

The mine was worked off and on for several years. But, apparently, most of the residents eventually moved down into Leadville. Nothing remains of Ibex today.

### HOWLAND

Howland was another small camp located on the east fork of the Arkansas River. It was said to be about seven miles northeast of Leadville, a short distance south of Birdseye. The town grew around some good mines, the best of which was the Little Doty. The city was in a small valley between the mountains.

A post office was installed in 1879. The town had a few business houses and a population of about 100. But apparently the mines, although paying well for a while, pinched out in a hurry. The population was down to twenty in 1882, and they left shortly after that.

### BIRDSEYE

Birdseye was a smaller camp located near the junction of Bird's Eye Gulch and the east fork of the Arkansas River . . . about eight miles above Leadville. The Gold Metal Lode was located here in 1879 and developed into a good quartz mine. Some other discoveries were made about the same time, primarily placer claims along the river.

There was some evidence that a small stamp mill was built here, but nothing definite. In fact, there's no evidence at the scene that a town even existed. The town and the gulch were named for the presence of Monzanite Porphyry, a speckled rock which suggests birds' eyes.

*TABOR* (Tabor City, Taylor City, Halfway House and Chalk Creek Ranch)

A lot of names for such a small camp—but there is a possibility Tabor City and Halfway House were two distinct camps, both on Chalk Creek Ranchland. The reason for the belief Tabor City and Halfway House may be separated is that early records show Halfway House served primarily as a rest and supply station for travelers over Fremont Pass, while Tabor City was a mining town.

However, if they weren't one and the same, they were mighty close together, both about ten miles northeast of Leadville.

Just one log cabin was here in 1879. In that year, a frame house was built and two competing restaurants were constructed. These were followed by two hotels, a blacksmith shop, livery stable and a general supply store.

This sudden development of the site may or may not be linked to the discovery of some good minerals along Chalk Creek in 1879.

Anyhow, records show a fellow by the name of Colonel Taylor purchased a site on Chalk Creek Ranch and laid out a city. He wanted it to be called Taylor City. But the miners called it Tabor for the Leadville carbonate king, who apparently had a finger in some pot here. After a while, even Taylor relented and Tabor City became the most remembered name for the little-remembered site.

Tabor City had several cabins, a half dozen business establishments and about 150 residents by 1880. Although the residents had high grade hopes, they found only low-grade ore. The post office was discontinued by 1881 and Tabor City was practially a ghost town by 1882.

Records show Halfway House was active longer than two or three years, which is another reason it is believed the two sites were separate. But both sites returned to ranchland—Chalk Creek ranch-land—within a few short years.

*ALICANTE* (Summit)

This town had two names, either one correct. The town and post office were officially named Alicante, for the nearby Alicante Mine. The mine was named for the city in Spain. The Denver and Rio Grande Railroad station here was named Summit—because it was high up on Fremont Pass. It wasn't at the summit of the pass, however. It was just south of the summit, near the present site of Climax.

A handful of good but little-developed mines were located here about 1880. A town grew near the mines. It had a post office in 1881 and a population of 100. The best mines were the John Reed, Gold Field, Walter Scott, Alicante and Miner's College. A 2,000-foot tramway system and a 20-stamp mill were built to develop the Walter Scott. The John Reed was noted for its fine rhodochrosite crystals—and that's something to be noted for!

But, despite the good ore, the season was short and water scarce. It cost too much to make a profit, and the area faded rapidly during the mid-80's and was gone by 1888.

## CLIMAX (Fremont Pass)

There was some mining activity during the early booms in this area, but Climax didn't achieve rightful importance until this century when the world's greatest supply of molybdenum was found here.

The site was originally named Fremont Pass, for the pass on which it rests. Fremont took the pass on one of his many exploratory thrusts into the Colorado mountains.

A small camp was located here during the time of the Leadville boom. A man named Charles Senter was credited with making the first strike. But the ores soon gave out and the site was deserted, although the peculiar stones remained a subject for curiosity. It was at first believed the rocks were galena, but when they showed little paying content, the curiosity was assuaged for a while.

The ore was identified as molybdenum in 1900, but there was little demand for it then, and its mining was not developed for another dozen years. The demand became great during the first World War and the development of molybdenum mining in Colorado got its start.

Among other things, molybdenum is used in the making of radio tubes, auto and plane parts, and in chemical compounds and dyes. The demand has increased through the years. The Climax Molybdenum Company has employed more than 1,000 people. Stock in the firm rose 116,900 per cent from 1926 to 1936. By 1938, production topped 20 million dollars, leading production of all minerals in the state.

A 1958 strike threatened to make a ghost town of Climax and greatly depopulate Leadville, where many of the company employees live. But an amicable solution, after months of negotiation, reopened the mines, and put what employees were left in the area back to work.

GOLD DUST: The population in 1917 was 200, and has slowly increased over the years . . . . the city was called Climax because it is near the summit of Fremont Pass, and the highest post office and railroad station in the United States . . . . the city itself is at the foot of Bartlett Mountain, called the Mountain of Molybdenum.

## LAKE CITY and HOMESTAKE (not on map)

Lake City and Homestake were the major camps in the Homestake Mining district on Homestake Mountain about twelve miles northwest of Leadville. Homestake was on the northern side of the mountain, and Lake

City, the larger of the two camps, was on the southern side of the mountain.

Lake City, for a small camp, was marked with more tragedy than most other camps in Colorado. The tragedy involves snow and snowslides, and there were plenty of both at this high altitude (11,500 feet).

In December of 1883, Albert Morrison led a party of three experienced men up the mountain to inspect some new holdings there. When the men didn't return, a large search party set out to look for them. Evidence of a giant snowslide was found. A cabin was eventually found some fifty feet below the surface of the snow. The four men were found within the cabin, frozen in the various peaceful positions they had been in when the snowslide hit. Death was apparently instantaneous from the vacuum created by the slide.

Another tragedy, or story of a tragedy, may be related in some way to the above.

Two miners came into Leadville, bearing the tale of two men found frozen in peaceful positions in a cabin in a ravine near the foot of Homestake Peak. The miners said evidence at the scene dated the tragedy as twenty years before—in 1859 or 1860. A search party set out in an effort to locate the cabin, but no trace of it was ever found.

Ten men were killed in another giant snowslide in 1885, which rolled virtually the entire city down the mountain.

Another story of the snow has no basis in fact.

Leadville newspaperman Orth Stein told the story of a woman prospector frozen to death near Homestake Peak. When found two weeks later, the woman's body was carried into Leadville and placed on a desk in the *Leadville Chronicle* composing room—near the potbellied stove.

The newspaperman told of watching the woman thaw, limb by limb. And, when completely thawed out, she got up, brushed herself off, and walked out of the office, never to be seen again.

As if the snow and snowslides weren't enough, Lake City had three murders and two lynchings in its short history.

A fellow named Merrick Rosencranz killed his friend H. A. Langmeyer, who caught Rosencranz rifling his trunks. Rosencranz was hanged with a man named Frank Gilbert, who murdered a man in nearby Tennessee Park. Another man was murdered shorty thereafter.

The Homestake region was settled after rich lead-silver ore was located in 1871 by three men who were only trying to find a trail over the range.

The men had the ore assayed. It ran about 30 to 60 per cent lead and from 200 to 500 ounces of silver per ton. It was valued at from $100 to $800 a ton. But the men were disappointed. The ore showed only a trace of gold. Gold was the thing—silver hadn't come of age yet.

But the men condescended to work the claims. In 1875, a small smelter was built at Malta to handle the ore, the first smelter to handle silver in the Leadville area.

The city contained about 40 cabins and several businesses. A road was built out from Oro City, but it was rough and dangerous, impassable much of the year.

The quality of the ores couldn't overcome the costs of production. And tragedy and transportation helped spell the end of Lake City and Homestake. Most of Lake City was erased by the slide of 1885. Countless slides since have carried away the rest.

### CAMP HARRINGTON and TENNESSEE PASS (Cooper)

Some mining was done near the top of Tennessee Pass in the early 80's. The miners' camp was called merely Tennessee Pass or Cooper. The population never did get over 100, if it reached that, and it was all gone by 1885.

The area was deserted until after the turn of the century when some more locations were found at about the same site. The new camp was called Camp Harrington for Jim Harrington, who made the original strike. But this camp wasn't very large either and didn't last long.

There were some placer and carbonate ores found in nearby East Tennessee Gulch, but there was no evidence of an organized camp here.

Now, the Cooper Hill ski area dominates the site near where Camp Harrington and Tennessee Pass were located.

### TENNESSEE PARK and SWEDE'S GULCH

Another small camp was located near the southern foot of Tennessee Pass and northeast of St. Kevins and Gleason Gulch. The camp, named Tennessee Park, was active for a while during the 90's.

The El Capitan, Lucy R. and Prendery were located on Taylor Hill above the town. The ores ran from about $15 to $120 of gold per ton with some traces of silver. Hardly enough to support a camp.

On the west side of Tennessee Park, about two miles north of Colorado Gulch, is Swede's Gulch. About twenty claims were staked out along the gulch. The best were Rock Island, Peerless, Vermont, Amity, Monte Carlo, Honest Dollar and Hattie K.

### ST. KEVINS and AMITY

St. Kevins was the major camp in the St. Kevins mining district, located north of present-day Turquoise Lake, about four miles west and a mile or two north of Leadville. The camp grew around the St. Kevins mine. The rock formations and mineral deposits were of an entirely different nature from that of Leadville—granite rock with some fissure veins of silver ore, with some lead, copper and gold.

The camp was not very large, but did have a stamp mill and a school. The peak period of the area was in the late 80's and 90's, although the Amity mine continued to produce after the turn of the century, and there was some placer mining as late as 1907.

There is evidence of another small camp here called *AMITY*, which probably grew around the Amity mine.

The Griffin and the President were two other mines here.

Thomas Walsh, who later became a multi-millionaire after the discovery of the famous Camp Bird mine near Ouray (see Camp Bird), was said to have made one of the first strikes in the region, in Sowbelly Gulch. He is also said to have been instrumental in planning the town and naming it St. Kevin.

## GLEASON GULCH

There were a number of haphazard dwellings just north of St. Kevins in Gleason Gulch while mining was going on here during the mid-90's. The two principal mines were the Huckleberry, which had some high-grade silver ore, and the Berdella mine, which had a stamp mill.

A large mill was built in 1895 to handle the ore in the gulch, but it burned down later the same year, and nobody bothered to rebuild it.

## CLIFTON

Clifton was a small camp around the Shields mill on Sugar Loaf Mountain, about two-and-a-half miles above Soda Springs.

The Shields, Venture and T. L. Welch mines were producing during the 70's. New locations were made in 1880, the best of which were the Gunnison and Birdie R.

The town of Clifton started about 1880. It had a general store and other businesses, but the population was seldom over a hundred. The biggest deal was the Shields 10-stamp mill, which handled most of the ore from Sugar Loaf Mountain (a part of Mount Massive) and Frying Pan Gulch.

The Tiger mine was tied up with litigation after it had produced $68,000. Many of the mines produced through the 80's, and there was a slight flutter of activity around the turn of the century.

## SODA SPRINGS

Soda Springs, west of Leadville, was the most popular resort of the early Leadville boom days. Some placer gold was found here at the mouth of Colorado Gulch in the early 60's. But after the gold gave out, the area was deserted until the Leadville boom, when it was turned into a resort.

There are several springs here. Despite its name, however, only one contains soda. The others contain sulphur and iron.

Activity centered around the Mount Massive Hotel. During its hoity-toity days it was also called Hotel de Mount Massive. It was famous for its cuisine and mixed drinks. The hotel and other facilities changed hands frequently. It reached its peak in 1881 when Judge H. S. Kimball and Nat Morton took over. The two introduced sleighing and other winter sports to Soda Springs and made a year-round resort out of it, where it had only been a summer thing in the past.

Soda Springs had a post office and a year-round population of about seventy-five by 1883. But the many changes in ownership and the lack of adequate management most of the time, generally hindered the profitable development of Soda Springs. The resort possibilities remain but the town of Soda Springs has long since disappeared.

## EVERGREEN LAKES

Evergreen Lakes was in another resort area, a favorite of the Leadville boom days. The lakes consist of four small but picturesque lakes just below Colorado Gulch. The Suburban Hotel was here and several cabins were built.

A permanent fish hatchery was built near here in the 80's. It is not only one of the oldest in the state, but also one of the largest.

Congress also appropriated $15,000 to turn the area into a park. In 1889, construction of recreation facilities began.

*An Then There Were* . . . . *HENRY* (not on map), not much is known about Henry except that is was registered as one of the many cities around Leadville in 1880. The town was said to be about three-and-one-half miles northeast of Leadville, possibly along the east fork of the Arkansas. In 1880, the town had a post office, two general stores and three saloons . . . . *ALEXANDER*, although some maps show Alexander as due north and even slightly northeast of Leadville, early sources say the town was about six miles northwest of Leadville on the Redcliff wagon road. It had a population of one hundred in 1883, but the directories didn't mention it after 1884 . . . . *WORTMAN* (or Wortsman), some maps show this town as Wortsman or even Wortmans, but the gazetteer and post office lists show the name as Wortman. The camp was located around the John Reed Mine a short distance from Alicante. The mine was owned by G. C. Wortman. Collier and Lewis later leased the mine and shipped several cars of high grade ore . . . . *JUNCTION CITY* (not on map), a small camp at the junction of Colorado and Rock Creek Gulches. The residents worked the nearby Kerby placers and there was a small mill here, but they couldn't get the capital to develop the workings and the site was abandoned after only a few cabins were built . . . . *PARK CITY* (not on map), an earlier camp on or very near the site of Adelaide. Some of the cabins in this town may have been used to start Adelaide . . . . *ARKANSAS JUNCTION* and *LEADVILLE JUNCTION*, two important railroad junctions during the Leadville boom years. Both were located along the Arkansas River. Arkansas Junction was located due west of Leadville, and Leadville Junction was about two-and-a-half miles north of Arkansas Junction. Both stops served Leadville.

210

## TWIN LAKES, INDEPENDENCE AND HAGERMAN PASSES

Twin Lakes
Dayton

### *From Bottom to Top*

Vicksburg, Winfield, Beaver City, Silver Dale and Rockdale

Granite

Cache Creek (Cash Creek)

Lost Canyon Placers

Georgia Bar

Everett (Halfway House, Seiden's Ranch)

Brumley (Bromley)

Independence (Chipeta, Mammoth City, Mount Hope, Farwell, Sparkill or
Sparkell)

Ruby (South Independence)

Massive City

Busk and Hagerman Pass

Ivanhoe

Hellgate, Nast, Sellar, Norrie, Biglow (Quinn's Spur), Muckawango

(Riley's), Thomasville, Calcium and Troutville (Wood's Lake)
*And Then There Were* .... *JUNCTION HOUSE, WELLER, LORIMER* (not on map),
*EAGLE SAMPLER* (not on map) *CRYSTAL LAKE, DOUGLASS CITY* (not
on map), and *HAMILTON* (not on map).

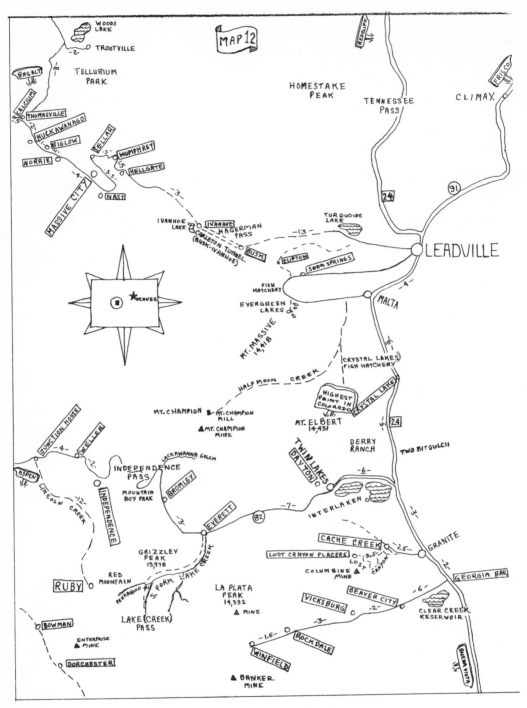

MAP 12

WOODS LAKE

TROUTVILLE

-2-

BASALT

TELLURIUM PARK

HOMESTAKE PEAK

REDCLIFF

FRISCO

TENNESSEE PASS

CLIMAX

CALCIUM

THOMASVILLE

HUCKAWANAGD

BIGLOW

SELLAR

NORRIE

HUMPHREY

HELLGATE

.5.5.

24

91

MASSIVE CITY

-4-

NAST

-3-

IVANHOE LAKE

IVANHOE

HAGERMAN PASS

CARLETON TUNNEL (BUSK-IVANHOE)

BUSK

CLIFTON

-13-

SODA SPRINGS

TURQUOISE LAKE

LEADVILLE

DENVER

FISH HATCHERY

EVERGREEN LAKES

MALTA

-4-

MT. MASSIVE 14,418

HALFMOON CREEK

CRYSTAL LAKES FISH HATCHERY

MT. CHAMPION

MT. CHAMPION MILL

MT. CHAMPION MINE

HIGHEST POINT IN COLORADO

CRYSTAL LAKE

MT. ELBERT 14,431

24

JUNCTION HOUSE

WELLER

-4-

-2-

INDEPENDENCE PASS

LACKAWANNA GULCH

DERRY RANCH

TWO BIT GULCH

TWIN LAKES

DAYTON

-6-

ASPEN

LINCOLN CREEK

-12-

INDEPENDENCE

MOUNTAIN BOY PARK

BROMLEY

-3-

EVERETT

82

-7-

INTERLAKEN

-3-

GRANITE

-2-

GRIZZLEY PEAK 13,978

RED MOUNTAIN

PEEKABOO GULCH

S FORK LAKE CREEK

LAKE CREEK

LA PLATA PEAK 14,332

CACHE CREEK

LOST CANYON PLACERS

LOST CANYON

COLUMBINE MINE

-2.5-

GEORGIA BAR

RUBY

MINE

VICKSBURG

-2-

BEAVER CITY

-6-

CLEAR CREEK RESERVOIR

BOWMAN

ENTERPRISE MINE

LAKE (CREEK) PASS

-1.5-

ROCKDALE

-3-

BUENA VISTA

DORCHESTER

WINFIELD

BANKER MINE

212

# XI. TWIN LAKES, INDEPENDENCE AND HAGERMAN PASSES

## TWIN LAKES

Twin Lakes is now a sleepy little summer resort. There are a hotel, a few cabins, an old school and a combination store and service station. Viewing the lakes and passing through the little village on the west side of the lakes, one wouldn't think the site had a fabulous past.

Twin Lakes, as a resort, was known from coast to coast during the Leadville boom days. The Leadville carbonate kings had lavish homes here, as did many other state officials and big shots. Twin Lakes also served as a center of an extensive mining area. It was a busy stage and freighter station on the run from Leadville to Aspen via Independence Pass.

Some say gondolas actually cruised over the lakes. Others say they were just talking about it. A story is told of the time gondolas were planned. The promoters weren't sure of the number to purchase. They put the question to John Morrissey, an ignorant man, made millionaire by the Leadville boom. Morrissey told the promoters the number of gondolas to buy wasn't a problem at all . . . "Just get a couple and let 'em breed," he said.

Twin Lakes took over from another important town of earlier days, Dayton. Dayton, the largest city in the county, and county seat for a while, in the middle-60's after Oro City faded, extended from the foot of Mount Elbert to, or near, the present site of Twin Lakes.

Dayton was last heard from in 1881. It is believed that what was left of the city was absorbed into fast-growing Twin Lakes. At any rate, the old Dayton Hotel was made over into a Twin Lakes hotel.

Twin Lakes got its start in 1879. By 1883 it had no less than six hotels, several lodges, and the lakes were surrounded by scores of cabins and cottages. Some were even built between the lakes. Everybody that was anybody in Leadville had a cabin here.

The biggest hotel at the time was the Interlaken (German for between the lakes), which was situated, curiously enough, between the lakes at the southern end. The Interlaken boasted of the "best cuisine in the country." It had a large dance pavilion, and many amusement facilities, including ice skating in the winter.

One of the biggest boosters of Twin Lakes was John Campion. Old John took a fortune out of the Little Jonny and put some $125,000 of it into a palatial home on Twin Lakes. They say he built the home for his new bride. While the lodge was under construction, he and his bride honeymooned in Europe, picking up the best furnishings the continent had to offer.

Campion talked many of the other carbonate kings, and several state big-wigs, into building summer lodges at Twin Lakes. And some of the top names of the day were guests at Campion's Lodge.

The lakes were more nearly twins in those days. But about 1880, a company came along and put in a dam that almost joined the lakes. The uproar caused by the action could be heard for miles and the company was forced to tear down the dam.

Later, however, the Twin Lakes Reservoir Company gained control of the lakes and put in a dam and headgates, that could lower or raise the level of the water at will. The uproar was again as loud, but this time the company did it legally. At least, the court upheld the action.

In disgust, Campion and many others moved away. Twin Lakes has never been the same since. For one thing, the lakes are no longer twins, and the shrubbery and trees around the lake—much of the lakes' early beauty—are gone.

Twin Lakes' life as a mining center and stage and freight stop was nearly as illustrious as its life as a resort kingdom.

During the Aspen boom and before the railroad got to that side of the divide, a constant stream of stages and freighter wagons rolled over long and grueling Independence Pass (first known as Hunter's Pass).

Concord stages would roar down to Twin Lakes from Leadville. At Twin Lakes the passengers and baggage would be transferred to canvas-top stages for the long haul over the pass. Four horses could pull the load much of the way, but one stretch required six horses.

Twin Lakes' gay resort days were marked by the sound of dynamite blasts heard in the hills. It was a reminder that much serious mining was going on. Twin Lakes managed to keep the smelters off the city proper, but many of the miners headquartered here. They would stock up here before heading into the mountains; the ore they dug passed through Twin Lakes; and the boys "Saturday-nighted" here.

Twin Lakes was the center of a mining area which extended from Mount Elbert in the north to Cache Creek in the south, and a good distance over Independence to the west, including Mount Champion and the Red Mountain district. Much of the ore was low-grade and a lot of it was difficult to reach. However, there were quite a few good claims, and much precious metal was produced in the region over the years. The Mount Elbert group was the nearest to Twin Lakes and had some of the best producers. The Gordon claim was located in 1880 and showed gold from the grass roots. There were some rich pockets found in the claim, and it had its own mill to treat the low-grade ore. It produced more than a half million dollars worth of metal in its 35 years. The mine sold for $200,000 in 1900.

Some steam shovel placering was done nearby just after the turn of the century. Although the work was profitable, it was hampered by huge boulders.

Then came the $125,000 dredge of 1911. The dredge was brought in by the Derry Ranch Gold Dredging Company. It produced up to a thousand dollars a day through 1911.

Some dry-land dredgers were working in Box Canyon, just north of Twin Lakes in the 1940's. The General Gold Corporation worked two dredges here until 1952, and are prepared to go back to work whenever the price of gold increases.

Perhaps, the Twin Lakes area hasn't seen its best days yet . . .but it's seen some pretty good ones.

GOLD DUST: The Interlaken was not only the most lavish hotel about, it was also the most expensive. Rooms went for as much as $3.50 and $4.00 a day . . . . after Campion sold out, his lodge was turned into a hotel called The Campion Hotel. It operated for many years . . . . during its peak, Twin Lakes had a permanent population of more than 200. But the transient population usually outnumbered the permanent residents many times over . . . . another well-known mine on Mount Elbert was the Little Joe . . . . Twin Lakes still has a post office.

## DAYTON

For a short while, Dayton was the top town in the Leadville area, and was the county seat.

Dayton was started in the early 60's about the same time as Oro City. When the town to the north faded suddenly, many of the prospectors moved to Dayton and the community at the foot of Mount Elbert was voted the new county seat in 1866. A 16-mile toll road from Oro City to Dayton was built to expedite the migration.

A two-story courthouse was built, the upper floor being used as a Masonic Hall. Dayton had three saloons and several other prosperous businesses. The peak population was more than 500 persons.

But the first ores found here could not support the population and the boom lasted only two more years. In 1868, the county courthouse was moved to the rapidly rising city of Granite.

Some mining was carried on here for several years. But when Twin Lakes was developed during the Leadville boom, the few remaining cabins of Dayton were absorbed into the resort town.

Some successful dredge mining was carried on several years later, for which Twin Lakes took the credit. Dayton was forgotten.

215

## VICKSBURG, WINFIELD, BEAVER CITY, SILVER DALE, and ROCK-DALE

The major cities along Clear Creek gulch, founded in the early 80's by some restless mules. The story goes that some Leadville prospectors, heading for Gunnison country, camped along the creek. During the night their burros wandered down along the creek. When the prospectors located the animals the next day they found good float at the spot.

Needless to say, the prospectors forgot about Gunnison country. The report of their find brought hundreds of other prospectors. Within weeks there was activity all up and down the gulch.

Beaver City and Vicksburg soon emerged as the top camps, but a short time later Winfield surpassed Beaver City. The two camps, Winfield and Vicksburg, had a peak population in the early 80's of between 200 and 300. A few log cabins in these two towns are all that remain of the early activity in the gulch.

Newer tourist cabins have sprouted up in recent years.

### GRANITE

Granite came to life in 1860, along with Cache Creek and Georgia Bar. As with the other two camps, Granite lost many of its inhabitants to Oro City, but its mines nearby did produce for a number of years.

The town was laid out when gold was found along the base of Cache Creek. Some good lode mines were located about 1870, giving the camp another spurt. The best mines were the Yankee Blade and Belle of Granite. Placer mining was, by far, the most profitable mining here. It was carried out from 1860 to 1889, when the hydraulic placers came in. The huge hydraulic finished scooping out the area in 1911.

Granite had a varying population through the years, with its peak years during the 60's and 70's when it had as many as 500 or 600 residents.

Granite had one of the state's more colorful hermits, George Woods, hermit of Golden Mountain, located about two miles down Cache Creek from Granite. Woods lived like an animal in a rude hut made by two boulders, covered by railroad wood. He was known to hide when anyone came near his residence. Yet, in his rare but necessary dealings with civilization, he was friendly and cooperative.

It is believed he lived here from 1912 to 1931. He existed on government charity his last years, although when he died in Salida in 1931, he had nearly $2,000 in cash and bank accounts.

Some believed he was the same George Woods who was reportedly killed in a 1912 mine accident in the Cripple Creek region. But the wife and the daughter of the victim did not claim any relationship with the hermit.

216

The Stark Store in St. Elmo. Annabelle Stark, "The Queen of St. Elmo," and her brother lived in the adjoining twelve-room house summer and winter for several years.

Main Street of St. Elmo, one of the best preserved and most colorful ghost towns in the mountains today.

Hancock in its heyday. Picture shows the Denver and South Park railway. *State Historical Society of Colorado photo.*

Alpine Station at the western end of the Alpine Tunnel. Well built railroad roundhouse was protection against the extreme weather conditions on the pass. Note track bed running from station. *Photo Courtesy Francis J. Rizzari.*

Monarch then. Time and highway construction have destroyed most of the town. *State Historical Society of Colorado photo.*

Denver and South Park RR pause at the remains of Woodstock west of the Alpine Tunnel. Note railway cars on tracks near top of photo. *William H. Jackson photo, State Historical Society of Colorado collection.*

The Angel of Shavano, visible as far away as Salida until mid summer. *U. S. Forest Service photo.*

The famous La Veta Hotel of Gunnison, the most lavish hotel west of the divide in Colorado. The La Veta featured one of the best cuisines in the west. *Picture courtesy of Gunnison Chamber of Commerce.*

Tin Cup just after the turn of the century. It had already begun its decline. *State Historical Society of Colorado photo.*

Tin Cup now. Only a couple of residents remain. Note old church in center of picture. The shot was taken from the opposite angle of the old photo. *Colorado Publicity Department photo.*

221

Spencer in 1912, already a ghost town. *U. S. Geological Survey photo.*

The Ruby-Anthracite mine at Floresta and town of Floresta. Note tracks and railroad cars. *U. S. Geological Survey photo.*

Irwin during its heyday in the early 80's. The town lived a full, colorful life in four short years. *Colorado State Historical Society photo.*

Gothic a few years after its boom. Little is left today. *Photo courtesy Gunnison Chamber of Commerce.*

Birdhouse at Bowerman. Ruins of the town show it had been liveable during its boon years.

Not Roman ruins but ruins at Marble. The largest single block of marble ever quarried came from here as did marble for the Lincoln Memorial and other famous structures. *Colorado Publicity Department photo.*

## CACHE CREEK (Cash Creek)

About two-and-a-half miles upstream from Granite was Cache Creek, predecessor to Granite and an important city in its day.

Cache Creek was headquarters for several small mining areas and camps along the stream, such as Ritchie's Patch, Gold Run, Gibson and Bertschey's Gulches, and Oregon and Lake Creeks.

There are two stories on the naming of the creek from which the town derived its title. One says early French trappers used to hide (or cache) their pelts here. Another story says a group of trappers, including Kit Carson and Lucien Maxwell, were ambushed by Indians near here in 1854, and hid their supplies along the creek to lighten their load in their escape. "Cash Creek" was a pet name given the site .

Some good gold discoveries were made here in 1860 and more than $200,000 worth of the precious metal was taken out of the district in the next seven years. Production here outlasted many of the other camps in the Leadville area. Peak population reached 3,000. Tabor tried his luck here while his wife ran a store and boarding house. Cache Creek was also the first post office in the county.

The Cache Creek Gulch is steep. Winters are severe. But some mining was done as late as 1929. However, long ago, Granite took over as the top town in the area and Cache Creek is little more than a memory.

## LOST CANYON PLACERS

There were many stories of hidden treasure in Lost Canyon, about three-and-one-half miles down the gulch from the present site of Granite.

It seems a group of prospectors became lost in the high canyon country on returning from the Gunnison area in 1860. More hungry for gold than civilization, the group decided to spend the time prospecting, and soon found nuggets "the size of eggs."

The group reportedly took out $60,000 in a few short weeks. They finally made their way out just before winter set in. The following spring, however, the prospectors were unable to locate the site.

Since that time there have been many stories of relocating the fabulously rich area, but most of the stories were mere hearsay. Some believe the Lost Canyon site located by those early prospectors was the same place some placer mining was done in the 80's. But this could be guesswork, and the rich field of nuggets "as big as eggs" may still be biding its time.

The canyon was named for the miners who got lost here in the early 60's. More than 1,000 men swarmed the canyon during the placer boom in the early 80's.

The area had a unique water system. Water was scarce so the miners built a reservoir, with headgates located in advantageous spots. Every half hour during the boom the headgates were opened. The water washed away the waste material, and the gold was picked up off the ground.

## GEORGIA BAR

Georgia Bar was founded about the same time as Oro City when ore was located along Clear Creek by a party of Georgia prospectors. Several thousands of dollars of placer gold was taken from the site during the first year, and many thought it had the best prospects in the county.

Came winter. The Georgians went back to warm Georgia and the others went back to Denver or up to California Gulch.

Came spring. Oro City had captured the imagination of the fortune hunters. Georgia Bar was all but forgotten, although there was some activity here now and again through the years.

## EVERETT (Halfway House, Seiden's Ranch)

Everett (sometimes spelled Everet) grew with the development of a toll road over Independence Pass. It became one of the most important stops on the stage run from Leadville to Aspen.

Known as Halfway House, or Seiden's Ranch in 1881, the site contained but two houses. Along came C. M. Everett who laid out the city which blossomed into quite a place by 1881-1882. By 1882, Everett had some 30 houses, a post office, three mills, several stores and two or three hotels, of which the Everett House was the most prominent.

There were some promising mines in the region. Everett's two stamp mills and one water power mill processed much of the ore. Eventually the mining petered out, and the pass fell into disuse with the coming of the railroad to Aspen. Everett was abandoned.

In 1918, W. S. Lorimer set up a sluicing plant near here and used some of the abandoned facilities at Everett.

A large two-story stage station, the last remaining building at Everett, tumbled to the ground in 1954.

There was some mining done south of Everett in what was known as the Red Mountain district. The district covered the Sayers and Peek-a-boo Gulches and the south fork of Lake Creek. The best mine here was the Bwlchgoch (Indian for Red Mountain) at the head of South Fork at an altitude of 13,000 feet. The mine operated off and on for thirty-five years and had a ten-stamp mill. There was a small revival of mining here around the turn of the century, but work was always hampered by the costly isolation of the area.

## BRUMLEY (or Bromley)

Brumley was another important stage and wagon station on Independence Pass. It also served as a toll gate and horse change as well as a mining

226

center. The town was named for the owner of the hotel here. His name was said to be Bromley and the station was originally named that. Somewhere along the way, however, the name came to be known as Brumley and it appeared on maps that way. Apparently Bromley pronounced his name that way—or he mumbled. His hotel was known for its hospitality and comfort.

About the only excitement recalled about Brumley was the near-fatal stabbing of a stage driver by another stage driver. They say it was over a woman.

Some mining was done in Mountain Boy Gulch just west of Brumley, the Apex properties on Star Mountain, and on Mount Champion to the north. The best known mine was the Mount Champion. The mine was situated near the summit on the south saddle. It was located in the late nineties. Independence Pass had pretty much outlived its usefulness by that time so a three-mile aerial tram was constructed to take the ore over the top of the peak and down into Halfmoon Gulch, where it was loaded onto wagons and taken in to Malta. A mill was built in Halfmoon Gulch to handle the low-grade ore. Cost of the aerial tram was $115,000.

Mount Champion produced for a number of years and had an enormous yield. Costs, however, held down the profits considerably. The mine property was sold in recent years for $1,800 in taxes.

The Eureka mine in Mountain Boy Gulch was a contemporary of Brumley. The mine was worked for a number of years. Generally the ore was hand-sorted and then packed on burros and shipped into Brumley.

There were some other good mines in Mountain Boy Gulch near Mount Champion.

*INDEPENDENCE* (Chipeta, Mammoth City, Mount Hope, Farwell and Sparkill or Sparkell)

Independence was the first camp in Aspen county. Charles Bennett, leading a party of prospectors into Aspen, discovered a lode mine on Independence day. Some say the Independence day strike was made by Dick Irwin. This may be true. It is just unusual that Irwin's name keeps popping up when various camps throughout Colorado are named—almost as if the name was automatic when historians couldn't think of any other.

Independence went through several names before it settled on the name of the mine. One of the longest used and most popular names was Chipeta, for Chief Ouray's wife. Some early maps show Sparkell (also shown as Sparkill) as a separate camp a short distance northwest of Independence, but the rebel camp was apparently absorbed by Independence.

Independence reached its peak during the 80's when the population

227

totaled more than 2,000. It was a wild town with the saloons and gambling halls the busiest places in town.

The Independence and Farwell were about the most productive mines here and were worked continuously until about 1900. There was another flutter of activity around 1908 and some lesser spurts of activity since. Some die-hard prospectors continue to try their luck even now during the summer months.

Ruins of the camp can be seen in a meadow far below Independence Pass, just west of the summit.

The 38-mile pass spreads through some of the most savage and beautiful country in Colorado. The state's highest peak, Mount Elbert (14,431 feet) is at the eastern end of the pass. Several other "fourteeners" can be seen from the pass.

About a half-mile off the road at the western foot of the pass are the grottos, a series of fantastic excavations whittled out of solid rock by centuries of rushing water. The grottos are in an ancient river bed. The river channel now is about fifty feet from the original channel.

The pass itself is the highest crossing of the divide in the state (12,095), and is closed most of the year by arctic weather. The pass was a development of the old Lake Creek trail to Aspen, and was originally called Hunters Pass. The route saw a steady stream of wagons and coaches during the early years of the Aspen boom. It was a rugged road. The first wagon over the trail took six weeks. Some later wagons didn't make it at all.

After the railroads were developed west of the range, Independence Pass fell into disuse. In 1919, state funds were allocated to rebuild the route.

The old mining town of Independence had a hermit, the Mayor of Independence, but he's long gone.

## RUBY (South Independence)

Ruby was laid out in the 90's about ten miles south of Independence on Lincoln Gulch, about equal distance between Aspen and Granite. Ruby silver found here was promising but costs of getting the silver out of the isolated area were almost prohibitive. A trail was built around 1900 and this helped some. A better road was constructed just before World War I, but it came too late, and little mining has been done since.

The mine produced mostly silver, but some gold, lead, iron and even some molybdenum were found here. The city itself was a mile-long row of cabins and stores that led up the mountain almost to the opening of the mine.

Since it was a latter-day camp and is fairly isolated from vandals, much of it remains, but a jeep is recommended in getting to it.

228

## MASSIVE CITY

A Denver newspaper predicted in 1879 that Massive City would be second to none—perhaps Leadville excepted—among the new boom cities of Colorado. The prediction read: "It is expected by those who know that there will be one thousand men there next season, hunting for hidden treasure . . . and it will hold a population of ten thousand souls ere the chilly winds of December again return, there can be found no rational reason for a doubt."

The stirring newspaper account said Massive City was the center of the richest carbonate belt in Colorado and within the limits of Massive City itself were the most valuable mineral springs of the state.

Despite the press notices, Massive City fell far short of expectations. However, it did see a good-sized rush the following spring. Several hundred treasure-hunters, no doubt lured by such newspaper predictions, rushed into the Massive City area. But "ere the chilly winds of December again returned," the bulk of them were fed up with Massive City and its false promises.

Massive City was another area opened up by the overflow of Leadville prospectors. It was located about halfway between Leadville and the Colorado River, at the junction of the Leadville, Eagle and Roaring Forks Rivers, on the western slopes of Mount Massive.

A few claims were made here in the summer of 1879. The best was the Massive, which did yield some unusually rich carbonate. However, before any of the claims could be developed extensively, the miners returned to Leadville to wait out the winter.

The following year, several dozen new claims were made and an elaborate city was planned. The Massive Mining Company was organized with a capital stock of three million dollars. The company offices were in Leadville, but the firm planned to develop holdings throughout the region, principally in the Massive City area. By the end of the summer of 1880, however, it was discovered that most of the claims weren't worth developing and the rich properties weren't as extensive as first believed. By 1881 the community had already passed its peak. Only about 100 or 200 miners were on hand to take what they could from the mountain. The residents had to make do with only two saloons and one gambling hall.

There was some excitement that year, however. It seems a German miner named Shults went beserk and shot up to the town. As far as is known, he didn't hurt anyone, but he made a lot of noise. He escaped capture and barricaded himself in his cabin where he continued to shoot up and down the Main Street from his own little fortress. The rest of the men in town hid themselves in a saloon a short distance away from Shults' cabin. Before long the German's bullets were spent and he came storming out of his cabin only to collapse in the street. He was captured and arrested. The town returned to normal—for another year or two. And Massive City died quietly.

## BUSK and HAGERMAN PASS

Herein lies a stormy little section of Colorado history, bringing on stage one of the state's lesser-known but more important tycoons, James J. Hagerman.

Hagerman accumulated his first fortune, and a bad case of tuberculosis, in Michigan and Wisconsin. He came to Colorado in 1884 when doctors warned him he wouldn't live more than a year or two if he remained in the moist Great Lakes region.

Hagerman didn't waste time. He invested in mines in the Leadville area and purchased controlling interest of the Mollie Gibson mine at Aspen, which brought him millions. He had a hand in some coal mines and other things around the state, but Hagerman's big interest was in the Cripple Creek boom.

He was president of the Isabel and Zenobia Mining and Milling Company. He had many other interests here and was one of the prime figures in the development of Cripple Creek city itself. But Hagerman is most remembered for his amazing little railroad, the Colorado-Midland.

The 238-mile railroad was the first standard gauge to cross the Rockies. It cut through some of the wildest and most difficult country in the state in its run from Colorado Springs to Aspen. It cost Hagerman millions to build, but it made him a fortune as well.

The run from Colorado Springs to Cripple Creek was one of the most popular tourist runs in the state. Teddy Roosevelt said the beauty of the surrounding countryside "bankrupts" the English language.

Hagerman encountered his most difficult problem in extending the railroad from Leadville to Aspen. He ran the track up and over Hagerman Pass and through Hagerman Tunnel near the top of Mount Massive. The short section cost him millions to build, and once it was built, it cost him millions to keep open. He did find some metals in making the tunnel.

In the winter of 1899, an army of snow-shovelers and the constant bucking of snow engines couldn't open the route. That winter forced Hagerman to buy the Busk-Ivanhoe tunnel, built some 500 feet down the hill. The two-mile long tunnel cost twenty lives and three million dollars in the building. Hagerman picked it up for four million. The run from Leadville to Aspen was one of the busiest from then on, important not only to mining but also to the tourist trade. But with the development of good highways and other railroads, the importance of the Colorado-Midland

230

slowly dwindled—the western end first. The last train roared through the Busk-Ivanhoe tunnel in 1918. The same year the tunnel was purchased by a fellow named Carleton, who renamed it the Carleton tunnel and operated it for a number of years as an auto toll tunnel with varying degrees of success.

Hagerman lost the last of his many fortunes in railroad and farming in New Mexico and Texas.

## IVANHOE

At the western end of the Busk-Ivanhoe tunnel was Ivanhoe, an improbable and nearly unlivable town which served as a railroad stop and a residence for construction workers. The town was named for nearby Lake Ivanhoe which was so called by a Scottish settler. He thought it reminded him of Lock Ivanhoe in his native land.

Ivanhoe had a post office in 1888. There were also a number of railroad buildings and cabins here. The Colorado-Midland track was routed by the lake. In 1908, an engine of a slow-moving passenger train capsized and almost slid into the lake. It took all the king's horses and all the king's men to right the engine again.

## HELLGATE, NAST, SELLAR, NORRIE, BIGLOW (Quinn's Spur), MUCKAWANGO (Riley's), THOMASVILLE, CALCIUM and TROUTVILLE (Wood's Lake)

Save for Troutville, these were all stations on the Colorado-Midland. Most of the towns had other occupations to keep them busy.

Hellgate was a point of greatest excitement on the Colorado-Midland run. It was little more than a lookout point, but the railroad would usually stop the trains here to give the passengers a thrill. From the point, passengers could get a chilling view of Nast, almost directly below, and a broad view of some of the most beautiful and primitive country in Colorado.

Nast was, and is, a resort village. A lodge-hotel, a store, several cabins and other buildings were constructed in the early 1900's and the town did a thriving business as long as the Midland ran. It has been kind of sleepy since.

Sellar was primarily a station, although some logging was done here. It had one of the first post offices in the valley. It was closed down in 1918.

Norrie was primarily a lumber camp. During the 90's, the camp had as many as 200 persons. There were a school, a post office, a large building which housed a store, sawmill, lumber yard and dancehall, and about fifty lumberjack houses.

Biglow was primarily a lodge and also a loading spur for lumber. The town was named for Mrs. Biglow, the first postmistress.

231

Muckawango (Indian for "place where bear walks") began as a lumber loading spur, but it developed into a favorite tourist area. There were a summer camp here and several picnic facilities. It is still a good picnic area, and there are some cabins around.

Thomasville was a settlement around the St. Louis and Colorado smelter. There was also a small mine, the Bessie, a short distance outside of town. This was in the very early 90's. The smelter closed down in 1892, but there was still some activity of various sorts for several years. From about 1912 to 1915 it was a construction camp for the Colorado Power Company's power line from Glenwood Springs to Denver. The town also served as a farm community. Thomas was a preacher who also ran the smelter for a while.

Calcium was one of the first settlements in the Upper Frying Pan area. It lasted a couple of years before it lost out to Thomasville, a half mile away. Limestone was quarried here by the Calcium Limestone Company.

Troutville is north of the Colorado-Midland run. It was made into a resort in the early 1890's, and still exists as such.

*And Then There were . . . . JUNCTION HOUSE, WELLER and LORIMER* (not on map) three more station stops on Independence Pass. Junction House was the first stop on the Aspen side and at the junction where the road turns off toward Ruby. Weller, stage stop, toll station and horse change, was twelve miles from Aspen. Lorimer was a short distance from Everett . . . . *EAGLE SAMPLER* (not on map) a small camp not far from Independence and around the mill for which it was named. It was large enough to have a post office . . . . *CRYSTAL LAKE*, a lesser resort between Twin Lakes and Leadville. The town and station stop was a short distance below the lake . . . . *DOUGLASS CITY* (not on map) a wild and woolly construction camp at the western opening of Hagerman Tunnel. The camp experienced a rowdy existence as long as the work lasted. Eight saloons and one dance hall were reportedly among the first buildings up in the town and they remained about the busiest places as long as the town lasted. Douglass City was apparently a few hundred feet above the site of latter-day Ivanhoe. . . . *HAMILTON*, there were some vague references to a town a short distance south and west of Winfield that was called Hamilton. The town lived during the mining excitement in that area.

# XII. WHITE GOLD

Skiing in Colorado is nothing new. Prospectors and miners learned early that the long boards were the fastest, and often the easiest, way to get them where they wanted to go.

In those early days skis were called "snow-shoes." What we call snow-shoes today were known as "webs." The skis, or snowshoes, were various shapes, often haphazard creations of the wearer. Some early photographs show them as narrow and short, about half the size of today's skis, but the longer European skis were not unknown in the early days of Colorado.

In many areas the miner would ski down to town after a day's work in the mines. He would use his skis for traveling long distances since they were much faster than webs. During the early days of the Aspen and Leadville booms, one man was said to have made the distance between the two cities in one day, still a record.

Father Dyer carried the word of God and the mail to distant snow-locked pockets of the mountains on his Norwegian-type skis which were nine to eleven feet in length. His skis are credited with saving his life. Losing his balance on a steep mountain incline, the snow-shoe itinerant used his skies to break his fall and to guide him safely into a snowbank and away from a precipice that would have meant certain death.

Skiing for pleasure is nothing new to Colorado either. Several areas had special hills where mine-town residents would spent their free time sledding and skiing. The hill running from Nevadaville to Black Hawk was one such pleasure hill. Some early ski clubs were formed in such places as the Crested Butte and Gold Hill areas. There was some competition too.

Modern skiing began in Colorado in the 20's and 30's when a few snow pioneers began spending their week-ends on the slopes. Ski tows were unheard of then. Cross country skiing was the thing.

One of these pioneers was Arthur Kidder. Kidder began skiing at the age of forty. He is still skiing. He has climbed some of Colorado's highest peaks, and traveled great distances on his ski. Yes, his ski! Kidder lost one leg while a child, and has become one of Colorado's best skiers, although one-legged.

Commercial skiing, although well-developed in many areas of Colorado, is relatively new to the state. In fact, virtually all of the slopes, the ski tows, and other facilities have been installed since World War II.

Aspen was one of the first areas to be developed. It is known the world over now, but it is still being developed. New facilities are added almost every year.

The idea of turning Aspen into a winter sports area began with Billy

Fiske, an international sportsman, and two Colorado natives, Thomas and Edward Flynn. The three talked of skiing one day in 1936 in sunny California. Fiske thought it was time to develop the popular European sport in the western United States. The elder Flynn suggested Aspen as a possible site for their project. Fiske, the Flynns, and others came to Colorado. Fiske fell in love with the Aspen area at first sight.

The group formed a company. They built the first lodge near the site of Highland, and began developing ski facilities. The most important part of their project was interesting others. It was slow moving, but attention picked up.

Then came World War II. Fiske was the first American pilot in the Royal Air Force to be killed. Without Fiske, Flynn and the others lacked a leader in the Aspen project. It was abandoned.

However, the war saw the beginning of a new kind of U. S. soldier, the ski-trooper. Most of these soldiers were trained at Camp Hale in Colorado. One of the top instructors was Friedl Pfeifer, an Austrian slats champion.

Pfeifer saw Aspen, and he too fell in love with it, and saw its possibilities as a winter sports area. After the war he returned to Colorado, determined to turn Aspen into the top ski resort in the country. He trained Aspen children in the fine art of skiing—free. Soon the whole town was behind him. Pfeifer was the leader, but virtually everyone had a hand in the Aspen renaissance.

The main idea was to keep the spirit of Aspen, the mining town, alive, and thus lend some atmosphere. This would mean restoring some of the houses a bit, fixing the streets. The idea caught on—and Aspen now sports many restaurants and boarding houses with such picturesque names as "The Roaring Fork," the "Red Onion," and the "Prospector."

After the long three-and-one-half mile chair lift—the world's longest—was built on Aspen Mountain, making available trails over four miles in length, Aspen really came into its own. To keep up the flavor of the mining atmosphere, many of the trails retained the name of the mining areas they crossed—Smugglers, Tourtelotte Park, Little Nell.

Walter Paepcke, a Chicago financier who owned the Perry Ranch near Colorado Springs, was the guiding force in the cultural renaissance of Aspen. Paepcke saw the possibilities of turning Aspen into a year-round resort. Since he came to Aspen right after World War II, top notch concerts, dramas and seminars have been held in the mountain kingdom. Leaders in many fields have come here. A unique tent-amphitheatre has been erected to give the cultural events a comfortable home. Several new symphonies have made their debuts in Aspen. Some of the world's greatest minds gather here to discuss and debate current and philosphical issues.

234

There is even an ultra modern health center where the tired businessman can spend a few weeks getting a physical and intellectual retread.

The old Hotel Jerome has been completely rejuvenated, although retaining its historical aura. The old opera house and other buildings have been restored. Aspen has a bright new look for an old mining town. It is a curious mixture of the new and the old, the foreign and domestic.

The nature lover and the outdoorsman are not neglected in the rebirth of Aspen country. Some of the state's most beautiful scenery is found in this area. Scores of fishing lakes and hundreds of miles of fishing stream are found within a short distance of Aspen.

But Aspenites know this rebirth is due to "King Snow," Colorado's White Gold. For years it was the state's biggest trouble-maker, the nemesis of prospectors, miners and travelers since Colorado territory began. Now it is giving Aspen another chance, as it is giving many other areas in Colorado a second chance.

In a few short years since World War II, more than thirty skiing areas in Colorado have been developed or are being developed. At least a dozen more are being planned. Frank Kistler of Denver has begun work to turn the Redstone area into a resort to rival even Aspen. In years to come, several other areas in Colorado will see commercial skiing, perhaps many areas now locked by the mountains and the snow and deserted since the prospectors left. Some of Colorado's most beautiful country is locked from view.

The possible ski runs in Colorado are endless. They rank with the longest and the best in the world. Colorado snow is the best. It blankets the hills longer than any other section in the country.

Mining is still carried out on a wide scale in Colorado. It will be for years. But snow is the element in Colorado's future. It is a multi-million dollar business—and the resource is replenished every year.

*MAP THIRTEEN*
### ASPEN COUNTRY
Ute City
Roaring Fork City
Aspen (Ute City, West Aspen, Ute Springs, Smuggler Mountain)
Tourtelotte (Tourtelotte Park)
Ashcroft (Castle Forks City)
Highland (Chloride)
Coopers Camp
Hell Gate and Maroon Creek
Carey's Camp

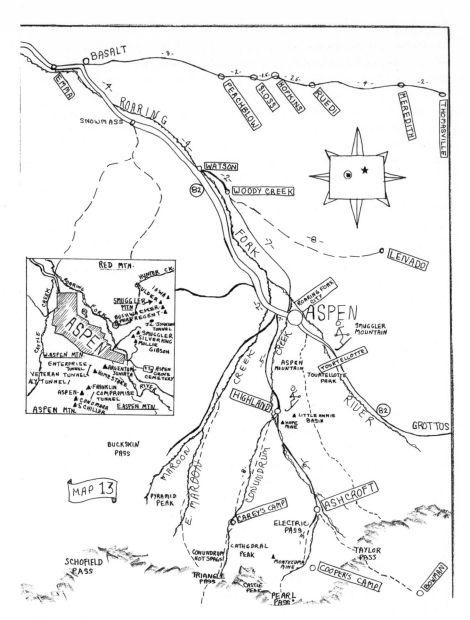

MAP 13

Lenado
Emma
Basalt (Frying Pan City, Aspen Junction)
Peachblow (Wilson's Quarries), Sloss (Sloane), Hopkins, Ruedi, Meredith

236

## UTE CITY

Ute City was one of the first "cities" laid out in the Aspen area by a group of prospectors whose hunger for gold was stronger than their fear of Indians. The city, which was little more than a tent city, was laid out in 1879, near where Maroon, Castle and Hunter Creeks run into the Roaring Fork. A large party came here, but many couldn't stomach the constant fear of Indians and returned to civilization. Those who remained kept a constant lookout for Indians. No campfires were allowed at night, no matter how cold. And a guard was on duty at all times.

The town was platted and elaborate plans were made, but by the following year another city was getting its start a short distance away, and the Ute City residents joined the crowd. The new city was to be known as Aspen.

## ROARING FORK CITY

Another promoter's city that didn't get much further than the drawing board. A group of Leadville town promoters laid out an elaborate city in 1879 on high land between Maroon and Castle Creeks, just west of the site of Aspen. The group, known as the Roaring Fork Townsite Company, named the site Roaring Fork City. The ballyhoo behind the planning was sufficient to cause the post office department to grant Roaring Fork City a post office rather than the nearby site of Aspen. But a post office was the only building erected in Roaring Fork City, and before it was used, Aspen, through sheer force of numbers, won title to the post office designation. The one building in Roaring Fork City was moved, lock, stock and pigeon hole, to Aspen.

## ASPEN (Ute City, Ute Springs, West Aspen, Smuggler Mountain)

Aspen's resplendant new life as one of the world's top year-round resorts is rapidly overshadowing its past as a mining town. But the "Crystal City of the Rockies" was at one time (1893) considered the richest silver-producing community in the world. The area ranks near the top in the production of precious metals in Colorado, and is second only to Leadville in the production of silver.

The Smuggler mine produced the largest "silver nugget" in the world, weighing 2,054 pounds. The nugget was more than 93 percent silver—purer than a silver dollar.

Aspen, however, had a slow start. Completely enclosed by towering mountains, and a stronghold of rampaging Indians, the Aspen area was neglected for several years while other mining camps bloomed in all directions.

The first hardy prospectors ventured into the region in the late 70's.

237

Fearing Indians, the party built a fortified encampment a short distance away from the present site of Aspen. They allowed no campfires, and a guard was posted at all times. The camp was called Ute City. The Indian fear was too much for many in the group. They returned to the "civilization" of Leadville in short order. The rest of the party left as winter approached.

In 1880, they returned. Some rich strikes were made. More prospectors came. The Indian fear lessened as the population grew. Soon small camps dotted the landscape: Old Ute City, Ute Springs, West Aspen, Smuggler, Roaring Fork City and Aspen City. Aspen soon overshadowed and absorbed the other camps.

Still the city grew slowly. Ashcroft, a dozen miles away, was favored by Taylor and Cottonwood Passes, still the only "good" roads into the area. Although the Aspen ore was rich, the cost of shipping it out was almost prohibitive.

The big rush came when New York financier Jerome B. Wheeler became interested in the area. His interest attracted others. B. Clark Wheeler (no relation), Henry Gillespie and other early Aspen settlers worked hard for the development of Aspen. They won support for the construction of a road over Independence Pass. Other roads were opened.

Aspen was on its way.

Its place as one of Colorado's top mining towns was solidified in 1887 when the Denver and Rio Grande entered the city. A few months later, in February of 1888, the Colorado-Midland train churned its way over Hagerman Pass and into Aspen, giving the city two railroads.

Most of the best mines were in production long before the railroads came. By the early 80's Aspen was producing in the millions. The city had a population of 12,000 by 1882. Banks, churches, schools and other businesses were going up. A $120,000 Opera House was built and a $90,000 hotel.

By 1887, Aspen's peak year, the population had increased to about 15,000. Three daily and three weekly newspapers were published. There were three large schools and a $20,000 hospital. The following year, Aspen became the first Colorado city to have electric lights.

The railroads were the greatest single factor in Aspen's prosperity. Previously, small and slow ore wagons ambled over the arduous mountain passes. There weren't enough wagons to carry all Aspen could produce. Lower grade ore wasn't touched and much good ore was stored while waiting its turn for shipment. The wagons charged from $50 to $100 a ton for ore shipped.

The railroads could ship out everything, quickly, and charged from $10 to $15 a ton.

Although Aspen was known as a gala "Saturday Night town," it lacked much of the violence and bloodshed that marked many other boom camps. Perhaps the unruly element was too rooted in Leadville to journey across the mountains. But most of the credit goes to the early settlers, a high-caliber lot who got things going smoothly and sanely, and kept them going that way.

Some boom cities never did have a church. Aspen had ten built during the eighties. Three schools were operating by 1882. Several social and intellectual clubs were formed those first years. The cultural atmosphere which marks present-day Aspen had its roots in the city's initial growth.

Aspen's early "elite" were conversant with the fashions of New York and Europe.

Opera wasn't out of place in Aspen. The story goes a widely-known concert singer was delayed on her trip to the remote mining camp. The capacity audience remained seated in the Opera House until two o'clock in the morning when the star arrived. And the curtain went up.

The Opera House was gutted by two fires in 1912. It was restored in 1947, and is still a favorite rendevous for the Aspen elite.

Wheeler (Jerome) was also one of the builders of the Hotel Jerome, a lavish three-story building that was completed in 1889 at a cost of one million dollars. The furnishings were imported from the east and from Europe at great expense. The Grand Ball which opened the hotel was one of the most colorful affairs those tired old mountains had ever seen.

In restoring the hotel in recent years, the owners kept most of the early furnishings intact.

Another early-comer to Aspen was Henry Tourtelotte. After a lifetime of unprofitable prospecting in Colorado, he struck it rich in Aspen, locating several mines. He located and developed the park near the mines on the mountain above Aspen.

Henry Gillespie had a big hand in the development of Aspen. He became rich and a civic leader. His efforts were successful in getting a telegraph line built over Independence Pass. He also gave Aspen a fire bell.

J. D. Hooper was another carpenter-turned-prospector. He leased the Aspen claim and discovered the amazing Hooper stope a few days before the lease expired and while working on credit. In the final days of his lease, he dug out $600,000 worth of ore.

Eben Smith, a partner of Chaffee in Central City, hit it richer in Aspen. He built a beautiful home in Aspen, then moved to Denver.

Another prominent man-about-town was D. H. Hyman, who made a fortune in the Aspen mines and spent a great deal of money in the city's first years.

B. Clark Wheeler was one of the very first civic leaders. In fact, he platted the townsite. He was vital to the early development of Aspen. He started the *Aspen Times* and married the daughter of Davis H. Waite, Aspen's most famous son.

Waite was a judge in Aspen. In 1892, at the age of 67, he was elected governor, the most controversial the state has ever had. He jumped into national prominence with his "bloody bridles" statement. He merely said: "It were better that blood should flow to the horses' bridles than that our national liberties should be destroyed." Waite claimed he took the term from the Bible and it was later proved that he did. But the source was ignored as newspapers around the world blasted Colorado's blood-thirsty governor.

"Bloody Bridles" Waite, as he was called, was one of the founders of the National Populist party. The party platform called for the direct election of senators by the voters, an eight-hour working day, the secret ballot, establishment of an income tax, the right of workers to organize and strike, and other things taken for granted today, but most radical in those days. During the depression which began in 1893, Waite made use of the *Union Era* newspaper to champion the nation's workers and farmers.

A result of the overall populist movement was the march on Washington by "Coxey's Army." The march was similar to the veteran's bonus march on Washington in 1932.

Waite's fair and expert handling of the first Cripple Creek strike brought about a just and relatively non-violent settlement. The union permitted Governor Waite to act as its arbitrator and the strike settlement favored the union miners. This was in 1893-94, years before the working man was given much bargaining power, if any at all.

One of the governor's greatest friends in later years was "Big" Bill Haywood, one of the national leaders in union development and Colorado history's top union man.

Despite the social living in early Aspen, mining was the thing. It remained so for several years.

Aspen itself rests on rich minerals, and some mining was actually done in the city. Several other good mines were located nearby in the mountains overlooking the city. Echoes of mine blasts were a constant reminder of the importance of mining to Aspen. For several years the miners carried candles to light their way to and from work in the mines. A change of shifts at night would mean an eerie parade snaking up and down the mountainside.

The Mollie (or Molly) Gibson was Aspen's most famous mine. It was located in 1880 and the ore assayed as high as $5,000 a ton. The large silver nugget was found on property that was later consolidated into the Mollie Gibson mine. The mine had many owners and several Coloradans outside of Aspen invested in the mine. It produced millions, although some of the profits were wasted on litigation.

The Aspen mine was second in dividends in the area. The mine, another early discovery, was owned by Wheeler and made the man a millionaire.

The Aspen, although only a small claim at first, produced $300,000 a month for years. One day's work paid as much as $100,000. The first electric tram ever built to haul ore down from a mine was installed here.

A half-mile from Aspen via a dirt road running from Ute Avenue is the Durant, another great mine which has been worked in recent years. The Durant was located in 1879, and purchased shortly thereafter by Hyman. Hyman developed the mine and soon had it paying an average of $150,000 a month. The property overlapped the Aspen property, resulting in lengthy litigation which cost a total of nearly a half-million dollars and finally ended in compromise. Now a waterfall high on the mountain disappears into one of the Durant shafts.

The Midnight, six miles over a winding dirt road, is located 200 feet east of the top of Roch ski run. One chamber of the Emma mine paid off a half-million dollars.

In 1884, the mines produced a total of $3,500,000. This was doubled by 1888, and tripled the following year, Aspen's best mining year. For the next couple of decades, Aspen produced an average of about $6,000,000 per year.

The city was hit hard by the silver panic of 1893 when Aspen was considered the greatest silver camp in the world. The city was never the same after that. Some 1,800 miners were thrown out of work. The population dropped to 2,000, where it remained for several years.

Gillespie and B. Clark Wheeler went broke. Jerome Wheeler took bankruptcy.

But Aspen survived. Shortly after the panic, miners agreed to take a cut in wages to keep the mines open. Within a few years, other minerals were discovered to keep the city going.

From 1899 to 1908, mines in the area produced nearly $16,000,000 in silver, more than ten million dollars in gold, plus millions in lead, copper and other metals.

Water was another problem at the Aspen mines. Work was stopped in 1910 at the Smuggler and other properties because of flooded shafts. Many suggestions were made in an effort to solve the problem, but the lower

241

pumps seemed hopelessly clogged and most people feared the mines were closed for good.

One of the most improbable solutions was made by Elias Cohn, general manager of the Smuggler and Aspen mines. Cohn suggested hiring deep sea divers to open the bottom pumps. The idea was generally scoffed at, but when every other plan had been discarded, he was given the go-ahead. Cohn hired a team of deep sea divers from back east at tremendous expense. But, within hours, the team had the pumps working and the mines dry. A short time later, however, the mines flooded again. The divers were called back; not only did they open the pumps but they stayed on to train some local talent in the art of deep sea diving.

After that, the mines produced for years.

Mining fell off during World War I and the twenties. The population dwindled. Several cabins were torn down. Many of Aspen's once-proud buildings were falling into ruin. Aspen seemed headed toward Colorado's vast "junk heap" of cities.

Then, the "White Gold," which had been there all the time, was discovered.

GOLD DUST: A famous legal battle in Colorado railroad history took place when the Colorado-Midland and the Denver and Rio Grande battled for right-of-way within Aspen. Since the D. & R.G. won the race to the city it had prior rights. The Colorado-Midland had to circle around Aspen to enter the community . . . . for several years during its boom, Aspen had as many as ten trains arrive at its station per day . . . . not only was Aspen considered the world's greatest silver mining camp, but during the late 80's and 90's, it served as the largest commercial center between Denver and Salt Lake City . . . . the Aspen Valley now serves as a fertile farming and ranching area . . . . as with most Colorado mining camps, Aspen was originally supported by placer mining with lode mining coming later . . . . During its heyday, Aspen had six fire companies, 33 lawyers and free mail delivery. The fire companies were among Colorado's best and prettiest, and frequently placed high in state competition . . . . the two mile long Cowenhaven tunnel carried ore from several of the mines.

BEST MINES: Mollie Gibson, Aspen, Durant, Midnight, Smuggler, Montezuma, Newman, Emma, Free Silver, Lone Pine, Argentum, Juniata, Castle, Washington, Vallejo, Compromise, Bush Whacker and Park Regent.

*TOURTELOTTE* (Tourtelotte Park)

Henry Tourtelotte came to Aspen early. He located several good claims up on Aspen Mountain, but he soon wearied of climbing up the hill every day to work on his diggings. He decided to build a home of his own in a grove on the mountain near his claims. His grove was named Tourtelotte Park, and the community that grew around his cabin was known as Tourtelotte.

Miners, who didn't care for the excitement in Aspen below, also built cabins here. During its peak Tourtelotte had more than 500 residents, most of them miners who worked in mines developed by Henry Tourtelotte.

More than four million dollars have been taken from the Tourtelotte mines.

In the old days an electric tramway ran from Aspen to Tourtelotte. Now a ski tow soars over the park to the top of Ajax Mountain and the Sun Deck. On the way down the mountain through the Dipsy Doodle Run, the skiers glide swiftly over the deserted site of the old mining camp.

## ASHCROFT (Castle Forks City)

Ashcroft got its start about the same time as Aspen, and for a while it threatened to outdistance the new community to the east. It was the railroad and the ores that made the difference.

At first, Ashcroft could only be reached over Taylor Pass, an arduous pass closed most of the winter and dangerous all of the time. To negotiate the pass it was necessary for stage or wagon drivers to disassemble the stage or wagon, and lower or raise it piece by piece over cliff walls as high as 40 feet.

Another arduous, though widely-used, pass which favored Ashcroft over Aspen was Cottonwood Pass. The route, which emptied into Taylor Pass, was the predecessor of Independence Pass and for a long while, until the latter was opened, was the major road from the Leadville side of the mountains into Aspen country.

During these years Ashcroft was the gateway to the Aspen area and therefore a more important city than Aspen.

But Aspen, through sheer perseverance and richer strikes, began to take over the limelight. And when the Denver and Rio Grande reached Aspen in 1887, the jig was up with Ashcroft. A few die-hards held out, hoping the railroad would be extended to Ashcroft. It wasn't, and eventually all the Ashcroftians moved into Aspen, many taking their cabins with them.

T. E. Ashcraft, early Colorado scout, mountain man, Indian fighter, miner and jack of all trades, was among the first prospectors to strike pay-dirt here in 1879.

Therein lies the confusion concerning the name. Many believed the community was named after Ashcraft, and the post office couldn't make out the spelling of the name. Others records show, however, the site was named for the ash trees abounding in the croft here. "Croft" is an Anglo-Saxon word meaning small enclosed field.

Fear of Indian attacks hampered the early development of the community, but a full-fledged city was established by 1880. During the boom, which lasted three years, Ashcroft had three hotels, a school, several saloons and many other busines enterprises.

Ashcroft was just as rowdy as the rest, if not more so. Other than Sam Ashcraft, the community was blessed with a visit by Bob Ford, the man who shot Jesse James and was shot himself ten years later in Creede, and H. A. W. Tabor and his lady love, Baby Doe.

Tabor purchased the Tam O'Shanter mines in 1881 and came to Ashcroft the following year. He built a lavish home, paneled with gold-encrusted wallpaper, for his new bride. Whenever Baby Doe came to town, Tabor declared a 24-hour holiday with free drinks for everybody. Baby Doe was well-liked in Ashcroft.

But even Tabor and all his millions couldn't keep a dead dog alive. Ashcroft faded rapidly. By the late 80's the city was all but deserted.

Only one man lived in Ashcroft for many years. His name was Jack Leahy, the hermit of Ashcroft. He died in 1939.

The Ashcroft region has come alive in recent years as a resort area. It has a mighty long way to go before it can compare with its ancient rival, Aspen, but it's got its start. And the phenomenal growth of Aspen as a resort may well spill over into Ashcroft.

The Four Seasons Club and Bavarian Lodge have been built near Ashcroft, and numerous cabins erected. Some skiing is done here, and the "croft" has excellent hunting and fishing possibilities. Alaskan dog sleds were introduced here as a special tourist attraction. Stuart Mace, who runs the dog teams, often hires them out for movie-making. Several movies have been made in this region.

BEST MINES: Tam O'Shanter and Montezuma

*HIGHLAND* (Chloride)

Highland was one of the towns founded by prospectors disgusted by their luck at Aspen. Some fairly good strikes were made in the surrounding hills in 1879. When about 500 others were lured to the area, the Highland Town Company laid out a city in a little protective cove at the foot of the mountains.

Some good mineral pockets were found but no good veins. There was little gold, but some good galena, silver, native copper, lead, carbonates and iron.

The population of Highland leveled off at about 300 in 1880. There were about 200 buildings in the town, including three stores and about the same number of saloons. The constant fear of Indians helped keep down the population.

The best part of the boom was over by 1881, although there was some activity here for several years. There was a slight upsurge around 1889, and 1890, although many of the new residents worked in the Little Annie Mill.

In 1910, the Hope Mining, Milling and Leasing Company started a tunnel a mile above Highland in an effort to hit the Little Annie Mine. The firm bored into the hill for a distance of three miles. Some ore was found but far below expectations. The tunnel was abandoned in the early twenties.

The first skiing experiments in the Aspen area centered near Highland. For the most part, the development was forgotten shortly after it began. Now they are taking it up again.

The nearby Highland-Bavarian Lodge represents the new life of the area; one old cabin represents the old mining life at Highland.

## COOPER'S CAMP

Another small camp around Ashcroft and Highland that grew around the iron mines found here. The mines and the camp weren't developed too much until the smelter was built in Aspen. Later, when the railroads were built into Aspen, it was cheaper to ship the iron in, and Cooper's Camp was soon forgotten.

Some old foundations and the ruins of some cabins at the end of a short trail mark the site of Cooper's Camp today.

## HELL GATE and MAROON CREEK

An 1882 newspaper made passing mention of Hell Gate as "that busy little mining town." Since the Hell Gate Mine was one of the larger mines on Maroon Creek, and since many large mines had camps around them, the Hell Gate referred to in the report probably was the Hell Gate on Maroon Creek.

(There was a Hell Gate on Hagerman Pass but it was a lookout point and little more.)

There were several fairly good mines up and down Maroon Creek, but with the possible exception of Hell Gate, they were just scattered settlements and no official towns. If there was a town it was called Maroon Creek since most reports referred to the section as if it could be either a town or area.

The best mines on the creek were Hell Gate, Dexter, Big Six, Montana, Sunset, Durango, Parallel, Johnstone, Occidental and Maroon Chief.

## CAREY'S CAMP

Carey's Camp is most remembered for the tragic snowslide of March, 1884, when the whole town was buried and five men—the only occupants of the camp at the time—were killed.

The bodies of the five men were found about a month later. A dog was found under 25 feet of snow at the same time. He must have been buried by the same slide, but miracle of miracles, he was still alive. The dog, "Bruiser" by name, was taken back to Aspen where he completely recovered. He became a hero of sorts and the town mascot. His badge of distinction was a solid silver collar, presented him by the citizens of Aspen.

A man named Abe Lee built a cabin here a year or two before the prospectors came. In 1882, a Captain Carey located some claims up Conundrum Gulch, about seven miles from Highland. His discovery started a small rush. Many claims were staked. Some fairly good placer finds were made but they never found the mother lode. In a short while most of the men who stayed were working for Carey.

The camp had a post office, store and about a dozen cabins. A wagon road was built up the gulch in 1883 and plans were being made to extend the road over the divide so there would be a direct route from Aspen to Gothic. But the road never materialized.

In 1912, years after Carey's Camp was deserted, a bathhouse and some cabins were built around the hot springs here. It was a popular camp grounds for a while. Everything but the springs is gone now.

The creek was originally named West Castle Creek. It was changed to Conundrum, however, after a disappointed prospector remarked: "Boys, it sure is a conundrum."

## LENADO

Lenado was a fairly small camp at the foot of Porphyry Mountain, where the only good mines on Woody Creek were located. About a quarter of a million dollars was taken from the mines here.

The site erupted with activity in the 80s when A. J. Varney located a rich vein of lead and zinc ore. He formed the Varney Tunnel Company and began to bore a tunnel into the mountain. There were several other claims staked, but few amounted to much. Before long, most of the men were working for Varney.

He employed 150 men at one time. At its peak, the town was inhabited by about 300 people. There were a post office, sawmill, large company boarding house, two saloons, a store, a number of cabins, and a large barn to house the company burros.

The road to Lenado was rugged. There was talk of improving and extending the trail for a more direct connection to Aspen, but little was done about it. In 1888, the Denver and Rio Grande made plans to run a spur to Lenado. The railroad graded the road bed, but never laid any tracks.

The town almost died, but was revived in the early 90's when a large lead mill was erected here. Then lead prices slumped. The mill closed down and Lenado was all but deserted again.

246

Varney and Company resumed operations about 1905, reopening the mine and mill, and erecting a sawmill. It wasn't too profitable, however, and the company closed down in 1906.

The mine was reopened for a short while in 1917 when zinc was needed for the war effort. The sawmill is still operating now and again.

## EMMA

Emma was a Denver and Rio Grande station, section house and water tank near Basalt, the corresponding station on the Colorado and Midland. In addition to the railroad facilities, there were several cabins, a store and a post office. The first postmistress was Mrs. Emma D. Garrison, for whom the town was named.

## BASALT (Aspen Junction, Frying Pan City)

Frying Pan City was a wild and woolly railroad construction town along the Colorado-Midland line going to Aspen. The railroad construction towns had their camp followers, including the gamblers and the gals.

It was still a pretty wild place after the construction crews moved on and the town became an important station stop. It was called Aspen Junction then. The big excitement was the train wreck.

On July 18, 1891, a Midland locomotive rammed into an excursion train. A check valve on the locomotive broke in the crash, shooting hot steam over passengers in one car of the other train. Ten persons were killed and almost every survivor in the car was badly scalded.

The town later settled back to a peaceful existence as a ranching and tourist center. The name was dignified by the title of Basalt, named for Basalt Peak which rises above the community.

## PEACHBLOW (Wilson's Quarries), SLOSS (Sloane), HOPKINS, RUEDI and MEREDITH

More stops along the Colorado and Midland run from Hagerman pass.

Peachblow was a small settlement where workers at the nearby red sandstone quarries lived. The quarries shipped out a lot of sandstone in its day. A Chicago builder once ordered 3,000 carloads in 1890.

Sloss was one of the original sidings on the Colorado and Midland. It was also a cattle camp operated by S. P. Sloss of Basalt.

Hopkins was a siding on the railway.

Ruedi was a railroad station and section house. The town was large. enough to have a school and post office. It was named for John Ruedi who built a cabin here before the railroad came through.

Meredith was also a limestone quarry town, as well as being a lumber camp. There were several buildings here and much activity during the nineties. Now it is mostly a resort area.

# XIII. THE QUEEN OF ST. ELMO

Annabelle Stark was the toast of Salida before she moved to St. Elmo. She had a college education. Her beauty, fashionable clothes, and queenly bearing made her the talk of the town.

When her mother died, Annabelle moved to St. Elmo to cook and care for her two brothers, just as her mother had done.

St. Elmo was a bustling, prosperous city at the time. And, as expected, Annabelle brought a touch of culture to the community. Her home soon became the social center of the area. But Annabelle was more than a social butterfly. She was an angel to those down on their luck. She ministered to the sick and feeble. She was an inspiration in time of trial.

One winter when the Alpine tunnel was blocked with up to 25 feet of snow, she baked bread continuously for 12 days, only getting a few minutes sleep here and there, so that the work crews shoveling the track could eat.

That's how Annabelle was. It was easy to understand why she was called the "Queen of St. Elmo."

Then, slowly, St. Elmo began to fade. One by one, or by groups, the miners, prospectors and camp followers began to move off to greener pastures. Annabelle stayed on. One of her brothers died many years ago, but Tony Stark and Annabelle stayed on in St. Elmo. They ran a grocery store and supply store for summer tourists. They rented cabins to fishermen during the summer. Brother and sister lived here summer and winter down through the years. Much of the time they were isolated from the outside world. Most of the time they were alone.

In 1958, Annabelle was injured in an auto accident near St. Elmo. Tony, after all the years, finally had to ask the outside world for help.

It was then that authorities discovered Annabelle and her brother were suffering from malnutrition, although their general store was well-stocked with food. It was learned they were living in filth and squalor although bags full of silver dollars were later found in their twelve-room house adjoining the store. Annabelle and Tony Stark, both in their seventies, were incapable of taking care of themselves.

They were taken to the hospital in Salida. Tony died a few weeks later. Annabelle lingered on. The faded ribbon in her hair had become part of her hair. Her once-beautiful tresses had to be cut off to remove the ribbon and the filth.

More shocking was the condition of their home.

One room was completely full of firewood—something Annabelle and Tony would need during the long winter they spent alone. Other rooms were piled high with newspapers, including many valuable early editions. Here and there, among the newspapers and elsewhere, were bones and decayed pieces of food, carefully preserved bottle caps and tin cans, articles of clothing—the fashions of yesteryear, a bag of money. Somewhere, under it all, was a grand piano.

The store still remains, its shelves stocked with canned goods. Authorities are carefully preserving the adjoining house and studying the quantities of things within—squalid memories of the Queen of St. Elmo.

*MAP FOURTEEN*

## ST. ELMO TO MONARCH

Buena Vista (Cottonwood)
Cottonwood Springs
Harvard City
Free Gold
Helena
Nathrop (Chalk Creek)
Mt. Princeton Hot Springs (Haywood Hot Springs)
Hortense (Chalk Creek Hot Springs)
Alpine
Iron City
St. Elmo (Forest City)
Romley (Murphys Switch)
Hancock
 *Salida Insert*
Salida
Cleora (Bale's Station)
Turret
Whitehorn
Calumet
Poncha Springs
Maysville (Crazy Camp, Marysville)
Arbour-Villa (Arborville, Arbourville)
Garfield (Junction City)
Monarch (Camp Monarch, Chaffee City)
Shavano (Clifton)
Babcock

*And Then There Were:* Brown's Canyon, Centerville (or Centreville), Midway, Hecla (not on map), Hecla Junction, Cree's Camp, Alton or Altman's camp (not on map), Columbus and Cascade (either on map), Hangman Camp, Nine Mile House (not on map), Bullion City (not on map), Hartville, Atlantic, Alpine Station, Manoa, J. R. S. and Cosden (Wagontown).

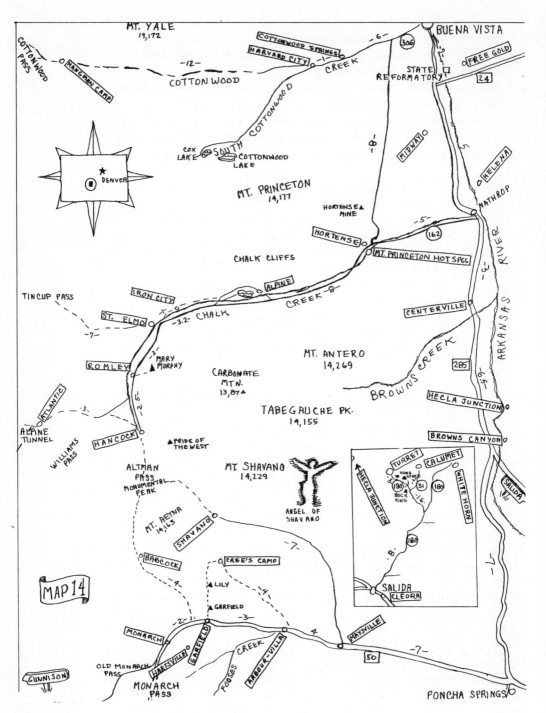

MT. YALE
19,172

COTTONWOOD SPRINGS

BUENA VISTA

COTTONWOOD PASS

HARGRAN CAMP

HARVARD CITY

306

COTTONWOOD

CREEK

STATE REFORMATORY

FREE GOLD

24

SOUTH

MIDWAY

HELENA

COX LAKE

COTTONWOOD

LAKE

NATHROP

MT. PRINCETON
14,177

HORTENSE MINE

162

HORTENSE

CHALK CLIFFS

MT. PRINCETON HOT SPGS

ARKANSAS RIVER

IRON CITY

ALPINE

CREEK

CENTERVILLE

TINCUP PASS

ST. ELMO

CHALK

MT. ANTERO
14,269

BROWNS CREEK

285

ROMLEY

MARY MURPHY

CARBONATE MTN.
13,874

HECLA JUNCTION

ATLANTIC

TABEGAUCHE PK.
14,155

BROWNS CANYON

ALPINE TUNNEL

HANCOCK

PRIDE OF THE WEST

TURRET

CALUMET

WILLIAMS PASS

ALTMAN PASS

MT. SHAVANO
14,229

MONUMENTAL PEAK

HORS LAKE

190

31

180

WHITE HORN

SALIDA

ANGEL OF SHAVANO

ROCK KING

MT. ETNA
14,163

SHAVANO

BABCOCK

CREE'S CAMP

MAP 14

LILY

SALIDA

CLEORA

GARFIELD

MONARCH

GARFIELD

MAYSVILLE

FORBES CREEK

ARBOUR-VILLA

50

GUNNISON

OLD MONARCH PASS

HARTSVILLE

MONARCH PASS

PONCHA SPRINGS

DENVER

250

## BUENA VISTA (Cottonwood)

Buena Vista (Spanish for beautiful view) was an important supply town in the development of the area.

Its growth paralleled that of Salida and there was much rivalry between the two points. In the county election of 1880, Buena Vista was voted the county seat by a large majority. But Salida appealed the vote, charging that Buena Vista cast 500 illegal votes. The state supreme court declared the election illegal but, nonetheless, awarded the county seat to Buena Vista.

The election was a telling blow against Salida, which was, even then, aspiring to be capitol of the state.

Buena Vista had a famous "hanging judge" named, oddly enough, Lynch. Judge Lynch handed out the death sentence with impunity and allowed no appeals of his convictions. Early visitors to Buena Vista found hanging bodies a common sight.

Today, Buena Vista is the site of the state reformatory and is still an important supply center for the ranching and farming area.

West of Buena Vista are three of the highest peaks in Colorado's towering Collegiate Range. To the southwest is Mount Princeton (14,200 feet), due west is Mount Yale (14,202), and to the northwest is Mount Harvard (14,417).

A couple of years back the eyes of the world were on a snow-locked 12,800-foot saddle between Mount Yale and Mount Harvard.

This was where Elijah spent the winter.

Elijah is an old bay horse, a lead horse in saddle jaunts out of Buena Vista. Elijah knows the mountains. His real name is Bugs, his owners said, because of his aversion to automobiles and women, especially women in slacks. His owners believe it was this aversion that finally made the horse "want to get away from it all."

An airplane sighted Elijah on the mountain during the winter of 1956-57. The animal became famous overnight. Pilots named him Elijah for the Biblical prophet who was fed by the ravens in the wilderness. "Operation Haylift" was launched and continued through the winter as planes dropped ton after ton of food to the horse. Money donations from throughout the nation helped finance the operation. Commercial airliners flew a few miles out of their way so the passengers could view Elijah's winter home. Running accounts of the horse's welfare appeared in newspapers as far away as London and Paris.

Came spring, Elijah was brought down from the mountain. All Buena Vista turned out in welcome. A few days later, Elijah was shunted into a

251

trailer for a series of personal appearances in Denver and other Colorado cities—filled with honking automobiles and women in slacks.

Then he went back to work in Buena Vista, his fling and moment of fame a thing of the past.

## COTTONWOOD SPRINGS

Historians have spent a lot of time battling over the location of this one-time town. Some say Cottonwood Springs was the predecessor of Buena Vista. Others contend it was a short distance outside of Buena and was eventually absorbed by it.

Its location is shown on early maps as about six miles west of Buena Vista. It would be an easy thing for a busy historian to get confused on something like that.

To add to the confusion, a source or two says Cottonwood Springs was once called Mahonville, for the two Mahon brothers who had land here. That wouldn't be so bad in itself, except for the fact there was a Mahon's Camp a short distance above Buena Vista.

See how things can get fouled up?

Anyhow, Cottonwood Springs was a favorite resort in the olden days. Hundreds would venture here to bathe in the medicinal hot springs (found six miles west of Buena Vista). The Indians used the place before the white men came.

The "springs" also served as a stop on the trail toward Cottonwood Pass. In fact, when the pass was active, around 1880, Cottonwood Springs was experiencing its biggest boom. When the trail lost its activity to Independence Pass, business at Cottonwood Springs dwindled.

Some say there was a little mining here, too, but then people would say anything.

## HARVARD CITY

Some gold was found in this area in the early 60's, but it wasn't until 1874 that a rich strike was made and Harvard City began. With the construction of Cottonwood Pass over the Divide, Harvard City also became an important supply center.

Cottonwood Pass was another perilous pass of the early mining days. It was frequently clogged with snow and always dangerous because of rock and snow slides. Many were killed in traveling the route. Records show one early merchant was forced to tunnel through 90 feet of snow and then lower his wares and wagon, piece by piece, over a 700 foot mountain wall.

Harvard City flourished through the 70's, boasting of a post office, a large dancehall and a number of saloons. It also became a voting precinct.

Then, when Independence Pass (first called Hunters Pass) was built over the Divide, and Cottonwood Pass was abandoned in 1882, Harvard City diminished rapidly and miners left for the newer and richer silver camps. Only a trace of this city remains.

## FREE GOLD

A small mining camp on the east bank of the Arkansas River, a mile and a half south of Buena Vista. The town was named for the mine on Gold Hill, believed to be about the only mining property around. The Free Gold Company was primarily a New York-owned organization. The town was pretty much a company town. There were a post office, store, saloon and modern stamp mill here. The peak population was about 150.

## HELENA

The town of Helena was located a short distance from Nathrop. Big John McPherson established the first post office in the county here in the mid-sixties and named it after his wife, Helena. The post office and town were soon taken over by Nathrop.

## NATHROP (Chalk Creek)

Although never a mining town, Nathrop once flourished as a supply station for the mining towns up Chalk Creek. It was also a farm town. The first grist mill in the Arkansas Valley was built here in 1868.

The site was originally called Chalk Creek and functioned as a stage stop in addition to its other duties. When the railroad came, the community was moved a mile and half to become a railroad station. At the same time the name was changed to Nathrop, believed to be a corruption of Nachtrieb, a merchant and freighter, who was part owner of the townsite. Nachtrieb was murdered in 1881.

This area is best remembered historically as the spot where Lt. Pike and his party spent a merry Christmas. The Pike party had traveled through deep snow for two days, eating snow and scraps of meat left on the ribs of wild animals. However, just before Christmas in 1807, the party killed eight buffalo and had a royal Christmas feast near here.

## MOUNT PRINCETON HOT SPRINGS (Haywood Hot Springs)

Here is another site first discovered and used by the Indians. It was a favorite camping ground for the red men. White men came along in later years and reaped a profit from it.

Development of the site began in the late 70's. Improvements were made through the years, until by 1917, the fabulous Antero Hotel was completed. The following year a small rock hotel and bathhouse was built below the larger structure.

For several years, the four-story Antero Hotel and its facilities represented a model of Victorian elegance and opulent living. Its many towers represented many forms of architecture.

It hit its peak in 1925, when the hotel cleared $12,000 and its owners (there were many) added a tennis court and golf course. The crash of 1929 caused its decline.

The hotel was razed in 1950, producing a million board feet of lumber. The foundation, including a swimming pool, can be seen from the road. The site recently became private property and was fenced off in 1958. The newer addition can be seen, almost intact, below the ruins of the Antero Hotel.

Mount Princeton Hot Springs may bloom again. A large youth camp has been built up the road. Several tourist cabins are near here and farther up Chalk Creek. Other camps have sprung up the hill toward Mount Princeton. The entire area is rapidly developing into an outdoorsman paradise, and perhaps in years to come, another lavish resort hotel will grow at Mount Princeton Hot Springs.

## HORTENSE (Chalk Creek Hot Springs)

A railroad station once stood opposite the exit of the Mount Princeton Hot Springs Hotel. The station and post office were called Hortense. But the cabins of Hortense were pretty much intermingled with those of the springs, a few above the station and more down around the creek.

It was difficult, if not impossible, to separate Hortense from Mount Princeton Hot Springs. Most of the miners who lived in the cabins worked in the Hortense mine, some 12,000 feet up Mount Princeton.

The mine was located in 1871, one of the first rich silver-producing mines in the area. Access to the mine was difficult and dangerous. Before Eugene Teats became manager of the mine and built a five mile wagon road to it, the ore was carried over a narrow ledge road which often spelled death if a misstep was made.

Teats, who was written up years later in the mining classic *Here They Dug the Gold*, managed the mine profitably for many years. But eventually the ore gave out, the mine was closed, and the part of Mount Princeton Hot Springs that was Hortense disappeared.

## ALPINE

There's a story of hidden treasure in the chalk cliffs above what used to be Alpine. It seems a party of Spanish gold-seekers passed through here many years ago—when the land belonged to the Indians. The Spaniards came upon an Indian village while the braves were off on a hunt. The invaders looted the village of many precious gold and silver trinkets and departed. But the braves returned shortly thereafter and gave chase. During the chase the Spaniards, to lighten their load, hid two mule skins full of their ill-gotten treasure somewhere among the chalk cliffs. Shortly thereafter, the Indians killed most of the looters, and if any escaped, they never came back.

They say those two muleskins of treasure remain until this day somewhere among the chalk cliffs on the side of Mt. Princeton. Whether the story is true or not, enough people have believed it to search the area for the treasure. Some have even lost their lives on the perilous cliffs, in search of the Indian treasure hidden many, many moons ago.

Many years after the origin of the legend, the city of Alpine arose, lived a short but exciting life, and then died.

The first cabin was built here in 1877. Then other cabins—then a town grew. Alpine flourished as a supply point for the other camps just starting farther along Chalk Creek, and was a jumping-off place for trips across the divide to Tin Cup, Pitkin and the cities beyond.

By 1880, when Alpine had an official population of just about 500 and an estimated or transient population up to ten times that figure, the city had two hotels, the Badger and Arcade, a lavish dance hall, 23 saloons, a newspaper *The True Fissure,* and several other less-colorful business houses.

When the Denver and South Park railroad arrived the following year, Alpine became even more of a center, and the railroad construction crews, among the toughest hombres of the early west, helped liven up the already live-wire town.

Alpine didn't have to take a back seat to anyplace as a rowdy town. Even after the ladies took over and brought in a school and a church, the competition between the good and the bad was pretty even. The story goes that a young boy was asked during one of the first Sunday school classes what Christ was doing on the Mount.

"Guess he was prospecting," the boy replied.

But just about the time Alpine was beginning to be quite a city, with three banks, a smelter or two and all the trimmings, the railroad reached St. Elmo, and St. Elmo became everything Alpine was.

The newspaper packed up and went to St. Elmo. So did the other businesses, and the miners and their families, many taking their cabins and stores with them.

Now only one tumbledown cabin remains from that earlier day, hidden among the cabins built in later years by outdoorsmen.

Alpine had its recluse. Madam Zabriski was called the Hermitess of Alpine, and spent much of her time looking for arrowheads in this old Indian stamping ground.

BEST MINE: Tilden.

## IRON CITY

Iron City, between St. Elmo and Alpine, had two excuses for being, and one was pretty flimsy.

A smelter was built here in 1880 which treated most of the ore of the Alpine District for many years. An electric generating plant was also built here that, for a very short period, furnished the power to run a dredge in Tin Cup. The power poles, all that remain of the ambitious but little used project, can still be seen running from the site, over Tin Cup Pass, and down toward Tin Cup.

After the railroad was built, and the ores could be shipped out by train, there was little excuse for Iron City and it didn't stay its welcome.

The Iron City reservoir was washed out many years ago and so was virtually all of the city. The site can be found a mile down a rugged side road just before the entrance of St. Elmo. The road curves around by Alpine and back to the main road. Fishermen take this route once in a while, but that's about all.

## ST. ELMO (Forest City)

St. Elmo, originally called Forest City, is one of the better preserved ghost towns, although tourist cabins have begun to mingle with the shanties of yesteryear. Sometimes it is difficult to distinguish between them.

Much of the old main street is still intact, including the Stark store (see above) and other false-fronted business houses that once did a thriving business. The old St. Elmo school is about two city blocks back from the main street in a clump of trees. A small stage, desks still in order, and the old pot-bellied stove can be seen inside the school. On the floor are the pages of several old school books. Apparently, when the school closed down, it did so with a vengeance.

St. Elmo was the biggest and most colorful city in the district. Although it derived much of its livelihood from the Mary Murphy mine, there were other mines around. It was a supply center and "Saturday Night Town" for the district, a jumping-off place for trips over Tin Cup and Alpine Passes, and it was a main station on the railroad.

The town came into being in the late 70's and was incorporated under the name of Forest City in 1880. The post office department balked at the name of Forest City because California had already made use of that name. So the post office was named St. Elmo, although the station remained Forest City for a few months.

St. Elmo flourished during the 80's and 90's and saw some activity until the 1920's. During its boom years it had a population of from 1,500 to 3,000, five hotels, a newspaper—*The St. Elmo Mountaineer*—and many other businesses. It was among the stops of Colorado's famous "itinerate

256

preacher," Father Dyer, and of Bishop Macheboeuf. The two men of God, in the early days, would preach wherever they could get a group together, often in saloons or gambling houses. But after the St. Elmo school was built in 1882, church services were held in the school.

Fire swept two blocks of the city in 1890. The post office was one of the buildings destroyed. The postmaster was both the hero and the goat in the conflagration. He saved the mail—at the expense of the liquor supply. BEST MINES: Mary Murphy, Pioneer, Iron Chest, Tressie C.

### ROMLEY (Murphy's Switch)

Romley grew around the Mary Murphy mine, by far the biggest mine in the Alpine district. Mary Murphy was a Denver nurse. A prospector, one of the men who located the mine, had been cared for by the nurse many months before and he never forgot her kindness.

The mine was located in the mid 70's by Dr. A. E. Wright and John Royal. The two soon sold the workings for $75,000. The new owners built a smelter in Alpine and further developed the mine, but the return they received was not encouraging and they sold the mine in 1880 for $80,000.

From then on, the Mary Murphy began to pay off—big. The mine made the three towns of Hancock, Romley and St. Elmo, and made the entire Alpine district prosperous.

The railroad arrived in Romley by 1883 which further stimulated development. A 5,000 foot tramway helped bring the ore down to the railroad.

An English company took over the operation of the mine in 1909 and spent an estimated $800,000 in improving it. Some 250 men were still working in the mine in 1916, but much of the activity ended abruptly the following year and the mine was completely closed by 1926.

It has been estimated the mines produced as much as sixty million dollars in gold, silver, lead, iron and zinc during its many years of operations. When it closed down, not only Romley died, but it spelled the death of the Alpine mining district.

As many as 2,000 people lived in or near Romley, called Murphy's Switch for a short time when the railroad came. The city was scattered among the trees all down the hill. Several well-preserved cabins can be seen on a flat just below the road, and many more cabins and the remains of cabins can be seen along the pathways winding back and forth down the hill. The ruins of a schoolhouse are about a quarter of a mile down a path which heads in the direction of Hancock.

### HANCOCK

The story of Hancock, for the most part, was the story of the Alpine Tunnel. Before the tunnel was completed in 1881, the miners, suppliers and

257

the like, had to take their chances with the unpredictable mountain passes: The Tin Cup pass from St. Elmo to Tin Cup, the Alpine Pass from Hancock to Pitkin and the Altman Pass from Hancock to Maysville. Snow closed these down much of the winter, and rock slides were always a danger.

Then the Denver and South Park railroad moved down Chalk Creek to Alpine, then to St. Elmo, and finally to Hancock. Then work on the tunnel began. The work was dangerous, and even after the tunnel was completed it took a lot of work to keep the tracks open because of the heavy snow. Large crews labored almost continuously during the winter months shoveling the deep snow from the tracks leading to the tunnel. Huge snowsheds were placed at strategic points along the incline, but they were not completely effective. Snowslides frequently roared down upon the trains, picking up railway cars on the way. One slide buried thirteen, men, women, and children under thirty feet of snow.

The grade from the tunnel entrance down to Hancock was one of the steepest railroad grades in the state. Locomotives were forced to use full brakes, and still the momentun was tremendous. Mark Twain reportedly made the trip just for the excitement, and later declared it was one of the most breath-taking experiences of his life.

It cost $100,000 a mile to build the tunnel—that's more than a million dollars a mile at today's prices. The initial outlay and the tremendous cost of upkeep drained profits from the Denver and South Park, and marked the beginning of the end for the historic railway.

The last train passed through the Alpine tunnel in 1910, and the project, a milestone in the development of the area, has long since fallen into ruin.

The old railroad grade up to the tunnel can be seen wending its way around the mountain behind the site of Hancock. The rails were torn up several years ago. Jeeps can sometimes make it up to the tunnel entrance, but cars—no!

Hancock also saw quite a bit of mining activity in its day. The Hancock Placer claim was the first, followed shortly thereafter by the Stonewall, the largest producer, which was located in 1879, and was worked until 1915.

Hancock had many faces, but its mining business was secondary to the fabulous Alpine Tunnel. From a busy population of more than a thousand during its peak years of the 80's and 90's, Hancock began to fade slowly. The closing of the tunnel hastened its death. The mines closed and finally, in 1926, the last passenger train roared down Chalk Creek to Hancock. The train's primary purpose was to cart the few remaining miners and their belongings out of the dead city. Now only a few crumbling cabins, a mine up behind the city, and the grade up to the Alpine Tunnel remain at Hancock.

OTHER MINES:   Allie Bell, Flora Bell and the Pat and Mary Murphy mines.

## SALIDA

When the railroads decided to make the site two miles above Cleora a main railroad junction, it marked the beginning of Salida and the end of Cleora. Cleora residents protested the railroad action to Governor Hunt. The chief executive said in reply: "God Almighty made some town-sites and Salida is one of them."

Salida grew so fast those first years its residents were boosting it for state capitol. The plan received a real setback, however, when it couldn't even win the county seat, losing to Buena Vista by almost a thousand votes.

Although Salida never became state capitol, it has been one of Colorado's most important cities down through the years. It was a gateway to mining camps in all directions. It has been a supply center for the mining areas and for the rich farm and ranchland surrounding it. It has also been a smelting and important railroad town.

Many famous figures paraded through here before and after Salida became a city. Zebulon Pike camped near here. Fremont was familiar with the area. Cy Warman (see Creede), who became a famous writer and journalist in his day, worked in Salida. Here he wrote *Sweet Marie*, a song dedicated to a lovely Denver girl who became his wife.

It was near the site of Salida that Col. Thomas Fauntleroy, on April 29, 1855, led a surprise attack on a band of Utes. The U. S. troops killed forty Indians and captured several others. It was a major victory in the long battle to set down the Indians in Colorado and in opening up the state for settlement.

## CLEORA (Bale's Station)

Cleora is one of the many towns throughout the west that was born of railroads and died by railroads.

The Santa Fe railroad laid out the town in 1878 and named it for the daughter of William Bale, operator of a stage station here. For a few short years Cleora grew rapidly as a railroad supply point for camps along the Arkansas River and on the other side of the divide. Then the Denver and Rio Grande rambled into the area and a dispute arose over the site of the railroad terminal. When the smoke cleared away another railroad terminal was laid out about two miles away. The new site was named Salida. With its growth, Cleora was soon forgotten. Now, only an old tombstone marks the spot where Cleora was.

## TURRET

George Corley returns to his claims in Turret every spring and digs for gold throughout the summer. Once in a while he rides down to Salida for supplies. Sometimes he has enough gold dust to pay for them, sometimes he has to dig into his pockets for minted money.

Frequently, during his trips to town, he tells of a rich new strike. But nobody gets very excited about it, and George goes back up into the mountains to dig by himself.

At one time, around the turn of the century, there were some 500 George Corleys here. They built a post office, a school house, a fancy hotel and had a newspaper *The Gold Belt*, and many other businesses. A bi-weekly stage ran from here to Salida.

The Independence was the big producer and copper and gold came out of it until 1916. The town was named for the nearby mountain.

Maybe, George will really hit a rich strike soon. Maybe he already has— and Turret will boom again.

OTHER MINES: Vivandiere and Gold Bug.

## WHITEHORN

Cattle now graze quietly in a field above Salida where the once-prosperous city of Whitehorn stood. A railroad worker, Derius Patro, was said to have found rich mineral here while cutting wood for railroad ties. The news of his find soon brought scores of fortune seekers. A camp was laid out in 1897 and named for Arthur Whitehorn, engineer, assayist, and a generous man who grubstaked some of the first prospectors.

So much was thought of the mineral prospects around Whitehorn, the Whitehorn Land and Tunnel Company was formed, and the company purchased more than 2,000 acres of land although it cost $500 to patent a single claim.

By 1900, Whitehorn was a city, with a schoolhouse, mill, several saloons, two brothels, a newspaper, *The Whitehorn News,* and all the other businesses that made a city a city. Fire destroyed some twenty buildings in 1902, but they were quickly rebuilt.

The surrounding mines were good producers, and there was some activity here until well into this century. But the post office closed its doors in 1918. The property was sold in 1946 for back taxes.

BEST MINES: Cameron, Golden Eagle and Independence.

## CALUMET

Calumet was once surrounded by vast beds of rich magnetic ores. Large deposits of white and variegated marble were found nearby also. The Colorado Fuel and Iron Company mined here for several years and named the town after the Calumet mine. The mine, along with the adjoining Hecla mine, had what was believed to be the deepest shaft in the world at the time. It was 4,900 feet deep, 380 feet less than a mile. It was begun in 1889 and completed in 1898. It had six equal compartments.

The Denver and Rio Grande built a spur here, and for a short while Calumet was a railroad terminal and supply point for the other camps around. When the railroad pushed on so did much of Calumet.

In recent years some felspar has been mined here but the town is dead.

## PONCHA SPRINGS

Indians first discovered the medicinal benefits of the 99 warm springs on the mountain on which Poncha Springs was later built.

The first white man here was said to have been Lt. Pike, who crossed the site in 1807 in search of the Red River of Texas.

A fellow by the name of James True came along in the early 1870's, saw the advantages of the site, and set up shop a few years before other towns in the area boomed.

When the boom came, True was ready. Poncha Springs rapidly became a supply center for camps in all directions. It served as a railroad junction in later years, and a miners' resort and health center.

There are two theories about the name. One says the springs were called "poncha" (warm) by the Indians, although the springs range in temperature from 90 to 185 degrees and contain salt, similar to those found in Hot Springs, Arkansas.

Another group says the city was originally called Pancho, Mexican raincape.

It was one of the few early cities that had a library. Many profitable businesses and resort facilities grew around True's place of business.

Fire destroyed most of the town in 1882—just about the time Poncha Springs hit its peak. Little of the city was rebuilt.

Perhaps the most significant thing about Poncha Pass, south of Poncha Springs, is that Otto Mears built a toll road over the pass to bring his wheat into the Arkansas Valley. It was the "little giant's" first attempt at road building and, although it wasn't a financial success, it started Mears on a roadbuilding career which—fortunately for Colorado—he developed to a fine point in later years.

## MAYSVILLE (Crazy Camp, Marysville)

This town was better known as Crazy Camp during its heyday.

Crazy Camp and Maysville (or Marysville) apparently were two nearby camps at first. An early newspaper item tells of a mill being built at Maysville to handle the ores from Crazy Camp. Then the camps must have

261

merged, with Crazy Camp the official title of the town for a while, and the pet name long after Maysville became the legal name. One newspaper said Maysville was formerly Crazy Camp "and it is thought by many the latter to be the most appropriate name of the two."

This writer could not find the derivation of the name Crazy Camp. In fact, nothing could be found concerning the derivation of Maysville. Early dispatches gave both Marysville and Maysville as names for the camp.

A rancher named Amasa Feathers set up shop here in the 70's when gold fever hit the Monarch District. The cattle were forgotten, and the prospectors took over. During the years 1879 and 1880, Crazy Camp (and/or Maysville) was the fastest growing camp in the district. Its early growth outstripped Monarch and the town was considered as a possible county seat.

The camp was situated in a "nice little park." Within the first few months a bank, lumber yard, two hotels and scores of other businesses and cabins were built. The camp also had two newspapers: one, *The Maysville Chronicle*, boasted a circulation of 1,000, the largest circulation of any newspaper in the county.

In addition to being a mining center, Maysville was an important travel junction. It was the eastern toll station for Monarch Pass. The Altman toll road from Hancock ended here and another toll road ran from Maysville to Shavano. The transient population often outnumbered the permanent population and kept the town prosperous and lively. The busiest places were the five supply stores, a half dozen saloons and gambling dens, and the large dance halls.

An 1879 newspaper report on Maysville said: "The camp has been very quiet until a few evenings since, when miners from above rode in, and, becoming intoxicated, passed word for word until they began shooting, making the camp lively for a half hour or so. Four were wounded, two of whom it is expected will die.

"The next evening while one of the wounded (Flynch) was lying in bed, Smith, one of the rioters of the night before, ascended to his room and shot him (Flynch) again, from which he will probably die."

Smith rode out of town passing six friends of Flynch's, who were riding into town. When the six friends learned what had happened they set out in hot pursuit of Smith. A sheriff's posse was also formed and it set out to capture Smith. Smith had not been captured within the next few days and this writer was unable to determine whether he was ever caught. One report expressed the belief Smith had made his getaway. There was reference to a double hanging a little later, but names were not given. It could have been another friendly little brawl. Maysville was a lively little town.

As a result of the Smith-Flynch incident the residents of Maysville petitioned for a justice of the peace, constable and a sheriff's deputy.

Maysville had a destructive fire in July of 1880 which destroyed five buildings in the heart of town. The remainder of the town was rescued through the valiant efforts of the bucket brigade.

The mining ended here with the crash of 1893, and Maysville died almost as fast as it had grown. A faded yellow house and a few cabins now mark the site.

## *ARBOUR-VILLA* (Arborville, Arbourville)

Arbourville, for a while, was the most important spot in the area—in one respect. It had the only parlor house in the entire district. In one early description of the Monarch district, a newspaper noted that while other towns in the area were busy and progessing rapidly "Arbourville was content with the dance hall building."

There were a little mining here, a little smelting, a stage station and some supplies sold—but the brothel was the big deal at Arbourville.

The city is more remembered now for its hermit, Frank Gimlett. Frank lived here for years and years after his neighbors had left. He kept busy, however—guarding the ice and snow on the mountaintops and writing letters.

After looking up at the mountains for a number of years, Frankie got sort of possessive about them. He thought he had a right to name them. He wanted to name them the Ginger Peaks after his favorite movie star, Ginger Rogers.

His letter-writing campaign went right up to the President. Eventually, the President answered, sympathizing with Gimlett's campaign. The President said Ginger Peaks was a fine name for a fine set of peaks, and Miss Rogers would be a fine person to name mountains after, but, the official feared, renaming the mountains would mean considerable trouble and expense for geographers, mapmakers and just about everybody else who dealt in mountains and things like that.

Gimlett couldn't see it that way, and he let everybody know it in no uncertain terms. In fact, in his wrath, he sat down and figured out how much the snow and ice on the mountaintops was worth on the open market, and how much his time was worth over the years. Gimlett sent the government a bill for $50,000 for all the years he spent guarding the snow and ice on the mountains. He said not one shovelful of ice or snow had been stolen during all the years he guarded the area.

The town name was spelled Arborville, Arbourville, and even Aberville, in the early days. It is generally believed the name came from the profusion of trees in the area, although one source said the town was named

263

after a Mr. Arbor, one of the first settlers. Gimlett insisted on calling the town Arbour-Villa, and since he was the last resident that is the last name given the site.

The town, which once rivaled Garfield and Monarch, has long since faded into history. The ruins of an old cabin, barn and outhouse mark the site.

Gimlett has gone and the snow and ice on the "Ginger Peaks" is easy prey to any and all snow and ice thieves.

## GARFIELD (Junction City)

A highway department camp now stands on what was once the colorful city of Garfield. Garfield erupted in 1879 and 1880 with the other camps in the area, and at the junction of two wagon roads. It was first called Junction City.

There were some good mines in the area and the population during its boom years exceeded 500. Fire hit the town on election night in 1883 while most of the menfolks were off to Salida to vote. When they returned they found their city in ashes.

The city was rebuilt of sturdier stuff and the post office department renamed the "new" city Garfield, in honor of President Garfield, who had been assassinated the year before.

Snow, as well as fire, was a big problem. There were many damaging slides and during the winter a heavy blanket of snow covered the high altitude community (8,800 feet). Stories of school children tunneling their way to school and miners tunneling their way to work through the snow mark Garfield's history.

BEST MINES:   Black Tiger, Columbus, Gunshot, Brighton and Monarch.

## MONARCH (Camp Monarch, Chaffee City)

Nicholas C. Creede, an unknown prospector at the time, was grubstaked for a go at the Monarch Pass area. He located paydirt in 1878, the rush started, and Camp Monarch began.

Within months, more than 3,000 gold seekers were in the area, and a helter-skelter tent and cabin camp blanketed the eastern foot of Monarch Pass. About 1880, the men took time out to plot a city, and they named it Chaffee City in honor of Jerome B. Chaffee, a widely-known Colorado banker who worked hard for statehood, and who became Colorado's first senator. The name was changed to Monarch in 1884.

The city had well over 100 houses, three hotels, several thriving businesses, including the usual large proportion of saloons and gambling houses.

264

At first the ore was hauled in wagons to Canon City but the railroad reached the site by 1881, and the transportation problem was settled.

Snow and rock slides were common and several mine accidents took their toll. In 1882, respected miner John Broll, a leader in the community, was killed in a mine explosion.

The Madonna mine was the big producer during the early years of the city, and during its peak employed 300 men around the clock and shipped up to 30 carloads of ore per day.

There were several other good mines. In fact, Monarch boasted of twenty to thirty mines within a half mile of the town which averaged "twenty to 150 ounces of silver to the ton, plus sixty per cent lead and a large per cent of iron."

But Monarch fell in the panic of '93. A few months later the last train through Monarch carried off most of the remaining residents. Those who stayed ripped up many of the cabins and stores for firewood. More of the city was torn down to make room for a new highway over the pass. Snowslides helped in the destruction.

The Colorado Fuel and Iron Company later operated limestone quarries here, but Monarch was dead. An old schoolhouse and a few tumble-down cabins, a little way off the highway, are all that remain of the old mining town.

BEST MINES:  Madonna, Monarch, Little Charm.

*SHAVANO* (Clifton)

Two legends surround the Angel of Shavano, formed by snow in deep crevices of the peak, and seen as far away as Salida in the late spring and much of the summer.

One legend, more widespread than the other, tells of an Indian chief's love for the famous white scout, George Beckwith. Chief Che-Wa-No of the Uncompahgre Utes had religious training in a friars' school in New Mexico. He had met Beckwith and had grown to respect him. In 1853 when Beckwith was fatally wounded in a riding accident, Chief Che-Wa-No came to the mountain to pray for his dying friend's soul. Since then, every spring, at the time Chief Che-Wa-No prayed at the foot of the peak, the Angel of Shavano returns to signal that the Indian's prayer has been answered.

The other legend, more popular with many of the oldtimers in the area, concerns an Indian princess and her love for her people. Many, many moons ago the drouth was driving the Indians from the land. The Indian princess came and knelt at the foot of the mountain to pray for rain and the end of the drouth. The Indian God of Plenty beckoned and the princess sacrificed herself so that her people could live. Each year thereafter, the Princess—the Angel of Shavano—reappears, and weeps once more for her people. Her tears—the melting snow—fall on the land below and make it fertile.

The land below the peak was also rich in precious metals, and the white man came and harvested what he could of it.

A strike was made in 1879, at the time of other strikes in the Monarch district. By the following year, more than one hundred hardy gold seekers probed the area and an elaborate city was planned. The townsite covered 120 acres, smelters were built, a sawmill, three general stores and the always-present saloon.

The boom lasted only three years, but long enough to have a murder and a hanging—a western trademark of civilization. The town faded rapidly once it started to die. There was a short rebirth in 1904 when silver was discovered here, but the boom didn't last long, and the area soon was returned to the Angel of Shavano.

Several cabins and a few business houses remain, and can be seen after a long, hard journey over a rutty, perilous road, more feasible for jeeps and hiking than standard automobiles.

## BABCOCK

There was some silver excitement in this remote area during the late 70's and early 80's. Newspapers at the time said there were five camps in this general vicinity: Jennings, Green's Gulch, Foosel, Hartz and Babcock.

Babcock was listed as the most promising camp. Ore from the Babcock strike assayed at "500 to 600 ounces of silver from a 2½-foot vein of galena and black sulphurets of silver." Babcock, of all the camps, won the distinction of being placed on the maps of the day. However, little fanfare accompanied the distinction as little is known of the camp.

The camp may or may not have anything to do with the Mountain Chief mine owned by a Colonel Babcock of Illinois, although Babcock's mine was also named as the mine at Cree's Camp.

No doubt, Babcock, the camp, had trouble with the weather and with transportation. It is isolated, although it was on the Altman Pass road. Nobody knows how long the camp lasted and even if it had a good life.

*And Then There Were* . . . . *BROWN'S CANYON, CENTERVILLE* (or Centreville) and *MIDWAY*, ex-railroad and post office towns between Buena Vista and Salida. All were also farm supply towns. Midway was named for its position halfway between Buena Vista and Northrop . . . . *HECLA* (not on map) mentioned earlier as one of the key towns in the Calumet area north of Salida. But after this early mention, nothing else is heard of the town. It wasn't even shown on early maps. Could be Hecla was an earlier name for one of the towns in the area . . . . *HECLA JUNCTION* is shown on the maps. It was a railroad junction and may well be a later name for the elusive Hecla . . . . in discussing the early camps and towns in the Monarch district, one newspaper mentions *CREE'S CAMP* that was "christened on a gallon of old rye." Cree's Camp had two mines: the Song Bird, owned by Alec Cree, for whom the camp was named; and the Mountain Chief, operated by Colonel Babcock. Babcock may be the namesake of Babcock, the town . . . . *ALTON'S* or *ALTMAN'S CAMP* (not on map). In the only reference found to this camp, the newspaper spelled the name two or three different ways. Since Colonel Altman and his pass were mentioned prominently in the write-up it seems safe to assume it was Altman's Camp. The write-up didn't tell the nature of the camp but did say it was "on the north fork of the South Arkansas and its northern branch." . . . . *COLUMBUS* and *CASCADE* (not on map), two obscure railroad stations in this area . . . . *HANGMAN CAMP*, an isolated camp located near a couple of mines just east of the summit of Cottonwood Pass. No one seems to know the reason for the name. It must have been interesting . . . . *NINE MILE HOUSE* (not on map) another stop on Cottonwood Pass trail. It was frequently mentioned as a popular stopover, but reports fail to mention what it was nine miles from. The owner of Nine Mile House, Martin Osborne, was killed in a brawl with a wagon driver in July of 1881 . . . . *BULLION CITY* (not on map) a transient camp laid out in 1879 near Monarch. The camp lost its residents to the other towns before much of Bullion City was built . . . . *HARTVILLE*, a small and relatively short-lived camp about a mile and a half from Monarch. It had a good start towards becoming a first class town—including a saloon—but that wasn't enough . . . . *ATLANTIC*, a railroad town at the eastern opening of the Alpine Tunnel. Railroad crews, working out of Atlantic, were kept busy during the winter months shoveling snow from the tracks and repairing snow sheds damaged by slides . . . . *ALPINE STATION* (just off map) was on the western end of the Alpine Tunnel. It was larger and apparently more important than Atlantic. Reports have it some of the railroad buildings were made of stone here, and that there was a roundhouse for the spare engines . . . . *MANOA* (not on map) was a camp around a mine about a mile and a half due east of Calumet and near Whitehorn. The camp was first heard from in 1902 and last heard from in 1908. The best mine was the American Flag, operated by the Sunset Consolidated Mining Corporation, "a Colorado corporation run by Iowa people." Other good workings were the Lizzie and Prairie . . . . 1904 *Mining Reporter* mentioned a "delightful little camp called *J.R.S.*" at Hawkings switch, on the Calumet Branch of the Rio Grande. The camp was sponsored by J. R. Smith, a hospitable man from Chicago, who wanted to make something of the site. He apparently didn't succeed . . . . *COSDEN* (Wagontown) was called "an interesting settlement" in Gunnison County. It was originally called Wagontown. It was located in Tomichi Valley where the valley narrows into the canyon. Early prospectors and settlers had to leave their wagons here to make their way into the canyon either on burro or on foot. The name was changed to Cosden during the 1880's for Dr. Cosden, an early settler. No trace is left of the town.

## EAST OF GUNNISON

Gunnison
White Pine
North Star (Lake's Camp)
Tomichi (Tomichiville, Tomichi Camp, Corning, Argenta)
Ohio City (Gold Creek, Eagle City)
Waunita Hot Springs
Bowerman (Nugget City)
Sherrod (Camp Sherrod, Sherrod Switch)
Woodstock, Camp Sterling (not on map), Lorraine (not on map) and
    Omega
Pitkin (Quartzville, Quartz)
Quartz
Tin Cup (Tincup Camp, Virginia City)
Abbeyville
Hillerton
Emma and Red Mountain
Dorchester
Bowman
Jack's Cabin (Howville)
Almont

*And Then There Were . . . . PIE PLANT, DOYLEVILLE, SARGENTS, GLACIER, CROOKTON or CROOKVILLE, TAYLOR CITY* (not on map), *FOREST HILL, GIVENS* and *DREW.*

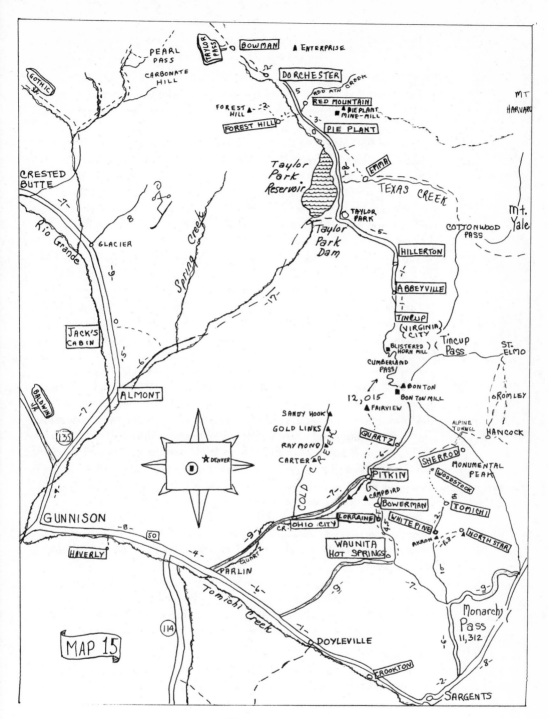

PEARL PASS

CARBONATE HILL

GOTHIC VE.

CRESTED BUTTE

—7—

Rio Grande

8

GLACIER

Spring Creek

—6—

—17—

JACK'S CABIN

—5—

—6—

BALDWIN VE.

—7—

135

ALMONT

GUNNISON

—8—

50

HAVERLY

—4—

PARLIN

114

QUARTZ

—6—

Tomichi Creek

—1—

MAP 15

TAYLOR PASS

BOWMAN

ENTERPRISE

DORCHESTER

5

RED MTN CREEK

RED MOUNTAIN

FOREST HILL

—2—

PIE PLANT MINE—MILL

FOREST HILL

3

PIE PLANT

0

Taylor Park Reservoir

EMMA

TEXAS CREEK

MT HARVARD

MT. YALE

TAYLOR PARK

—5—

COTTONWOOD PASS

Taylor Park Dam

HILLERTON

ABBEYVILLE

TINCUP (VIRGINIA CITY)

Tincup Pass

ST. ELMO

BLISTERED HORN MILL

CUMBERLAND PASS

BONTON

BON TON MILL

oROMLEY

12,015

FAIRVIEW

ALPINE TUNNEL

HANCOCK

SANDY HOOK

GOLD LINKS

RAYMOND

CARTER

COLD CREEK

QUARTZ

—6—

SHERROD

MONUMENTAL PEAK

WOODSTOCK

★ DENVER

PITKIN

CAMPBIRD

BOWERMAN

TOMICHI

—7—

LORRAINE

WHITE PINE

—2—

CR. OHIO CITY

AKRON

—6.3—

NORTH STAR

WAUNITA HOT SPRINGS

QUARTZ

—9—

—7—

—9—

—6—

—6—

Monarch Pass 11,312

DOYLEVILLE

—6—

—8—

CROOKTON

—2—

SARGENTS

## XIV. EAST OF GUNNISON

*GUNNISON*

Now the heart of one of the richest ranch and recreational areas in Colorado, Gunnison has been many things to many people in the past. It was a favorite stomping ground for Indians. Spanish explorers, searching for the fabled City of Gold in Colorado, didn't find the city here, but apparently were as attracted to the region as man has been since.

Some of the first silver in Colorado was found near here—in the early 70's. But the red man wasn't ready to give up the land yet, and the white men retreated. About the same time, the government saw the range possibilities and established a cow and sheep camp about five miles below the present site of Gunnison.

And despite the Indians, the fortune seekers were not to be denied. In the late 70's good gold and silver were found in all directions from Gunnison. The site was the logical location for a shipping and supply center. The fortune seekers stocked up in Gunnison for another go at the mountains. They wintered here when the mountains wouldn't let them in. Gunnison smelters processed the metals the miners found. Trains, first built to Gunnison, shipped out the metals for use by the outside world. The Gunnison area later furnished the granite for the State Capitol building.

By 1880, Gunnison was a roaring frontier town of 10,000 people, all kinds of people. It rivaled Denver. The lavish four-story La Veta Hotel, built in 1884, was the finest west of the mountains. The same year, two more smelters were built and a street railroad system was installed.

The city was named after Capt. John W. Gunnison who passed through here in 1853, leading a party of government topographical engineers in search for a central railroad route from the Mississippi to the Pacific. The captain was killed by Indians a few weeks later in Utah.

But the river he traveled and the city along its bank lived on. For after the gold and silver seekers drained the mountains dry of their metals, the cattlemen and ranchers took over. Then came the fishermen, the hunters and the sightseers.

It is only a shell of the fabulous frontier city of yesterday, but it has begun to boom again. The population has doubled within the last twenty years, and it will soon have 4,000 people—living in a serene and colorful city, surrounded by the mountains that have many stories to tell.

*WHITE PINE*

The legend of "Snow Blind Gulch" kept prospectors a-looking in this area throughout the 60's and 70's. And when the legend turned out to be true, the story of White Pine and its suburban camps of Tomichi and North Star began.

It seems two old prospectors discovered rich gold here in the early 60's. They set up sluices and began to develop the property. But, in their eagerness to work it as much as they could before winter set in, they waited too long. Winter caught them on the way out of the area, and, the story goes, they became snowblind, lost and/or killed by Indians.

No one bothered to pass on how their story leaked out, but anyhow, prospectors searched for "Snow Blind Gulch" for many years to come. Years later, a trace of a sluice was found on Tomichi Creek, near the sites of the prosperous camps of a later year.

The first strike (outside of legend) was made in 1878. By the following year the area was crawling with prospectors, and by 1881 the town company was formed, and White Pine was born.

The city thrived throughout the 80's and was known as a bustling, sociable place. The peak population was 3,000 and the residents were served by several thriving businesses.

During its heyday, White Pine was also known for *The White Pine Cone* edited by witty, sarcastic George S. Irwin from 1883 to 1893. His mining tips and saucy columns were quoted and re-quoted throughout the area, and have since been a great source for researchers.

White Pine was another camp that suffered from a traffic problem. Roads were often clogged by snow. A stage coach enroute to White Pine was held up and robbed.

The mining slump hit White Pine in the early 90's, and the panic of 1893 just about finished the job. The camp was deserted until 1901 when another boom hit the area, aided and abetted by the Tomichi Valley Smelter. The mines have been worked off and on since. A revival (mining type) was held in the mid-40's, but the activity has been hit by the decline in lead and zinc prices in recent years.

TOP MINES: May-Mazeppa, Morning Star, Evening Star, North Star, (see North Star), Copper Queen, Copper Bottom and Black Warrior.

## NORTH STAR (Lake's Camp)

A delapidated building with the original false front, surrounded by a few old cabins, marks the site of the once-prosperous city of North Star. The city was usually considered a suburb of White Pine and the site was owned by the May-Mazeppa company of White Pine. But North Star had a life of its own.

Rich veins of galena ore were found in 1878 and the North Star Lode was located the following year. A town arose at the site. At first it was called Lake's Camp, apparently for some fellow named Lake, but the name was later changed to North Star.

Like White Pine, it was known as a happy-go-lucky sociable town, and was most proud of its Soup Bone Musical Club which exploited the dubious talents of the area.

But before the mines had been properly developed, the panic of '93 hit, and the miners left for the booming gold camps of Creede or Cripple Creek. However, the camp was in full swing again by 1901. The Leadville House Hotel and a post office were opened that year. And the camp has seen activity off and on until recent years.

*TOMICHI* (Argenta, Corning, Tomichi Camp, Tomichiville)

At one point in its history, Tomichi was a larger camp than White Pine. That was the time Tomichi had a population of 1,500, and White Pine didn't. But now nothing is left. A snowslide in 1899 completely covered the site and did much to bring about its death.

The slide hit shortly after Tomichi experienced a slight revival. As White Pine and North Star, Tomichi prospered throughout the 80's, all-but-died from the silver panic in '93, and had a short comeback three years later. Apparently, however, most everyone was gone again by 1899, because the records show the slide buried the town, though only six people were trapped in one building. Every available man in the area pitched in to rescue the six, and although some reports say all six were dead when found, actually two were pulled out alive.

Slides were common here as snow was heavy. Records show notary Sam Hyde was crushed by snow falling off a building. Another story has been passed on about a dog digging himself out after being buried for more than a week in a snowslide. Anyhow, after the slide of '99, what could be salvaged from Tomichi was taken to White Pine.

The first post office here was called Argenta, but somewhere along the line it was changed to Tomichi, which is Indian for "hot water." By 1882, there were a bank, assay office, smelter and a newspaper, *The Tomichi Herald*. Paper for the newspaper was delayed for a while in 1885, but the *Herald* was published just the same—on wrapping paper. And the smelter burned down in 1883. Just everything happened.

But it had good mines. The Magna Charta was the best. Its tunnel reached for a mile and a half, under White Pine and North Star.

OTHER MINES: Lewiston and Sleeping Pet, the first lodes located; Eureka, Brittle Silver, Little Carrie.

The still-thriving city of Telluride, nestled at the foot of the towering mountains. The mountain in the center is Ajax Mountain. *Photo by Homer Reid.*

The Tomboy Mine near Telluride. Note all the workings up the valley. *U. S. Geological Survey photo.*

The mill on the side of the hill, the Smuggler. Note workings above mill. There were cabins and a boarding house here for the workers. A larger Smuggler-Union mill was built in the San Miguel Valley near Pandora. *U. S. Geological Survey photo.*

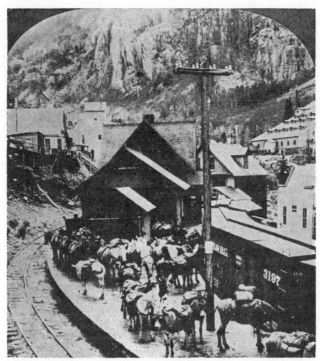

Rocky Mountain Canaries unloading concentrated ore in railroad cars at Ophir. Picture taken in 1906. *State Historical Society of Colorado photo.*

Rico during the first of its many booms. The Enterprise Mines are to the right behind the city. *William H. Jackson photo, State Historical Society of Colorado.*

David Frakes Day, longtime editor of Ouray *Solid Muldoon* and *Durango Democrat*, as bold and as biting as the land in which he lived. *State Historical Society of Colorado.*

The little man who conquered the mountains, Otto Mears. *State Historical Society of Colorado.*

It's a long way down. An early trail in the Silverton area. One source says this was part of Otto Mears Million Dollar Highway, but it is probably a trail in Cunningham Gulch. The picture was taken by William H. Jackson in 1874. *Colorado Highway Department photo.*

Silverton and magnificent Sultan Mountain. The picture was taken in 1900 from Boulder Mountain. Note Silverton reservoir in foreground. *U. S. Geological Survey photo.*

Notorious Blair Street in Silverton. The Bent Elbow is at right.

Eureka then, looking down the main street. *State Historical Society of Colorado.*

Eureka now. Picture taken at far end of street shown above. Other buildings shown above are gone. *Colorado Publicity Department.*

The amazing little railroad unloading passengers and baggage at Red Mountain Town in 1888. Otto Mears standing at rear platform to right of woman. *Denver Public Library Western Collection.*

Narrow gauge at Silverton.

*OHIO CITY* (Gold Creek, Eagle City)

Gold was found near here in the 60's, but the rush didn't come until 1879 when silver was found. During the 80's, Ohio City was one of the most prosperous camps in the area. It was originally called Eagle City, changed to Ohio, later changed to Gold Creek, then to Ohio City.

By 1880, there were nearly fifty cabins and tents at the site. Later a lumber mill was erected two miles away, and the place began to thrive for real. A hotel was built, restaurants, saloons, assay offices and many other businesses. A daily stage was run from Pitkin, and by 1882 the Denver and South Park Railroad lent itself to the boom. Millions were spent in carefully developing the area, including the construction of several stamp mills and tunnels from the mines.

Ohio City was hit by the silver panic of 1893. Within months, the camp was all but deserted. But gold was re-discovered three years later and the area bloomed again.

The top mines were the Carter, in which millions were spent in developing and millions were returned; the Raymond, which produced seven million dollars worth of metals in its day; and the Gold Links, which produced nearly a million dollars in gold and silver. The Calumet, Eagle and Roller lodes were within the limits of Ohio City.

Some mining has been done down through the years, and the area also became a favorite hunting and fishing region. The year-round population was seventy-eight in 1940 and has been slightly less in recent years, although Ohio City has retained a school, combination post office and general store, and one telephone.

It was on the road a short distance out of Ohio City many years ago, that a faithful old mule died. Its master buried the animal on the spot and placed a marker on the grave which read:

> "Death went prospecting
> And he was no fool.
> Here he struck faithful Pete
> **The emigrant mule.**"

The marker has long since gone, but the story lives on.

The Carter, still in operation off and on, is the first big mine up Gold Creek. Next comes the Raymond and finally the Gold Links. All are easily accessible by car and well worth the visit. Each of the mines has small camps around, especially the Gold Links, which has a delightful community with four large boarding houses and a few lesser buildings. However, as far as could be determined, none of the camps was an official town with an official name unless it took the name of the mine.

281

## WAUNITA HOT SPRINGS

Early miners and prospectors first discovered the health advantages of the soda and sulphur springs here. By 1880 a trail to the spot had been worn through the wilderness and it rapidly developed into a favorite camping spot. In 1885, a two-story hotel was built along with swimming pools and bathhouses. A post office was established, and the springs became an elaborate resort area for the next fifteen years.

But business began to fall off around the turn of the century as the population of the nearby camps began to fade. In 1904, when Waunita had but fifty patrons, the post office was closed. The site was virtually empty the next ten years, save for a wayward prospector or tourist now and again.

Then, in 1916, Waunita saw another rise as a resort area. New radium hot springs, large hotel and cottage facilities, and a sanitarium were built. But, alas, interest soon dwindled a second time and the resort slowly fell back to sleep. By 1941, only fourteen summer residents were recorded.

## BOWERMAN (Nugget City)

Bowerman was perhaps the most widely trumpeted city in Colorado in its day. But it turned out to be one of the biggest duds. Newspaper descriptions called Bowerman "a new Cripple Creek," and the "greatest gold camp of the twentieth century." One newspaper went so far as to claim only one other camp in the nation had richer ore than Bowerman—and that was in South Dakota.

Despite the newspapers' claims, and despite the fact Bowerman residents tried hard to make this another Cripple Creek, the two booms here only lasted a few months each, and the gold produced was almost negligible.

The story of the "fabulous dud' began because a woman couldn't keep a secret.

J. C. Bowerman had worked most of the mining areas in the state for a period of thirty years without having any luck. As with H. A. W. Tabor, Bowerman's wife did chores and took in boarders to keep her husband in prospecting money. Finally, Bowerman was forced to advertise for a grubstake. A railroad official in Pueblo answered the ad, promising to furnish Bowerman $50 a month in supplies.

It wasn't long before Bowerman hit rich ore. He worked the area secretly for some time, storing the ore, and making certain he had the best claim worked out.

Accounts vary as to what happened next. Some say Bowerman, when sure of his find, sent for his wife whom he had left behind in the last camp. Mrs. Bowerman, unable to keep the find secret after all the years of bad luck, let the cat out of the bag before she traipsed off to join her husband.

Another account claims Mrs. Bowerman was with her husband all along, and that she took a shine to the "fancy baubles" found on her "husband's hill." She carried some of the nuggets with her, and showed them off on a shopping trip to Waunita Hot Springs one day.

Either way it happened, the rush was on. Only a handful of prospectors showed up at first. But after the ballyhoo began, and within weeks hundreds of fortune seekers were swarming all over her "husband's hill."

That was in the summer of 1903. The 500 and some prospectors founded a town, built up a bunch of businesses, including five saloons and five gambling halls, and set out for the hills.

The big trouble at Bowerman was there were too many chiefs and not enough Indians—all prospectors and not enough miners to work the mines. And it wasn't long before it was discovered the Bowerman property was about the only good property around, although the others refused to admit this.

A cloak of mystery covered the Bowerman diggings. The first ore he had assayed was said to be worth more than $70,000 a ton. Most of the press notices concerned this first ore. But more ore was a long time in coming. Bowerman let it be known the ore was so rich that tourist could cart off thousands of dollars in one visit. So he fenced off his property. Time after time, his first major shipment of ore was scheduled, and time after time the shipping date arrived and no ore was sent out. Many of the smaller satellite camps shipped out ore before Bowerman did.

But all this time, the town was still living it up—thinking big, acting big. The first church sermon was held in August, 1903. The log church wasn't large enough to accomodate the crowd that had gathered to hear famed speaker, The Reverend J. J. Mackay. So the sermon was held out-of-doors, and the event drew miners and onlookers from miles around.

Most Bowerman saloons were closed for the sermon, but some stayed open. The saloon right across the street from the meeting stayed open and its patrons joined in the singing. A churchgoer would have to tell the saloon crowd when the songs were finished, because the lusty drinkers didn't want to stop singing.

The town was incorporated in 1904 and the town officials were named. Then came a wild celebration. E. K. Lore came over from Gunnison and started *The Bowerman Herald*. Two hotels were built, and the city had the services of two lawyers and three mining engineers.

Still, Bowerman did not ship out any ore. Some of the residents had begun to lose interest and drifted off. Finally, another good strike was made and it was called the Camp Bird mine, after the mine near Ouray. The Camp Bird shipped out before Bowerman's Independent did. The shipment fanned some new interest in the town, and the population got back up there about where it was.

For the next two years, Bowerman experienced a normal existence. There were some ore shipments out, even from Bowerman's claim. But, all in all, it wasn't anything like they had expected. As soon as the miners realized this they began drifting off. There were only 200 in town by 1907, and the site was deserted by 1911. Many interesting remains of the fabulous dud remain at the foot of Wuanita Pass.

### SHERROD (Camp Sherrod, Sherrod Switch)

If surveyor Hayden hadn't been so busy measuring the fields and mountains of Colorado he could have made a fortune in mining. In making his surveys of Colorado, Hayden passed through some of the richest sections in the state, often before the booms had begun. In many cases he predicted where the gold was to be found.

For example, in 1872, he predicted a ten-mile radius around Monumental Peak would be one of the richest mining areas in the state.

Within the next few years the fabulous mining towns of Ohio City, Hancock, Romley, Pitkin, White Pine, Tomichi and Monarch erupted within the area referred to by Hayden.

One camp located on Monumental Peak itself was Sherrod, the most important of the satellite camps in the latter-day Bowerman boom. Good gold ore, running as high as $1,700 a ton, was found here in the late summer of 1903 by W. H. Sherrod and others.

By September some fifty tents were pitched at the site, near the head of Missouri Gulch, and several permanent buildings were going up.

Sherrod promised to be an important camp. Its promise was so good, in fact, the Colorado and Southern Railroad deemed it necessary to run a spur to the new camp. Sherrod shipped out ore even before Bowerman did. The two-story Nathan Hotel was completed and could accommodate fifty people.

Several thousands of dollars in gold were taken from the mines around Sherrod, the best of which were the Brittle Silver, Paywell and Ejan lodes. The Brittle Silver was sold to a Denver tycoon for $25,000 in 1903. The Lopez was sold during the winter for $30,000.

But Sherrod was another camp that couldn't beat the winter. Located at 12,000 feet, snow prohibited work in the winter and snowslides were always a danger. The ores, which played out fairly rapidly, just weren't worth it.

Sherrod was all but dead by 1906. Now, only the rapidly deteriorating ruins of a couple of cabins mark the site.

*WOODSTOCK, CAMP STERLING* (not on map), *LORRAINE* and *OMEGA* (not on map)

Four of the more important small camps around Pitkin and Bowerman.

Woodstock was an earlier camp, located on Monumental Mountain just below the site of Sherrod, which came some twenty years later. About the only history known of the place was a tragic snowslide in March of 1884, which completely destroyed the camp and killed fourteen of the seventeen residents, including five children.

Camp Sterling was a small camp about three-fourths of a mile beyond the Independent mine of Bowerman. The camp was located around a claim owned by K. C. Sterling.

Lorraine and Omega were two other camps located around claims in the Bowerman area. Lorraine was situated about a mile south of town. That's more than is known about Omega. Several cabins remain at Lorraine.

*PITKIN* (Quartzville, Quartz)

Another boom town that arose about the same time as Leadville, and some of its early citizens firmly believed it might outdistance the silver city to the north. The growth was so rapid, the first few months, a huge tent hotel and tent restaurant, both making use of mother earth with a sprinkling of sawdust for a floor, were constantly "full up." A would-be merchant sold $3,000 in hardware merchandise set out in front of the location where his store was under construction.

In no time the area was so populated one man complained: "We have three women, eight children, three fiddlers, 180 dogs, two burros and one cat —and need a newspaper and a sawmill."

He had only to wait.

By 1880, the boom camp had a newspaper, *The Pitkin Independent*, a bank, several more saloons and several more women, and a population of more than 1,000. The following year more than 2,500 persons were in the area and there were nearly 100 businesses, including four hotels, eight restaurants and more than a dozen saloons.

Pitkin wasn't lacking in confidence either. *The Silver World*, the voice of mining in the early west, carried a dispute between Pitkin and another booming town of Colorado, Lake City. Said the Pitkin correspondent:

"There is not now, nor has there ever been, a mining camp or district in Colorado where the average grade of ores it produced was as high as it is in the Quartz Creek district . . . . I will wager a copy of the *Silver World* as long as it shall be published, that I can name fifteen mines within a radius of five miles of this place—Pitkin—from which the average grade of the vein will exceed that of any five mines you can name within a radius of ten miles of Lake City."

The community was originally named Quartz, then Quartzville, for the nearby creek. But the residents soon named it after Colorado Governor Frederick W. Pitkin and the town was incorporated under that name in 1880.

Pitkin was rich in silver and was another camp that they say was discovered by accident. It seems two old prospectors had combed the area for about two years without much luck and were about to take off for greener pastures, when one of the men hit on a rock in disgust, and the chip disclosed rich silver wire within the rock.

Pitkin had its rough element and its share of shootings and the like. During the construction of the Alpine Tunnel (see Alpine) the tough construction crews helped liven up Saturday nights in Pitkin. The arrival of the Denver and South Park in 1882 caused new excitement.

Like other Colorado silver cities, Pitkin was hit by the silver crash of 1893. But, although many left, some never have. The population remained around 200 through the years, falling to about sixty in recent years.

The city's outstanding feature today is the huge state fish hatchery about a half mile south of town. It is the largest in the state, producing some 91,000 pounds of trout in 1956. Good hunting is found here and Pitkin has become a tourist center.

BEST MINES: Fairview, Tycoon, Little Roy, Red Jacket, Silver Islet, Silent Friend, Iron Cap, Silver Age, Western Hemisphere, Terrible, Blue River, Green Mountain, Silver Link, Good Hope, Independence, Dobson, and Little Addie Addie.

## QUARTZ

There was a small mining camp near the summit of Cumberland Pass about six and a half miles north of Pitkin. Early maps give the place the name of Quartz.

It may be only coincidence that an early name for Pitkin was Quartz, too.

Little information could be found concerning the Cumberland Pass camp. It may be some of the early references to this Quartz were regarded as references to Pitkin. According to the appearance of Quartz on the maps, however, it existed about the same time as Pitkin and the other boom towns in the area.

Also, it apparently was a fairly substantial settlement since there are still some ruins remaining, including a large mine building.

## TIN CUP (Tincup Camp, Virginia City)

This near ghost town with the quaint name is fast becoming a popular display spot of the many, many skeletons in Colorado's closet. Tin Cup is a good representative of the past. Not so big as many places but larger than most, Tin Cup had its ups and downs. It was a once-bustling, once prosperous city, albeit more rowdy than the average—much more rowdy.

As with Creede, Leadville and others, the underworld element actually ruled the town. In 1880, the year the rush to Tin Cup really began, the underworld staffed the city offices with their own men, and they told the sheriff the first man he arrested, other than those specified, would be his last. He only lasted a few months. The second marshal was also under the thumb of the rough element, but he attempted to display a little more authority by periodically rounding up a few harmless drunks, if for no other reason than to have someone in jail. Harry Rivers became marshal in 1882. An honest man, Rivers too soon discovered that honesty was not the best policy in Tin Cup. He was shot and killed by Charles La Tourette, saloon keeper and tough underworld leader. The next marshal committed suicide and his successor was killed in a gun battle.

That's how things were in Tin Cup.

But it did give color to the Tin Cup cemetery.

The story is told about the conversion of Jack Ward. Old Jack was just about the roughest, toughest, drinkingest no-good around. He used to come to town just to get drunk and pick a fight. He got in more gun battles than just about anyone, and one battle was said to have set some kind of record in that more than 100 shots were fired. Well, one day, "Honest" Marshal Harry Rivers decided fun is fun but enough is enough. So he set out to take old Jack Ward in. He did—but only after a gun battle, of course. Somehow, during the experience of sitting in jail and being fined for cutting up, old Jack got religion. He reformed. Next time he was heard from was from the pulpit in Glenwood Springs, preaching hell-fire and damnation against gamblers and other rowdy-like characters.

The noises of mining soon outdistanced the sound of gunfire, however. By 1882, Tin Cup was the biggest silver producer in the Gunnison area and the population soared to 6,000.

Some placer claims were located north of Tin Cup in 1859, but weren't developed. The silver strike of '79 brought the fortune hunters out in force. The gulch and district had already been named Tin Cup, because one of the early prospectors carried out gold dust in a tin cup.

The booming, helter-skelter tent and cabin community became known as Tin Cup Camp. But soon the residents thought a dignified name would be more appropriate, and believing Virginia City, Nevada, would have nothing on the new Colorado camp, the city fathers renamed the camp Virginia City. The site was incorporated under that name in 1880. This started the big debate.

Many thought this was a unique camp in itself, and deserved a unique name—Tin Cup, for example. The post office was rooting for this latter group, as it had enough Virginia Cities as it was. (There was also one in Montana.) So, the Tin Cup movement grew and eventually won out. Not, however, without a lot of bitterness and, perhaps, even a few gun battles here and there.

In addition to the rich mines nearby, Tin Cup also became a supply and "social center" for the area. Many prospectors from nearby camps wintered in Tin Cup. Several smelters were built.

The big problem was transportation. At first, ore had to be carted out by pack train over difficult, and often snow-bound, Tin Cup Pass to Forest City (St. Elmo), Iron City or Alpine. Then roads were built the other direction, so ore could be taken to Almont or Gunnison. Eventually, the railroad was extended to Almont. The fabulous Alpine tunnel was built and the railroad ran to Pitkin. This expedited shipments—but not enough to satisfy the residents of Tin Cup. Here it was the biggest producer around, but no railroad. Tin Cup suffered and brooded about this fact for many years, and never did get over it completely.

The Gold Cup, which produced $7,000,000, the Jimmy Mack and other mines, kept turning out the silver and gold. There was a mild recession here in the mid-80's, but Tin Cup kept going. It even weathered the panic of '93. And just when things were getting slow again, another boom came in 1902, and 2,000 fortune hunters rushed back to Tin Cup.

Finally, things began to quiet down for good. By 1912, Tin Cup's day as a mining center was over, although the Gold Cup didn't close down until 1917. It opened up for short periods up until 1936.

Now, Tin Cup is little more than a fishing and recreation area with a memory. Only a handful of people live here the year around. Most of the early cabins and business houses are gone. The biggest thing left is the cemetery just south of town.

TOP MINES: Gold Cup, seen three miles south of town on Cemetery Road; Jimmy Mack and Tin Cup, adjoining Gold Cup; Drew, Mayflower, Iron Bonnet, El Capitan, Anna Dedricka, and the Blistered Horn Mine at the summit of Cumberland Pass.

GOLD DUST: There were several newspapers in Tin Cup's past, including the *Tin Cup Record* and *Tin Cup Miner*, among the first, and then the *Tin Cup Banner* and the *Tin Cup Times* . . . . . the most famous saloon and gambling joint was Frenchie's . . . . some fire plugs. installed in 1891, are still standing . . . . the Town Hall was built in 1906, and repainted in 1951 . . . . the first cabin on the site was built by Saul Bloom in 1879 . . . . the graveyard is called "The Cemetery of Four Knolls," each knoll represented a different group—one each for the Jewish, Catholic and Protestant religions, and the fourth and most active in the early days, was for those who had no religion but survival (they lost)—those who died with their boots on

.... by 1882, every mining property that had reached fifty feet was in pay dirt .... Tin Cup was represented in a mineral exposition in Denver in 1882 .... many tunnels were built to develop the mines .... Robert Clark, who took over the Gold Cup in 1896, was killed three weeks later when he was thrown from a toboggan going through a tunnel .... southwest of Tin Cup is Cross Mountain (12,200 feet), a miniature Mount of the Holy Cross. The Mountain's snow cross, although smaller than the famous mountain north of Leadville, melts much later in the year .... leader in the resurgence of Tin Cup popularity is Denver Radio and TV personality Pete Smythe who broadcasts from "East Tin Cup" daily over the "Bobwire Network." (The program actually originates in Denver.)

## ABBEYVILLE

A small camp one mile north of Tin Cup. The camp grew around the C. F. Abbey smelter, built in 1881 to handle the ores from the Virginia City mines. Shortly after the smelter was built, however, most of the construction workers returned to the excitement of Tin Cup, many taking their cabins with them. Workers at the smelter, the short time it was operating, generally lived in Tin Cup.

## HILLERTON

Hillerton erupted about the same time as Virginia City, and for a while some believed it might outdistance the city two miles to the south. It was named for Edward Hiller, one of the founders who started a bank there in 1879.

Cause for confidence in the town was construction, during the first few months, of a smelter, a large hotel, The New England House, a bank, several sawmills, several other businesses, and a toll road to Jack's Cabin. This road was the quickest route to Crested Butte and Ruby. And the population the first few months kept apace with that of Virginia City. By 1880, some 1,500 miners were here.

But the ores in the area didn't support the confidence.

A newspaper, *The Hillerton Occident*, moved to Virginia City just a few months after its establishment in 1879. The residents soon followed and the town went downhill rapidly.

Now, nothing remains of the site.

BEST MINES: Adeline, What Is It, and Little Earl.

## RED MOUNTAIN and EMMA

Two little-known towns along the Red Mountain Trail, an extension of the Taylor Pass Trail and a busy road in the boom years of the area.

Red Mountain is mentioned by F. V. Hayden, Colorado's noted suveryor-explorer, in his travels through the region in 1873. He said the town was on the south fork of Lake Creek along the Red Mountain road. Hayden said the camp was deserted and the cabins falling to ruins. So it must have been a very early camp for this region, possibly the earliest.

289

Emma was an almost untraceable camp south of Red Mountain. It was shown on many early maps as between Hillerton and Red Mountain, and is listed as having a post office in 1882. Little else is known about it.

## DORCHESTER

Gold was discovered in the Italian Mountains in 1900, and soon Dorchester became the camp of the area. More than 1,000 prospectors and miners were within the section within a short time, many of them coming from Tin Cup and Aspen.

The early settlers had high hopes for the city, and an eastern mining expert, after a short visit, even went as far as to call Dorchester the "coming mining camp of the new century."

But snow covered the area much of the year, hindering the work. Snowslides were frequent. Nonetheless, some of the mines remained open all winter long. One time, work didn't stop until fifteen snowslides were counted in one day.

Getting the ore in and out was often difficult and at times impossible. However, mining continued through the early years of this century. Some lead and zinc were mined during the first World War, but after the war the mines closed and the camp was deserted.

Now the site is a picnic and camping area, reached over a rough, but passable, road.

BEST MINES: Bull-Domingo, Doctor, Star, Enterprise and Forest Hill.

## BOWMAN

Oldest camp in Taylor Park, outside of Tin Cup, Bowman was known not only for its mining but also as a shipping point. It was the last stop before the rugged trip over Taylor Pass into Aspen.

The perilous route, often clogged by snow and rock slides, was a busy road during the 80's and 90's, although it often took weeks to negotiate the round trip. Apparently, the oldtimers were more hardy than the late-comers to the area, because the road has been closed for years.

Some prospecting was done in the area in the early 60's and some ore was found. But the rush didn't get off the ground for another twenty years.

Bowman was a main stop on the stage route from St. Elmo to Aspen, and apparently much of Bowman's population was made up of travelers waiting for storms to clear over the pass. Some lives were lost on the pass, and once a stage was stranded for three weeks in a storm.

The population was about 100 through the 80's. And in addition to the stage depot, there were a smelter, a log hotel, a couple of general stores and a few scattered cabins.

The smelter, a two-story building and a few foundations are all that remain.

## JACK'S CABIN (Howville)

An important junction in the early days for traffic going to and from Gunnison and the mining towns to the northeast and northwest.

A cabin town grew up around a cabin built by Jack Howe. Before long the site boasted of two hotels, two saloons, two restaurants and two grocery stores, all in two buildings. The site was first called Howville, but was more commonly known as Jack's Cabin, and that eventually became its official name.

One of the buildings and a small, half-hidden cemetery, remain.

## ALMONT

Apparently the sole reason this remained an important town in the Gunnison area for so long was the fact the Denver and South Park railroad was only built this far.

Great pressure was brought to extend the railroad to other camps (even Tin Cup), but this was never done. Ore from many of the camps (even Tin Cup) was brought here for shipment to Gunnison.

Some lead and zinc from mines along the Taylor River were shipped from here during World War I.

After the mining faded and the railroad was junked, Almont continued to live (especially during the summer) as a resort area. The camp is popular with fishermen and a picnic area was developed. The Taylor Park camp grounds are five miles from the site along the road toward the Taylor Dam and Reservoir.

*And Then There Were . . . . PIE PLANT*, actually a part of the activity of Dorchester. But Pie Plant had a life of its own. The camp grew around the Pie Plant mill which handled the ores from the mines up the Taylor River. There was also some lead and silver mining in the area of the mill itself. In later years the site became a cow camp . . . . *TAYLOR CITY* (not on map), a proposed city near Dorchester on the Taylor River road. It may actually have been a predecessor of Dorchester. All that is known is that an elaborate city was platted but little or nothing was built . . . . *GLACIER* a Denver and Rio Grande station near Crested Butte. It was named for the nearby glacier. Some skiing is done here now . . . . *CROOKTON* or *CROOK-VILLE*, a D & RG station along Tomichi Creek, twenty-four miles from Gunnison. It was named for C. E. Crook, a pioneer in the area . . . . *SARGENTS* and *DOYLE-VILLE*, two more supply towns and railroad stops along the main route from Salida to Gunnison. The towns are little more than stops in the road today . . . . *FOREST HILL*, a small camp around a mill not far from Red Mountain. The mill processed the ores from the Forest Hill mine a couple of miles above the mill . . . . *GIVENS* (not on map), an obscure camp between Bowerman and Sherrod which grew during the boom in that area. An early newspaper said the camp was around the Kimball group of six claims. The 1904 report said the site was named for G. S. Givens, general manager of the mine workings, who purchased 60 acres "and plans to build a modern camp" . . . . *DREW* was a small, obscure mining town at the southern foot of Cumberland Pass, north of Pitkin. Ruins of the old camp can still be seen.

## SOUTH OF GUNNISON

Chance
Iris
Vulcan (Camp Creek)
Spencer (Cameron)
Dubois
Powderhorn (White Earth)
Cochitopa
West Gunnison
Sapinero
Parlin

*And Then There Were* . . . . *HAVERLY, IOLA, CEBOLLA, TOLIAFERO* (Nugget City) (not on map), *GOOSE CREEK, MIDWAY, GATEVIEW, BARNUM, ELK-HORN, ELK CREEK, LAKE CITY JUNCTION, MADERA SIDING.*

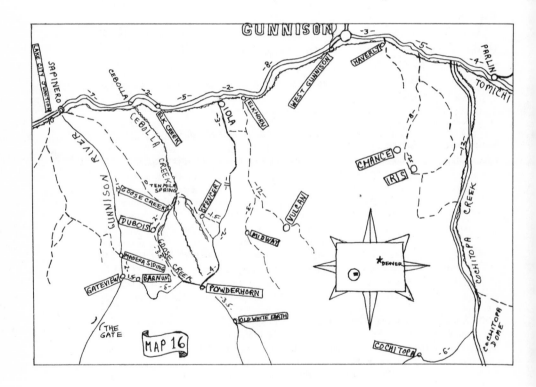

# XV. SOUTH OF GUNNISON

## CHANCE

Chance was established in 1894, the same year as was Iris, and just a mile from the other camp. The name was suggested by the first inhabitants for the luck of the camp. Its history ran parallel to that of Iris, except Chance produced more gold. The Mineral Hill property was between the two towns.

As many as 1,000 miners and prospectors lived in the area during its short boom. There were many shops and businesses. The town even had a telephone system.

Much money was invested in the town's development, but little was returned. A. E. Reynolds, who had some workings here, built a $50,000 mill. But it closed down about a year later, producing only about $30,000 in processed ore.

The camp died down about 1897 but had a brief revival shortly after the turn of the century.

## IRIS

Not so good a producer as Chance, Iris was nevertheless the larger of the two camps which sprang up about 1894. By the following year, Iris had many stores and saloons, had tri-weekly mail service, and was connected to Gunnison by telephone.

About 1,000 miners and prospectors lived in the Iris-Chance area during its short boom.

Better public relations brought more capital into developing Iris mines than those of Chance. But the ore was not very good and was spread too thin for a profitable return.

As with Chance, Iris faded rapidly about 1897, had a short revival in 1901-02, and then died out completely.

Iris was named for the flowers by that name growing here.

## VULCAN (Camp Creek)

Vulcan was by far the biggest and most productive camp in the so-called "Gunnison Gold Belt" south of Gunnison. The Vulcan and Mammoth Chimney Mines were located in 1895, bringing hundreds of fortune-seekers into the area. A town was laid out. It was first called Camp Creek, but the name was changed to Vulcan in 1897. Vulcan was the Roman god of fire. The town received its name from the nearby Vulcan Crest and Vulcan Hill which was caused by ancient volcanic action.

That same year, a newspaper—*The Vulcan Enterprise*—was published.

Rumors of English and French investments in the mines here brought new interest and new miners.

The Vulcan worked 200 men during its boom and shipped two carloads of ore a week to the smelter. A fire raged through the mine for several days about the turn of the century and did untold damage.

The Good Hope, Lincoln, and Vulcan produced nearly a half million in gold and other metals around the turn of the century. These and the other mines were eventually closed. But the Vulcan Mines Company later purchased most of the big mines and worked them for copper, sulphide and quartz.

Several buildings and cabins remain at the site, to be found over a rough twelve-mile road from the highway.

### SPENCER (Cameron)

A twin city to Dubois, Spencer was established around 1894 with the other camps in the area. The camp was first called Cameron, but the name was later changed to Spencer. Some say the name was in honor of S. P. Spencer, county clerk and recorder. Another source says the camp was named after a Milton Spencer, a store owner.

Everybody seemed pretty excited about the camp at first. Some went so far as to call it another Cripple Creek. Hundreds of prospectors probed the hills. Several Creede businesses opened branches here. C. A. Frederick, who published *The Tin Cup Times,* moved his presses here and put out *The Spencer Times.*

But the enthusiasm was not matched by the ores. The camp was all but deserted by 1898. Some good copper finds brought a revival at the turn of the century and about 500 men returned to the area. But litigation and poor management soon spelled an end to Spencer's last boom.

Spencer is cattle country now, and only one old cabin remains.

### DUBOIS

Another camp in what was called the Gunnison Gold Belt. Dubois was laid out in 1894. The first issue of *The Dubois Chronicle,* published in April of the same year, said: "We are here to stay."

Another newspaper, *The Dubois Pick and Drill,* was published for a short time in 1894.

But, despite the deluge of newsprint, the camp faded rapidly after a short prosperity. Some good ore was found but little money was invested to develop the workings.

### POWDERHORN (White Earth)

The recent discovery of a high-grade body of rare columbium near Powderhorn has caused some new excitement in this area which may rival the silver and gold rushes in the past. Some mining experts say the columbium find may be one of the richest, if not the richest pockets of the metal-hardening mineral in the U.S. The mineral is vital to the missile program. Previously, only limited quantities of generally low-grade columbium has been found in the U.S. The Powderhorn discovery has led some experts to believe more of the same can be found in the Colorado Rockies. The search is on.

There has been some mining in the Powderhorn area in the past, but the properties were not too rich or too extensive. Powderhorn had to make do with being a trading center and a resort of sorts. The Cebolla hot springs are nearby.

The site was first settled in 1876. It soon absorbed the village of White Earth which was located a short distance away. There is some evidence that Powderhorn was also called White Earth for a short while.

There are two theories about the name Powderhorn. One says the creek and the town were named such because of the shape of the valley. The most told story, however, is that the town was named for the nearby creek which was named when one of the first settlers found a powderhorn along its bank.

## COCHITOPA

There was a little mining near Cochitopa, but the town was primarily a Ute agency settlement which also functioned as a stop on the Cochitopa Trail, an important one in the development of the west. The trail was used frequently by the mountain men and early explorers in their trips across the mountains. Before that it was an important Indian route.

S. F. Beale was said to have carried a bag of gold over the trail in 1853 on his trip from Sutter's Fort in California to Washington.

Cochitopa comes from the Utes and means "buffalo high place" or "pass of the buffalo."

## WEST GUNNISON

The founding fathers of West Gunnison laid out an attractive town a mile west of the mother city in an effort to lure the railroad. They believed their site would be more appealing because it was nearer the river.

The town had a population of 200 at one time; a fairly good hotel, the Cuenin; a weekly newspaper, *The Gunnison Review;* and several businesses.

The railroad didn't cooperate, however. West Gunnison soon lost out to Gunnison.

## SAPINERO

Sapinero was primarily a supply town and stage stop on the route to Gunnison.

It is most noted for its cultured hermit. Old timers believed the hermit, who lived a short distance out of town, was an English nobleman. He subscribed to many newspapers which were thrown off the train near his crude abode. About once a year he would meander into town for supplies and reading material—a year's supply of books and magazines.

The old Rainbow Hotel here was the most famous landmark along the D&RG narrow gauge from Salida to Montrose. Built in 1908 by H. S. Carpenter, it was a busy resort hotel through the 1920's, especially to weekend fishermen. The hotel later became a roominghouse and part of ranch buildings. The hotel and its lavish furnishings came to an ignoble end during the summer of 1962 when it went under the auctioneer's block, in preparation for the inundation of the area by the reservoir behind the Blue Mesa Dam, part of the vast Curecanti reclamation project.

## PARLIN

Parlin was once a railroad stop. It seems John Parlin, local dairy rancher, gave the site to the railroad free of charge back about 1877. There were only two stipulations: the railroad had to build a depot; and the trains had to stop for at least five minutes so the passengers could buy milk. The pact was kept for a while.

Parlin is still a ranching center.

*And Then There Were . . . . HAVERLY,* a Denver and Rio Grande railroad stop three miles east of Gunnison. The town also served as a supply point for the mining camps south of here . . . . *ELKHORN, IOLA, CEBOLLA, ELK CREEK,* other Denver and Rio Grande railway stops along the Gunnison which served also as supply towns for the mining camps . . . . *LAKE CITY JUNCTION* and *MADERA SIDING* key railroad points on the D & RG run to Lake City. The run began at Lake City Junction, just west of Sapinero . . . . *MIDWAY, GATEVIEW* and *BARNUM,* three lesser supply towns south of Gunnison. Midway, a short distance west of Vulcan, may have had a little mining, but there were no outstanding mines registered here. Gateview and Barnum were within a mile and a half of each other. Gateview was a railroad stop, and Barnum was primarily a supply town. It was named after P. T., the master showman . . . . *TOLIAFERO* (Nugget City) and *GOOSE CREEK,* two obscure mining towns in the Dubois area. Goose Creek was also the name of the mining district, and the town by that name was the district headquarters for a short time. Toliafero was originally called Nugget City but the name was changed to Toliafero at the request of the post office because there was another Nugget City in Colorado. The town flourished in the mid-nineties. Reports said a Colorado Springs group was erecting a hotel and new gold finds were being made every day.

### IRWIN-GOTHIC and the CRYSTAL RIVER

Crested Butte
Irwin (Haverly, Silver Gate, Ruby Camp and Ruby)
Haverly and Silver Gate
Ruby (Ruby City and Ruby Camp)
Cloud City
White Cloud
Baldwin
Floresta (Ruby and Ruby-Anthracite)
Pittsburg
Smith Hill (Anthracite)
Gothic
Elko
Schofield
Crystal (Crystal City)
Marble (Yule Creek, Clarence)
Placita
Redstone
Coal Basin
Avalanche, Prospect, McClure House (McClure Flats)
Janeway (Mobley's Camp)
Marion and Spring Gulch (Gulch)
Sunshine (Sunlight)
Carbondale
Satank (Cooperton, Rockford, Moffat)

*And Then There Were . . . . KEBLER PASS, ROCK CREEK* (not on map), *SILVER NIGHT* (not on map), *ELK MOUNTAIN* (not on map), *KUBLER, GALENA, BELLEVIEW* and *ELKTON*

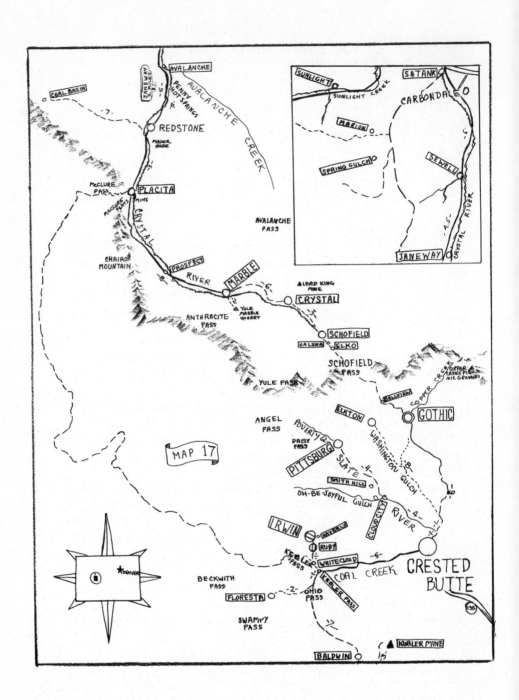

# XVI IRWIN-GOTHIC AND THE CRYSTAL RIVER

## CRESTED BUTTE

Crested Butte was, and is, a lot of things. It was a mining town, stage and railroad center, supply center, smelting center, and is now a tourist and ranching center.

The city was particularly noted for its coal production. For this reason the fact is often overlooked that Crested Butte started out as a gold camp. They say some $350,000 in nuggets were found in nearby Washington Gulch. When they had picked up just about all the nuggets lying around, then they got after the coal.

It wasn't much of a camp until the coal was located in the late 70's. The only bituminous coal found west of the Pennsylvania coal fields was mined here. And coal has kept the city going all these years.

Crested Butte had some fifty dwellings and businesses by 1880, and a population of more than 250. The camp also had a newspaper, *The Crested Butte Republican.*

The railroad came the following year, and Crested Butte became an important travel center. Its importance increased in 1882, when the road over Pearl Pass to Aspen cut some fifty miles off the distance between the two cities.

The Colorado Fuel and Iron Company took over the operation of some of the mines in 1882-83, and Crested Butte hit its stride. There were three anthracite and three bituminous mines near town and some 150 coke ovens were built. The Elk Mountain Hotel, which opened in 1882, was going full blast and boasted the best food this side of New York.

Deep snow covered the area half the year but the residents didn't miss the conveniences because of it. They built two-story outhouses, using the top floor during the winter.

In 1952, the Colorado Fuel and Iron Company closed down the mines because of the expense of getting the coal out. Overnight, the population of Crested Butte dropped from 800 to 400.

But things picked up the following year when work started on the new $400,000 refining mill for lead and zinc.

Crested Butte is still going strong. A city with so many interests doesn't die easily.

COAL DUST: Pearl Pass from Crested Butte to Aspen, long-since closed, was a difficult trail at best. Stage drivers often had to disassemble the stage and lower it over drops up to 100 feet, for re-assembly . . . . during Crested Butte's gold days, thousands of burros carried down the ore to town over the steep trails above Crested

Butte. In later years, when the burros were no longer needed as much, many of them were turned loose. They say there are still packs of wild burros running loose in the hills around Crested Butte . . . . the city was named for the mountain standing 3,300 feet above the town . . . . Howard Smith, who founded Smith Hill, was said to have platted Crested Butte. Smith also had the first sawmill in the Elk Mountains, shipped in at great expense . . . . Crested Butte had, perhaps, the first ski club in Colorado and the first skiing competition.

## IRWIN (Haverly, Silver Gate, Ruby Camp, Ruby)

Irwin's history was as short and as interesting as Gothic's. Both cities crowded a lot of color into the years 1879-1885.

Dick Irwin and a couple of other men struck good ore here in late 1879. Irwin sent his ore to be assayed in Denver. That's no way to keep a secret. Within weeks the gold seekers came a-running. The first ones didn't wait for spring. They built their cabins and stores in the dead of winter.

When spring came and the snow started melting, some of the stumps of the trees they had cut down for cabins turned out to be ten-feet high. The tall tree stumps became a trademark of Irwin. There are still several mighty tall stumps around the site.

The first cabins and stores were built in helter-skelter fashion, forming many camps which all became Irwin during the second year, except Ruby, which took a little longer.

The city was on Ute land and a fear of the Indians hovered over the site most of the time. A company of Minute Men was organized in case of an attack. But the Indians never caused any trouble.

Irwin reached its peak at 1882 and none of the residents could guess that the city would be a ghost town in three or four years. It had been laid out to last forever. They installed fire hydrants and even iron street signs.

The main street was a mile long and every business imaginable was pushing against the wooden walks. There were several hotels, a couple of them as fine as could be found anywhere. There were twenty-three saloons, and plenty of gambling halls and parlor houses.

Irwin needed two marshals to keep the law, and the law kept the marshals busy. There were a sturdy jail, a good-sized school, and later on there were Methodist, Presbyterian and Episcopal churches. Before the churches were built, Bishop Spaulding preached hell-fire and damnation wherever he could get an audience, usually on the main street. One of the first sermons held was in a cabin next to a dance hall and gambling house. The bishop went into the place and asked if it could be closed during the sermon. The owner said he couldn't do that, but he'd donate the next roll of the dice and turn of the cards to the collection.

Irwin had many distinguished visitors and the city didn't cut any corners in showing welcome. Irwin's welcome of General Grant was as lavish as Gothic's, if not more so. The general stayed in Irwin for two days and was royally entertained at the exclusive Irwin Club.

Teddy Roosevelt, not as well known as Grant at the time, was another visitor. Wild Bill Hickok spent some time at the camp, as did Bill Nuttal, vaudeville king of the day.

The Irwin Club was just about as exclusive as a club could get. The furnishing were ornate. The original membership was 100 of the biggest men in the camp. The men met so frequently and were so secretive about it all, the womenfolk began to believe they were carrying on. To dispel the rumors, the ladies were allowed to visit the club one or two nights a week and a grand ball was scheduled. It was one of the grandest balls ever held in the Colorado hills. It was such a success that the members wasted no time scheduling another one. That was the big mistake.

Someone, believed to be a disgusted holdout against letting women in the club, spread cow itch all over the place. The ladies left in short order, scratching themselves like crazy.

The club membership numbered only five in 1884, so rapidly had Irwin faded. The five members got together and decided to auction off the club furnishings and hold one last feast. The auction brought in nine dollars, but by that time there were only two members left, and they didn't feel like feasting.

As it did everything else, Irwin died with a flourish. It died so fast in late 1883 and 1884, that many of the cabins still had dishes on tables and beds unmade.

Recalling the life and sudden death of Irwin has brought many a lump to the threats of oldtimers and amateur historians. Maybe Irwin wouldn't have been so interesting if it had overstayed its usefulness. Colorado cities have come and gone by the hundreds in the last hundred years. Irwin was just one of the casualties, one sorely mourned.

BEST MINES: Forest Queen, Bullion King, Lead King and Lead Queen, Ruby Chief.

GOLD DUST: When the first prospectors appeared in the spring of 1880 after the site had been laid out, they couldn't see the town until they got to it—and then they would have missed it if smoke hadn't been coming out of the holes in the snow where the cabins were . . . . Irwin had six sawmills going at top speed during the boom . . . . Irwin had its share of newspapers, the first and most important being the *Elk Mountain Pilot*. The first issue that came off the press on June 17, 1880, sold for $55, and the first six issues sold for a total of $158 . . . . one of the publishers was J. E. Phillips, who also laid out the graveyard and was the first man to be buried in it. He was killed in an explosion while dynamiting fish . . . . the stone marker for a little girl is the only one left in the Irwin graveyard . . . . as with many other camps, snow was a constant problem here. Scores of persons were killed in snowslides in

this region. Four miners were killed in a slide over the Bullion King mine in 1891
. . . . Irwin's Bullion King, and the Forest Queen and Ruby Chief were the big
producers . . . . the Forest Queen, whose owner once rejected a million dollar bid
on the mine, was sold for $40.45 taxes in 1932. The Queen was worked continuously
until 1891, and has experienced short bursts of activity since . . . . a half interest
in the Forest Queen a few days after its discovery brought $100,000 . . . . the camp
was so hard to get to that first winter, supplies cost a fortune. As an example, butter
cost ninety cents a pound and coffee was as high as sixty-five cents a pound . . . . lots
selling for $10 to $25 the first year, sold for $5,000 in 1880.

### HAVERLY and SILVER GATE

Two of the larger camps in the Irwin and Ruby area. Early maps show
all the camps as distinct locations, although all were within about a half-
mile radius.

Evidence leads historians to believe Haverly and Silver Gate were on
the same site as Ruby and were absorbed by Ruby before the whole shebang became Irwin.

Jack Haverly, a noted theatre and minstrel agent of the time, took to
town promoting. This attempt failed. Haverly laid out the town and gave
it his name, but he over-promoted it. The first forty residents jumped the
site and left Haverly out in the cold.

### RUBY (Ruby City, Ruby Camp)

Ruby was built about a quarter-mile south of Irwin and threatened to
outdo Irwin for a while before it eventually was absorbed by the other
camp. The only reason Ruby's history is worth a separate section is a
story of its nefarious beginning.

It seems a promoter from Leadville came here during the first part of
the boom. He laid out an elaborate city a short distance away from Irwin
which he wanted to call Ruby City. The promoter promised to build a six-
story hotel (almost unheard-of outside Denver), an office building almost as
large, a grocery store and other things. He sold lots reasonably . . . .
not cheap, but reasonable.

When all the lots were sold—and they went pretty fast—the promoter
disappeared and was never heard from again.

The small camp bustled for a short while in the fall of 1880 when some
silver and copper were found here.

### CLOUD CITY

After legal battles just about stopped all the work in Cloud City, the
disgusted miners put up a sign at the entrance to the town: "No lawyers
allowed within city limits." The sign didn't work, however, as Cloud City
died within two years of its founding and litigation caused most of the
trouble.

## WHITE CLOUD

White Cloud was the first camp on the old road to Ruby and Irwin. It was located at the base of Ruby Peaks, about eight miles from Crested Butte. It was named for its location, in a basin of high peaks on which clouds often rested. The camp was born of the Irwin rush, but soon lost most of its residents to Irwin.

## BALDWIN

There was some gold in Baldwin's past. A rich strike was found nearby in 1897. However, the town was mostly concerned with coal and cattle. The original town was across the hill from the present site. It was one of the better coal camps in the state. It apparently changed locations to accomodate the D. & R.G. which ran a branch to Baldwin from Gunnison.

The present town is also a ranching center in addition to its being a coal town. The surrounding valley is noted for its timothy hay which is used for the winter feed of the prize Herefords raised here.

## FLORESTA (Ruby and Ruby-Anthracite)

The Colorado Fuel and Iron Company used the Floresta coal mine here extensively before the turn of the century. The mine was still worked off and on until 1936.

For a while Floresta was a shipping point for several of the mines in the area. The site was originally named Ruby or Ruby-Anthracite, but later took on the name of the coal mine. Floresta is Spanish for "Forest," or "fine country place."

## PITTSBURG

If Pittsburg had been located on a nice flat meadow, say, or even a narrow little valley, it could have been one of the more fabulous places of the day. But, as it was, Pittsburg was built on the side of a hill near timberline. It wasn't worth the men killed in snowslides and the tremendous costs of getting the ore out.

They say the Pittsburg area still abounds in wealth, and it is being worked off and on, but the problem of transportation still deters its development.

The Augusta mine was one of the most famous mines in the state during the 80's. The mine was said to have had a vein, from ten to thirty feet wide, of almost solid gold, silver and lead. The lead was the richest in the nation.

The Augusta was the big mine and most of the history of the area is concerned with this mine. Colonel Stanford, brother of California's Leland Stanford, procured options on the mine in 1886, and went to London to raise money. Before investing, the English capitalists sent a man over in

303

the dead of winter to investigate. The place is always closed up tight by snow in the winter, but the investigator investigated, almost killing himself doing so.

Dozens of persons did lose their lives in snowslides here. In 1904, six Augusta miners were killed in a single slide. The mine could only be worked for three or four months of the year, and the road from Crested Butte to Pittsburg was almost always blocked off by rock and snowslides. If it wasn't for the sure-footed burros, this camp may not have existed at all.

One of the Augusta owners attempted to build an overhead cable from the mine to the town below, but just before the cable was ready for operation, a big snowslide destroyed the whole shebang.

One other story is told of Pittsburg. It concerns Yank Baxter, famous Indian fighter, buffalo hunter and express rider of early-day Colorado. Seems Yank got hold of the Excelsior property here in Poverty Gulch, and was working it one day, when a man came along and asked Yank how much he wanted for his diggings. Yank right off said $35,000, thinking to startle the stranger.

But, instead of being startled, the stranger began counting out the money. Baxter got mad—and told the stranger if he had that kind of money he didn't need the claim. Baxter told the stranger what he could do with his money, and to get off his property. Baxter died a few years later in Salida. He was penniless and had to be buried by the county.

The city of Pittsburg never amounted to much. It was a summer town and never had a population of more than three or four hundred. The mine is still good; some of the ore during its early years ran as high as $10,000 a ton. It was just getting it out that was, and is, the problem.

## SMITH HILL (Anthracite)

Smith Hill was not an official town, but a company settlement built around the Smith Anthracite mine. The coal land was located in 1876, and was later developed by H. F. Smith. At its peak the mine employed about 200 men and shipped between ten to twenty carloads of coal per day over a Denver and Rio Grande spur built to the site.

There are still some cabins left, a half-mile hike off the road to Pittsburg.

## GOTHIC

If people lived in places just for the beauty of it, Gothic would be thriving. The spot is still a mecca for nature lovers, but Gothic as a hustling, bustling mining city is no more.

It had its day, however. It had a peak population of more than 8,000 and was one of the wildest towns in Colorado. But despite all the gambling, drinking and shady ladies, the city boasted a minimum of stealing and only two murders—one an unarmed man on Main Street during broad daylight. Of course, it had a lynching—but that wasn't murder, that was early Colorado justice.

Rich gold and silver ore was found at the foot of Gothic Mountain in June of 1879. Within one week of the time the news was out, there were some 100 tents and cabins up. Within four months there were 170 buildings, including a hotel, three stores, a butcher shop, barber shop, two sawmills, only one saloon and NO GAMBLING DENS. By the following year, the population topped 1,000 and Gothic was the richest city in Gunnison County, surpassing Virginia City and Hillerton.

The city hit its stride during the next two years when millions of dollars in gold and silver were taken out of the surrounding hills. Some of the ore was valued up to $15,000 a ton.

By 1884, most of the gold and silver was gone, and the city faded almost overnight.

But Gothic, as nearby Irwin, did a lot of living during its short lifetime.

The first big deal was an Indian scare, which emptied the town in hours. The Indians never showed up and the miners and their families drifted back and went to work.

The big event of 1880 was a visit by General Grant. The general visited a good many of the boom towns of Colorado. He had the time of his life and the residents of the boom towns had a big time entertaining him. Each city tried to outdo the other in welcoming the general, and Gothic was no exception. They—the citizens—went out to meet him and the parade back to town was one of the noisiest in Colorado history. The general, of course, led the procession, driving his own stage.

Much of the rest of the history of Gothic was made up of horse racing, newspaper reading and people being killed in snowslides.

Horse racing was a big sport in most of the boom towns, and Gothic had some of the best races of them all. The city had more than its share of newspapers, as many as four at one time. *The Gothic Bonanza* was the best. *The Gothic Miner*, a crusading newspaper, urged the wearing of a badge of mourning by the residents for thirty days after the death of President Garfield. Many of the citizens complied.

People were always getting themselves killed in snowslides, and snow was always blocking off the town or blocking the roads to the mines. The first winter was one of the hardest, and twenty-six families were stranded at one time.

Gothic also served as a supply, transportation and smelting center. The city had two schools and three sawmills working to capacity, two big hotels, known as the Olds and the Bums, two "real" doctors, two lawyers, two big dance halls and plenty of saloons. The Gothic shady ladies were notorious for wearing their dresses all the way up to their knees.

Newspapermen Lee Wait and G. H. Judd were both in the running for mayor, so they rolled out the dice and Wait won. But Wait was only mayor for a short time before the boom was over. He left with the others.

Judd stayed on and was mayor of a deserted city. When Irwin and Pittsburg became deserted, Judd extended his jurisdiction over these empty cities. He stayed, and stayed, and stayed. Summer and winter, he remained in Gothic all by himself. A few years ago, they found Judd dead in his cabin. They cremated him and spread his dust around Gothic as he had wanted them to. Judd's still there.

In recent years, the Rocky Mountain Biological Laboratory has taken over the site of Gothic for advanced study in plant and animal life. There's a lot of plant and animal life here.

BEST MINES: Silver Night, Independent, Silver Spruce, Native Silver, Rensselaer, Vermont, Jenny Ling, Wolverine, Triumph, Keno, Buckeye, Hoyt, Terror and East Wing.

GOLD DUST: the Rocky Mountain Biological Laboratory tore down Gothic's big hotel and many of the cabins, remodeling others for its own use . . . . Judd was the subject of numerous magazine articles and one movie, made in 1928 . . . . Gothic was named for the nearby mountain which appears to be of Gothic architecture . . . . The Silver Night, located on Copper Creek, was about the best mine around. It had rich pockets of native and wire silver which assayed at between 6,000 to 15,000 ounces per ton . . . . the Sylvanite group of mines was among the biggest producers, although they were about four miles away over a rough road that was frequently closed by snow . . . . Gothic was not platted by a town company, and so the lots were cheaper . . . . a newspaper report from Gothic in 1879 said the town "has not had a death or sickness since it started. It is a very healthy place."

## ELKO

A smaller camp a couple of miles from Schofield at the foot of Galena Mountain. The town was laid out in 1881 by a group of men from Crested Butte. The men had high hopes for the town but most of the prospectors left after the first big rush and only a handful of people remained in Elko. Some stayed on through the 80's and into the 90's.

Elko, although smaller than Schofield, lasted longer.

## SCHOFIELD

Some silver was found here as early as 1872, but fear of Indians held off settlement for another seven years. In 1879, after Chief Ouray had quieted the Utes, and after more strikes had been made here, between 200 and 300 prospectors rushed into the area.

The town was getting its start in 1880 when General Grant rode in on a white mule. The illustrious guest was accompanied by ex-Colorado Governor Routt.

There wasn't much to show the guests, but the residents rolled out a barrel of whiskey. It was enough to make the general's visit to Schofield one of his most pleasant visits to any Colorado town.

Perhaps the most colorful resident in town was "Old Lady Jack," a niece of the famed Indian scout, Jim Bridger. Old Lady Jack wore a gunny sack as a shawl and was partial to cleanliness and cats. She kept an army of cats and would wash them frequently, hanging them out to dry by the napes of their necks. She would even wash her firewood so she wouldn't get her hands dirty.

A mill was built in 1881, and by 1882, when Schofield hit its peak, the town had a hotel, restaurant, post office, store, carpenter, blacksmith, barber and daily mail-stages to Gothic and Crested Butte.

Schofield was at the foot of Schofield Pass and served as a station for stages going over the pass. Being one of the more rugged passes of the day, people didn't go over it unless they had to.

The transportation problem, plus the mediocre ores, soon spelled the end of Schofield. By 1885, when the post office was discontinued, the town was virtually deserted. A few people, like Old Lady Jack, lingered on until the 90's.

Only a trace of the isolated camp remains. Just north of town is a deep, dark canyon that was called "Sonofabitch Basin" by old-timers. General Grant thought it was an appropriate name.

### CRYSTAL (Crystal City)

The kingdom of Crystal is well protected today by a fortress of high and mighty mountains. About the only entrance to it is a harrowing road from Marble.

The mountains didn't hold back the early prospectors, but they did hinder the area's development. The first prospectors entered the beautiful kingdom in the mid-60's, but largely because of the lack of good roads, little was done to develop the area until the early 80's when some rich silver strikes were made.

The first roads entered from Gunnison country, primarily Schofield Pass. Later, a road was built out to Carbondale, and Crystal got its biggest boost.

A half dozen mines produced good silver, lead and zinc here until the panic of '93. One of the biggest producers, the Lead King, recovered from the panic and continued to shell out the metal until 1913. A little mining activity has been carried on since, but not much.

Crystal, or Crystal City as it was known during its heyday, prospered through the 80's and early 90's. The population averaged about 500. There were a fancy hotel, a post office, two newspapers, several general stores and saloons, some pool halls, and the popular Crystal Club.

Brothers Al and Fred Johnson just about ran the town. Al published the *Crystal River Current* ( a newspaper), and operated the hotel, post office and a general store. Brother Fred carried the mail back and forth to Crested Butte on snowshoes during the winter.

Crystal was represented in the Chicago World's Fair of 1893 with a display of silver ore from the Black Queen Mine.

Although there were still a lot of precious metals left in the hills around Crystal, the city pretty much faded after the silver panic. By 1899, there were only a weekly newspaper, *The Silver Lance,* a general store and a saloon, and a handful of people.

But Crystal City has never been deserted for long. The summer population through the years has varied, but usually has stayed around fifty. The few people who live here now are mostly sportsmen. Some talk has circulated about restoring the city and fixing up the road, but nothing much has been done about it yet.

Perhaps, in the near future, the beautiful mountain kingdom will thrive again. Several cabins are left at the site, and the impressive Sheep Mountain Tunnel mine can be seen on the side of the cliff nearby.

BEST MINES: Black Queen, Lead Queen, Black Eagle, Sheep Mountain Tunnel, Inez, Catalpa, Harrison Farley, all good mines.

## *MARBLE* (Yule Creek, Clarence)

The fabulous "Mountain of Marble" near this site has furnished marble for the Lincoln Memorial in Washington, the Tomb of the Unknown Soldier in Arlington, the municipal buildings in New York and San Francisco, the New Customs building and Colorado National Bank building in Denver, and many other buildings throughout the country. The mountain furnished the largest single block of marble ever quarried, for the World Columbian Exposition in 1892. The one block cost $1,700.

The marble here was said to have been the best and the most plentiful in the world. There is still plenty left. But people just don't use marble as they used to, or if they do, they use a marble substitute. So the city of Marble is fighting off oblivion with a meager tourist trade during the summer months.

Some gold and silver were found here in the late 70's and early 80's, but the area was pretty much overlooked until the mountain of marble was uncovered in 1882. Some credit the discovery to George Yule, while others claim a couple of fellows named William Woods and W. D. Parry did the discovering.

308

The marble was pure white. Some had pink, gray or blue serpentine gizmos in it. It was good stuff. The trouble encountered at first was transportation.

Marble is difficult to handle. The first marble was taken out by wagon over the long, rough road to Carbondale. During the winter, it was usually taken out on sleds. This was costly and slow. Nonetheless, a considerable amount was hauled out this way, before the railroad finally reached the city in 1907.

Several smelters and quarries were opened here during the 90's. A number of companies and individuals aided in the development of the marble deposits here: the Kelly Brothers, the Colorado-Yule Marble Company, the Vermont Marble Company. The best known figure in Marble's history was J. C. Osgood, a man of mystery, but a man of tremendous power. He stood toe-to-toe with the other financial titans of the day, including Rockefeller, for control of the Colorado Fuel and Iron Company, and he won. (See Redstone).

Two camps, one called Clarence and other Yule Creek, started out about the same time in the early 1880's. As the camps grew, they combined and were named Marble. Much of the town, especially the important buildings, were constructed of marble, and therefore have remained through the years. But, even at that, much of the city has been destroyed by fire, snow and rock slides, and even the big flood of 1941. Marble has had more than its share of misery.

The city has had its ups and downs as far as work was concerned, too. The population varied from a low of 100-200 during its early years and during World War I to more than 2,000 during the early 1900's and 1920's. In 1926, the year of Marble's most disastrous fire, the mill here was the largest marble-finishing plant in the world.

Personal disasters did much to bring about Marble's downfall, but the greatest blow was the fall in popularity of genuine marble. The Vermont Marble Company closed down its quarries in 1941. The same year, a cloudburst up the Crystal River sent a huge tidal wave down the valley and it wiped out most of the city.

Little marble mining has been done since, except by and for tourists. The city isn't dead. In fact, the summer population has been increasing the past few years. As Colorado's tourist trade grows, the Crystal River Valley can't help but grow in popularity. Marble will remain an important point in the valley.

MIGS: Marble had three or four newspapers in its day. Perhaps the most important was the *Marble Times*, published from 1892 until the early 1900's. One of the editors was Sylvia Smith, a sharp-tongued crusader against many people and things, especially mine owners. Her "I told you so" attitude over a mine disaster was finally too much, and the lady was escorted out of town . . . . the first piano was brought into Marble in 1889 after a long, difficult trip from the east. The trip didn't do the piano much good—in fact, it sounded terrible and was soon put out of its misery once and for all . . . . several of the early-day buildings, including the school and churches, are still standing. The city had a good band during the 20's and the old bandstand is still erect . . . . the main marble quarries can be reached via a four-mile hike . . . . the original population of Marble was made up of Italians, brought to this country because of their experience in working in the quarries in Italy . . . . the mile-long Treasure Mountain Lines' locomotive remains on the tracks at the end of the line, just where New York banker Strauss left it before he went down with the Lusitania. . . . the marvelous marble ruins, including the frames of the giant conveyor, line the river in Marble. It is much like wandering through the ruins of an ancient Roman city. One of the few marble levees in the world can be found here, too.

## PLACITA

Some old cabins and an old coal mine about halfway down the Crystal River Valley from Marble, mark the site of Placita. The Colorado Fuel and Iron Company opened the mine in 1899, took out 6,500 tons of coal that first year. The C. F. & I. sold the mine in 1901. It was later operated for several years by the Rapini brothers.

The coal mine gave rise to the town, but the town also served as a railroad center. Laid out in a wide and level part of the valley, Placita was ideal for railroad use. For a while, before the railroad was built on up the valley, Placita was the main shipping point for the marble quarries.

When the Crystal River Valley was booming, the Crystal River and San Juan Railroad (Marble railroad) ran along one side of the river and the Elk Mountain Railroad, heading for Gunnison country, ran along the other side of the river.

The first entry into the Crystal River Valley was made from Gunnison country, over perilous Schofield Pass. When the Aspen country was opened up and Carbondale came into being, the Crystal River got its big boost.

Schofield and the other passes from Gunnison country have long since been closed. The Crystal River Valley is a one-way road from Carbondale to Marble. The area from Marble to the divide, over which thousands of wagons, coaches, mules and men once rode down into Crystal country, is empty of people—one of the most beautiful sections of the state is now a no-man's land.

Placita was a lesser city along the Crystal. It still is, but from this site there is a commanding view of the beautiful valley. At the far end of the expansive valley from Placita is majestic Chair Mountain. When the Indians roamed here, the mountain played an important part in their legends and rituals.

The valley was headquarters for Chief Colorow of the outlaw Utes that terrorized the entire region for several years, postponing settlement by the white men.

One of the early characters in the valley was "Boilbeef Jim," a Civil War veteran who lived out his life with bullets imbedded in his leg. He was noted all up and down the valley for his cooking. But all he would ever cook was boiled beef.

All the aspen in the valley whisper of the legend here. They tell of the Devil's Punch Bowl, a rock cavern at the southern end of the valley, where, legend says, one of the first white men fell into the hole, and his skeleton still remains under the snow. The skeleton of the man's horse was found above the hole, still tied to the tree.

The top personages of the day passed through the Crystal River Valley. J. P. Morgan and John Rockefeller once dined at the Osgood mansion. Jay Gould was here, they say. The valley is still a mecca for artists. Frank Mechau, one of the west's most famous artists, died in recent years, near his favorite view—Mount Sopris.

Ben Turner, another popular western artist, still spends half the year in and around Redstone. On good days he heads out with his painting and fishing equipment, returning at evening with two or three landscapes and his limit of fish. On bad days he remains in his studio overlooking Redstone, painting still life and Indian portraits, for which he is famous.

Some historians have named this the "Valley of the Jinx" for the many failures—money failures—seen here. How can people, including historians, speak of money in a valley so rich in beauty—and promise? The history of the Crystal River Valley has just begun.

## REDSTONE

Redstone was a fairy city built by J. G. Osgood. It may soon become a recreation wonderland, known throughout the world. The area is ripe for development, and now it has a sponsor. Work has already begun.

John Osgood reportedly purchased the land around the turn of the century for $100,000. On the land he built his fabulous 42-room manor house, a 40-room inn and a model village for his workers. Cleveholm, his mansion, is a Tudor castle. No expense was spared in bringing in the best furnishings from throughout the world. The best Italian artists came to hand-stencil the oak panel walls. Many of the ceilings were done in gold-leaf. The library was done in hand-tooled green leather and elephant hide, the music room in green silk brocade, the dining room in ruby velvet. A huge, hand-cut stone fireplace dominates the drawing room. Even the stables were done in oak.

The inn at the edge of town was furnished almost as lavishly, and was intended originally as a club house for the workers.

The city itself was a novel experiment in employer-employee relationship. Attractive homes were built for the workers, each one unique and each one a different color. The best in cultural and educational facilities was provided. The top artists of the day appeared here, and European talent was imported to give the workers instruction in many fields of endeavor.

No more fabulous character burst and bloomed upon the pages of Colorado history than John G. Osgood. He was a giant among the giants of his day. But, at times, he was a reluctant dragon, a man of tempest, or a man of peace and beauty—a man of mystery.

Little is known of his history. He was born in Brooklyn on March 6, 1851. He worked at a number of white collar jobs before making his way to Colorado in 1882. He worked every boom town of the day. He must have made a fortune, nobody's quite sure. He may have just had the minimum of money and the maximum of organization genius.

With this he organized the Colorado Fuel Company. Soon he acquired the Colorado Coal and Iron Company, and named the new larger company the Colorado Fuel and Iron Company. Osgood defeated John W. Gates for leadership of the firm, and successfully held off Morgan, Gould and Rockefeller for control of the company. He is believed to be the last independant to stand up against the financial titans of the time. The C. F. & I., with Osgood at the wheel, secured an investment of more than forty million dollars in coal and iron business in Colorado. He broke with the company in 1903, and spent the few remaining months of his life in his castle on the Crystal. After he died, his wife, known as "Lady Bountiful" along the Crystal, remarried. But her allegiance remained with Redstone and the Crystal River Valley.

Now, some fifty years later, another man of money and vision is back in the valley. Frank Kistler wants to turn Redstone into another Sun Valley, only with better scenery. Kistler's plans call for a network of ski runs, several tourist cabins and cottages, and many other recreational facilities to make Redstone a year-round outdoor wonderland. The Osgood mansion will be a country club, the inn will be the hub of activities.

In a few years, Redstone, "the Ruby of the Rockies," may bloom as it's never bloomed before. Osgood would be proud.

## COAL BASIN

A good coal seam was located here in 1881 by W. P. Parry and G. P. Griffith. The two were more interested in gold and silver. They sold the claim to J. C. Osgood a short time later.

Osgood and his C.F.&I. operated mines here for a number of years. Another coal mine was located in 1892. A spur of the railroad was built to Coal Basin in 1900, greatly boosting the effectiveness of the area.

The community was primarily a company town. There were a store and post office, some boarding houses and a number of cabins. The peak population was around 300.

A miner was shot and killed in a drunken brawl in 1908—about the only excitement Coal Basin ever had.

The C.F.&I. closed the mines in 1909.

### AVALANCHE, PROSPECT and McCLURE HOUSE (McClure Flats)

Three of the smaller locations along the Crystal River.

Avalanche was a stop on the Crystal River Railroad. The small community was named for the nearby mountain. In 1880, the U. S. Forest Service asked the postmaster of Redstone to designate the name of the mountain. He named it Avalanche Mountain. There are scars of past avalanche activity on the peak.

Some coal mining was done at Prospect. The C.F.&I. operated some mines here in the late 90's. It was also a freighting, mail and supply town. The peak population was about 200. It was a fairly sociable community. The town was named when one of the early settlers found a mining pan near the river. Prospect was granted a post office in 1886.

The McClure cabin was a favorite stopover on the journey up and down the Crystal. In the 90's when a pass was developed over the divide it was called McClure Pass and McClure House became a junction point. A few other cabins were built around his house. McClure Pass, although a fairly rough road, is still open part of the year. It is a part of State Highway 133.

### JANEWAY (Mobley's Camp)

There was a little gold mining on Avalanche Creek during the 80's and 90's and the small community of Janeway, at the mouth of the creek, served as headquarters. The town was named for Mrs. Jane Francis of Carbondale who was part owner of the Skobeloff and M. J. mines.

The first strike was made by Hugh Pattison in 1880. In the following years there were a number of claims staked out up and down the creek, but none of them produced much. About the best was the Silver Queen.

Janeway had a post office some of the time and a store most of the time during the community's existence. There were never more than 100 people living here at any one time.

### MARION and SPRING GULCH (Gulch)

Two neighboring coal camps not far from Carbondale that were busy off and on from the late 80's until about the beginning of World War I.

Spring Gulch was the larger of the two camps with a population running all the way from 100 to about 300.

Marion's population fluctuated between 100 and 200.

313

Both towns were run much of the time by the C.F.&I. and were very much alike. Both had active unions. Both were sociable, had glee clubs, athletic teams, usually competing against one another.

The towns died away when the C.F.&I. closed the mines in the early years of this century.

## SUNSHINE (Sunlight)

Sunshine was one of the larger coal towns in the Carbondale area. The mine was opened about 1887. When Satank faded, many of that city's residents came here. The town had a large store, a saloon, blacksmith shop, post office, a boarding house and several cabins. The post office was given the name of "Sunlight" because there were too many "Sunshines" around already.

The C.F.&I. operated the mine in 1892 and 1893, then shut it down. The mine was re-opened in 1897 and stayed open this time until 1904.

In 1907, the Rocky Mountain Fuel Company leased the mine until 1921, but when the Colorado and Midland closed operations in 1917, the mine was closed for good. When the mine closed only fifty miners were living in the town, and the total production for the year was 350 tons.

## CARBONDALE

Carbondale is now a ranch and farm center. Years ago, Carbondale was a coal and railroad center for the towns up the Crystal River.

The city was named by John Mankin, one of the founders, for his home in Pennsylvania. When the railroad came to Carbondale, the city was important in shipping out marble, until the marble interests up the Crystal found it was too much trouble to take the marble out by wagon. So they built the railroad on up to where the marble was taken out of the mountain.

Carbondale was not important any more after that, as far as mining was concerned. It is now famous for its potatoes, developed by Eugene Grubb.

## SATANK (Moffat, Cooperton, Rockford)

Satank rivaled Carbondale for a number of years, eventually losing out when the C.F.&I. influenced the railroad to by-pass Satank in favor of Carbondale.

Satank had been a railroad stop, one of the first and most important on the D.&R.G. for the area. But the C.F.&I. made plans to establish large-scale coking operations at Carbondale. The D.&R.G. extended the line and built the main station a mile away near Carbondale.

Then when the move was accomplished and Satank began to fade over-night and Carbondale boomed, the C.F.&I. decided not to build the coke ovens after all.

Satank was laid out in 1885. When the railroad came two years later,

Satank thrived. During its heyday, Satank had a large restaurant, seven saloons, a school, post office and the Hotel Moffat. The grand ball opening the hotel brought guests from all the way up the Crystal River and as far away as Glenwood Springs. The railroad ran a special train to Satank for the event.

Satank was named for Setanta (Standing Bear), a well known Kiowa Chief.

*And Then There were . . . . KEBLER PASS,* a Denver & Rio Grande Station at the 9,946-foot level of the pass for which it was named . . . . *KUBLER,* a town around the Kubler mine southwest of Crested Butte. The mine was operated by the Colorado Fuel and Iron Company . . . . *ELK MOUNTAIN* (not on map), a rather large camp in Elk Park east of Gothic. The top mines here were the Lake View, Silver Queen, Jenny Lind and Silver Moon . . . . *ROCK CREEK* and *SILVER NIGHT* (neither on map), small camps located near some of the best Gothic mines. Rock Creek was at the head of the East River, about seven miles from Gothic. Nearby mines were the Cliff, North Star, Shakespeare, Colora, Wild Oat, International, Whopper and Legal Tender. Silver Night was near the famous Silver Night mine, perhaps Gothic's richest mine . . . . *GALENA* and *BELLEVIEW,* two more small mining camps between Gothic and Schofield. Galena was about midway between Schofield and Elko. Belleview was a short distance north of Gothic . . . . *ELKTON,* a fairly large but little known camp around some mines at the end of Washington Gulch, a short distance west of Gothic.

## XVII. THE LITTLE MAN AND THE MOUNTAINS

When poet Sam Foss said, "Send me men to match my mountains," he could have been more specific had he said, "Send me more men like Otto Mears."

Not as poetic, perhaps, but Otto Mears was more than a match for any mountain. A midget of a man, Otto Mears stood toe-to-toe with some of the mightiest mountains in Colorado and whittled them down to size.

The history of southern Colorado, particularly the San Juans, would have been much different without him. The development of the west would have been extremely more difficult without men like him.

Born in Russia in 1841, Mears came to San Francisco with his family when he was ten years old. His name first appeared as a member of the First California Volunteers in the war between the states. He served with Kit Carson in the Indian Campaign against the Navajos.

Otto came to Colorado in the 60's. He opened a store in Saguache, then an Indian agency. He took up farming in the San Luis Valley. With Major Lafayette Head, he operated a sawmill and grist mill, and brought one of the first mowers and steam threshers into the Valley in 1867. But the Mexicans refused to have wheat threshed by a machine, claiming the process robbed the grain of much of its food value.

Needing a market for his grain, Mears eventually decided to take a gigantic gamble. He would build a road over Poncha Pass to sell his wheat in the Arkansas Valley.

It was a crude road that he built, little better than functional. But it was enough of a success that the government granted him permission to operate it as a toll road. The road was important to Colorado in that it provided his imaginative mind with a challenge.

Road-building was in his blood. Before he was through, Otto Mears built a network of roads in the San Luis Valley spanning some 300 miles. Many of his roads were used later as railroad beds. No place remained the same after it was touched by his golden hand.

A short time later he was appointed one of five commissioners to make a new treaty with the Indians for eleven million acres of land, encompassing much of western Colorado. The government was prepared to pay $1,800,000 to the Indians for the land. Mears paid the Indians two dollars each to sign the treaty, spending a total of $2,800. Although he saved the government nearly the entire $1,800,000, he was charged with bribery and brought to trial. The case was dismissed when Mears pointed out the Indians would rather have the small cash payment than the promised much larger payment.

It was probably during the time he was negotiating the treaty that Mears saw the golden opportunities and the great challenge of the San Juans.

The Silverton-Red Mountain area, although some of the richest mineral country in the state, was all but boxed in by those rugged mountains. Otto Mears wasn't an engineer. "Impossible" wasn't a part of his vocabulary, either. He was a little man who saw the mountains staring defiantly down on him. He was a giant of a man who accepted the challenge.

By this time, he was an accomplished road-builder. Although he lacked the engineer's and geologist's knowledge and modern tools, he had a genius for choosing the right pathway to follow, and above all, he knew where the roads were needed.

With amazing skill and speed his roads took shape, despite the almost constant threat of snow and rock slides, the sometimes threat of Indians, and the frequent threat of losing the work force to a new gold or silver rush. Soon, his roads connected the major boom towns in the San Juans. Supplies and new fortune-seekers entered the once-isolated area. Millions in rich ores were hauled out over his roads.

Perhaps, his biggest challenge was the road over Red Mountain Pass. Many laymen and many engineers said such a road was impossible. But Otto Mears was to hear and disregard that word many times before he was through. His road over Red Mountain Pass cost $10,000 a mile—equivalent to more than $100,000 a mile at today's prices. It soon became one of the most traveled roads in southern Colorado. The later-built Million Dollar Highway follows much of Mears' early road.

The step from road-building to railroad-building may seem a small one. Actually, however, it provides many more challenges, especially in mountain country. Railroad grades can't be as steep, curves must be much gentler, and the tracks must be more sheltered from possible snow and rock slides.

But when the recently-organized Denver and Rio Grande considered building a railroad into the San Juans, the railroad's most logical choice for the job of builder was Otto Mears. When a job was fraught with challenges, who but Otto Mears would accept with alacrity?

Mears used many of his earlier road beds in laying out a network of tracks connecting the boom towns of the San Juans. Then he would build another road.

Every new link brought its new challenge and a new cry of "impossible" from the grandstands. But Otto Mears whipped 'em all, or almost all.

His greatest challenge, perhaps, was the line from Telluride to Rico down to Durango over Lizard Head Pass and "Ophir-land." Otto Mears built

317

his famous Ophir Loop, where the trestles were sometimes 100 feet high and the track actually swings around until it is directly above the track below.

Legend says Otto Mears himself was so terrified at his first ride over "the loop" he wanted to get out and walk.

Another amazing thing about "the Loop" was the safety in which it was built. Railroad building was one of the most dangerous pastimes in the early west. Hundreds lost their lives. The Ophir Run was a grueling and dangerous stretch. Workmen sometimes dangled 1,000 feet over sheer cliffs to chip out a pathway for the tracks. Yet not one man lost his life in the construction of the Ophir Loop.

Otto Mears opened up the San Juans, and the endless treasures of the San Juan poured forth. A wild celebration met the entry of one of his trains into a boom town. Cities died when ignored by those all-important tracks. New cities were born. The clackity-clack of his puffing locomotives set up a constant chant to mimic the early cries of "Impossible!"

Otto Mears, hired as a track-builder, soon owned the railroad. He lived a long and useful life. He died in Pasadena, California, in 1931. He was buried under a simple marker which should have read: "He thought 'Impossible' was a naughty word."

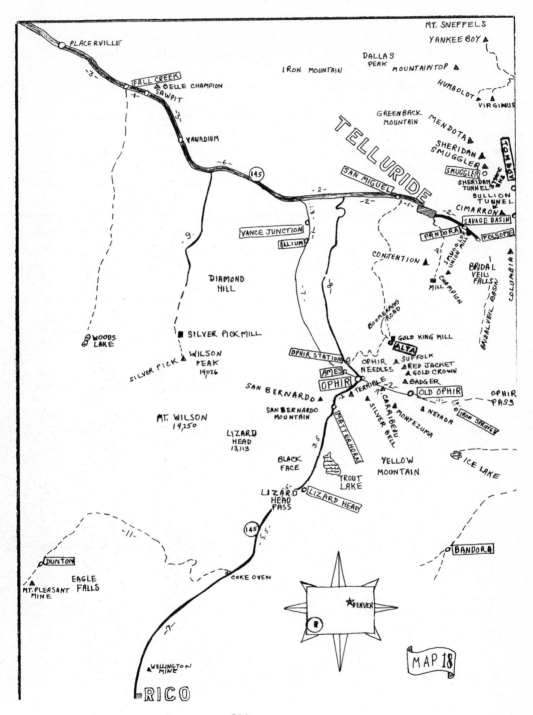

MAP 18

## TELLURIDE TO RICO

| | |
|---|---|
| Telluride (Columbia) | Folsome |
| Placerville | Ames |
| Fall Creek (Seymore, Silver Pick) | Ophir (Howards Fork) |
| Sawpit | Old Ophir |
| San Miguel City | Matterhorn (San Bernardo) |
| Savage Basin Camp | Dunton |
| Pandora (Newport) | Lizard Head |
| Rico (Carbon City, Carbonateville, Lead City, Dolores City) | |

*And Then There Were* .... *SMUGGLER, ALDER CREEK* (not on map), *OMEGA* (not on map), *LEOPARD* (not on map), *VANADIUM, VANCE JUNCTION, ILLIUM, OPHIR STATION, IRON SPRINGS, TOMBOY, ALTA.*

*TELLURIDE* (Columbia)

Telluride is another city that may see better days. And it's seen some great days already.

In all, its mines have produced about a quarter of a billion dollars in precious metals. Many of its best mines are still operating, and some geologists estimate there are enough rich minerals in the surrounding hills to withstand another 40 or 50 years of full production. A neat and attractive little town, Telluride is just beginning to exploit the tourist possibilities of the region.

Telluride, first known as Columbia, was just another camp along the San Miguel River in the late 70's. San Miguel City, about a mile down the river, was larger and could well have outdistanced Telluride. However, Telluride was more convenient to the better mines, and as the mines were developed, Telluride eventually took over as the leading city in the section.

But Telluride and the other camps around were still extremely isolated. Although the mines proved prosperous the costs of shipping them out ate up much of the profit. Consequently, Telluride grew slowly during the 80's. The boom came in 1890, when Otto Mears' little railroad chugged into Telluride, opening the fabulous region to the world.

The mines were already well-developed and now, with the railroad to take out the ores quickly and economically, Telluride lost little time in recovering the lost ground. The town was already platted and many of the buildings and cabins were built, so the sudden growth was more orderly than that found in other boom camps.

The boom lasted until 1893 and the Silver Crash. Silver being the primary metal of the camp, Telluride was all but deserted when rich gold properties were found and another boom began. The town has been going strong ever since.

Several placer claims were made on or near what is now the Smuggler property in 1874. Several more prospectors ventured into the area and other rich claims were located and developed.

The two top mines were the Sheridan and the Union. In 1876, J. B. Ingram came along and noticed that the two claims extended 500 feet more than was legally allowed. He set up shop on the middle ground and called it the Smuggler.

The Smuggler developed into one of the best mines in the area. It bought up most of the other paying properties around and became one of the largest mines in the state. The ores were found from the surface down. The main vein extended a mile in length. The property had more than thirty-five miles of tunnels by 1900, and was even further exploited when rich zinc deposits were found in 1915.

The two other important mines were the Liberty Bell, about two miles north of Telluride, and the Tomboy, located on Savage Fork of Marshall Basin, 3,000 feet above Telluride. The Liberty Bell was one of the first locations but was considered all but worthless and was neglected until the late 90's when rich deposits were found. The Tomboy, on the contrary, paid from the beginning. In 1897, the mine was sold to the Rothchilds of London for two million dollars.

In 1894, the Columbia and Japan lodes were located near the Tomboy.

Telluride had its labor wars about the same time Cripple Creek did, and they were almost as vicious. The first major strike was called in 1901 by union miners in protest against the recently-installed system of contract work, which meant a large loss in pay to most miners.

Things proceeded peaceably enough until the mine owners, refusing arbitration, reopened the mines using scab labor. The incensed union miners organized a small army, surrounded the mine, and waited for a shift change. Four men were killed and several were injured in the ensuing free-for-all. The battered scabs were herded to the top of the hill and ordered to make tracks.

A story is told of the first strike. It seems some scab miners, including one badly-injured man, sought refuge from the free-for-all in the mine. A courageous mailman, waving an American flag, braved the union blockade and entered the mine. The mailman reappeared a few moments later with the injured scab who was wearing a mail bag with leg holes cut in it. The union miners, rather than face charges of tampering with the U. S. Mail, permitted the mailman and his "bag of mail" to pass.

As with Cripple Creek, the Telluride miners won the first round. The contract system of work was abolished and a standard hour and wage scale adopted. But an uneasy peace reigned. A year later, mine manager Arthur Collins was shot and killed by unknown assailants.

And the labor war broke out with new fury in 1903. Union miners at the Tomboy walked off their jobs when non-union labor was put to work in force. The union miners lost little time in gaining the upper hand. The mine owners appealed to Governor Peabody for help. The Governor appealed to President Teddy Roosevelt for troops. The President declined to answer the petition. So, in January 1904, Governor Peabody sent State Troops to Telluride under the leadership of Major Z. T. Hill. Hill took over the city and the surrounding mines. Hill and his soldiers arrested the union leaders and several other miners, beat up some, and booted them all out of town. A mine-owners committee, with the blessing of Hill, kicked sixty more miners out of town. Hill ruled the area with an iron hand, censoring all communications and supervising virtually all the activity in the city.

His methods gained sympathy for the miners, as did a widely-circulated picture of a union official chained to a telephone pole. But it did the union little good.

The union leaders kicked out of camp took over an abandoned mine near Ouray and began planning and drilling for the recapture of the Telluride area.

Governor Peabody was blamed for the situation, and it was during this time, and as a result of this strike, that Harry Orchard attempted to blast the governor to Kingdom Come with a few well-placed sticks of dynamite. His plan almost worked but the governor was spared by a last-second quirk of fate. Harry, however, further developed his "art" and became more effective in Cripple Creek and Idaho (see Cripple Creek).

Despite the growing feeling of sympathy for the miners and all their elaborate plans to regain lost ground, the mine owners won. The union was broken and the mines continued to operate with non-union labor.

Telluride also had its snowslides. The worst years were 1902 and 1906, when scores of lives were lost in avalanches. One hundred persons lost their lives in the winter of 1905-06.

Nineteen men were killed in successive slides in 1902 which carried away the aerial tramway to the Liberty Bell mine. Several men were buried in the slide. A second slide buried several members of the rescue party. A third cut off the second rescue party and killed one man.

Perhaps the two most notable characters in Telluride history were Marshal Jim Clark and Banker Charles Waggoner. Clark was an early day character on the right side of the law, but greatly hated and feared. Waggoner was a latter-day figure, on the wrong side of the law, but deeply loved by the citizens of Telluride.

Clark was a sadistic gun-slinger, who used to keep in practice by beating up innocent miners, and shooting out signs in Telluride. He was hated by virtually everyone but no one dared speak up against him. He bullied the debtors into paying their bills. Knowing he was hated, Clark lived in constant fear of ambush. To be ready in case of emergency, he cached guns at various places around town.

He was shot in the back one night by a man hiding in the shadows between two stores. The murderer was never found. Nobody really cared to look.

Waggoner, a small-town banker, was the talk of the banking world a few years ago. He achieved his reputation by swindling some of the best banking brains in the nation out of half a million dollars in order to keep Telluride solvent.

It began with the crash of 1929. Banks were closing throughout the country. Workers who had scrimped to save a small nest egg were penniless. Waggoner saw the same thing happening to his bank and his long-time friends. But he couldn't cover the deposits. Something had to be done.

Waggoner went to Denver. Using a system of banking codes, he wired the top New York banks and told them, on authority of their Denver branches, to deposit huge drafts to the credit of the Telluride Bank.

Then he went to New York, showed his credentials, and withdrew the money. He sent a large sum in cash to the Telluride bank to cover the deposits. He deposited the rest in the name of the Telluride Bank in so many banks around the country that much of it was impossible to trace.

When he was arrested a few days later in Wyoming, he took full blame for the swindle, and stated that the bank, its employees and depositors were in no way responsible. He was sentenced to fifteen years in prison, but his friends in Telluride didn't lose a cent of their savings.

BEST MINES: Liberty Bell, Tomboy, Smuggler, Union, Medata, Cimmaron, Argentine, Sheridan, Cleveland, Bullion, Hidden Treasure and Alta.

GOLD DUST: Another near-legendary character in early Telluride was Reverend Bradley who preached hell and damnation from newspaper articles rather than the Bible . . . . Telluride also had a notorious red light district until a fire roared through the area, destroying twenty-two saloons and all eight parlor houses. The Pick and Gad was the best known parlor house and the most noted "Gambling Hell" was the Pacific Hall . . . . "Casey Jones," the Galloping Goose, half bus and half train, roared into Telluride until recent years on its run from Ridgeway to Durango . . . . Telluride produced gold, silver, copper, lead zinc, tungsten, manganese, and now some uranium . . . . The Idarado Mining Company mill, using new methods, produces 1,800 tons of processed ore per day, biggest operation in Telluride history. . . . in the

323

90's, Telluride was considered one of the best-lighted cities in the world. L. L. Mum built the first long-distance, high-powered transmission lines to the city. The first hydrogenerator is now in the Henry Ford Museum . . . . there were many foreign groups involved in Telluride's history. The camp saw many European engineers and musicians . . . . the Gold Run mill below the Liberty Bell was the third largest mill in the state . . . . the slack from ore dumps was reworked in recent years and produced much profit . . . . the Telluride district produced 60 million in precious metals by 1909 . . . . the peak population was between 5,000 and 10,000 . . . . another famous Telluride family was the Costigans. George Costigan, Sr., a Virginia lawyer, operated the Liberty Bell for several years and was a famous Colorado judge. One son, George, Jr., wrote several legal textbooks, and the other son, Edward, was a U. S. Senator from Colorado . . . . miners attempted to send the ore down the hill to the mills on toboggans, but a considerable amount of the ore was lost and the plan was soon abandoned. The miners also attempted to steady the sleds by putting wings on them. A couple of sleds "flew" down the mountain before this plan was abandoned too . . . . Sometimes the hills were too steep even for burros. So, a novel plan was devised here to lash huge logs to the burros, which went up in tandem fashion . . . . the Tomboy operated 60 years before it closed down in 1928.

## PLACERVILLE

This city was named for the placer gold found here. The name has remained although the placer gold has long since played out and the city became one of the top livestock shipping points in western Colorado.

A prospecting party from Del Norte, led by Colonel S. H. Baker, was credited with finding rich gold-bearing sands here in 1876. The story of the growth of the city demonstrates the flexibility of the early miners and the cities in which they lived.

The city was platted and several cabins were built in 1877. Trouble was one young fellow liked the site a mile and a half away. Ordinarily, this might not have made any difference. But the rebel built a general store and the only saloon around. As a result the first settlers pulled up their stakes and their cabins and relocated the city around the store and saloon. The camp grew slowly, even after the railroad came to town. It wasn't until ranching came into its own here, that Placerville really boomed.

The cattle came first, then the sheep. Therein lies the most exciting part of Placerville's history. As happened throughout the west, cattlemen hated sheepmen the most. The area underwent a violent range war and several sheep ranchers were killed before the two elements finally learned to live side by side.

Much of the business section of Placerville was destroyed by fire in 1919 but was rapidly rebuilt of sturdier material. Placerville is situated in beautiful country and has good resort possibilities, but at present much of the neighboring land is fenced off.

## FALL CREEK (Seymore, Silver Pick)

During the 80's Seymore was a busy mining camp, center of the placer diggings along Fall Creek, and shipping point for the famed Silver Pick Mine for several years after that. During its peak it had a fine hotel and many other businesses.

The post office was moved to Silver Pick Mine in 1894 and then to Saw Pit two years later.

Seymore was little more than a name for years, and even that was changed to Fall Creek in 1922. It was named for the creek which was named for the waterfall near the town.

## SAWPIT

A blacksmith was the cause for Sawpit. The smithie, James Blake, located good ore here in 1895. He named his claim the Champion Belle. The first three carloads of ore brought him $1,800, and hundreds of other fortune seekers came into the area. The Commercial mine was located the following year, and Sawpit came into its own. The town was laid out in 1895 and several frame buildings were put up. The town was named for the nearby creek.

Mining hit its peak here just before the turn of the century. Sawpit shipped out sixty-eight cars of ore in 1896, 151 in 1897, and sometimes averaged as much as fifteen to eighteen cars per week the next couple of years.

## SAN MIGUEL CITY

San Miguel City rivaled Telluride for a spell. Although the rivalry didn't last long and Telluride soon overshadowed its neighbor to the east, San Miguel City was the scene of much activity for several years. The city was laid out in the mid-70's when some good ore was found here. The city fathers took advantage of the natural beauty of the area in laying out the town, and few trees were uprooted within the townsite.

Several paying gold and silver mines were located around the town, a stamp mill and concentrating works were set up. The town also had a post office, saw mill, restaurant and hotel. A large dairy herd was brought in. By 1880, the city population was 200 men and five women. Little wonder most of the town soon left for Telluride where it was more exciting. The cattle remained, however, and San Miguel City is primarily a ranching area today. Several old cabins can be seen, but it's mostly cows.

About the only juicy gossip that could be found about San Miguel City concerned its easily disgusted postman. It seems the mail carrier was robbed enroute to San Miguel from Silverton in 1879. It was his first trip, but he became so disillusioned by it all, he quit his job and left the area for good.

## SAVAGE BASIN CAMP

A small camp for miners working in the Tomboy mine above Telluride.

The camp accomodated those miners who didn't care to travel back and forth to Pandora every day. If you travel up to the mine from Pandora you can understand their position. It is a ledge road most of the way. The camp had its own school, livery stable and several stores. It is still being used off and on in recent years.

## PANDORA (Newport)

Pandora was laid out shortly after the Pandora mine was located in 1875 and attracted scores of miners. The town was originally called Newport for Newport, Kentucky—hometown of one of the founders—but was later given the name of the mine.

Although the Pandora was the first mine, the primary source of livelihood for the town was the Smuggler-Union mill, a flotation mill which handled the ore from the Smuggler-Union on the hill high above the town. Aerial trams ran from the mine to the mill in Pandora, bringing down ore and carting men and supplies back and forth. The Smuggler-Union, which contained one of the longest ore shoots ever opened, was worked for several years. It was reopened in 1933 after being closed down for a number of years.

Snowslides were common on the hills above the city, and many people were killed. In 1902, one of Colorado's worst winters, one gigantic slide threatened to destroy the town completely, but miraculously stopped just short of the mark.

Several cabins and ruins of cabins remain in Pandora today, and the city sees many tourists who visit the Bridal Veil Falls a half mile south of town. Water cascades some 365 feet down the rough cliff face in a beautiful, misty, lacy foam.

Pandora was at the foot of Imogene Pass to Camp Bird in the olden days, and although the road has long since been closed, its route is a favorite trail of hiking enthusiasts and provides some magnificent scenery.

## FOLSOME (with Pandora)

Dave Day's *Solid Muldoon* said in 1881: "The post office in the upper San Miguel Valley which was once San Miguel City is now Folsome and it is incorporated. San Miguel City never was. Another town a few rods away is Telluride."

The *Solid Muldoon* didn't think the valley could support more than one town, two at the most. Day, in his own caustic way, suggested the people in the valley get together and decide upon a townsite and a name. Day thought San Miguel City and Folsome should merge, and the name of the place should be San Miguel.

Of course, San Miguel City soon reclaimed its post office from Folsome, and San Miguel and Telluride became the main cities in the San Miguel Valley.

Pandora grew just west of Folsome, and absorbed the earlier town, or possibly Pandora was simply a later name for Folsome. Reports of Folsome don't mention Pandora at all.

Folsome ranked with Telluride and San Miguel as one of the first cities in the valley. The town was platted near the Folsome and Company mines on Water Fall Gulch, later called Bridal Veil Falls. There were several good finds here, and in 1892, the company began construction of a 300-foot tunnel into the gulch.

The last Folsome is heard from was around 1881. Then Pandora got the press notices.

## AMES

Ames was a small camp laid out below the Gold King mine. The Gold King was important in that it employed the world's first commercial transmissions of high-pressure electricity. The amazing electrical power plant and transmission line was the brain-child of L. L. Nunn, who, like Otto Mears, was a midget of a man but a giant in the development of mining in Colorado.

Nunn was a lawyer, not an engineer. And they say he became a lawyer when he was hit over the head by a law book in a barroom brawl. But he was a genius, with an imagination as big as the mountain. His success in engineering feats was probably due to the fact he was a lawyer and not an engineer, and therefore not hampered by the engineering restrictions of the day.

They say Nunn compiled his first modest fortune by installing a bathtub in his cabin and charging miners, bound for a Saturday in Telluride, fifty cents per dip.

Nunn became involved in electricity because of his law practice. The Gold King, although a rich mine, never made much profit because of its altitude (12,000 feet) and because of the high costs of operating, especially in fuel.

In 1888, the mine was attached by creditors, and Nunn was hired to represent the hard-pressed mine owners. Nunn succeeded in obtaining a stay in the proceedings and then systematically went about a study of the mine's problems. Of course, the problem was financial, caused by the extravagant costs of fuel.

Nunn, however, saw the potential power in the San Miguel River flowing below, and suggested building an electrical power plant. Just about everyone scoffed at the idea, including the engineers. But Nunn went ahead and did it anyway.

The new electrical power trimmed expenses at the mine tremendously and saved the day for the owners. In fact, it worked out so well Nunn built high-tension lines across 13,000-foot Imogene Pass to serve other mines in the Camp Bird area. Before long, the use of electricity in mining became widespread in Colorado and throughout the world.

### OPHIR (Howard's Fork)

There were Ophirs (or Ofers) in the Pueblo and Empire areas, but this Ophir was, and is, the best known—if only because of the famous Ophir Loop. The loop, still visible, was perhaps the most amazing feat in Colorado railroad history. The loop consists of three tiers of railway tracks, overlapping each other and employing a 100-foot trestle.

The city, founded in the middle 70's, was originally named Howard's Fork for Lieutenant Howard, godfather of Howardsville. But the name was soon changed to Ophir for the nearby Ophir needles. Historians generally agree the site was named after the Biblical city where gold was found. A couple of sources, however, claim the town was named after a remark by Lt. Howard on seeing a yawning cavern: "*O fer* God's sake, lookit that hole!"

Lieutenant Howard led the first group into the area. The Yellow Mountain was the first claim, made in 1875. Other prospectors began traipsing into the area and made other strikes. The most notable were the Osceola and Gold King, made in 1879, and the Alta, made a year earlier.

A good-sized mill was erected and the city was just about hitting its stride when Rico's first excitement lured away most of Ophir's residents. The Rico excitement proved to be a false alarm, however, and most of the miners returned to Ophir.

The second Rico boom, which proved genuine, kept most of the miners, and the Ophir area died out, although some mining has been done here off and on until recent years.

Ophir has had only two permanent residents through the years. Jim Noise was the mayor of the town. His only steady constituent was Nellie Tatum. Some say there was something serious between them. The town has had enough "off and on" residents to retain a post office.

BEST MINES: Butterfly-Terrible, Alta, Yellow Mountain, Osceola, Gold King, Silver Bell, Suffolk, Carribean, all good producers.

OPHIR DUST: The old Galloping Goose station is now used as the post office . . . . other buildings still standing include an old hotel and the Butterfly-Terrible Stamp Mill, and some cabins. Some of the old water hydrants are still visible also . . . . most of the early ore from Ophir was shipped to Silverton by burro train . . . . Ophir had its share of death and destruction, mostly attributed to the long, harsh winters. There was also a mail robbery or two here.

## OLD OPHIR

Although Old Ophir preceded new Ophir, more is left of the old town and more people live (at least part of the year) in the old city than in new Ophir. Even in modern times, a handful of prospectors, who firmly believe the best claims are still to be found here, return to Ophir faithfully each year.

Despite the name, Old Ophir did not precede Ophir by long, and, different from many of the other cities in Colorado which had a new and an old, the two cities lived side-by-side for years.

Old Ophir is at the foot of Ophir Pass, a rugged but much-traveled pass in its day. The most remembered story of the pass concerns Sven Nilson, a conscientious mailman who carted the mail to Ophir from Silverton year in and year out in all sorts of weather. Much against the advice of everybody in Silverton, Sven set out in a blizzard on December 23, 1883, to deliver the Christmas mail to Ophir and Old Ophir.

Sven never reached Ophir. Some people, people who didn't know Sven very well, said he absconded with the mail. Most people knew better. Search party after search party combed the pass for old Sven. Finally, two years later, Sven's body was found at the bottom of a ravine below the old trail. The mail was still strapped to his back and still intact.

Old Ophir was a progressive little town. By 1898, the city had its own electricity, a water works, several churches and a school to serve the population of about 500. Two cars of ore were shipped out daily.

Don't miss the interesting cemetery just outside the town.

## MATTERHORN (San Bernardo)

Matterhorn was a small camp located on the Lake fork of the San Miguel River at the foot of Yellow Mountain. The mountain was nicknamed Matterhorn by the old timers because of its resemblance to the Swiss peak. The town here was originally called San Bernardo, but the post office got the name confused with a California town, so the miners changed the name to Matterhorn.

There has been some mining here through the years. Two or three cabins are frequently occupied in recent years. The 1940 population was nine, not counting dogs.

The sole occupants of the town, Mr. and Mrs. Jack Montgomery, who operate the Silver Hat Mining Company, recently were instructed to tear down the old Matterhorn dance hall and saloon by the Forest Service. The old house was noted for the gals of ill repute who lounged around on its balcony and enticed the miners inside.

## DUNTON

Dunton, or the spot where Dunton used to be, is becoming a popular resort area now. The section gives access to Navajo Lake and other good fishing streams, and the mountain climbers pass by here enroute to Mount Wilson, El Diente, and other good-sized mountains around.

The town was first established in 1885 on the discovery of the Emma, Smuggler, American and many other claims along the West Dolores River. Cabins were said to line the river for a mile or so, population topped 300, and there was no lacking for revelry. The town dwindled slowly. It was a ghost town by 1918 when Joe and Dominica Roscio bought it for ranch land. The family still runs a dude ranch at the site, taking advantage of the many natural fishing and hunting grounds here. Two of the old saloons have been converted into cabins. One of the old dance halls is a public meeting place where dances are held once or twice a year. Another old saloon, is still just that. It has the old honky-tonk piano in the corner and other items of the past.

## LIZARD HEAD

Lizard Head, at the northern foot of Lizard Head Pass, was another small camp that didn't last too long. The pass and the town were named for Lizard Head Mountain (13,113 feet), so named for the grotesque formation of rotten rocks which looks somewhat similar to a lizard's head.

The mountain is one of the most dangerous peaks in Colorado to climb, and the daredevils who have attempted it in recent years claim the rocks are becoming more rotten each year and therefore more dangerous.

Lizard Head Pass (10,200 feet) runs between Black Face Mountain (12,100 feet) to the east and Sheep Mountain (13,200) to the west. Although the pass is mild for cars, it posed quite a problem for trains, primarily due to the heavy snows. No less than a quarter of a mile of track near the top of the pass was covered with snowsheds, and snow plows were almost in constant use during the winter to keep the tracks open.

## RICO (Carbon City, Carbonateville, Lead City and Dolores City)

Rico (Spanish for rich) was well named. The surrounding land has poured forth millions in valuable minerals and metals over the years—and its best days are still to come.

The present boom is equal to anything in the past. Rico is fast developing into a uranium center. And the Rico Argentine Company recently built a huge sulphuric acid plant, plus twenty new housing units and other accomodations for Indian employees. There is an estimated half million tons of pyrite in Nigger Baby Hill, enough to keep the new plant in full operation for five years.

The Blaine, Argentine and Mountain Springs, all run by the Rico-Argentine Company, have been in continuous operation since 1938, and the Rico mill turns out an average of 150 tons of lead and zinc daily.

Rico boomed early and never stopped. It was one of the last outposts in the old west. Horse thieves were active here as late as the 1930's. The posses gave chase in cars and on motorcycles.

Many of the early Spanish ventures into Colorado passed through here. Mountain men worked the area as early as 1830. There are conflicting reports as to the identity of the prospector who made the first strike. Some reports say two prospectors bound for Montana, Joe Fearheiler and Sheldon Shafer, made the first location. Other reports show a Texan named Colonel Nash was first. But the reports agree on the year—1866.

Trouble was the Indians didn't want to give up the land. The red men generally harassed anyone daring to venture into the region, chased most of them out and killed some. The Indians were successful in holding back the development of the area for about a dozen years, until about 1874 when the prospectors were not to be denied.

The Indian trouble continued for several years. The Rico area was on the edge of Indian panic most of the time. One of the biggest scares came in 1881, when a ranch a short distance from Rico was burned to the ground and its occupants slaughtered.

Despite the Indians, however, many locations were made in the years 1866 to 1878, and some mining was done. The Montana was started in 1869. Other locations were made the following year. A small adobe shelter was built in 1872. But the initial profit was not worth the trouble.

Suddenly, in 1878, rich finds were made and within weeks hundreds of prospectors poured into the region, locating new claims and further developing the claims already made. The town fathers thought this would be another Leadville. This apparently influenced the first names used for the camp: Lead City, Carbonateville, and others. But none of the names was completely satisfactory to the early residents, so a meeting was held and the name of Rico was finally selected.

By 1879, there were some thirty businesses here, including a sawmill, four assay offices and seven saloons. The population topped 600.

The first big Indian scare came the same year. All the women and children were herded into one of the stores, and the menfolk turned the city into an armed garrison. The Indians never came.

The Grand View Smelter was built in 1880. The *Rico News* was published in Silverton until the presses were installed in Rico. Another smelter was built in 1882. About this time, government forces chased some 250 Indians out of the region and more people ventured into Rico.

The Enterprise mine, located in the early 80's, was one of the biggest producers here and has a most interesting beginning. The mine was located by David Swickheimer, town handyman, whose wife ran a boarding house. Swickheimer spent all of his spare time and money prospecting. He located a mine he called the Enterprise just above the town. The couple had spent just about every penny they had on the claim and had no other course but to sell it, when Mrs. Swickheimer spent her last dollar on a lottery ticket.

The ticket paid off $5,000. The money was spent in further developing the claim into one of the top mines in the state. The Swickheimers made a fortune on it and sold the mine to an English Syndicate in 1891 for one and a quarter million dollars.

Rico's early development was also hampered by its isolation. Shipping out the ore ate up much of the profits. Roads were eventually built here from Silverton and Durango and were improved upon, but the expense of shipping was still great. Supplies were expensive. Flour was $50 a sack, and eggs were $3 a dozen. The arrival of a wagon train of supplies during the winter time was usually the cause of a wild celebration.

331

Then, in 1891, Otto Mears' amazing railroad reached Rico. The celebration was tremendous and lasted for days—and Rico boomed as it had never boomed before.

A story is told of the first piano to reach Rico. The piano was to be a surprise for Helen Marsh, but apparently everyone else in town knew it was coming and kept a sharp lookout for its arrival.

When it finally arrived, no less than 100 grizzly miners quietly hid outside the Marsh home for the sound of the town's first piano. But the long, jarring trip hadn't done the piano much good—it was horribly out of tune. In fact, the tone of the instrument caused one of the hidden miners to curse—loud enough to be heard inside the house. Old man Marsh jerked up the window shades to catch the redfaced miners.

Rico saw many ups and downs, but it never died out completely. Usually, just about the time the city began to go downhill, new strikes or new minerals were found, or new ways were installed to treat the ore. Rico produced millions in gold, silver, lead, zinc, copper, tin and now uranium. TOP MINES: Atlantic Cable, Montana, Aztec, Yellow Jacket, Enterprise, Alma Mater, Phoenix, Pelican, Argentine, Blaine, Mountain Springs, Grand View, Pelican and Electric Light.

*And Then There Were* . . . . *SMUGGLER*, a fairly large camp around the famous Smuggler mine. The mine was only about three miles from Pandora, but it was uphill all the way. The miners found it handier to live near the mine . . . not as enjoyable, but handier. As many as 200 to 300 miners and mine officials lived here. There were a post office and commissary. The mine offices closed in 1928 but the camp remained . . . . *TOMBOY*, a mile up the draw from the Smuggler was another good-sized camp built around the Tomboy Mine. The camp had a population as high as 900 during the boom years but gradually faded, ceasing mining operations altogether in 1927. Between Smuggler and Tomboy was a renegade settlement known as "The Jungle," populated by the gamblers and the "girls of the line." The mine owners spent several thousands trying to clean out The Jungle, but with little success . . . . . *ALTA*, a town that grew on a bench a mile north of the Gold King and the Alta Mines. Several hundred lived here at one time, then it dwindled, saw some new life during World War II, then died again. The Alta mill burned in 1948, vandals and the weather have almost completed the destruction . . . . *ALDER CREEK* (not on map) a small placer mining camp located thirty miles west of Ouray on Alder Creek, a branch of the San Miguel . . . . *OMEGA* (not on map), a one-time village near Placerville. Omega is the last letter of the Greek Alphabet, and the letter represented the ultimate goal of the first settlers . . . . *LEOPARD* (not on map), an 1882 newspaper said, "a new town by this name (Leopard) has been started on Leopard Creek, on the San Miguel Road." The town was never heard from again . . . . *VANADIUM*, a town that grew around the huge mill operated by the U. S. Vanadium Corporation. The town is little more than a store and post office now, but there are many buildings left from the past . . . . *VANCE JUNCTION*, *ILLIUM* and *OPHIR STATION*, three important junctions on Otto Mears' "amazing little railroad." Vance Junction was a junction point for the run to Telluride. Illium was named for the ancient city. Ophir Station served Ophir and Old Ophir . . . . *IRON SPRINGS*, a small village a short distance from Old Ophir toward Ophir Pass. Although there was much mining in the neighborhood this was also a resort community. There were limonite deposits, an important ore of iron, in this area.

## XVIII.  DAY'S DAY

Newspapers played an important part in the early west. They were read by all. A new boom town wasn't officially a town until it had a newspaper— or two, or three, or fourteen. Cripple Creek, during its heyday, had as many as fourteen. Even some of the minor towns had three or four.

Boulder felt neglected. So a group of public-spirited citizens stole the press away from Valmont and kidnapped the editor. Editor Scouten decided it was too much trouble to move back, so he went right on publishing, in Boulder.

Some of the first printing presses were hauled over the plains and mountains by ox team. Some were brought in by sleds and sleighs. Some newspapers were printed on wall paper or wrapping paper when printing paper was hard to come by.

Newspapering was a fighting profession then. Newspapermen were usually a crusty bunch, often representing the conscience and integrity of the community, much more so than the law enforcement agencies. It was often a dangerous profession, especially for a fearless, outspoken man. Editors were beaten up on many occasions, but strangely enough, few of them were killed.

Newspapers were frequently a family affair. Women also had a hand in the business.

Sylvia Smith, mentioned before, a sharp-tongued crusader for the *Marble Times*, was eventually run out of town for her blatant "I told you so" attitude after a mine disaster.

Mrs. C. W. Rommey, fearless editor of the *Durango Record* during the city's early years, defied threats by the notorious Stockton gang and her editorials were instrumental in running the gang out of town.

Many of the early newspapermen hadn't had a day's experience when they began publishing. They merely had something to say and wanted to be heard. A newspaper was the best way to do it. Colorado had some good newspapermen, known throughout the west and the world. There were Cy Warman (see Creede), Eugene Field, Damon Runyan, Gene Fowler, to mention but a few. Even Bat Masterson, better known as a tough western sheriff, got a touch of journalism in Colorado, and spent the last eighteen years of his life as a New York boxing writer.

But perhaps the fightingest, most colorful one of the bunch was Dave Day—David Frakes Day—who edited the *Solid Muldoon* in Ouray for thirteen years, and then went down and published the *Durango Democrat* until 1914.

Nobody could out-speak this outspoken crusader. He was quoted and requoted throughout Colorado and the nation. He was always stirring up something, but it was usually for the good of his city or for Colorado. He didn't care whose toes he stepped on as long as he thought he was right. At one time he had forty-two libel suits against him. He won all that came to court. The others were dropped.

Day was always needling communities to spruce up. The residents of Ophir became so incensed when Day criticized the town for not living up to its biblical name that they led a parade of burros through Ouray with the names of prominent Ouray citizens wagging behind each animal.

He had two pet peeves: women and politicians, especially professional-type women and Republican-type politicians.

Jim Belford, western Colorado's first Congressman, was a particular example of the latter. Day never missed a chance to throw a barb at Belford. One day Belford came to Ouray on a campaign tour. Day stretched out on the lawn during the speech. Belford said something about cutting his speech short since it was apparently tiring to some of the audience.

Day called out: "Don't mind me, Jim. I can lie here as long as you can lie up there."

Although through the years he expressed a strong feeling of sympathy for the parlor-house ladies, he hated women in business. He thought women belonged in the home, and when one or another of them made a name for herself, he thought she was getting out of line. Once he wrote: ". . . . the Queen-Bee statesman indulges in a quarter-column article on 'nursing children.' An individual with a pair of bosoms that look like two gingersnaps pinned onto a cottonwood shingle, must be an excellent authority on such subjects . . . ."

As with Warman and several other early newsmen, Day put much of his news into poetry. He had a lusty tang about his writing, as bold and as biting as the land in which it was printed.

An example was his obituary for a local prostitute, who died while still quite young:

> "Charlotte,
> Born a virgin, died a harlot.
> For 14 years she kept her virginity,
> An all-time record for this vicinity."

## FROM SILVERTON TO OURAY

Baker City and Baker Park
Silverton
Titusville
Arastra (Arastra Gulch, also spelled Arrastra)
Silver Lake
Bandora
Howardsville (Bullion City)
Niegoldtown (or Neigoldston)
Highland Mary
Middleton
Eureka
Animas Forks
Engineer City (American Flats)
Mineral Point
Poughkeepsie
Gladstone
Fisherville
Chattanooga (Sheridan Junction)
Red Mountain City, Upper Red Mountain Town and Old Congress Town
Red Mountain Town (Sky City, Upper Red Mountain Town)
Guston
Ironton (Copper Glen)
Ouray (Uncompahgre City)
Camp Bird
Sneffels
Ruby (Ruby City)
Dallas (Dallas City, Dallas Station, Gold City, Uniweep) (north of map)

*And Then There Were . . . . LeMOYNE CITY* (not on map), *YANKEE GIRL,
BURRO BRIDGE* and *SUMMIT, NEEDLETOWN, COLUMBINE, CASCADE CITY*
(Cascade Siding)—(the last three south of map)—*ALBANY,* and *TUCKERVILLE*
(not on map)

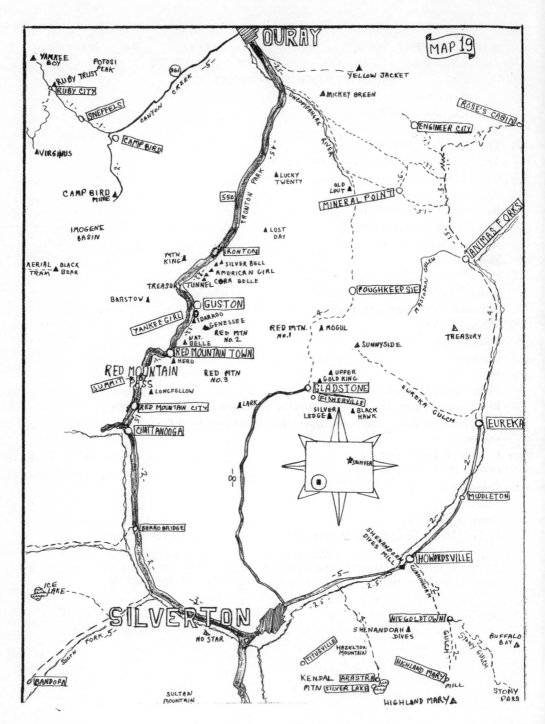

MAP 19

OURAY

YANKEE BOY ▲
POTOSI PEAK
RUBY TRUST
RUBY CITY
SNEFFELS
361
CANYON CREEK
YELLOW JACKET ▲
MICKEY BREEN ▲
UNCOMPAHGRE RIVER
ROSE'S CABIN
ENGINEER CITY
CAMP BIRD
VIRGINIUS ▲
CAMP BIRD MINE ▲
550
TRONTON PARK
-45-
LUCKY TWENTY ▲
OLD LOUT ▲
MINERAL POINT
ANIMAS FORKS
IMOGENE BASIN
AERIAL TRAM ▲  BLACK BEAR ▲
MTN. KING ▲
IRONTON
SILVER BELL ▲
AMERICAN GIRL ▲
CORA BELLE ▲
TREASURY TUNNEL
BARSTOW ▲
GUSTON
IDARADO
GENESSEE
RED MTN No.2
LOST DAY ▲
POUGHKEEPSIE
MASTODON GULCH
RED MTN. No.1
MOGUL ▲
TREASURY ▲
YANKEE GIRL
NAT. BELLE ▲
RED MOUNTAIN TOWN
HERO ▲
SUNNYSIDE ▲
RED MOUNTAIN PASS
SUMMIT
LONGFELLOW ▲
RED MTN No.3
LARK ▲
UPPER GOLD KING ▲
GLADSTONE
FISHERVILLE
SILVER LEDGE ▲
BLACK HAWK ▲
EUREKA GULCH
EUREKA
RED MOUNTAIN CITY
CHATTANOODA
-8-
DENVER ★
MIDDLETON
BURRO BRIDGE
ICE LAKE
SILVERTON
SHENANDOAH DIVES MILL
HOWARDSVILLE
CUNNINGHAM
-5-
2.5
NO STAR ▲
SHENANDOAH DIVES ▲
WIEGOLDTOWN
BUFFALO BOY ▲
SOUTH FORK -5-
BANDORA
SULTAN MOUNTAIN
KENDAL MTN
TITUSVILLE
HAZELTON MOUNTAIN
ARASTRA
SILVER LAKE
HIGHLAND MARY MILL
HIGHLAND MARY ▲
STONY GULCH
STONY PASS

## BAKER CITY and BAKER PARK

Although no more than small, temporary camps, these were the first settlements in the San Juans. Famed scout, Indian fighter, mountain man and jack-of-all-trades Jim Baker heard tales of gold from the Indians. Although much of the land was uncharted, and all of it still belonged to the Indians, Baker organized a small party of prospectors and headed north from Fort Garland in 1860.

It is believed his first camp was established on or near the present site of Silverton, but that the party later moved on and established their camp on the site which later became Eureka, although both campsites were little more than conjecture.

Legend says the party faced many hardships. Travel was difficult at best. Storms continually hampered their progress. Provisions ran low, and fear of Indians was constant. To top it off, the group found little evidence of gold. All the blame fell on Baker.

The story goes that the other prospectors held a mock trial, forcing Baker to show cause why he should not be hanged. In a surprise move by the defense, Baker said he could pan gold on the spot. Court was recessed temporarily while Baker attempted to prove his point.

And, as the story goes, Baker did pan out some gold—a few pennies worth. It saved his life but didn't save the expedition. The party soon returned to Fort Garland.

The San Juans were forgotten for another dozen years, but the story was largely responsible for later prospecting expeditions into the area, and the birth of one of the richest gold and silver regions in the west.

## SILVERTON

They call Silverton "the mining town that never quit." Forsooth, it is just beginning.

Ranking among Colorado's richest regions historically and geologically, Silverton is currently experiencing its greatest tourist boom in history. And the scenic mountains on all sides, which have produced nearly a quarter of a billion dollars in gold, silver, lead, copper and zinc since 1870, still hide perhaps an equal amount of rich minerals.

Silverton was "big-time" from the beginning. It is truly one of Colorado's greatest cities. It has been well-named the "Silver Queen of Colorado" (Leadville is the Silver King) and the "Treasure Chest of the Silvery San Juans."

Some prospecting was done around here before the Brunot Treaty with the Indians in 1874. Charles Baker camped near the site when he led a prospecting party into the San Jauns. They knew the treasure was there, but most of them waited until the Indians relinquished the land.

Within weeks of the signing of the Brunot Treaty, thousands of fortune seekers were scampering all over the San Jauns. Many good strikes were made around Silverton and a city was founded in the center, at the most logical site. By late summer of 1874, some 4,000 persons lived here while a larger number lived and worked in the nearby hills. There was little question about the name of the town after a prospector declared he didn't find much gold, but he found "silver by the ton."

Those baby years, Silverton was as raw and wide-open as they came. Murders and shootings, resulting from claim-jumpings, gambling arguments and drunken brawls were a dime a dozen. Hastily-organized vigilante groups were busy capturing and lynching the most notable miscreants.

Various versions of the most infamous incident are told. When the notorious Clint Stockton gang found it too hot in Durango they fled northward. Some say they actually were seen in Silverton. In fact, it was rumored they got drunk here and shot up a saloon. When night marshall Clayton Ogsbury dashed into the saloon, he was cut down by stray bullets.

Another story goes that the marshal was merely on the lookout for the gang. When he saw two suspicious characters along Blair Street he crossed the road for a better look and was cut down in the street. Tellers of this tale say the murderers may or may not have been members of the Stockton gang.

Anyhow, the marshal was dead. The Stockton gang was held responsible for the act. But they disappeared. The blood-thirsty vigilantes, frustrated in their attempts to find Stockton and his gang, had to make do with lynching an unarmed Negro, who had only the most remote relationship with the gang and didn't have anything at all to do with shooting up the saloon, if the saloon was shot up in the first place. This uncalled-for lynching has been preying on the Silverton conscience since.

Blair Street, on which the shooting and lynching occurred, ranks with the most notorious "gaming streets" in state history. It had nearly forty saloons and a vast array of gambling dens, dance halls and parlor houses that never closed. Many of the top gamblers and "portable" prostitutes in the west worked the street.

Blair Street was headquarters of the unruly element in Silverton and this element was controlling the city. Things were getting out of hand. Finally, the town council took drastic action. They hired Bat Masterson as sheriff and attempted to close down Blair Street. Bat and his hand-picked, fast-drawing deputies soon restored some semblance of law and order to Silverton. But they never did close down Blair Street. They say Bat didn't particularly want it closed in the first place.

Even before Bat came to town, the itinerant preachers and other crusaders were working quietly for men's souls. Churches soon rose and church societies flourished to challenge the influence of Blair Street. The Congregationalists, Catholics, Methodists and Episcopalians all erected churches in the early 80's. The Negro population even purchased an abandoned building and made it into their church. These meeting houses and the societies and religious groups they sponsored were the core of much of Silverton's early and legitimate social activity. Dances, benefits, bazaars, or just plain socials were rife.

Silverton was the birthplace of perhaps the best known band in its day. Jack Sinclair organized the band in the late 80's. Within a couple of years it was known throughout the west and then the nation. In 1891, the band accompanied Governor Routt's inauguration trip. It also played at Governor Adams' inauguration. It played at President Harrison's inauguration in Washington and at major events throughout the nation. Part of the band's trademark was their ten-gallon hats and cowboy suits. It eventually called itself the "original Dodge City Cowboy Band," although they weren't cowboys and were organized in Silverton.

Much of Silverton's early social activity centered around its race track and boxing arena. Some of the top race horses and fighters of the day did their bit in Silverton.

A story is told of one of the early fights, matching an inept challenger and the local champion. The champion was finding possible contenders scarce and his financial condition haphazard. During this one match, the champ endeavored to play the challenger along in an effort to get a rematch out of it. The crowd soon became displeased over the style of fighting used by the champ and expressed their displeasure with sky-shattering jeers. It didn't help. But a few rounds later the referee strapped on his six-guns, drew one, cocked it and pointed it menacingly at the champ. The champ, after looking down the gun barrel, lost little time in putting his opponent away.

Another source of competition at the time was furnished by the Reese Hook and Ladder Company, organized in 1878 and the first volunteer fire department in the San Jauns. The fire departments in those days would compete with the units in other cities. Competition included appearance, speed at getting to appointed spots, and effectiveness in organizing for fighting the fire.

The Reese unit of Silverton ranked among Colorado's best. Its uniforms were certainly among the most colorful, and its equipment was the latest. The Hook and Ladder truck was purchased in the east, and when it finally got to the San Juans about half the male population of Silverton met it on

Stony Pass to help bring it into town. Its arrival was cause for a wild and prolonged celebration—but then just about everything was.

The wildest celebration took place, however, when Otto Mears brought his fantastic railroad into town in 1882.

The railroad, more than anything else, brought Silverton a feeling of permanency. Although the surrounding mines had already produced in the millions, the railroad made the shipping of ore cheaper and many times as fast. Production stepped up considerably. And, with the railroad, Silverton itself had an easy link to the outside world where she had been all but isolated before, especially in winter.

Silverton was now a true Queen City. Her famous Grand Imperial Hotel, the second finest in western Colorado (the La Veta of Gunnison was the first), built in the early 1880's, could have speedier access to the delicacies it was noted for.

The smelters, and there were many, worked to capacity and more were built. Low-grade ore, not processed before because of the cost of milling and shipping, were now processed and produced additional millions.

The 80's and 90's were great years for Silverton. Blair Street was still going full blast, but the many churches overshadowed its influence. The *Silverton Miner* was published daily, and eventually the *Silverton Standard* began to compete. Several other lesser newspapers were published from time to time.

And Silverton had one of the largest breweries in the state. Charles Fischer erected his brewery in Howardsville but soon rebuilt it in Silverton when that city became county seat and outgrew Howardsville. The brewery was built of stone and its huge cellars were cut into the solid granite of the mountain. Fischer once advertised that his beer was produced as a tonic and not as an intoxicant.

Silverton had become so sophisticated by the 90's, the citizens raised a rumpus about cattle wandering through town. In 1901, the city's own public utility system was complete, the first in the U. S. owned by the city itself. A library was started in 1903, and soon became one of the finest in the state. (It still is.) The courthouse was built in 1907. The second floor of the Grand Imperial had been used for a courthouse.

All the while, the nearby mines poured forth their riches, and mining methods were developed and improved upon. Aerial trams replaced burros and even toboggans. The area boasted one of the first aerial tramlines in the state. It ran 10,000 feet, from the mines high on the mountains on the other side of the divide to the mills down below, sometimes swinging back and forth as much as 3,000 feet above the hillside. The tram, built more like a high bucket than a tram, was used to haul men and supplies to the mines, and bring back ore and the injured or dead. Many oldtimers in the area say the ride in the tram was the most frightening experience in their lives.

Milling methods were perfected here. J. J. Crooke's mill was the first in the nation to produce both gold and silver. Crooke invented the process. He also invented the tin-foiling process and a copper process. He received royalties for all tin-foil produced in the U. S. and copper produced under his process.

The first successful waterjacket type of mill in Colorado was built here.

Eastern and European money was invested in mining around Silverton. Part of the fabulous Guggenheim fortune came from here. Colorado's famed multi-millionaire Thomas Walsh (see Camp Bird) had milling and mining interests in the Silverton region.

Silverton's mineral millions came from, and continue to come from, Cuningham Gulch, the Silver Lake Area, Solomon Mountain and many another gulch, creek and mountain. Each section produced in the millions, and some are still producing.

But due to the price of silver and gold today, Silverton isn't producing what it could. Only a half-dozen mills are open, and only a few companies run the bulk of the mines. Even many of the small companies have merged to make mining more economical and profitable.

The Shenandoah-Dives Company is about the biggest producer. It includes property in the Silver Lake area and the large North Star, Terrible, and Shenandoah-Dives Mines. The company wasn't formed until 1929, and its huge mill wasn't built until 1933.

Silverton never did quit. It made it through the panic of the mid 90's by substituting gold for silver as its top metal. It made it through the depression of the 30's. It's still going strong in mining, and the tourist trade is increasing every year.

BEST MINES: In addition to the Silver Lake and Arastra Gulch mines, some of Silverton's best mines were in Solomon and Sultan Mountains. Most of the Solomon mines opened at 12,000 feet or higher, The North Star opens at 13,300 feet and is said to be the highest operating mine in Colorado. There was another North Star on Sultan Mountain. Its mill produced more than seven million dollars in processed ore. Other, but by no means lesser mines, were, and in many cases, are, the Shenandoah, Dives (now combined), Mayflower, Little Dora, Martha Rose, Terrible and Slide.

SILVER DUST: The Grand Hotel (the "Imperial" was added later) was built in 1882 by an Englishman, W. S. Thompson, and has changed hands frequently. In 1950, the Texas Housing Company, headed by Winfield Morton, bought it and spent $350,-000 in remodeling. It was sold again in 1958 to settle mortgage foreclosure. An owner for many years was Henry Frecker, who left his family in Victor and became a hermit in the Silverton region. His family didn't know where he was until his daughter Edna inherited the hotel about 40 years after his disappearance . . . a fire that started in the kitchen did an estimated $100,000 damage to the hotel in 1958. But the damaged area was repaired. The hotel, center of the tourist trade as it was a center of the social activity in the past, serves as a museum as well as a hotel today . . . . the first cabin here was built by Francis M. Snowden. Many of Silverton's early dances and socials were held in this cabin . . . . In the early days, water was sometimes as scarce as supplies. The first water was brought in by barrels and sold for fifty cents a bucket. . . . Silverton was often isolated during the winter by snow, and snowslides caused hundreds of deaths in the area. In 1906, snow fell for more than a week and there were scores of slides. Twenty miners were killed in a slide at the Shenandoah-Dives mine. Several others were killed that same season. That year, a huge slide cut off the river and immediately turned to ice, causing a high nature-made dam. The water backed up hundreds of feet and froze over the railroad tracks. The late 30's were also bad years for slides. Spring snows in 1936 carried some twenty miles of trees, rocks and snow down the mountains in slides. But one of the worst slides occurred in 1938, knocking over some of the towers holding up the aerial tramway . . . . some say the tune "There'll Be a Hot Time in the Old Town Tonight" was written here instead of at Cripple Creek . . . . a stone marker constructed in front of the court house in 1941 contains specimens of ore from nearby mines in the base, and lists fifty-one of the top mines in the San Juans . . . . the modern 700-ton selective flotation mill in Silverton employs more people than any other in the southwest . . .. the first Silverton smelter was built in 1875 by Greene and Company. The machinery was packed on burros for the trip over Stony Pass and each brick in the furnace and stack cost $1.15 each . . . . as with many another silver town, Silverton suffered greatly from the panic, but soon overcame much of the loss by increasing production of gold and other metals. Due to the silver panic, only sixteen Silverton residents voted for McKinley . . . . , and only two of them would admit it . . . . Silverton still produces almost as much as it did during its heyday. Silverton costs now plus the low metal prices, however, don't make for so much profit. Automation and new mining and milling methods permit about 1,500 persons to do the work of 3,000 a few years ago . . . . in 1902, members of the Silverton cooks and waiters union placed nooses around the Chinese who were competing for the restaurant jobs, led them to the edge of the city and bade them begone . . . . dog sleds once carried freight into Silverton. The story goes that the dogs were rewarded after each trip with a jolt of whiskey . . . . another Silverton hermit was George Washington Posvar, who kept armed guard over the Kitty Mack mines for a number of years, fending off a battery of lawyers who were attempting to take away the mine for the American Smelting and Refining Company . . . . a Thomas Hole died as a result of injuries he received when he fell into the North Star mine shaft in 1882 . . . . an example of Silverton life and Colorado journalism in 1884 is contained in the following item found in the *Rocky Mountain News*: "Henry White, who killed Charles Gill in Silverton, has been found not guilty by the jury" . . . . the interesting Silverton cemetery is on a hill east of town in the direction of Howardsville. Many of the graves were filled during the disastrous flu epidemic in 1918 which claimed the lives of about a third of the people in the area, including Silverton's only undertaker . . . . the first big mine to the left in the direction of Howardsville is the Lackawanna. It is still being worked by its owner. The natives call it the Lackamoney because of the lack of working capital . . . . Blair street is beginning to bustle again with some of the color of the past

342

although the name of the street has been officially changed in recent years because some residents disliked living on a street with such a bad reputation. The newly-painted shops and stores, however, retain the name and the flavor of early-day Blair Street . . . . the Silverton jail, directly behind the court house, is, and has been, empty. There has been some talk of turning it into a museum . . . . there is hope in Silverton the giant Shenandoah-Dives mill will be running again soon. They say the giant G-shaped vein which runs from the Shenandoah-Dives around under Silver Lake still has plenty of good ore. The major problem is the water, but Silvertonites hope the planned American Tunnel (see Gladstone) will remedy the water problem . . . . although the tourist business is increasing yearly, the prosperity of Silverton is dependent on the mining in the area. Mining activity is on the upswing and there is great confidence of continued activity in Silverton.

## TITUSVILLE

Titusville was a short-lived camp south of Silverton on Kendall Mountain. About the best mining property was the Belle of Titusville.

The town, while it lived, had several saloons and other businesses. The peak population was more than 600 people. The ores weren't too extensive, however, and Titusville was soon deserted. Broken and rusted machinery mark the site today.

## ARASTRA (Arastra Gulch, Arrastra)

The first arastras in Colorado were built in the Fairplay region by the Spanish. In fact, the "arastra" is a Spanish device for grinding out gold ore.

The arastra is a circular, enclosed stone bed. Ore fragments are spread out in the bed. A burro, led by one arm of an upright shaft, walks round and round, dragging heavy stones after him which grind out the quartz. The arastra was similar in appearance and operation to the old fashioned cider mill. It wasn't very effective for mining purposes. That is the reason so few of them were built by the Yankees.

One of the rare Yankee arastras in Colorado was built in a gulch below Silverton. The gulch was named Arastra Gulch and a small camp near the crude device was named Arastra. There was some mining along the gulch, too, and some miners lived in the camp. The camp was never very large and it didn't last too long. It did, however, last long enough to have a post office.

The top mines on the gulch were the Iowa and Tiger.

## SILVER LAKE

Although this was apparently a scattered group of camps rather than one official town, there was a post office at Silver Lake for several years. The camps were around the mines, some of the best in the Silverton area. The Silver Lake mines have produced more than eleven million dollars in precious metals since 1901.

343

Part of the Guggenheim fortune came from this region.

There is a long-standing joke in the Silverton area about draining Silver Lake, for the precious metals dumped here by high-graders (see glossary for definition of high grading). It seems the miners used to cache their ill-gotten ore in the lake. Much of it was washed away or whisked away before it could be recovered. They say the American tunnel (see Gladstone) may eventually be cut under Silver Lake and the lake may be drained after all.

They say the road into Silver Lake is almost impossible now, even for jeeps. Nonetheless, it is still a favorite spot for fishermen, even if they have to pack in. There is still ore in there. If the tunnel brings new life into the area, Silver Lake will be bustling again.

## BANDORA

No buildings, only some mine workings, some still active, mark the site of Bandora.

Ore was found along Mineral Creek as early as 1882. Several other rich claims were located during the next few years, some in the Ice Lake district.

The Blanco Mining Company bought up many of the claims in 1940, and has been doing a little work here since. The Esmeralda is still being worked off and on.

But the workers generally stay in Silverton. There's no place to live in Bandora anymore.

## HOWARDSVILLE (Bullion City)

Howardsville was quite a large city in its day — and a prosperous one. It grew at the head of Cunningham Gulch. The gulch contained several good mines on the way up to Stony Pass, a dangerous pass closed much of the time by snow. But the pass was about the only entrance into the San Juans during those early years.

The city erupted in 1874, about the same time as Silverton. It appeared for a while as if Howardsville might outdistance her neighbor, so it was given the county seat of newly-formed San Juan county—the first county seat west of the divide in Colorado. The distinction didn't last long, as Silverton was voted county seat the following year.

The city was laid out in 1874 by the Bullion City Company, and was named Bullion City until the residents got together later the same year and decided upon Howardsville. Some reports say the city was named for Lieutenant Howard, an important figure in the area, and other reports show the city was named for George Howard, who had a cabin here when the others came. It may have been named after both of them—seems the only fair thing to do.

344

Although the city had a post office, a court house and numerous stores and businesses, it never did have the population of the gulch, except on Saturday night.

The mines up the gulch produced for years, turning out millions. Some have been worked off and on up to recent times. But as transportation got better, most of the Howardsville residents moved into Silverton to live. Howardsville lost its post office in 1939. A few scattered families still live in Howardsville cabins.

*OTHER MINES*: Pride of the West, one of the first in the gulch, located in 1874, and still being worked; King William, Green Mountain, Leopard, Flat Broke, Osceola and Old Hammer.

*GOLD DUST*: The two-room cabin which served as the original court house is still standing in Howardsville . . . . Cunningham Gulch was named for a Major Cunningham, who led a party of Illinois prospectors into the region and made some of the first discoveries here . . . . the Old Hundred mine, the first one in the gulch, sent a gold brick weighing fifty pounds and valued at $10,000 into the Denver Mint in 1906 . . . . the Old Hundred was worked up to the top of the mountain and a large boarding house was built at each new level.

## NIEGOLDTOWN (or Neigoldston)

Niegoldtown, also spelled Neigoldston by some early sources, was located about halfway up Cunningham Gulch, equal distance from Howardsville and Highland Mary and about seven-and-a-half miles from Silverton.

The town was larger than Highland Mary. The population was generally between 200 and 300 miners. The town was usually deserted on Saturday night when the miners joined in the excitement of Howardsville or Silverton.

Niegoldtown had a post office.

## HIGHLAND MARY

The Highland Mary was a town around the Highland Mary Mill a short distance below the Highland Mary mine, the second biggest producer in Cunningham gulch—and by far the most interesting.

It seems the two Ennis brothers of New York City, suddenly decided to go into mining. They had their own way of going about it. They went to a spiritualist who, for a fat fee, pointed to a spot on the map where the brothers would find their fortune. The spot was at or near the end of Cunningham Gulch.

The brothers staked out the site and called it Highland Mary. The spiritualist, for additional moola, continued to instruct the pair on where and how to drill into the mountain. The mystic took them on a zigzag course, which must have by-passed countless good veins by a few feet. Although they found evidence of precious metal, they found little to make the work worthwhile.

Finally, in 1885, after they had sunk one million dollars into the mine—not including the $50,000 paid to the spiritualist—the brothers were forced into bankruptcy. They sold their mine and the fancy house they built nearby and returned to New York. The next owners developed the mine along more orthodox lines and it started paying immediately.

The mill and the town were situated high on Stoney Pass at an altitude of 12,000. Winters were bad. But the mine made the town worthwhile for a number of years. There were a post office and several businesses.

The ruins of the giant mill can be seen at the end of Cunningham Gulch. The site affords a majestic view of the gulch. An attractive little valley where several cabins and mine workings once stood can be seen via the Highland Mary Trail. The uppermost mine opening is near the end of the trail, almost at the top of the divide.

## MIDDLETON

Some 100 claims were laid out at the foot of Middle Mountain in the early 90's. The first strike was made in 1893 by a couple of fellows named Gotlieb and Konneker, and the town got its start the following year. The site was apparently named for Middle Mountain which was apparently named for its situation about halfway between Howardsville and Eureka.

Middleton never achieved the position of its neighbors, although there were some good-paying mines here. In later years, many of the miners moved to either Howardsville or Eureka.

The top mines were the Golden Nugget, Hamlet and Kittimac.

## EUREKA

The story of Eureka is the story of the Sunnyside Mine. Although other mines were located around Eureka, the fortunes of the city through the years were based on the fortunes of the Sunnyside and Sunnyside extension mines, and the Sunnyside Mill, one of the largest in the state.

The Sunnyside was located in 1873, and the extension, the following year. But like all good things, it was slow in developing.

Perhaps the most prominent name mentioned in connection with the Sunnyside was John (later Judge) Terry. Terry poured what money he had into the development of the mine. Broke, he was forced to sell the property to a New York syndicate. He got a good price—$300,000, much more than the natives thought the mine was worth. The syndicate paid Terry $75,000 cash and agreed to pay the rest in easy installments. But the eastern outfit, after spending additional thousands on the development of the property, became disgusted with the mine before another payment was due.

346

They agreed to let Terry keep the $75,000 if he would just take the property back. With the new capital, Terry went back to work on the mine and almost immediately discovered what he was looking for.

With the aid of expert mining man Rasmus Hanson, Terry turned the Sunnyside into one of the richest mines in the state, making him, and many of the owners after him, millionaires. The mine was worked almost continuously for more than 50 years. It was finally closed down in 1938. Later, the U. S. Smelting, Refining and Mining Company purchased the property for taxes and salvaged what it could from the extensive workings.

The giant Sunnyside mill was the fourth mill built to handle ore from the mines. It employed up to 500 persons, and as many as 300 employees worked full time in the mill during the 20's and 30's.

The Gold Prince mill, another giant, was moved to Eureka from Animas Forks. But before it could be put in operation it was greatly damaged by fire. It was rebuilt and set in operation in 1919.

As many as 2,000 people lived in Eureka during its boom, most of them working in the mines and mill. The city itself was protected on all sides from snow and rock slides. But the surrounding hills were constantly a danger. Many were buried by avalanches. The story is told of a miner being killed when a slide carried away the Silver Wing bunkhouse in 1906.

The miner's two brothers came to take the victim back to Durango. But a sudden storm forced them to leave the body along the way. When they returned the next day they found a huge snowslide covered the area and they were forced to dig the body out from tons of snow.

Otto Mears extended his fabulous railroad to Eureka in 1896 and then built a spur up to Animas Forks.

The ruins of the Sunnyside can be seen on the hill overlooking the dead city of Eureka. The winding road on the mountain behind the mill heads up Eureka Gulch to the mine. The road up the gulch is impossible much of the time now. However, the American Tunnel is expected to drain the mine enough to make it workable.

OTHER MINES: Mastoden, Golden Fleece, Toltec, Scatia, Tom Moore and Sound Democrat.

### AINMAS FORKS

An Animas Forks justice of the peace, threatened with an appeal of a conviction, once told the defendant that an appeal to a higher court was impossible— ". . . . this is the highest court in the United States." Animas Forks once boasted of being the largest city in the world at an altitude of 11,300 feet. There may have been higher communities, many in Colorado, but few if any were as big and hustling as Animas Forks in its boom days.

The first prospectors came here during the 70's and the first strike was made in 1875. The town was laid out two years later. Lots were given away free and settlers were offered aid in building a home, if they would come to the isolated, and often-snowed-in community, to settle. More than 1000 hardy men and women ventured to the spot.

Much of the activity surrounded the huge mill, built here in the 70's, to treat ore from the Red Cloud mine in Mineral Point. Animas Forks also became an important junction on the road to other camps in all directions.

To the north was the road to Mineral Point, with routes veering off to the east and west—one heading for Rose's cabin and Lake City—and the other, a difficult trail, heading for Ouray. Directly to the east was the trail to Whitecross, Sherman and on to Lake City. To the south were Eureka and Silverton. Animas Forks had a telephone system, running from Lake City and over the divide at 12,500 feet.

In the last years of the 19th century, Otto Mears, the railroad genius of the San Juans, built a perilous railway spur up the four-mile grade from Eureka on the dirt road he had built earlier.

Snow, as usual, was the big problem of Animas Forks. Most of the settlers left during the winter, but some of the sturdiest remained all winter, braving snow drifts up to twenty-five feet deep and chancing dangerous slides. It was full-time work during the winter keeping the trails and the railroad tracks open. Mears planned an elaborate series of snow sheds that would not necessarily block off the snow, but would shuttle it off harmlessly. The first big slide took the first shed with it and the experiment was abandoned.

Several persons were killed in slides.

A Mrs. Eckard was the first woman in town. She ran a boarding house and was quite popular with the miners, often carrying them on credit for weeks until their luck changed. A vigilante committee was formed when it was discovered a man had run off without paying his tab for three months' lodging. The committee caught up with the free-loader in Silverton, and—waving a noose in his face—the committee said the man had better pay up or be hanged. The man paid up and no one else attempted to cheat Mrs. Eckard.

When a rule was made in the district that all mining patent notices had to appear in a newspaper, Sol Raymond quickly took advantage of the situation and started up the *Animas Forks Pioneer*. The first issue was sold to a mine owner in Mineral Point for $500. After that it sold for as much as $25 and never less than a dollar per issue. Despite the price, the paper had a big circulation as long as new claims were made, but when prospecting fell off, the paper folded.

348

Animas Forks prospered in the late 70's and throughout the 80's, but started to wane during the 90's. The Gold Prince mill was moved to Eureka in 1917 and Animas Forks was all but deserted by the early 20's, although some mining continued through the 30's.

The ruins of Animas Forks are dominated by a large house with a window seat. The house was once owned by Thomas Walsh, just before he struck it rich on the Camp Bird mine. His daughter, Evelyn Walsh McLean, is said to have spent some time here while she was writing the book about her father.

TOP MINES: Columbia and Early Bird, worked during the 30's; the Silver Coin, the last to close; and the Gold Prince, the largest mine.

### ENGINEER CITY (American Flats)

For a short while, Engineer City boasted of being the largest city in the state without a saloon. That was in 1875, when the city had as many as 400 prospectors who were too busy attempting to locate a rich silver lode to spend their time in a bar.

The Polar Star, near the top of Engineer Mountain, was the big producer in the area. Its location was a matter of the early bird's getting the worm.

H. A. Woods, who had located some good silver lodes on nearby Siegel Mountain the year before, had heard about a party of prospectors in Howardsville planning to stake out the spot on Engineer Mountain. That was in the early spring of 1875. Woods made like he was going the other way, but instead, circled around and beat the prospecting party to the site by several hours. Woods had arrived at the spot at daybreak, and the chilled clear morning suggested the name of the location. Another rich strike in 1882 brought hundreds of fortune hunters swarming into the area. Cabins and tents were thrown up around a huge tent boarding-house erected by Jack Davison, who boarded fifty men.

The camp was located on the eastern slope of Engineer Mountain on what is known as American Flats. There is some evidence the camp was first known by that name.

Good silver was found in Engineer and Siegel Mountains, but it was another case of good ore losing out to bad roads. Most of the claims were located above timberline—the entrance to the Annie Woods was at 13,000 feet—virtually impossible to reach in the winter and difficult under ideal conditions. Some of the roads were narrow cliff ledges, barely wide enough for the wagons and the crew. The road down to Rose's cabin and on down to Howardsville was no better.

Now, only a rugged trail for jeeps will take you to the spot.

BEST MINES: Polar Star, Syracuse Pride, Annie Woods and Siegel, located by H. A. Woods; Palmetto, Little Fraud and Bill Young.

349

## MINERAL POINT

Despite its high and isolated location, Mineral Point was one of the most prosperous and colorful cities in the San Juans during its short existence. And, had it not been for the many millions squandered here promiscuously, it might have lived much longer.

Some minerals were located and a few cabins built in 1873 by Charles McIntyre and Abe Burrows. The rush started and most of the good locations were made during the first few months.

Mineral Point was named for the sixty-foot knob of quartz on which it sits. Several mineral veins, including the famed Mastodan vein, converge within the knob. The Mastodan vein was one of the best in Colorado mining history. It ran in a perfect line, over hill and dale, for several miles. On it were several locations which supported many camps and cities.

Mineral Point, along with many other camps in the area, had its transportation problem and was also bothered by extremely harsh winters. But one of the primary causes of its death was the over-enthusiastic ventures of many of the entrepreneurs.

To drum up interest in the camp, all sorts of far-fetched propaganda were circulated far and wide. One advertising scheme pictured steamships on the Animas River and trolley-cars running from Mineral Point to Animas Forks. Another scheme to build a tunnel here cost four million dollars before its ambitious supporters gave the whole thing up as a bad job.

One expensive plan came within a hair's breath of failing. The Old Lout company sank a 300-foot shaft without finding anything worthwhile. The men were ordered out of the shaft. There are two versions of what happened next. One says one of the miners just had one shot left and decided to get rid of it, and another story says the miner decided to fire one more shot out of curiosity. Anyhow, the result was the same. The last shot uncovered one of the richest bodies of ore in the area. The first carload was worth $8,000 and the mine produced $86,000 the first month.

While some were satisfied to spend money and reap little reward, others worked and became rich. Much good ore was shipped over rough roads to Silverton via Animas Forks or to Lake City via Rose's cabin. Some was even packed on mules and shipped to Ouray over two or three near-impossible trails.

And the city prospered. The peak population was near the thousand mark, and Mineral Point boasted of a hotel, several restaurants, a post office, justice of the peace, and enough saloons to accomodate the residents. The big man about town was Ed Tonkyn, who was not only mayor, postmaster, street supervisor, hotel operator, but also deacon of all churches.

The camp began to wane in the late 80's and died quickly in the early

90's. Not much is left of the city high in the mountains, but what there is can be reached over a rugged jeep road from Animas Forks, or Rose's Cabin. The road is closed much of the year, and is difficult to travel when open. It is the scene of a difficult but beautiful jeep run. The remains of the San Jaun Chief Mill still stand above the city.

BEST MINES: Old Lout, Mastodan, Bill Young, Burrows, Vermillion, Dacotah, Red Cloud, Yankton and Ben Butler.

## POUGHKEEPSIE

Poughkeepsie was called "the biggest little camp in the San Juans." There were a number of good mines here but the remoteness of the area hindered the development. It was high in the Uncompahgre Mountains, seven miles south of Ouray and about twelve miles up Cement Creek from Silverton. Winters were cruel and so the mining was limited to a couple of months or so in the summer. Summer residents numbered about 250 during the boom days of the late 70's and early 80's.

Despite its size and the few months of the year that the town was occupied, Poughkeepsie was a fairly complete settlement. There was a post office here as early as 1880. L. P. Kendall was postmaster. He also started up *The Poughkeepsie Telegraph*. There were stores, restaurants, saloons and other businesses.

The ores were generally galena and gray copper carrying gold and silver. The ore was sent over rough roads, usually by burro train, to Lake City and Silverton. There was also a rough trail to Ouray, and sometimes the ore was sent there. The top mines were the Alaska, Saxon, Alpha, Adelpha, Red and Rogers. There were also some mines in Poughkeepsie Basin below.

Although there were still plenty of ores left in the mines, the mine owners, after a while, decided the profits didn't compensate for the travel and weather problems. Poughkeepsie was abandoned after a few short years. The area has been returned to nature. There may be some ruins left, but it would take a long hike and then a long climb to get to them.

## GLADSTONE

Although there were some other good mines around, the story of Gladstone is the story of the Gold King mine. The mine became one of the best mines in the county and produced some eight or nine million dollars in gold.

The Gold King wasn't the first mine here. In fact, Olaf Nelson, who located the Gold King, was a miner in the Sampson mine which had been working since 1882.

In 1887, Olaf hit a good vein at a sharp angle while working in the Sampson. The discovery led him to believe a better mine could be

351

located nearby. He staked out the next claim to the Sampson in the direction of the vein. Olaf worked the property by himself in his spare time, until he got enough from his discovery to work on it full time. Nelson died in 1890 but already had made a tidy sum out of the Gold King.

In 1894, Cyrus Davis and Henry Soule bought the mine from Olaf's widow for $15,000. They hired as manager Willis Kinney, who suggested the purchase. Within a year, Kinney had the Gold King paying off big. Gradually it bought up the other claims around and during its peak shipped up to 300 tons of processed ore per day.

The population of the town was reflected in the activity of Gold King. As the mine expanded, so did the town, until as many as 2,000 persons lived in the city.

Fire destroyed the surface buildings of the Gold King in 1907, trapping three men inside the mine. A huge rescue party was organized, but before the men could be saved, two of them died along with four members of the rescue party—all killed by fumes.

Litigation among heirs and stockholders closed down the mine in 1910, but it was reopened in 1918 and Kinney was called back as manager. The mine was worked profitably for several more years.

Heavy equipment and tons of pipe mark the site of Gladstone today. Work has begun on the American Tunnel. The tunnel, as planned, will be one of the longest tunnels of its kind in the world. It is planned to under-cut the Gladstone mine, cut through Eureka Gulch, swing around to the Shenandoah-Dives, and, eventually, run through the Silver Lake region. When the immense task is completed it will mean a great new boom for the entire Silverton region.

GOLD DUST: The biggest boost to the development of the Gold King and the city of Gladstone was the coming of the Silverton, Gladstone and Northerly Railroad in 1899—cause for a wild celebration . . . . the railroad tracks were torn up in 1915. Many of the buildings are gone, but there is still plenty to see, including a smelter and the workings of the Gold King. The road to Gladstone is not the best in the world, but is usually passable . . . . at one time a rough road—more of a trail—ran up Poughkeepsie Gulch to Poughkeepsie and on into Ouray . . . . the town was named for the prime minister of England.

## FISHERVILLE

Fisherville was a suburb of Gladstone. It grew around Fisher's stamp mill, located a half-mile south of Gladstone. The town was laid out in 1889 at the time the mill was built. The mill worked ore from the Exposition mine, a good quartz property.

## CHATTANOOGA (Sheridan Junction)

Chattanooga led three lives. One life involved silver, one gold, and one transportation.

Some good silver was located here in the late 70's. Silver wasn't nearly as valuable as gold and therefore more had to be shipped to make the effort worthwhile. Therein was Chattanooga's main problem. The railroad hadn't come into Silverton yet, and the Chattanooga mines had to ship their ore by wagons as much as 200 miles. Nonetheless, the local mines, primarily the Silver Crown mines, shipped a lot of silver. The coming of the railroad to Silverton aided silver production in Chattanooga.

During the same time, Chattanooga, at the southern foot of Red Mountain Pass, was a key stop on the route from Silverton to Ouray and the camps in between. Wagons coming from Silverton would make their terminal at Chattanooga, and the wagon supplies would be loaded onto pack trains for the trip over the pass. The procedure would be reversed with traffic coming down off the pass enroute to Silverton.

The key man then was Jim Sheridan, who ran a hotel, saloon and livery stable. Chattanooga was called Sheridan Junction for quite a while.

Just about the time Chattanooga seemed doomed by the silver panic, gold was discovered in the Hoosier Boy mine. The silver crash upset just about everybody's apple carts. Within days, hundreds of silver mines throughout Colorado closed down, and thousands of miners were thrown out of work. That's why the gold strikes—especially in Cripple Creek and Creede—brought forth more fortune seekers than the area could handle.

Chattanooga was no exception. There was good gold here. In fact, for a time, they thought it might rival Cripple Creek's. Hundreds of prospectors and miners rushed to the site. Within weeks almost every foot of available land was staked out. Trouble was, Chattanooga wasn't another Cripple Creek, and with everybody digging so feverishly, the gold soon played out.

To add to the confusion of the time—or maybe because of it—a fire swept through the city and destroyed the majority of the buildings and homes. The new miners and prospectors were too hungry for gold to worry about shelter, and little of the town was rebuilt. A huge snowslide has since destroyed much of what was left by the fire.

In later years, Chattanooga earned the distinction of having the first mill in the country which used magnetized machines to separate lead and zinc ore. The mill was the Silver Ledge.

Only a few scattered buildings remain at the site, although some mining has been done in recent years in the hills and gulches nearby.

GOLD DUST: The Silver Ledge mine, which also played an important role in Chattanooga's gold excitement, is on the hill above town . . . . the shafthouses of the Silver Ledge were destroyed by fire in 1891 . . . . Chattanooga also had its hermit, who had a ramshackle cabin in his small mining claim, which produced enough ore to keep him alive from 1908 to 1940.

## RED MOUNTAIN CITY, UPPER RED MOUNTAIN TOWN and OLD CONGRESS TOWN

A number of camps erupted on Red Mountain Pass during the mining boom in the early 80's. Eventually, Red Mountain Town and Guston emerged as the top ones.

Of the other camps, Red Mountain City was the largest. Up until recently, historians believed the city was a predecessor to, or even another name for, Red Mountain Town. But more recent evidence shows Red Mountain City was just over the crest of the pass from Red Mountain Town, on the Silverton side. In fact, there was at one time a great rivalry between the two camps. Red Mountain City lasted for several years before the last hold-outs finally gave up the ghost and moved to the Town. The last trace of Red Mountain City was destroyed in a forest fire in 1939, although there are still some mine buildings left.

Old Congress Town was on Congress Hill around the Congress mine. The town was laid out while up to six feet of snow was still on the ground, so it was unsteady from the start. When Red Mountain Town emerged as the town of Red Mountain Pass, Old Congress residents moved there, cabins and all.

A similar, but shorter history, accompanies Upper Red Mountain Town.

## RED MOUNTAIN TOWN (Sky City, Upper Red Mountain Town)

A few crumbling buildings and cabins about a half mile off the highway north of the summit of Red Mountain Pass mark the site of Red Mountain Town. It was one of the most fabulous cities during the golden years of the San Juans.

Rich metal was found on the pass in the late 70's, but the lack of transportation and the severe winters held back the stampede for two or three more years. When the rush did come, claims virtually covered the pass. There was one camp right after another up one side and down the other.

There was great rivalry between the camps. Brawls and bloodshed were common. Eventually, of all the camps on the pass, three or four took shape and absorbed the others. On the northern side were Guston, Ironton and Red Mountain Town. Just over the summit of the pass was Red Mountain City (which is believed to have absorbed old Congress Town).

There was still great rivalry between the cities. A Saturday night drunk more than likely would end in a free-for-all. But there was no doubt about it, Red Mountain Town soon became King of the Mountain—and remained that way.

Of course, Red Mountain Town had a hard time getting settled. They say its location was moved a time or two before everyone was satisfied. Different reasons have been given for the moves. Some say the town

354

moved to be near the toll road built by Mears over the pass. Others say it was moved to a spot more level and open and better suited for a town. Yet others say an obstinate liquor dealer set up shop a short distance away, and the town up and moved to the source of the nectar.

Anyhow, once settled, Red Mountain Town soon became one of the most colorful and prosperous towns of its day.

The ores around rivaled the metals of Leadville. Eastern and European investors poured millions into the region, and took out millions. And Red Mountain Town, with a population in the thousands, became one of the most bustling cities in the state.

As with Creede ten years later, Red Mountain Town had no night-time. The saloons and gambling halls were always open and the doors were always swinging. Brawls and shootings were common and not worth worrying about.

Nearly 100 businessmen prospered. Never less than two newspapers were published. By 1886, Red Mountain Town had its own water works. A school was built later. They didn't bother with a church.

The population during those early boom years has been estimated as high as 10,000. The output in precious metal was said to be second only to Leadville for a while.

Of course, transportation those first years was the major problem. A fellow named Otto Mears, already established as a pretty fair country road builder, soon solved this problem. His first road over the pass was as great an accomplishment as the latter-day Million Dollar Highway, much of which followed Mears' early road. Mears spent $10,000 a mile in building the road, equivalent to at least ten times that amount at today's prices. The Million Dollar Highway cost $20,000 a mile, and the prices were much closer to today's level.

The steepest grade on the Million Dollar Highway is six per cent. Some grades on Mears' early highway topped twenty per cent.

Mears soon realized his highway, called the "grandest highway in the Rockies," was not enough to do the job. He started work on his famous railroad line. It was completed from Silverton to Red Mountain Town by 1888 and had dropped down into Ironton by the following year.

A celebration heard throughout the southwestern corner of the state greeted the arrival of the first train into Red Mountain Town.

The railroad, of course, only added to the prosperity of the town. During the first years, the railroad carried out an average of 20,000 to 25,000 tons of ore per year and brought in an average of 15,000 tons of coal.

About the only obstacle in the prosperity of Red Mountain Town were the winters. Snow several feet deep buried the town, and only the hardiest stayed the winter. Armies of snow shovelers were in almost constant use, keeping the railroad tracks open. Scores were killed in snowslides and from exposure. Stages were rigged out like sleighs during the winter, and chains and claw-like anchors were needed to go downhill.

One sleigh, similarly rigged, containing vital supplies for Red Mountain Town, plus two drunken miners, went out of control and shot over a 100-foot cliff on Red Mountain Pass. The stage driver jumped clear. The supplies were completely lost. The two miners miraculously survived, rescued near-dead but totally sober, in a creek at the foot of the cliff.

The city also had its share of fires. A fire started in the Red Mountain Hotel in 1892 and roared through the town in a matter of hours. The townspeople piled most of their belongings in the streets upwind of the fire, but the wind changed and burned up everything.

Much of the town—but not all—was rebuilt. Part of it was destroyed a few years later in another fire. Much that remained was burned in a fire in 1937.

Despite the winters, the fires and the other troubles found here, the Red Mountain area was one of the leading metal producing areas in the state for several years.

The National Belle was one of the first mines, and produced for years. Other mines located shortly thereafter were the Congress and the Summit. The Enterprise was said to be "solid copper from the grass roots."

The Yankee Girl was the best, producing more than eight million dollars in precious metals. The mine was developed at twelve levels and employed more than 2,000 men at its peak.

The Guston was nearly as rich.

Some prospectors opened a cave in a knoll above the town, found the walls rich in lead carbonates, and were soon shipping fifty to ninety tons a day.

In all, an estimated thirty million dollars in gold, silver, lead, zinc and copper has been taken from the Red Mountain and Guston mines.

A big boost to the mining in later years was the Treasury Tunnel, built at a cost of more than a million and a half dollars. The tunnel tapped mines as far away as Telluride, and more than paid for itself in two years. The tunnel is still being used in the operation of some mines in the area.

GOLD DUST: News of the first discoveries became known during the winter. Despite ten feet of snow, several miners poured in, staking their claims on top of the snow . . . . there were two or three hazardous but well-traveled routes from Mineral Point to Red Mountain Town . . . . Red Mountain Town had one of the most complete and efficient hook-and-ladder fire companies in southern Colorado . . . . This was a very sociable town. Dances and get-togethers were frequent. The residents often put on their own plays and musicals. There was plenty of debating and athletic competition . . . . Red Mountain balls were famous and often brought visitors from as far away as Ouray and Silverton . . . . Mears' railroad climbed at an average of 212 feet to a mile and crossed the pass at the 11,650-foot mark.

## GUSTON

About midway between Ironton and Red Mountain Town was the prosperous city of Guston. The town was named for the Guston mines. There were several well-paying mines around, many of which Guston shared with its neighboring cities.

The Yankee Girl, whose wealth was shared by Red Mountain Town, was the most famous.

There were several stories about the Yankee Girl. A John Robinson, who located the Guston mine, was said to have located a piece of pure galena while deer hunting, and staked a claim at the source. When his shaft was only twenty feet deep he sold the property for $125,000 and quickly staked claims on both sides, believing the vein of the Yankee Girl would extend in both directions. He was right and his claims, the Robinson and Orphan Boy, both paid well.

Another story about the Yankee Girl tells of three prospectors failing to locate a vein after digging hole after hole for three years. They were about to give up on it when they returned to one of their earliest diggings, put just a tiny bit more work into it, and hit a bonanza.

Other than its good mines, Guston's main badge of distinction was the fact it had the only church in the entire Red Mountain district for several years.

In 1891, Reverend William Davis, a young eager minister, recently arrived from London, was sent into this unholy Red Mountain district by the Congregational Church in Denver. Reverend Davis received a cold reception, to say the least. The coldest reception came from Red Mountain Town, "The King of the Hill." The good reverend did the best he could by preaching the word wherever a few men would gather. His take was hardly worth the trouble. It was enough to discourage an ordinary man. But it merely made the reverend more determined to bring religion to this pagan region. He knew he needed a church and set out to get one.

After several weeks of bullying, browbeating, badgering and begging from individuals and groups all up and down Red Mountain, and as far away as Ouray and Silverton, Reverend Davis finally had enough to buy the material to begin his church. He won title to a small hill near the heart of Guston. The reverend did most of the building himself, although now and again a miner would donate some of his time.

The townspeople finally began taking some pride in the building as it neared completion. Some Cornish miners thought the church needed a bell. So they built a belfrey, collected enough to buy a bell, and installed it.

Another miner, used to doing things all of his life to the sound of a whistle, suggested a whistle be installed also. It was. And the Guston church became the only church in the state known to have called meetings via a mine whistle.

The church held its grand opening during November of 1891. The Reverend Davis and a few other men of God journeyed into the wilderness on Red Mountain, and miners frequently journeyed to Guston from up the hill or down the hill on Sunday. The little church in Guston was the only symbol of Christianity on Red Mountain through the years.

The little church on the hill was protected from fire, the ravages of weather, but lost to the ravages of time. After one final look around, it fell flat on its face in recent years.

Guston grew during the early 90's, just a few hundred feet away from the Yankee Girl mine. Although many of the miners chose to live in Red Mountain Town, many others chose convenience to excitement, and lived in Guston.

Guston thrived during the 1890's and early 1900's, and has seen mining activity off and on ever since. Peak population varied from 500 to 1,000.

BEST MINES: Yankee Girl, Robinson, Orphan Boy, Guston, Saratoga, Cardice, Silver Bell, Genessee-Canderbilt and Paymaster.

## IRONTON (Copper Glen)

Another town that shared the wealth of the mines on the north side of Red Mountain Pass. As with Guston and Red Mountain Town, Ironton owed much of its livelihood to the Yankee Girl and Guston Mines. Ironton also served as a major transportation junction between Ouray and Red Mountain.

John Robinson and others staked out the Guston claim during the summer of 1881. They got little return that first year and were seriously considering abandoning it. But they decided to give it another go the following year, and hit a rich lode almost immediately.

Before good roads were built up the mountain, Ironton played a key role in the development of the area, serving as a transportation and supply center for the region.

Stage and supply wagons arrived at Ironton at regular intervals and ore wagons headed out from the city continuously. The community lost some of its activity to Guston and Red Mountain Town when the Mears toll road was extended up the mountain, but the coming of the railroad boosted activity here considerably. The beauty of the surrounding countryside made

Ironton a top tourist center. During its peak, two trains arrived daily at Ironton from Silverton.

As with mines throughout Colorado, the Red Mountain Mines were hampered by water. They also had a unique problem—sulphuric acid in the water. The sulphuric acid continually wore through the machinery and mine props, making constant and expensive replacements necessary. The sulphuric water eventually caused many good mines—including the Yankee Girl—to be closed down.

George Crawford, who had worked the district from the first, believed a tunnel built below the mines would alleviate the problem. Despite the apparent soundness of the idea, it took Crawford several months to obtain backing for the tunnel.

Work on the tunnel began in 1904 and was completed in two years. It cut below the main shaft of the Yankee Girl, which had not been worked for twelve years. The tunnel drained the Yankee Girl at the rate of 1200 gallons per minute, permitting the mine to return to full operation almost immediately.

Since that time, several other mines in the region have been drained through the tunnel, which brought new prosperity to the entire area.

During its heyday, Ironton had a population of more than one thousand, had ten saloons and branch stores of many Silverton and Ouray merchants. The community began to fade during the early years of this century. Much remains of the old city.

## OURAY (Uncompahgre City)

Chief Ouray's life must have been a most difficult one. But Colorado is very fortunate he lived when he did. He, more than any one man, white or Indian, was the guiding force in bringing peace between the white man and the Indians in Colorado.

Often distrusted by the whites, considered a traitor by his Indian brothers, Chief Ouray, nonetheless, prevented an unestimable amount of bloodshed and eventually brought about peace through sheer force of character. It is proper that one of Colorado's fairest cities was named for him. Here, Chief Ouray and his wife, Chipeta, spent much of their time.

Ouray, the city, is nestled in a beautiful valley surrounded on all sides by near-14,000 foot peaks. It has been called the "Opal of the Mountains" and "Queen City of the San Jauns."

From its inception, it was a trading and transportation center for the rich camps around. It was naturally a very popular tourist gathering place, and it had a rich mining life of its own. Ouray has remained important for these reasons down through the years.

Shortly after the Brunot Treaty with the Indians, prospectors swarmed into the San Juans. Most bypassed Ouray for a try at the lush regions to the south. But some tarried on their way to scout the Ouray region. Evidence of paydirt was found but no rich strikes were made until a couple of Mineral Point prospectors, A. J. Staley and Logan Whitlock, discovered the Trout and Fisherman lodes while on a fishing trip here.

News of the strike brought hundreds of prospectors into the region. Several more rich strikes were made. Judge Long and Captain Cline laid out a city. Ouray was on the map.

The first building was a saloon, where whiskey glasses were used faster than they could be washed. Shortly thereafter, when Ouray became county seat, the saloon was turned into a court house.

The first woman in the town was Mrs. Dixon who ran the first boarding house. She did so well, she soon was able to put up a hotel, The Dixon House Hotel, Ouray's pride and joy. Tabor, Thomas Walsh, and many other personages of the day stayed at the hotel at one time or another.

The first church service was held in a saloon. Beer kegs and whiskey cases were used as seats.

Newspapers played a vital part in the early days of Ouray. Of course, David Frakes Day and his *Solid Muldoon* were legend (see above), but there were other important papers. There were the *San Juan Sentinel* and the *Ouray Times,* later called the *Plaindealer.* Both were read and quoted throughout the San Juans.

The city was well established by 1877. The residents noted the fact with a gala Fourth of July celebration. A huge twenty-foot flag was presented at that time. Perhaps incongruously large and majestic for the cabin town below, it nonetheless waved proudly above the city for years.

The area around Ouray, and further south, on Red Mountain Pass, and in the Silverton district, is perhaps the worst area in the world for snowslides. Countless tales are told of the many slides here. Scores lost their lives to winter.

Two miners at the Terrible were injured by a mine accident. A four-man rescue party from the Virginius was killed in an avalanche while enroute to aid Terrible miners take the injured men to Ouray.

Another slide, in the early 1900's, claimed the lives of seven miners and twenty-seven horses and mules.

In addition to the endless slides, dozens more died from pneumonia and exposure during the long hard winters, especially in the Terrible, Virginius and Camp Bird areas. More than 100 died or were killed during the disastrous winter of 1905-06, one of the worst in Colorado history.

But there were also tales of survival. The story is told of a man buried in a mine by a snowslide. He tunneled out after two days and walked into

360

Ouray to find his name in the obituary column. Another man dug out of a snowbank with his bare fingers, turning them into bloody stumps.

The cruel winters intensified the isolation of Ouray. This isolation came to a screeching halt with the coming of the railroad from Montrose, then from Ridgeway

Each new entry into Ouray by the railroad was sufficient cause for a wild celebration.

By the mid-80's, the Ouray region ranked third in the state in mineral production (topped only by Leadville and Aspen), the bulk was silver until 1893, when it turned to gold. Ouray suffered little from the panic with the many rich mines around, the growth and development of the fabulous Camp Bird Mine, and the other reasons for being of the city.

In fact, Ouray has suffered only minor ups and downs through the years. Many of its mines are still producing, the tourist trade is better than ever and growing yearly. It is still a trading center and important junction on the railroad.

One needn't worry about Ouray's future.

GOLD DUST: Nearby Vinegar Hill was named in 1875 when miners, lacking the usual spirits for the occasion, drank vinegar to celebrate Christmas Day . . . . Ouray has an interesting graveyard . . . . the public library in Ouray, one of the finest in western Colorado, was donated to the city by Thomas Walsh . . . . Bear Creek Falls, two miles south of Ouray, falls 210 feet, more than Niagara Falls. There is a plaque here commemorating railroad giant Otto Mears. This is the site of one of his toll gates . . . . White House Mountain (13,493 feet) is to the west of Ouray; Hayden Mountain (13,100 feet) to the south, and Cascade Mountain (12,100 feet) to the northwest . . . . the Beaumont Hotel, at Fifth and Main Streets, was one of Ouray's first . . . . the early red light district was at the northern edge of the city, and is now a cottage camp . . . . two large, natural hot springs are in the southwest corner of town . . . . presses for the *Ouray Times*, first newspaper in the region, were brought over the mountains in a six-wagon train . . . . Dave Day also dabbled in mining. Among the many mines in which he invested was the El Mahoi, one of the richest in the region . . . . a couple of random items about Ouray taken from the *Rocky Mountain News*: (In 1882) "Ed Bigger, sentenced for murder at Ouray has been reprieved—it is said against his wishes."; (in 1885) "Ouray has nine saloons and gambling houses but not one resident preacher." . . . . Chief Ouray died in 1880 at the age of 47 and was buried secretly by brother Indians. What was believed to be his grave was discovered forty-two years later on a rocky mesa two miles south of Ignacio. Chipeta remarried and moved to Utah where she lived until her death in 1924 when she was 81 years ago.
BEST MINES: The Sneffels and Camp Bird mines, Terrible, Virginius, El Mahoi, Begale, Bachelor, American Nettie, Chief Ouray, Consolidated, Wedge, Khedive, and Banner American. Many of the mines are still producing.

361

## CAMP BIRD

Thomas Walsh came to America from Ireland when he was 19. He worked at many things on his way across the country. Mostly he was a carpenter like Winfield Scott Stratton (see Winfield). He worked on building bridges for the Colorado Central Railway.

That was how he made his living. At heart, he was a prospector. His ambition was to get rich quick. There were thousands with the same ambition but only a handful achieved their goal.

Walsh was one of the more illustrious to fall into step with fickle Dame Fortune. But it didn't come easy. He worked many of the boom areas in Colorado, and even tried his luck in South Dakota. He wasn't very lucky.

Then came Leadville. They say he did acquire a small fortune in buying up some mining properties. But what fortune he did have was all but erased in the silver crash of '93.

That might have been enough for some men—but not old Tom. Instead of following the crowds to Cripple Creek and Creede, Tom Walsh moved to the Silverton area.

The next part of the story is obscure. One side says Old Tom was out prospecting, himself, when he became interested in the ore samples around the site and hired prospector Andy Richardson to go into the subject further.

Another side says Mister Walsh was running a mill in Silverton and was looking for some silicous ores for flux, and hired old Andy to look around for some. (Andy couldn't pronounce it, but he knew what it looked like.)

No matter, it all turned out the same. Andy ran across the old workings this side of Sneffels, became interested and studied it som᾿ more. On pausing one day, Andy returned to his burro and found camp birds had eaten his lunch. Camp Birds, Camp Robbers or Whiskey Jacks, were Canada Jays— a common bird around mining camps, who ate many a miner's lunch.

It's not particulary important to Walsh's story, but it does give some insight into early Colorado birds and explain why this particular site was named Camp Bird.

Anyhow, lunchless Andy took some of the ore he had found back to Walsh. Some of the samples ran as high as $3,000 a ton. Walsh bought up most of the claims around for only $20,000, letting Richardson stake a claim.

The claim started paying off from the start, but Walsh, one of the smartest men in Colorado mining history, spent much of the profits those first years buying up more claims and improving the property. By 1900, he had spent a half million dollars in improving his workings, including one of the finest miners' boarding houses in the state. The property soon covered some 900 acres.

Under Walsh's leadership, Camp Bird became one of the largest and most productive gold mines in the world, and the second largest in Colorado, trailing only the Portland in the Cripple Creek area.

Walsh was already a millionaire in 1902 when he sold the property to an English syndicate for $5,200,000, getting $3,500,000 in cash and the rest in easy installments.

Walsh, one-time poor immigrant boy, became a U. S. Senator, and one of the most impressive figures in Washington. He purchased the fabulous Hope Diamond for his wife (it was later given to his daughter). His Washington home became the meeting-place for the great the world over. His wife was one of Washington's all-time famous hostesses.

In 1900, Walsh was appointed a commissioner of the Paris Exposition. During the last years of his life, he joined King Leopold in mining enterprises in the Belguim Congo.

But, as with another gold king, Winfield Scott Stratton, Walsh's fortunes came too late. Both had only a few short years to enjoy or use their wealth. Senator Tom Walsh died in Washington in 1909.

Meanwhile, back at the gold mine—

An Englishman, George Barber, and his partner, Bill Weston, located the Gertrude and Una here in the late 70's, but after doing some work at the site, gave it up for a bad job and turned the property over to the Reed brothers in 1880. The brothers drove a cross-cut tunnel between the Gertrude and the Una, but the ore gave out and Barber and Weston sold out for $50,000 the following year.

The next owner was scared off by the snowslides and the claims were virtually left alone until Walsh and old Andy Richardson came along fifteen years later.

Walsh built a tremendous boarding house to accomodate 400 men. But it was much more than just a barracks. It had electric lights, steam heat, modern sewage, marble-topped lavatories and reading rooms.

A two-mile tramway was built to bring the ore into the mill. The free milling gold was filtered out on the crushing tables and the lower grade ore was treated by cyanide which recovered more than ninety per cent of the paying metal.

Snow was always the problem. Miners had to tunnel through huge snowdrifts during the winter, and several men have been killed down through the years by snowslides.

Three men were killed in early 1958, one slide burying one miner, and a subsequent slide burying two members of the rescue party. The threat of more slides hampered rescue operations and the three bodies weren't found for several days.

Estimates on the total of production of the Camp Bird mine vary considerably, running from a low of about thirty million to a high of more than fifty million dollars. Walsh took out several million, but he put a lot back into the mine. The English syndicate took out more than twenty-three million dollars from 1902 to 1916. At its peak, Camp Bird produced as much as three or four million per year.

It's still a good producer. Maybe it will outdistance the Portland and be Colorado's top mine.

GOLD DUST: It's a steep, sometimes narrow road up to Camp Bird from Ouray —but trucks make it back and forth every day—just don't get in their way . . . . a story goes that two masked men robbed a stage between Camp Bird and Ouray in 1899, but passed by some $12,000 in gold shipments. A large posse almost caught the bandits, but they later escaped in a burst of gunfire . . . . the story of Walsh is told in *My Father Struck It Rich*, written by his daughter, Evelyn Walsh McLean.

## SNEFFELS

Had not the Camp Bird mines been so close, Sneffels' rich mines might well have had a more prominent part in the history of the area. The Sneffels area got a better start than Camp Bird and produced almost as well. An estimated twenty-seven million dollars in precious metals poured from Mt. Sneffels during the boom years of 1881 to 1919. It has been in production much of the time since.

The greatest thing that happened to mining here was the Revenue Tunnel, built in the 80's by the Thatcher brothers, Ouray financiers, at a cost of $600,000. The tunnel was cut some three miles into the mountain about 3,000 feet below the original shaft, solving the water and ventilation problems of the mine, and opening up enough ore to keep the mills running for nearly forty years. The tunnel has paid for itself many times over.

Good strikes were made here in the early and mid-70's, even before Ouray and two or three years before the first locations were made at Camp Bird. There was another difference between the two camps. Camp Bird, at first, didn't look too promising and the area was soon deserted.

Sneffels began paying off from the first. Some of the first ore assayed as high as $40,000 a ton. A road was cut down the mountain to Ouray, passing close to the later site of Camp Bird. Hundreds of supply and ore wagons, prospectors, and miners passed by Camp Bird before Tom Walsh developed the section in the 90's, and made himself a multi-millionaire.

Mines were located along the route from Camp Bird to the Ruby Trust and Yankee Boy, the latter about three miles above Sneffels. Some smaller camps were located around the more distant mines, but the miners generally headquartered at Sneffels. As many as 3,000 persons worked in the district during its boom days.

Work was usually kept at a minimum in winter but some mines stayed open all winter long, even if it meant tunneling through snow drifts several feet high. The road down into Ouray was not a million-dollar highway. The narrow ledges and steep grades spelled danger and sometimes death. Rock and snow slides were common. Nonetheless, thousands of wagons, and later trucks, made their way safely down to the big city.

Although some of the mines here are still being worked, few people live in Sneffels and most of the cabins of yesterday are gone.

The town was named for the majestic mountain on which it is located. The mountain was named for the Icelandic Peak in Jules Verne's book *A Journey to the Center of the Earth*, although another amateur historian went so far as to claim the mountain and the town were named for a Professor Sneffels, a member of the Hayden survey team.

BEST MINES: Virginius, Wheel of Fortune, Ruby Trust, Yankee Boy, Hidden Treasure, Revenue-Tunnel, Governor, Atlas, Humboldt, Senator.

### RUBY (Ruby City)

A small camp near Sneffels, was handicapped from the first by transportation and costs. The ore wasn't too good anyway. The camp got its start about 1880 with some locations being made here. Only a few cabins were built. Until a crude road was built, ore had to be shipped out on burros.

The area got its biggest boost about the turn of the century when the Ruby Trust mine, the biggest mine here, was connected with the mill at the mouth of Yankee Boy Basin. Mining has been done at the Ruby Trust off and on ever since.

### DALLAS (Dallas City, Dallas Station, Gold City and Uniweep)
### (north of map)

Placer gold was located in Uniweep Valley in 1879, and within days hundreds of fortune seekers poured in, all but deserting the established cities of Silverton and Ouray. Hundreds of tents and huts were thrown up. The makeshift community was named Gold City.

But almost as quickly as the excitement had erupted, disappointment set in, and the site was all but deserted a few weeks later.

A more organized stampede began the following year and a permanent town was platted. It was named for George V. Dallas, then vice president of the United States.

Although gold was the reason for the city, it soon became a major stage and wagon train station on the road to Telluride and Ouray. It remained so during the 80's as the population wavered between 100 and 200.

Much to the disappointment of Dallasites, the railroad made a spot two and a half miles south of their town the main junction, although a spur was run to Dallas. Dallas, also called Dallas Station, then faded proportionately with the rise of Ridgeway to the south. Dallas was all but dead by 1900.

*And Then There Were* . . . . *LE MOYNE CITY* (not on map), an elusive city that was more planning than being. The plans called for a compact town four blocks in each direction, but only five or six cabins were actually built. The town was platted in 1883 at the foot of Boulder Mountain, where some locations were made. The town only lasted a few months . . . . *YANKEE GIRL*, although Yankee Girl miners lived in several towns and cities from Red Mountain Town to Ouray, there was a rather large camp right at the mine, situated less than a mile from Guston. As many as 200 miners lived here, and there were a post office, commissary and other facilities . . . . *BURRO BRIDGE* and *SUMMIT*, two important stage and railroad stops on the road between Silverton and Ouray. Burro Bridge was at the junction of the road and the road over Ophir Pass. Thousands of burros traveled over the pass in its time. Summit was at the summit of Red Mountain Pass. A busy saloon here allowed the travelers a chance to catch their breath after the trip up the pass and fortify themselves for the trip down. There were also some working mines near the town and some miners lived near or in the town . . . . *NEEDLETON* and *COLUMBINE* (both south of map), two towns between Durango and Silverton which had little or nothing to do with mining. Needleton was a station stop on the Denver and Rio Grande. Columbine was the name of a lake and a mountain pass as well . . . . *CASCADE CITY* (Cascade Siding) (south of map), many Hollywood movies have been made around the site of old Cascade City, a minor community at the junction of the Animas River and Cascade Creek, about twenty-two miles south of Silverton. It was a stage station during the 70's and 80's and later became a siding for the Denver and Rio Grande . . . . *ALBANY*, a little known town, six miles south of Ouray, toward Silverton. It was apparently very near Ironton and was apparently a siding on the railroad, where it met with the Milion Dollar Highway . . . . *TUCKERVILLE*, a remote and small mining camp at the southern end of the Needles Mountain. A few ruins can be found about nine miles up Los Pinos Canyon over a rough jeep road.

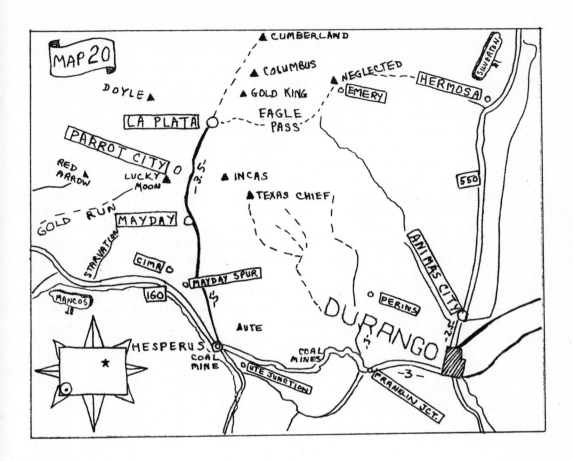

*MAP TWENTY*

DURANGO

Durango
Animas City
Hesperus
Mayday
Parrot City
La Plata (La Plata City)
Cima, Mayday Spur, Mayday Station, Ute Junction and Franklin Junction
Perins (Perrins)

*And Then There Were . . . . HERMOSA, CAMP STARVATION* (not on map),
*EMERY, MINERAL CITY* and *WEBTOWN*

367

# XIX. DURANGO

## DURANGO

It is only reasonable that tales of hidden treasure and lost mines should permeate the dark pockets of the mysterious Colorado mountains. Some of the tales concern Indian treasure, many concern Spanish gold. Still others are told about the ill-gotten loot of highwaymen and bandits. Some are more recent and perhaps more authentic.

Durango and the San Juans have more than their share of these legends. Two of the most-told in Durango concern recent times.

Legend? Call them legend if you like, but fifty million Durango-ites swear to their truth.

The first lost mine has three skeletons in its closet.

An old prospector walked into Durango in 1905 with a bag full of almost pure gold ore. The prospector wanted to sell the ore to buy supplies so he could go back up in the mountains and work the old mine he had found.

He paused in Durango just long enough to give some details of the mine. He said he ran across it while prospecting in the Bear Creek area. He said the mine was pretty well developed, a tunnel shaft and all. The timbers were rotted and old, but the mine was rich. Some sacks of gold ore similar to the bag he had were inside the entrance, and evidence of equally rich ore was all over the place.

But the most unusual part of the mine—and that which became a trade-mark of this particular mine—was the tenants. They were as dead as they could be. In fact, their skeletons were just sitting there inside the entrance, collecting dust. The old prospector said he could find no identification or any evidence of how or when the three died—and he didn't stop to ask questions.

The old prospector sold his rich gold ore in Durango, bought supplies and headed back into the mountain, never to be seen again.

In 1918, a fellow by the name of Pedro Martinez came into town with a sack of the same rich gold ore and the same story of the lost mine. But before Pedro could go back into the mountains, he died of flu and the secret of the mine died with him.

Twenty years later an old sheepherder came in with some gold and told of finding the mine with the bones of three very dead men guarding the entrance.

The Durango-ites worked fast before the sheepherder could get away. They organized a search party. But the sheepherder must have been more at home in front of a herd of sheep, because he couldn't lead the search party back to the elusive mine, and the search was eventually abandoned.

Perhaps the next person to run across the mine and its eerie inhabitants will have a better sense of direction.

The other story is as recent and as frustrating as the first.

During the depression many an unemployed man set out to win his fortune by prospecting. One of this army of latter-day prospectors was an earnest young man who walked into Newton's cafe in Durango one day, told the owner he had studied rocks a little, and would be willing to split any or all of the gold and silver he found for a grubstake.

Newton took an instant liking to the youth and agreed to the deal. The youth, loaded down with supplies, set off for the mysterious mountains.

Two weeks later he was back and plopped a number of fascinating rocks on the counter of the cafe. He said he knew where there were tons more just as pretty.

Newton, the youth, and several other customers admired the shining rocks for a spell, before a gnarled old prospector made his way through the crowd, looked at the rocks for a moment and began laughing.

He said the rocks sparkled from iron pyrite—better known as "fools' gold."

The crestfallen youth disappeared and was never seen again. Newton threw the rocks up on shelf as a reminder of the time he thought he had a fortune.

A few weeks later, a mining engineer noticed the rocks while eating at the restaurant. He asked to look at them. After inspection, he said it was some of the richest gold ore he had ever seen.

But after falling so hard before, Newton still wasn't convinced. However, he did have the rocks assayed. They assayed at better than $5,000 a ton.

Newton still has half-interest in a gold mine—but he doesn't know where it is.

Durango was, and is, a railroad and smelting center as well as being a major exporter of legend.

The city was founded in 1880 with the construction of the Denver and Rio Grande Railway here. The first smelter was built in 1882. From then on there was no stopping the progress of the city, and it remains a railroad and smelting center today, and has added a couple of new lines—ranching and tourists.

The city figured in the Tabor story. The Carbonate King owned a livery stable and stage line here. It was here that Tabor filed secret divorce papers against his wife. Later, after his marriage to Baby Doe, the divorce was declared invalid. It was a good thing Tabor was a U. S. Senator and filthy rich, or it could have ruined his reputation.

Carbon Peak, Durango's moving mountain, is a puzzler to geologists for

369

its tummy-rumbling. A few years back, a large fissure appeared on the mountain face, followed by a roar and several giant rockslides. Some believe it was caused by spontaneous combustion in some of the old coal mine shafts in the mountain, but nobody's sure.

The Durango area had been a favorite romping ground for Indians, and the red men fought viciously to keep the white men out of the region.

Many of the Spanish explorers passed by here in their quest for gold and silver.

When Durango finally took over from Animas City as *the* city of the region, it rapidly became a brawling, rowdy frontier town. It was the smelting city, a supply and Saturday Night Town, a ranching town. There were almost constant brawls between the different elements. Naturally the red light and gambling section was the most rowdy of all.

The victim of the first lynching in the town was gambler Henry Moorman, who shot and killed James Prindle over a gambling debt.

Perhaps most of the city's early violence stemmed from the range and cattle wars.

The grand opening of the West End Hotel in 1881 was postponed when feuding cowboys shot up the hotel. One of the brawlers was lynched.

To protect their property, most of the cattle barons hired well-known gunslingers. The most notorious of these groups was the Stockton gang. The Stockton bunch pretty much ran the Durango area as they pleased. The gang's greatest rivalry was with the Frank Simmons gang of Farmington, New Mexico. A "pay-day binge" often wound up in a gun-battle between the two groups.

One Christmas season, the Stockton bunch, in high spirits, invaded the Farmington region. Unable to find any of the Simmons gang, they crashed a Christmas party held by one of the ranchers. It wasn't long before the gang started shooting up the place, and one of the guests was killed by a stray bullet.

The Stockton gang escaped, but a Farmington "necktie party" set out in hot pursuit. The Stockton bunch barricaded themselves up at the outskirts of Durango. The ensuing gun-battle lasted two hours and wounded two bystanders before the Farmington group retreated.

The gun-battle was just about the last straw as far as Durango was concerned. Nobody wanted the Stockton gang around, but it took a fearless newspaper editor to say what all Durango felt. In a blaring editorial on the front page of the *Durango Record,* the editor demanded that the gang leave town.

Ike Stockton himself clumped into the *Record* offices to straighten out the editor and demand a retraction. He was amazed to discover the editor was a woman, Mrs. C. W. Romney.

Mrs. Romney did not apologize nor promise a retraction. Instead she promised to continue the editorials until the Stockton gang was out of town. Her words and her bravery were instrumental in getting the townspeople up in arms against the Stockton gang. And they left town.

After the slaying of Marshal Ogsbury in Silverton (see Silverton), the residents of that city offered $2,500 each for the killers.

Ike Stockton, who had nothing to do with the shooting, captured a member of his own gang near Rico and turned him in for the reward money.

The betrayed gang member was lynched. Ike Stockton himself was shot down a few days later by Silverton Deputy Sheriff Jim Sullivan, who hated a traitor more than a murderer.

## ANIMAS CITY

Animas City was one of the first settlements in southwestern Colorado. It led a full and exciting life for about twenty years before it was stabbed in the back by the railroad and died without regaining consciousness.

Famed scout Jim Baker learned of the gold in the region through the Indians and laid out a small camp on or near the site of Animas City in 1860. But the Indians weren't about to give up the area yet. Constant Indian intimidation plus the under-abundance of rich gold ore caused a partial abandonment of the site the following year.

Animas City was all but deserted until 1873 when the Indians signed the Brunot treaty, opening up much of the land for prospecting. Within weeks Animas City was in full bloom with dozens of flourishing businesses and cabins.

Animas City was just about hitting its stride in 1880. The city anticipated a greater prosperity with the coming of the railroad. But the Denver and Rio Grande didn't build to Animas City. The closest it came was two and a half miles to the south. That point became an important railroad and smelting center almost overnight. It was named Durango and it grew so fast that many Animas City citizens just picked up their belongings and cabins and moved there. What little was left of Animas City soon became a suburb of Durango.

Animas City had an exciting life while it lasted. Much of the excitement generated from the Indians. Animas City was on an almost constant alert for the red men, even after the Brunot treaty.

Perhaps the biggest Indian scare came in 1879, shortly after the Meeker Massacre. The men of the city drilled every day, and lookouts were posted every night. Women and children spent much of the time barricaded here and there—but only after the womenfolk had buried their carpets, their most prized possessions.

One time the townspeople were so sure the Indians were coming they sent a fast rider up North to get help. The trouble was he stopped at a bar in Howardsville. After a quick drink, he shouted breathlessly: "The Indians have burned down Animas City and wiped out the whole town."

It worked—he got himself a free drink. And as the drinks continued he elaborated on the gory—although false—story.

They say he used the same system of shock to get free drinks at other towns, but his one stop in Howardsville had been enough. His story greatly added to the scare that was felt throughout Colorado and caused many small communities and camps to be abandoned, at least temporarily.

U. S. Troops did come to Animas City. They camped nearby at Fort Flagler until the scare was over.

All the characters of that region traipsed through Animas City at one time or another.

Port Stockton, brother of the notorious turncoat gangleader, Ike Stockton, was marshal for a while in Animas City.

His trouble began in the barber shop.

Seems the barber, no doubt shaken by the notoriety of his customer, nicked Port during a shave.

Port, as with so many men, didn't like to be nicked while shaving, so he threatened to kill the barber if it happened again. This, of course, didn't steady the barber's nerves and Port was nicked again.

The next thing Animas City knew a very frightened barber was seen dashing down Main Street, with the Marshal, still wearing apron and plenty of shaving cream, in close pursuit, his guns blazing.

The barber managed to stay ahead of all but one of the bullets, which creased his head.

The barber was later deputized and aided in the capture of Stockton. But no jail was strong enough to hold a Stockton. Port escaped to make his way south to Farmington, New Mexico. Here he killed a man who happened to complain about having his claim jumped. Port was killed in the ensuing gun battle with the posse.

## HESPERUS

Hesperus was principally a coal mining town, but it also served as a supply and railroad center for the rich gold regions to the north. The site was settled when the Hesperus Coal Mine was opened by John A. Porter in 1882. The Rio Grand Southern Railroad named the site Hesperus. The mine and the city were named for Hesperus Peak (13,225 feet) which was twelve miles to the northwest. The peak was named for its western position among the state's highest peaks.

Hesperus has remained a coal mining center to this day.

To the west of Hesperus is Sleeping Ute Mountain. According to Indian legend a tribe of giants as large as this mountain once inhabited this region. One year all the braves but one went off on a hunting expedition. The brave was left to guard the possessions, which he did, year after year. In fact, he was on the alert for centuries because the other braves didn't return and didn't return. Finally the faithful brave could take it no longer, his head fell in sleep. When the rest of the tribe returned they were reduced in size as punishment for tarrying. Only the one faithful sentinel remained a giant—and he still sleeps.

## MAYDAY

The Mayday district north of Hesperus produced many millions in gold in its day. New gold strikes in the 30's brought a new flood of prospectors. One nugget found here was worth $4,000. The area is still producing and many riches are believed still locked in the hills nearby.

## PARROT CITY

Ranchland now covers the site of Parrot City. The founding and development of Parrot City was due to one John Moss. Returning from the California gold fields, Moss prospected through this region and located some good placer gold near the mouth of the La Plata River. But the Indians still held the land.

Before the Brunot treaty was signed, Moss returned to the site. He located some quartz in addition to more placer gold. Moss made his own treaty with Ignacio, Chief of the southern Utes, for the right to farm and mine a 25-mile square area. Armed with the treaty and ore samples, Moss headed for San Francisco for funds. He received the backing of Banker Tiburcia Parrot.

When Moss and his party returned, they found an Arizona group working the property. Moss made a deal with the new group, partitioning up the land to allow both sides to work it. Both groups pitched in to lay out a city and build cabins. The group also worked together in building irrigation ditches and flumes for the various workings.

About this time, the prospectors were swarming into the area after the Brunot treaty, and Parrot City was becoming quite a community. Moss still wasn't happy. He wanted Parrot City to be county seat. Despite his efforts, however, Howardsville won the distinction.

This was in 1877. Two years later there was talk of forming a new county to split the large and now thickly-populated La Plata county. So once again, John Moss began to wheel and deal.

He led an army of miners to the county meeting in Silverton. He helped vote in and establish San Juan county. He made a deal with Silverton citizens to support their bid for county seat if they would support Parrot City for county seat of La Plata County. It worked!

Parrot City had already hit its peak. It had a school, post office, dozens of prosperous businesses, and a population that varied between 500 and a thousand. The community began to dwindle very slowly at first, but more rapidly during the early 80's. Durango was made county seat and Parrot City was all but deserted by 1883.

The cattle came in about the same time Moss made his treaty with Ignacio. Of course, the Indians didn't like it but the cattle soon outnumbered the braves. When the gold and silver played out the cattle took over. There's nothing left of Parrot City but foundations. The last building burned down within recent years.

Of the nearly 500 locations staked, only a handful were developed to any extent. The best of these were the Comstock, Isabel, Bulldozer, Snowstorm, Ashland and Tenbrook.

### LA PLATA (La Plata City)

The Spanish explorer Juan Maria de Rivera was believed to have been the first discoverer of gold when he led a party through here in 1775. Exactly 100 years later several good mines were located by Yankee fortune hunters. The city grew overnight. Within weeks hundreds of gold and silver seekers were in the area.

Silver was mined along with the gold, and when the town was hard hit by the silver panic in 1893, new gold discoveries put La Plata back in business.

But the mining began to play out after the turn of the century. There has been some activity in the mines up until modern times, but La Plata City has long since fallen into ruin.

Some of the better mines in the region were the Comstock, La Plata, Lady Eleanor, Cumberland, Snowstorm, Neglected, Gold King, Red Cloud, Swamp Angel, Idaho and Mayday.

The La Plata Gold Mining Corporation, headquartered in Salt Lake City, recently spent $150,000 to reopen the Bessie G mine, which produced over three quarters of a million dollars up to the time of its closing in 1955. The mine was first opened in 1889 under the name of the Egyptian Queen.

### CIMA, MAYDAY SPUR, MAYDAY STATION, UTE JUNCTION and FRANKLIN JUNCTION

D&RG railroad stops in the Durango area.

Cima and Mayday Spur were located a short distance apart and south of Mayday. Much of the rich ore that was shipped from the mines passed through these two stops. There was also some mining near the towns. Mayday Spur was at the junction of the spur that ran north to Mayday, passing closely to old Parrot City, and to Mayday Station, close to some of the northernmost mines in the area.

Ute Junction was just what it said it was, a railway junction point for the spur that ran up to the Ute Mine.

Franklin Junction, three miles west of Durango, was located at the cutoff of a spur that ran up to Perrins.

## PERINS (Perrins)

In 1891 G. C. Franklin found a seven-foot-thick outcropping of coal on Perins Peak. With eastern capital he organized the Boston Coal and Fuel Company and set out to develop the mine. Key item in the development was a railroad spur to the workings.

Work began on the railway spur in 1901. Although it had to run slightly less than five miles to tie up with the Rio Grande Southern at Franklin Junction, it was rugged country and had unique problems. Some 500 Navaho Indians were employed in the construction. The rails wound around the mountain on grades up to four and one-half per cent and curves of 32 degrees.

A gala celebration was held when the line reached Perins. On November 25, several flat cars loaded with people from Durango and the surrounding area arrived in Perins for the festivities. Miss Edna Newman drove in the silver spike to cap the celebration.

The railroad's arrival put the new town to work. The Boston Company operated its own trains. At the peak of its operations it was running three trips daily back and forth to the camp, hauling 17 cars of ore to Franklin Junction to fulfill the D&RG's order for 80 carloads a week and the Rio Grande Southern's order for 40. At least three times a week a large tank of water was hauled into camp.

Falling demand for coal and old-fashioned methods slowly brought the activity at Perins to an end. The mine and the rail branch were abandoned in 1926. A few years later the rails were torn up. The echo of the celebration a few years before had long departed.

*And Then There Were . . .. HERMOSA* a stage station and later a Denver and Rio Grande railroad station between Durango and Silverton. Hermosa had a post office. It is little more than a stop on the road today . . . . *CAMP STARVATION* (not on map) after discovering gold in the Parrot City area, Capt. Moss and a group of his followers headed back to civilization in 1873 to pick up supplies. One of the party accidentally shot himself on the trip and couldn't continue. Moss took a few men with him to get supplies and help while the rest of the party remained behind with the wounded man. They lived here for 18 days on berries, bark, roots and any small game they could catch until Moss got back with the supplies. They dubbed the spot Camp Starvation . . . . *EMERY*, a small camp around the Neglected Mine at the head of Junction Creek. There was no information available on how the names Emery and Neglected came to be. In fact, there was little information on either . . . . *MINERAL CITY* (not on map) was mentioned as a new town in La Plata County in 1875. In 1876 it was said to be a prospectors' camp of about 20 cabins. Its location was never pinpointed and nothing was heard from it after 1876 . . . . *WEBTOWN* was a smelter town on the Animas River a short distance from Durango. A flood in September of 1909 virtually washed the town away as the 100 families living there watched from higher ground.

# XX. CANNIBAL COUNTRY

Perhaps primitive and beautiful Hinsdale county is more isolated and unpopulated today than it was at any time in its recent past. The land around San Cristobal, the state's most beautiful lake, was a favorite stamping ground for Indians. Later it served as a gateway to the San Juans and was, itself, one of the richest mining areas in the State.

All this was in the past. Only two hundred people live in the entire county today, and they live in the county's only community, Lake City. Some day soon, an entrepreneur with an eye for beauty will discover the resort possibilities in the area, and Hinsdale county may thrive again. Until then, serene San Cristobal will rock lazily in its mountain cradle and the aspen-covered hills will sleep—and dream bad dreams.

For Hinsdale county is haunted.

At the foot of Slumgullion Pass, not far from beautiful Lake San Cristobal, is a memorial to Alfred Packer, and the men he ate here. Alfred Packer is the only man ever tried for cannibalism in the United States.

This, perhaps, is the strangest part of his strange story. Cannibalism, although never reaching craze proportions, was well known in the westward movement.

The Donner party, one of the earliest and the most tragic wagon trains bound for California, practiced cannibalism openly in the vain effort to keep alive in the snow-covered Sierra Nevadas. The only restriction put upon eating the dead was that relative would not eat relative, but would eat only somebody else's relative.

One of the four advance scouts of John Fremont's 1848 ill-fated fourth expedition into the Colorado Rockies died. When the famed pathfinder came upon the group he found evidence the other three had partaken of the dead man's flesh.

Henry Villard, later a railroad king but then a correspondent for a Cincinnati newspaper, and traveling companion of Horace Greeley, wrote of widespread rumors of cannibalism in the early Pikes Peak fiasco. He even obtained a written confession of one Daniel Blue, who told of eating his two brothers near the Colorado-Kansas border.

A grotesque character of early Denver, known as Old Phil the cannibal, boasted of the men he ate. He said the heads, hands and feet, when well-cooked, tasted good . . . not unlike pork. But the rest of the body was too grisly and tough for a satisfying meal.

A famous western scout, John "Liver Eating" Johnston, declared war

A room with a view. Ruins of activity at Poughkeepsie, at the end of Poughkeepsie Gulch. Picture, taken in 1901, looks up the gulch toward Abrams Mountain and Ouray. *U. S. Geological Survey photo.*

Yankee Girl and Yankee Girl Mines above Guston. *State Historical Society of Colorado.*

Red mountain in 1901. Corkscrew gulch is at left center. Ironton is below it, hidden by the hill. Picture looks southeast toward Red Mountain Town. Guston is clearly visible at right center. *U. S. Geological Survey photo.*

Ironton in 1900. Note railroad turntable on Corkscrew Gulch above town. Trains ran into turntable and backed down the hill. Evidence of activity at Guston can be seen in distance. *U. S. Geological Survey photo.*

Fourth of July celebration during the early 90's in Ouray. Parade was on main street. *State Historical Society of Colorado.*

Animas City in 1897. It had already lost much of its population and cabins
to Durango, two-and-a-half miles to the south. *U. S. Geological Survey
photo.*

Durango at the turn of the century, taken from Waterworks Mesa. The
photo looks northwest across the river and up the valley of Junction Creek.
On the right is the Dakota dip slope from Animas City mountain. In the
distance on the left the eastern La Plata summits. *U. S. Geological Survey
photo.*

380

Alfred Packer, the man eater, as he looked in 1883. *Denver Public Library Western Collection.*

Thomas Walsh. He became a multi-millionaire with the development of the Camp Bird Mine. *State Historical Society of Colorado.*

Lake City in 1908. Picture taken from trail to Crystal Lake. Round Mountain is behind the town and snowcapped Red Mountain directly behind that. *U. S. Geological Survey photo.*

The camp of Lake Shore, around the Golden Fleece Mines on Lake San Cristobal, 1904. *U. S. Geological Survey photo.*

An isolated place called Carson, another Colorado camp sitting on an ancient volcano. Picture was taken after the turn of the century, after Carson's day. *U. S. Geological Survey photo* .

Antelope Springs, once an important stage stop on the run from Del Norte to Silverton. Picture was taken in 1905 when site was resort country. *U. S. Geological Survey photo.*

Creede going up during the early 90's. The streets were crowded all day and there was no night in Creede. *State Historical Society of Colorado.*

Creede now.

against the Crow Indians, whom he believed killed his wife and child. Johnston was said to have killed more than 300 Crows, scalped them and eaten their livers. He claimed the only good thing about an Indian was his liver. Johnston later denied his butchery. But by that time his story had reached such proportions in the old west, mothers threatened their children: "Liver-eating Johnston will get you if you don't behave."

No doubt, the harsh and secluded pockets of the early west have seen many another grisly meal made up of man. It had to stop somewhere. Packer was caught and made an example of so men would stop eating one another.

In 1873, Packer led a party of five Utah men on a prospecting journey into the San Juan mountains. Against the advice of Chief Ouray, the men pushed on in face of approaching winter. Packer returned alone to the Los Pinos agency, seventy-five miles from Lake City.

He said others in the group left him, and that he was forced to eat roots and small game until he could reach civilization again. A few weeks later an Indian turned up at the agency with strips of flesh—human flesh—he had found along Packer's route. Packer's conflicting stories further aroused suspicion. That spring, a photographer for *Harper's Weekly* stumbled upon a grisly sight at the foot of Slumgullion Pass. Here were the bodies of five men; their skulls had been crushed and strips of their flesh had been removed.

Packer was arrested, escaped, and was recaptured several years later in Wyoming. Despite his contention that another member of the party, a fellow named Bell, had killed the other four members and eaten upon them, and that he (Packer) killed Bell in self-defense, Packer was convicted.

Some historians say the Lake City judge, a Democrat, declared: "Packer, you so and so, there were seven Democrats in Hinsdale County and you ate five of them . . . I sentence you to be hanged by the neck until you are dead, dead, dead."

But Packer was not hanged. He was granted a new trial and was sentenced to forty years for manslaughter. A few years later, an early Denver sob sister, Polly Pry, reopened the case with an interview of Packer in prison and helped Packer win release. He worked for a while as a doorman for the *Denver Post* and later became a recluse. He died in 1907. A simple stone marker on a hill near Littleton marks his grave. But Packer was one of those rare individuals who became a hero in his own lifetime, and his fame has spread since his death.

During the first years of the century, a young Denver Republican group, headed by Gene Fowler, organized the Alfred Packer Club. In recent years the Packer story has been turned into no less than two plays. Poetry has been written about him. The small plateau at the foot of Slumgullion Pass, near Lake San Cristobal, has been named Cannibal Plateau and a marker was placed at the site to commemorate Alfred Packer and what he did here many years ago—when he was hungry.

Packer maintained until his death that Bell was the cannibal and that he killed Bell in self-defense. Wouldn't it be ironic if we are eulogizing the wrong man? Serene Lake Cristobal knows the secret . . . and it won't tell.

## MAP TWENTY-ONE
### CANNIBAL COUNTRY (LAKE CITY)

Lake City
Henson
Capitol City (Galena City)
Rose's Cabin
Carson (Carson Camp, Carson City)
Sherman
Whitecross
Tellurium
Lost Trail Camp
Timber Hill
Junction City

Beartown (Gold Run, Bear Creek, Silvertip, Sylvanite)
*And Then There Were* . . . . *STERLING* and *BURROWS PARK* (Argentum), *CROOKE* or *CROOKE CITY* (not on map), *HERMIT* and *LAKE SHORE.*

## LAKE CITY

Lake City is now a sleepy little town nestled near the center of colorful Hinsdale County. In fact, Lake City's 200 residents are Hinsdale County. It costs Colorado more to maintain the county than it receives in revenue from the residents.

Lake City is a lovely old lady now, but she had a rich and boisterous past. In her day, she was one of the busiest cities in Colorado. She was the queen bee in a rich beehive of activity. And she has grown old gracefully.

There is evidence that some of the first gold in Colorado was found near here, not by a prospector, and the find was forgotten. Other valuable minerals were located in the years that followed, but the Indians successfully held back the tide of white men until the Brunot Treaty of 1873 opened up the area. Still the Indian menace wasn't over. There were reports of Indian trouble here for several years after the treaty. And a big Indian battle was fought near Lake City as late as 1879.

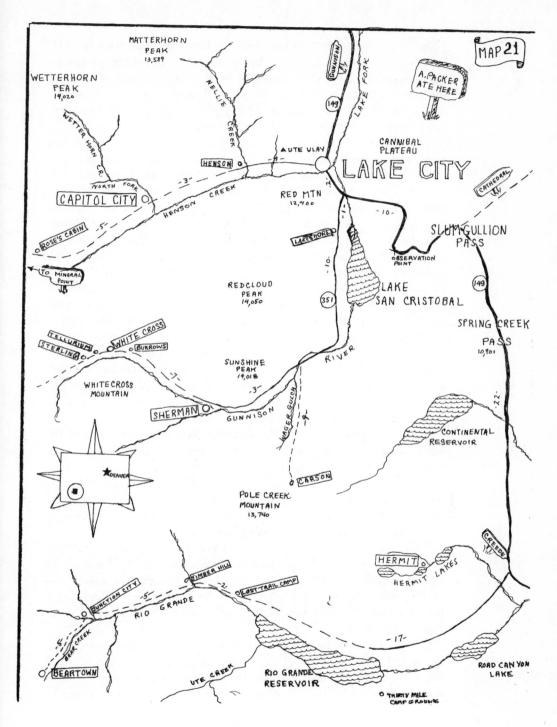

MAP 21

MATTERHORN PEAK 13,589

WETTERHORN PEAK 14,020

WETTER HORN CR.

NELLIE CREEK

GUNNISON W.

LAKE FORK

A. PACKER ATE HERE

CANNIBAL PLATEAU

149

HENSON

UTE ULAY

LAKE CITY

CATHEDRAL

NORTH FORK

CAPITOL CITY

HENSON CREEK

— 3 —

RED MTN 12,400

LAKESHORE

— 10 —

SLUMGULLION PASS

ROSE'S CABIN

— 5 —

OBSERVATION POINT

TO MINERAL POINT

REDCLOUD PEAK 14,050

— 10 —

LAKE SAN CRISTOBAL

149

351

SPRING CREEK PASS 10,901

TELLURIUM

WHITE CROSS

STERLING

BURROWS

SUNSHINE PEAK 14,018

RIVER

— 22 —

WHITECROSS MOUNTAIN

— 7 —

— 3 —

WAGER GULCH

— 9 —

SHERMAN

GUNNISON

CONTINENTAL RESERVOIR

DENVER

CARSON

POLE CREEK MOUNTAIN 13,740

CREEDE

HERMIT

HERMIT LAKES

TIMBER HILL

JUNCTION CITY

— 5 —

— 2 —

LOST TRAIL CAMP

— 17 —

BEAR CREEK

RIO GRANDE

BEARTOWN

UTE CREEK

RIO GRANDE RESERVOIR

ROAD CANYON LAKE

THIRTY MILE CAMP GROUNDS

387

One of the richest finds in the area—the Ute-Ulay—was made in 1871, but it wasn't developed until after the treaty when the land was opened up for prospecting. Lake City, registered in 1875, became one of the first communities in the area. It was named for beautiful Lake San Cristobal. It soon became the hub of all the activity in the region, and an important link between the rich regions to East and West.

Naturally, it suffered growing pains. Other than Alfred Packer, it had many another questionable acquaintance in its unruly youth. Life was cheap. With so many deaths in mine accidents and snowslides, the residents thought little of the many men killed in gun battles. Men were killed almost daily in arguments over gambling tables and mining claims. A saloon keeper, an important figure in any mining town, was laid low by bullets.

In 1882, Sheriff E. N. Campbell and a party of deputies waited in ambush for two saloon keepers with a sideline in burglary. But the ambush backfired. The suspects escaped in a blaze of gunfire which killed the sheriff and wounded some of the deputies. A posse finally captured the suspects and threw them in jail. Their imprisonment almost tore the town apart. The unruly element worked itself into a lynching lather. The "rights" turned the jail into an armed fortress. But the "wrongs" were by far the most powerful. Two hundred strong stormed the jail and dragged off the suspects, hanging them from the nearest bridge. The bodies were left dangling for several hours to serve as a reminder for any other would-be criminal. School was excused the next day and the students were paraded by the bridge. A lurid lesson in early Colorado justice.

And, of course, there were the gamblers, con men and ladies of the street. However, there was the better element that struggled for, and eventually won, the upper hand.

There was the legendary Reverend George M. Darley, who could stand up to any man alive. He preached the word of God anywhere and everywhere he could get an audience, and his largest audiences were found in the gambling halls and other unholy places.

The first church on the western slope was built here in 1876—the Presbyterian church. Soon other meeting houses were built. Four of the earliest churches are still standing. In 1882, a gala musical benefit was held to earn money to buy a bell—the best bell to be found. The bell has been used as a combination church, fire, and celebration signal down through the years.

Lake City was not lacking in cultural and social life. There were much drama and music to pass the time. Dances were held at the drop of a hat. Some of the top personages of the day passed through the city. Most of the city gathered in 1877 to cheer or jeer Susan B. Anthony's talk on women's suffrage. But there was no jeering. Even the most cynical gambler and skeptical miner was held spellbound by the dedicated speaker.

Harry M. Woods began publishing the *Silver World* in 1875. It was the first newspaper on the western slope. Other newspapers followed including the *Mining Register, Lake City Phonograph* and *San Cristobal Magazine.*

During its heyday, Lake City had as many as 2,500 residents and hundreds more passed through the community each week. There were scores of business houses, a fair share of saloons, gambling dens and parlor houses, several hotels, two banks, a library, sawmill and several mills.

The transportation problem bothered Lake City somewhat during its early months, but eventually roads were cut in all directions. Stage coaches passed through the city daily. The situation improved further in 1889, when the Denver and Rio Grande reached here. During the 90's, two passenger trains arrived in Lake City each day, and ore shipments left regularly. Lake City even had one of the earliest telephone systems in the state.

The best mine was the Golden Fleece, which changed hands many times and was known under other names. A story is told about the Golden Fleece. It seems one of its first owners got down to his last stick of dynamite before giving up on the location. The next owner used the stick of dynamite left by his predecessor and uncovered a rich lode. Many of the mines were worked until recent years, and some uranium has been found here.

GOLD DUST: The main hotel was the Occidental until it burned down in 1944 . . . . Otto Mears was one of the builders of the toll road from Saguache, completed in 1874 . . . . the Golden Fleece was finally sold in 1943 for taxes . . . . one of the more unusual reduction plants was built above the city in 1874 at Granite Falls. It was powered by a 70-foot water drop . . . . 15 charcoal kilns were built here in 1882 . . . . many of the early homes and buildings were made of stone and are standing today. The large stone schoolhouse was built in 1882 . . . . the D & RG lines were ripped up in 1937 . . . . there is a story told by oldtimers of a prospector here who taught his burro to use snowshoes for his many journeys into the mountains . . . . picturesque Slumgullion Pass was named for the stew-like concoction the early miners and prospectors used to cook while traversing the pass . . . . the first baptism in St. James Episcopal log church, still standing, was of a child born in Silverton, and carried 65 miles on horseback in 1875.

## HENSON

Henson, a comparatively small and isolated camp, probably had more excitement and significance per capita than even Creede or Fairplay. The city was laid out near the Ute-Ulay, Ocean Wave and Hidden Treasure mines, about the richest group of mines in all the San Juans.

Much of the excitement here centered around the big strike. In 1899, the mine owners of the Ute-Ulay and the Hidden Treasure declared all single men must board at the company boarding house. In protest, some

389

eighty Italian miners, all members of the Western Federation of Miners, went out on strike.

The mine owners added insult to injury by keeping the mines open, using non-union workers. The union miners put a quick stop to this by waylaying the scabs, manhandling a few and chasing most of them out of camp. The union had the situation pretty much under control when the mine owners asked for and got state troops. Governor Charles Thomas dispatched four companies of cavalry and two companies of infantry to the scene.

This is when the Italian consul in Colorado interceded. The consul, Dr. Cuneo, hastily dispatched himself to the area, intercepting the troops a few miles outside of town. He respectfully requested a chance to talk to the strikers first in an effort to prevent bloodshed. The permission was granted and thus began the most unusual procession those hills have ever seen.

Leading the procession was Dr. Cuneo, in full diplomatic dress, despite a raging snowstorm. Dr. Cuneo promised the miners to do his utmost to secure a fair hearing and just settlement. Under his insistence, the miners submitted. But they—and Dr. Cuneo—were double-crossed. Instead of a fair hearing, the unmarried strikers were ordered to leave the area within three days and the married strikers were given sixty days in which to leave town. The mine owners were successful, with the aid of government troops, in breaking the union—and the owners refused to employ Italians after that.

Henson was a rough, tough town. Shootings and mine accidents occurred with tragic frequency. The city had eight doctors (unusual for a smaller mining town), and these doctors were kept busy day and night. The worst accident occurred when, due to miscalculations, the mine tunnels of the Ute-Ulay and the Hidden Treasure accidently came together, causing a tremendous gas explosion. When the smoke had cleared, twenty Ute-Ulay and sixteen Hidden Treasure miners were dead.

The first gold strikes were made here in 1871, but little was done to develop the claims until after the Brunot Treaty with the Indians was signed in 1873. The camp began to take shape and prosper in 1877 when the Henson Creek and Uncompahgre Toll Road was completed. The early settlers in the area all pitched in to have the road extended to connect with the Animas Forks Road, and it soon became one of the busiest highways in the San Juans. It crossed the divide at 12,200 feet.

The Ute-Ulay and other rich mines continued to produce for years, but the harsh winters here and the growth of Lake City, a short distance away, eventually spelled the end of Henson. Ruins of many of the cabins can be seen at the site, and a frame schoolhouse—once the pride and joy of Henson—is still visible.

*CAPITOL CITY* (Galena City)

The large brick building on the edge of Capitol City might well have been the governor's mansion if George T. Lee had had his way. Lee, the master-mind of Capitol City, built his home with this purpose in mind, they say. He led the movement to change the name of the city from Galena to Capitol, because he believed it would soon surpass Denver and become the capitol of all Colorado. He wanted his home to be the largest and most beautiful in all southern Colorado. He invited the top figures in the state to his home. He entertained lavishly.

Alas, all his efforts went for naught. Capitol City wasn't even made county seat. As with many other early cities with big ambitions, the ores, although they paid well for awhile, played out too soon. Litigation aided in the downfall of Capitol City, as did transportation problems. But George Lee had fun with his dream while it lasted, for Capitol City was George Lee's city.

Other than the "governor's mansion" Lee built the Henson Creek smelter a mile below the city. He owned the saw and planing mill in town. He also took over the other mill at the other end of town. He had his finger in just about every other pot that boiled in Capitol City.

Rich finds in 1877 gave the camp its start and hundreds of prospectors poured into the area during the first years. But, probably inspired by Lee, the city planners were over-ambitious. The 200-acre townsite was over-planned and over-built. Almost before the need arose, the camp had several hotels, restaurants, saloons, smelters, a sawmill, post office and several houses. A schoolhouse was built in 1883 for $1,500. But the population never did exceed 800, if it reached that.

Lee's smelters handled ore from mines for miles around. The mines paid off well while they paid, but that wasn't enough. Many of the early claims overlapped and as early as 1880 litigation bogged down much of the work.

Population fell off gradually through the 80's and 90's, and Capitol City was almost empty when some gold was found in 1902 and another short-lived boom began. Now only a few crumbling buildings, the schoolhouse and "the governor's mansion" remain of the site.

BEST MINES: Capitol City, Ocean Wave, Polar Star, Yellow Medicine, Morning Star, High Muck-a-Muck, Great Eastern, San Bruno, Incas, Ajar and Moro.

GOLD DUST: The Ocean Wave mine, one of the big producers here, can be seen between Henson and Capitol City . . . . Lee's house contained a miniature theatre . . . . the Morning Star mine was worked almost exclusively by Negroes. Many French miners also worked in the area . . . . Capitol City was the center of a joint telephone musical recital held in 1881. Camps from Lake City to Ouray and Silverton participated in the unique event . . . . the mines produced gold, silver, lead, iron and other minerals . . . . the trial run of Lee's smelter in 1879 produced $3,900 in bullion . . . . Capitol City did have ample water power, fed by a 1,000-foot flume.

## ROSE'S CABIN

Rose wasn't a girl. The cabin belonged to Corydon Rose. It was one of the first structures built in the area after the land was opened to prospecting by the Brunot Treaty in 1873. And it wasn't just a plain ordinary cabin. It had tavern and dormitory accommodations. Rose gradually expanded upon it during the years and, as mining camps arose in all directions and roads were built—past Roses' Cabin naturally—the place became more important.

Until social facilities were brought into Lake City, Rose's Cabin was the only place of entertainment on this side of the range. It also served as a post office and restaurant.

When some minerals were found nearby and mining was done on Copper Hill, American Flats and Palmetto in the late 70's and 80's, many of the miners built cabins at the site, until there were as many as 100 there. In 1882, Rose expanded the dormitory facilities and enlarged the bar, so that it was the largest in the area. Rose also hired out a sixty-animal pack train that was in constant use. The Cabin was remodeled in recent years and used as an office for the Galconda mines, and was taken over even later by a private owner. The cabin is gone now, but its stable remains. It can be seen over a rough road, more for a jeep than a car.

## CARSON (Carson Camp, Carson City)

Carson had the rather unique distinction of sitting on top of the Continental Divide. Snow—and there was plenty of snow—melting on one side of the town would eventually work its way into the Gulf of Mexico. Snow melting on the other side would eventually find itself in the Pacific.

Carson was one of the most inaccessible camps in Colorado, and its winters were among the most severe. Despite this, good gold and silver was found here and it sustained the camp for several years. In fact, the founding fathers thought it would be the biggest camp in all the San Juans. If it weren't for its location, it might well have been.

Chris Carson found traces of ore here and later staked out the Bonanza King. The district was organized in 1881, and the camp established the following year. More than 150 claims were worked the first few years, and several good mines were located. The construction of a wagon road up Lost Trail Creek in 1887 stimulated the activity. Carson reached its peak during the 90's and early 1900's, when 400 to 500 men worked the mountaintop. There was a slight lull after the silver crash of 1893, but Carson recovered three years later with some good gold finds.

But Carson couldn't buck the winter. Situated at nearly 12,000 feet, the

392

site was blanketed with heavy snow much of the year, and little or no work could be done in the winter. Despite the construction of roads from the north and south, they were always dangerous and often impassable. So, no sooner had Carson reached its peak in 1901,1902, than the decline set in, and the camp was deserted within months. Now, the camp with its many mining relics and tumbledown cabins, can be seen via a treacherous jeep road from the north and a hiking or horse trail from the south.

BEST MINES: St. Jacob's, top producer, Maid of Carson, Thor, Chandler, Legal Tender, Kit Carson, George III, Lost Trail, St. John's, Cresco, Iron Mask, Dunderberg.

The St. Jacob's produced more than $300,000 in gold and silver and hit its peak in 1898 when it produced $190,000 in minerals.

## SHERMAN

Sherman was located at the junction of Lake Fork and Cottonwood Creeks. The spring run-offs were always heavy and often disastrous. It wasn't until the turn of the century that some enterprising folk decided to build a 150-foot dam to hold back the churning waters. The company went broke when the dam was only half finished, but a short time later another company was formed to complete the job. A few days after the project was completed a cloudburst flooded down the mountainside, ripped the dam to pieces, and carried off much of Sherman as well.

In addition to the spring floods, Sherman was generally deserted in the winter because of the snow. The elements combined to hold back the full development of this potentially rich area.

Some rich strikes were made here in the late 70's and early 80's, but it wasn't until the Sherman House Hotel was built that the camp took on the appearance of a permanent city. The city fathers platted a handsome town with wide streets and alleyways. Several cabins and frame houses were built. There were some small business places located here and there, but much of the community's activity centered around one large building which housed a dormitory, grocery and general store, butcher shop and slaughter house, bakery, and storage and forwarding house. The summer population during Sherman's peak years was around 300.

There was some mining here throughout the 80's, 90's and early 1900's, and off and on until 1925. The top mine was the Black Wonder which produced well for several years. An eastern company took over the mine in 1897 and spent more than $200,000 in improvements.

A few cabins which escaped the flood remain at the ghost site.

Other mines were Smile of Fortune, Monster, Minnie Lee, George Washington, New Hope, Mountain View and Clinton.

## WHITECROSS

Long, hard winters and cruel, tortuous roads didn't keep the fortune hunters out of Whitecross, center of several small camps located near the top of Cinnamon Pass. Even during its boom days in the 90's, the camp was virtually closed down in the winter and transportation was costly and travel was dangerous all the time. Although a railroad was only five miles away at Animas Forks, it was often easier to haul out the ore by wagons to Lake City, twenty miles away.

Activity began here around 1880 and a haphazard camp of tents and shanties was first called Burrows Park for the area in which it is located. In 1882, the post office name was changed to Whitecross, for the cross of quartz seen on the mountain nearby.

The peak population was seldom more than 300. The Hotel de Clauson was the social center of the camp and surrounding camps. There were several other businesses. A mill was built in 1901 near the top of Cimarron Pass. Thanks to Tom Byron, who devoted much of his life to carrying mail between the camps on both sides of the mountains, Whitecross had almost daily mail service, even in the worst weather.

Although the Champion mine was opened briefly in 1916 after being closed for 15 years, Whitecross was never fully developed because of its handicaps. Today, the Tobasco mill and the ruins of several mines, and a few of the cabins in which the miners lived still stand. They can be seen by hardy jeepsters over not-quite-so-hardy a trail.

BEST MINES: Tobasco, Champion, Bonhomme and Cracker Jack.

## TELLURIUM

A short-lived camp beyond Whitecross. It started during the mid-seventies, about the same time as Whitecross, but was practically empty by 1880.

During its first months, Tellurium had delusions of grandeur. An elaborate townsite was laid out and an expensive mill was built. But much of the planning didn't get beyond the paper stage. The mill was only used for a short time.

Tellurium can be reached by a jeep road, but only a trace of the town remains.

BEST MINES: Providence, Mountain King, Little Sarah, Troy, and Allen Dale.

## LOST TRAIL CAMP

Lost Trail Camp was a popular stage stop, tourist center and prospector's rendezvous back in the 80's and 90's. It was located at the western end of the Rio Grande Reservoir. There were a ranch office, post office, store, saloon and several cabins.  Activity here faded during the 90's and was all but dead by the turn of the century, although it has remained a good camping spot for sportsmen.

## TIMBER HILL

Timber Hill was a favorite spot for highwaymen on the long, isolated run from Silverton to Del Norte.

One time three particularly rich wagons of ore out of Beartown headed up Timber Hill. Three scouts rode ahead of the wagons on the lookout for highwaymen. They were ambushed by bandits. Two were killed, but the third escaped and dashed back to warn the wagon crews. The crews hurriedly dumped two of the wagons in a nearby hiding place. But before they could cache the third wagonful of ore, the bandits were upon them and the wagon crews and the third scout were killed. The bandits rode off with the third wagon and the first two wagonloads of ore are still hiding and waiting for lost-treasure hunters.

Timber Hill was a stage stop on the run. It apparently wasn't active for long, just long enough to have a post office in the early eighties.

## JUNCTION CITY

Another city that suffered from delusions of grandeur but didn't have the minerals to support the ambition. Some ore was found in 1894. A town was platted, but even before many cabins were built, many of the miners became disgusted and left. Only one cabin near the junction of Bear and Pole Creeks with the Rio Grande marks the site of the overconfident city of yesterday.

## BEARTOWN (Gold Run, Bear Creek, Silvertip, Sylvanite)

Some paydirt was found in this area in the early 70's, but it wasn't until 1893 that a rich strike brought hundreds of prospectors. Within weeks some 400 prospectors were in the region, bedding down wherever they could.

It was weeks later before some of them took time off to build cabins. The mines here looked like good producers and the early prosperity of the settlement encouraged many Creede merchants to open branches of their businesses here. The operators of the *Creede Candle* even began publication of the *Gold Run Silvertip*.

The residents here dreamed up several names for the camp, and even tried out a few of them before finally settling for Beartown. The mines did turn out pretty well and there was activity until far into this century. The Sylvanite mine, which netted up to $4,000 a ton, was a big producer and was worked until recent years. All the mines are closed now. The pros-

395

pectors have left. An old mill and some cabins mark the spot where Beartown thrived.

OTHER MINES:   Gold Bug, Silver Bug, Yankakee, and Good Hope.

*And Then There Were* .... *STERLING* and *BURROWS PARK* (Argentum), small communities located near Whitecross. Sterling was located a short distance beyond Tellurium toward Animas Forks. Burrows Park was in a small valley five miles long and a half mile wide which was also named Burrows Park. At one time there were some 100 locations here, but only a handful were worth developing. The best mines were the Undine, Napoleon and Onida. The ore assayed from $100 to $600 a ton .... *CROOKE* or *CROOKE CITY*, believed to have been a small camp around the Crooke Reduction Works at Granite Falls, a mile above Lake City. At any rate, a Crooke City in Hinsdale County had a post office .... *HERMIT*, a town listed as a post office in Hinsdale County a number of years ago but this writer could find no other information about it. Hermit was mentioned as a new post office in 1880 .... *LAKE SHORE*, a small camp at the northern end of Lake San Cristobal, three miles south of Lake City. The Golden Fleece Mines were the big workings here. The Michigan mine was a little farther to the west.

# XXI. SLEEPLESS CREEDE

Most men came to Colorado to win their fortune in silver and gold. But in 1880, a 25-year-old youngster came to Colorado to satisfy his passion for locomotives. Trains, all sorts of trains, were being built to the new boom towns as fast as Colorado's railroad pioneers could build them. Cy Warman wanted to be a part of this new railroad era.

He did a little prospecting and mining too—everyone did. But mostly he worked on the railroads, all over Colorado. They say he began composing poetry to the clackety-clack of the rail wheels. It was a short step—in those days—into journalism.

It was as a journalist that he came to the new boom town of Creede. He became editor of the *Creede Candle,* an integral part of the Creede story. "The Poet of Cochitopa," as Warman was called, did big things. His poems and stories were published in national magazines. His song, "Sweet Marie," a tribute to a beautiful Denver girl who became his wife, became an all-time classic. He later became editor of the *New York Sun.*

Few people in Colorado recall the name of Cy Warman today. But one poem he wrote will be remembered as long as Creede is remembered— and as long as men recall that crazy, hungry quest for gold:

> Here's a land where all are equal—
>   Of high and lowly birth—
> A land where men make millions,
>   Dug from the dreary earth.
> Here meek and mild-eyed burros
>   On mineral mountains feed.
> It's day all day in the daytime
>   And there is no night in Creede.
>
> The cliffs are solid silver
>   With wondrous wealth untold,
> And the beds of the running rivers
>   Are lined with the purest gold.
> While the world is filled with sorrow,
>   And hearts must break and bleed—
> It's day all day in the daytime,
>   And there is no night in Creede.

## CREEDE

San Juan City
Antelope Springs
Spar City (Fisher, Lime Creek)
Creede
Jimtown (Gintown, New Town and Others)
Weaver
North Creede (Upper Creede, Creede, Creedetown)
Bachelor (Teller)
Sunnyside
Wason (sometimes spelled Wasson)
Wagon Wheel Gap
Embargo
Sky City
Del Norte
Loma
Biedell
Carnero

Commodore Camp

*And Then There Were*: Willow City, Amethyst, Creedemoore, South Creede, Mexican Town (not on map), Crystal Hill and Cathedral.

### SAN JUAN CITY

San Juan City was believed to be the first city in the San Juans. When Hinsdale County was first organized in 1874, the year after the Brunot Treaty, San Juan City became the county seat. The distinction didn't last long, however, as the county seat was moved to Lake City the following year.

San Juan City was on the stage route from Del Norte to Silverton and some mining was carried on here for a short while during the 70's. The city had a merchant who filled in as postmaster. But, despite its early distinction, San Juan City slipped quietly into history, leaving little evidence of its having been at all.

### ANTELOPE SPRINGS

Antelope Springs was an important stop on the stage run from Del Norte to Silverton during the late 70's and until the railroad was built in 1882. The stop was established in 1875 on the site of old Salt Lick, a favorite feeding grounds for hundreds of deer and antelope.

Being rather isolated, it was also a favorite feeding ground for highwaymen after it became a stage station. There were many robberies near here (for one, see Del Norte).

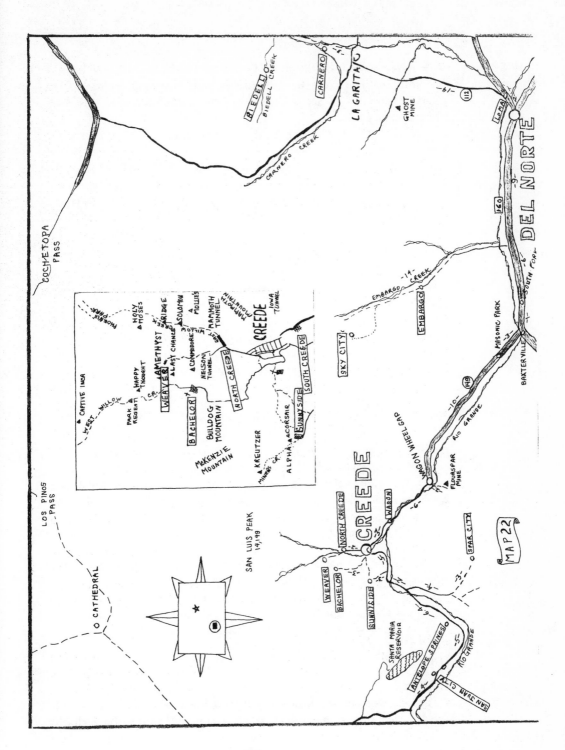

399

One gold stage from Silverton, bound for Del Norte, was caught in a blizzard. The stage crew chucked the load beside the road and dashed for safety. The stage returned in the spring and found their load of gold bars under 20-foot drifts.

Antelope Springs underwent the same Indian scare in 1879 that Howardsville experienced when a false messenger, more interested in attention and free drinks than authenticity, passed through Antelope Springs claiming the Indians had slaughtered all the citizens of Animas City (see Animas City).

With the construction of the railroad, Antelope Springs was no longer needed, and it died quickly. Only a hint of its existence can be found about a half-mile north of the highway. A natural swimming pool fed by warm springs is another half mile west of the site.

## SPAR CITY (Fisher, Lime Creek)

Much remains of Spar City, including the jail, a saloon, dance hall, parlor house, and many other business houses and cabins. But the people have gone. Creede's "long-distance" suburb was founded in 1892 as Fisher City. Some 300 persons were here within weeks, and the number was doubled by the following year, with an almost equal number in the surrounding hills. Some 200 worked in the Denver Tunnel Mine.

A regular coach line was established between Spar City and Creede. And many Creede businessmen opened branches here. The newspaper, *Spar City Spark,* was operated by owners of the *Creede Candle.*

The route between Creede and Spar City was a dangerous one, since the road passes over "Robbers Hill," a favorite ambush station for highwaymen. Many a stagecoach and ore wagon was waylaid here.

Spar City's main claim to fame was the big pine bar, behind which Bob Ford, the killer of Jesse James, was shot in Creede. The bar was crated and shipped to Spar City at much trouble and expense.

Spar City was hard hit by the panic of '93. Those who couldn't afford to leave soon became destitute. But the day was saved when a unique relief system was worked out with Creede. Spar City was put to work to earn food and lodging.

The city never fully recovered, however, and was deserted by 1905, when a group of Kansans purchased the site and built their summer homes here. They carried on some mining and remodeled some of the city. The Kansans have left by now.

TOP MINES: Big Spar, Headlight and Fairview.

## CREEDE

They say one can tell a town by its people. That couldn't work with Creede. They were all here—as dazzling a cross section of the underworld as could be found anywhere in the west, the crusaders and men of God scrambling from gulch to gambling hall to spread the gospel, the merchants, businessmen and men of vision, the mining barons who hit it lucky or played it smart, the grimy, hard-working miners and prospectors who sometimes did, and sometimes didn't, rake gold out of the mountains by the fistful.

Those first few months of Creede, when more than 10,000 men, women and children scampered all over the mountains for a rich claim or a place to sleep, were most noted for the underworld characters that came here—and found a place to sleep. Bob Ford was not the least nor the most. He walked into town early and announced he was boss. And he was (for a while); he had a reputation. He gunned down "Mr. Howard"—Jesse James. Ford opened up the Exchange, about the biggest saloon and gambling joint in town. Creede, during Bob Ford's reign, got so bad an official vigilantes committee and a mayor were elected to run the camp. About the first thing the vigilantes did was to run Bob Ford out of town. Then, after much pleading by Ford, the committee relented and allowed Ford to return to town for forty-eight hours to close out his business. Ford was promised protection if he would behave himself.

It was during this two-day period that Ed O'Kelley walked into Ford's Exchange and gunned down "that dirty little coward." Some say O'Kelley shot Ford in the back. Some say he didn't. Ford was expecting trouble most of the time and usually kept a gun handy and an eye on the door.

There were three motives given for O'Kelley's deed. Some say O'Kelley was married to a sister of the Younger brothers, members of Jesse James' gang. Others say the two merely quarreled over a gambling debt, and others say Ford intimidated O'Kelley's parents. Whatever the motive, Bob Ford was dead, dead, dead.

There were no tears shed over Ford's death, but O'Kelley was almost lynched anyhow for defying the vigilantes committee. He was arrested, received a jury trial, was convicted, imprisoned and pardoned a few years later.

The Creede underworld financed Ford's funeral. The ceremonies weren't too impressive, but the wake was tremendous. They broke out the whiskey at the burial site on Boot Hill, and began dancing on the grave. The party lasted for days—until the whiskey and the women gave out.

Even before Ford's death, a young fellow by the name of Soapy Smith had taken over Creede, lock, stock and parlor house. Smith was too powerful for Ford, and even the vigilantes, to buck. In fact, some stories intimate that Soapy Smith gave the vigilantes the idea of running Ford out of town.

Soapy was named for his special con game. It worked wonders in boom towns throughout the west. Soapy would sell soap on a street corner, wrapping some of the bars in hundred dollar bills, tens and twenties. The purchaser was allowed to keep any bill he found around the bar of soap he could buy for as little as five to twenty-five dollars. Usually a cohort bought the first bar of soap and found a large bill in the package. But to everybody else, Soapy's hands were quicker than the sucker's eye. Of course, he was a graduate from the penny-ante con-game racket by the time he came to Creede from Denver. Soapy ran the Creede underworld. He got a cut of every gambling concession in the city. After Soapy got tired of Creede, he made his way up to the Klondike and ran things there until he overplayed his hand and was shot down by a poor loser.

Lou Blonger was another underworld dictator at Creede. Bat Masterson was a well-known figure about town. Writer Richard Harding Davis, they say, lost many a dollar at the gambling tables.

Poker Alice and Killarney Kate were famous lady gamblers and cigar smokers. Lillie Lovell and six-foot-two Rose Vastine, better known as Timberline, were the top madams. Timberline went up into the hills one day, intent on suicide. They say she pumped six bullets into her chest before she fell. She didn't die, though, but pretty much messed up her dress.

Those first few months it was difficult to tell which camp came first and where one camp left off and another one took up. But Creede had emerged by 1891, and within the next few months overran most of the other smaller camps up and down the gulch. Some 5,000 people were here by 1892, 8,000 by the following year, and 10,000 by 1894. Real estate soared and more than a few made a fortune in just buying and selling lots. Lot jumpers were as common, if not more so, than claim jumpers. Guns were a way of life in Creede and shootings over a small section of land were common. The rule was that a man had to start building on the land the same day he got it or he had no claim to it by nightfall. One woman stood by, night and day, until carpenters finished building her home. Then she turned around and sold it the next week for $10,000.

Counteracting the overwhelming underworld element were the men of God, who, until the churches were built, preached in saloons, gambling halls, and mines—anywhere a group of men gathered. The record assembly of 300 hardened miners and gamblers was held spellbound by Reverend Joseph Guston of Ouray in a busy gambling house. All joined in on the Lord's Prayer at the end of the sermon.

There is also the story of one itinerant preacher who had his pants stolen shortly after his sermon. But Soapy Smith made the thief give the pants back and add a little to the kitty besides.

402

Creede had its sentimental side. The whole city pitched in on the relief of Spar City when that community was hit by the panic of 1893. And the first baby born in town was cause for a celebration as wild as Ford's wake. The proud papa was made mayor of Jimtown for a week. The baby was showered with gifts from everyone, including lavish presents from N. C. Creede himself. The baby remained nameless for several weeks because the city couldn't agree upon a name—no name was good enough.

There was some prospecting in the area in the 80's, and minerals were found in 1885. But the rush didn't start until Creede located the Holy Moses in 1890. Then the stampede didn't really get underway until David Moffat showed his faith and interest in the region by purchasing the claim for $70,000. Other rich claims were located in short order. Within a year, six million dollars in silver was taken out of the hills.

A branch of the Denver & Rio Grande rolled into town in 1891, another cause for celebration. Creede became county seat of the newly-organized Mineral County in 1893 (see Wason).

Creede had more than its share of fires and floods. In 1892, a fire, which started in a saloon, destroyed most of the business district. A fire at the Amethyst mine destroyed all the surface buildings and killed four men. Another fire in 1936 destroyed about a third of the business district. Ten years later another fire burned down the frame county courthouse. There were many other fires and accidents. Willow Creek, swollen from run-offs every spring, washed out much of Creede's northern suburbs and damaged Creede proper several times.

But Creede has survived all the Bob Fords, Soapy Smiths, fires and floods, and is very much alive today. There are only about 500 persons living here now, but there is still much mining being done and much mining left to do.

To date, millions in gold, silver, zinc and other minerals have been taken from the area. For a while, Creede led the state in the production of silver. They say the original boom would have been much bigger had not Cripple Creek happened about the same time. Nonetheless, it couldn't have boomed much more than it did.

TOP MINES: Holy Moses, Ridge, Solomon, Last Chance, Amethyst, Bachelor, Commodore and New York.

GOLD DUST: Bob Ford's body remained in Shotgun Hill for several years before his family took it back to Missouri . . . . a short time later, another murderer was buried in Ford's grave . . . . a huge turbine on a hill above Creede kept the city lights burning for twenty-four hours a day and furnished electricity for a light placed high on a cliff to signal the entrance to the canyon . . . . many Creede merchants and businessmen established branches in other camps throughout southern Colorado . . . . the Last Chance mine, one of the top producers, was located by a butcher's helper who was grubstaked by the butcher . . . . Ford's saloon is still standing, although his elaborate bar was shipped to Spar City at great expense . . . . there was very little racial discrimination in Creede although many Chinese, Negro, Indians and other nationalities were attracted to the boom town . . . . many of the top entertainers of the day did their bit in Creede. There were also many local entertainment groups and social clubs. Among the many social clubs were the "Creede Study Club," "Ladies' Social Club," and the "Ladies Bicycle Club." The latter was a large organization and it was a common sight to see the female population cycling through Creede in their bloomer outfits. The story goes that a prominent man-about-town was so embarrassed to see his wife so, he ordered her to keep right on pedaling, right on back to Illinois. She took the train . . . . during the hectic beginning of Creede it was discovered that due to faulty surveys the Creede area touched on three counties but was not in any one. After much confusion, Mineral County was created and Creede was made county seat . . . . N. C. Creede, who started all this, died in Los Angeles in 1897, not so rich and not so happy as he could have been. In fact, he committed suicide by taking morphine. He had separated from his wife a short time before. As the *Apex Pine Cone* put it: "His wife wanted to live with him again and he preferred death." . . . . in case you haven't heard the story before, Creede paused for lunch one day in 1890, disgusted with prospecting and just plain disgusted. In his disgust, he slammed his pick into the ground. Sure enough, there was pay dirt. "Holy Moses, I've struck it rich," he cried. That was the start of the Holy Moses mine and the start of Creede.

## JIMTOWN (Gintown, New Town and others)

Camps arose so quickly and haphazardly during the first months of the Creede boom, it was difficult to keep an accurate account of them. Some reports say Jimtown was one of the first camps to emerge with its own identity. Other reports say Jimtown was created when the population of Creede spilled over. Some reports tell of Jimtown as an outgrowth of several small camps around, while other reports give these camps a separate identity. Some say Gintown was actually the name of Jimtown for a while, while others say Gintown was just a pet name for the city. The latter seems more reasonable.

Nonetheless, Jimtown emerged and became one of the larger camps around. It grew so fast, reports say 200 carpenters worked full time to build homes and businesses.

Jimtown also had the distinction of having the first organized church service in the entire district. Previously, services were held in bars, gambling halls and mine shafts—wherever the men of God could get a small group together. Then the Denver Congregationalists donated a huge tent to the area. It was set up in Jimtown as the area's first church. The tent, much like a circus tent, was kept busy. When not used as a church, it was made useful as a meeting house of all sorts. One Easter, church services were held in the morning and a boxing match was held in the same tent the same night.

## WEAVER

Weaver, along with Willow City, erupted in late 1890 or early 1891 above North Creede and was one of the first of the many small towns around Creede. They say the city was named for the many Weaver families among the first residents. Most of the mines here closed down in 1893, although the ore was far from exhausted. They were reopened from time to time until recent years. Some cabins remain of the site.

## NORTH CREEDE (Upper Creede, Creede, Creedetown)

Before settling down as a residential suburb of Creede, North Creede had a life of its own. The city was built in a narrow gap along Willow Creek and was always troubled with floods during the spring run-off. The worst flood occurred in 1918, when a torrent of water washed out much of the city, including the Cliff Hotel and the Holy Moses saloon. A devastating fire in 1902 destroyed two hotels and twenty houses.

North Creede had many names in its day. It was first called Upper Creede. In 1910, when Creede toyed with Creede City for a while, North Creede became just Creede. Then it returned to North Creede, via Creedetown. The city had hundreds of residents during its boom years, 150 in 1910, and about twenty today.

## BACHELOR (Teller)

About the time the Amethyst and Last Chance mines were located on Bachelor Mountain, hundreds of fortune seekers began staking and digging out claims throughout the area—even on the site of the planned city where schools and public buildings were to be constructed. The governor had to intervene personally to bring some order to the chaos on Bachelor Mountain. His visit saved the townsite and also brought new interest and new miners to Bachelor Mountain.

A balky burro is credited with one of the first discoveries here. Legend says the animal wandered from camp one night. When found on Bachelor Mountain the next day, the burro refused to budge. The prospector picked up a stone to throw at the animal and found the rock heavy with lead. He staked a claim on the site.

Some minerals were found here in the mid-80's, when the prospectors combed Bachelor Mountain and started the city of Sunnyside, around the hill from Bachelor. But Bachelor itself didn't begin to boom until the Creede excitement in the early 90's.

By 1893 it was the largest and busiest "suburb" of Creede. The first three "businesses" thrown up—two saloons and a parlor house—gave an indication of the city's stormy future. Accidents and shootings were an everyday occurrence. Fires were common. One in 1892 burned down a hotel and two saloons. Other fires took their toll. But, largely due to Bachelor's excellent volunteer fire-fighting unit, the city on the hill didn't suffer an all-destroying conflagration.

When Bachelor petitioned for a post office in 1892, the government refused to accept the name because there was already a Bachelor in California. Instead, the post office was named Teller, in honor of Colorado's popular governor. The residents refused to accept the post office name and continued to call their city Bachelor, although they got their mail in the Teller Post Office.

Life on Bachelor Mountain was a difficult one. To compensate, the residents went all out to amuse themselves. Other than the many saloons, gambing halls and parlor houses, there was much "legitimate" entertainment. Dances were common, and plays and musical benefits were very popular. One of the most boisterous benefits ever held was staged to raise money for the construction of a Catholic church. Bachelor had its own opera house, and the Bachelor City Dramatic Club was one of the best.

The Amethyst and Last Chance and other good mines were located near Bachelor and by 1893 the city was doing two-thirds of the mining business in the entire Creede area. Population was estimated as high as 6,000 during the boom years.

In February of 1893, 20 mines produced 9,000 tons of highgrade ore valued at $800,000. And this was only the beginning. But later on in the same year, the silver panic rendered Bachelor a blow from which it never fully recovered.

However, Bachelor kept going all through the 90's and the early 1900's, but eventually most of the residents moved down to Creede or moved out of the area altogether. Now, only some ruins of wooden sidewalks and a few foundations, well hidden by brush and shrubbery, mark the site of Bachelor. Its cemetery is a short distance down the hill toward Creede.

## SUNNYSIDE

Minerals were first located here in the early 70's. More finds in the mid-80's brought on the rush, and the camp just got its second wind during the Creede excitement in the early 90's.

Dick Irwin of Irwin and Rosita fame located some good mines in the mid-80's and helped develop them. Other good finds were made in 1892 when prospectors from Creede combed the hills.

After Bachelor came into being, a crude road was built around the mountain to Sunnyside. This helped things somewhat, but transportation remained Sunnyside's major problem. One has to hike there today, and then there isn't anything to see.

BEST MINES: Hidden Treasure, Nelson, Diamond I, Irwin finds, Sunnyside, Yellow Jack, Kreutzer Sonata, Corsair.

## WASON (or Wasson)

Wason was the result of one man's ambitions, but like so many dreams of the day, they never panned out. M. H. Wason ran a cattle ranch here when the stampede to Creede began. He saw the opportunities and lost no time in platting a city. In short order he started the first newspaper in the area, built a courthouse which he hoped would be the county courthouse, and sponsored a gala Fourth of July celebration—all to capture the market on county seats.

Although there is some scant evidence Wason was actually the county seat for a few days, Wason's grandiloquent plans were all in vain. The courthouse stood empty for several weeks until, one night, a group of Creede citizens, filled with community spirit, stole down to Wason, disassembled the courthouse piece by piece, carted it back to Creede, and reassembled it.

Now, Wason is a resort and ranch area again.

## WAGON WHEEL GAP

There are two stories of how Wagon Wheel Gap came by its name.

The most frequently heard story tells of the early travelers naming it for an old wagon wheel found here and believed to have belonged to the George Baker party that passed through the region before the mining boom.

The other story is that a band of Indians ambushed a party of white men, killed them, scalped them and strung the scalps across the gap, weighing the whole mess down with a wagon wheel.

Wagon Wheel Gap was, and is, a supply town. It was also an important stage stop, and later a railroad station. The town figured prominently in the Creede story.

The community came into the news again in 1958, when road construction crews uncovered what is believed to be prehistoric ice. The ice was in two layers, separated by a layer of gravel and dirt. It may take scientists years to learn all the secrets of this freak of nature.

Sportsmen and scientists now comprise the bulk of the residents at Wagon Wheel Gap.

## EMBARGO

Only one cabin and some mine dumps mark the site of Embargo. During its boom years there were a hotel, saw mill and several other businesses and cabins.

There were some prospectors here in 1878, but things didn't get going until four years later. Most of the locations soon played out, although some work continued until the early years of this century. There was a mild rebirth about 1919, but it flickered out almost as fast as it fluttered in.

The best mines were Tornado, Golden Income and Little Ray.

## SKY CITY

Sky City never was much of a mining town, but it is rich in history. At least, the surrounding country is. A short distance northwest of here, John C. Fremont's ill-fated fourth expedition (of 1848) was forced to turn back by the cold and snow. It was one of the few exploratory failures in Fremont's career and almost cost him his life.

South of the site of Sky City was the scene of the last great Indian battle between the Commanches and the Utes. Some hastily-erected stone barricades are still standing on South Fork.

The town itself was another mining area in which Tom Bowen (see Summitville) had a hand. Bowen had some mining interests here, built a road to the site and drove a tunnel into the mountain, in an effort to make the mines pay. But the mines didn't pay very much, especially in comparison to the money put into them.

The gold camp was established in the late 80's and died in the early 90's, although there has been a little activity off and on since. The site is twenty-one miles off the main road.

## DEL NORTE

One of Colorado's first cities, Del Norte, was once in the consideration for the state capitol. Never a mining town, Del Norte served as a supply point and gateway to the San Juans, the most important in southern Colorado. Being such, it was a wide-open frontier town and one of the busiest in the state.

There was an active vigilante group in the early days. The vigilantes stormed the jail one night to lynch two rustlers, but the rustlers beat their way to freedom. Thus thwarted, the necktie party went on a binge and shot up the town. They didn't sober up until after they had shot and killed one of their own members and injured several others.

But the vigilantes weren't always so ineffective. In 1881, highwaymen held up a stage on the Del Norte to Silverton run. A sheriff's posse captured two of the three suspects, but didn't bring them back to town until nightfall to avert any trouble. All was quiet when the posse and the prisoners returned to Del Norte. So the sheriff locked up the two highwaymen and went to bed. When he awoke the next morning, he learned that a mob had stormed the jail during the night, hanged the suspects, and returned their bodies to their cell.

When the railroad came in, Del Norte became a shipping center. Its smelters processed ore from throughout southern Colorado. And the city was the commercial and banking capitol of the southern part of the state.

Colorful Senator Tom Bowen was a big man here. Mark Biedell was one of Del Norte's leading merchants and citizens. He invested in many mines throughout the area and helped develop several mining camps.

Del Norte was much in the news during those early years. Some social items during the early 80's:

"Horse thieves infest the vicinity of Del Norte. A hemp festival is maturing."

". . . the *Del Norte Prospector* has been presented with a turnip weighing twenty pounds and a dozen potatoes weighing 38 pounds, and still there are people who insist on believing that Colorado is not a fruit state."

"Ice, an inch in thickness, formed at Del Norte last week. The *Democrat* gives the fact as a hint to organizers of church oyster festivals."

The founding fathers of Del Norte must have had confidence in the permanence of the city. Many of the early buildings constructed in the sixties were made of stone, and are still standing. Del Norte has remained a supply center and shipping point. Farmers and ranchers have replaced the miners and prospectors.

## LOMA

One of the small hamlets near Del Norte that eventually became absorbed by the booming frontier town. Loma was founded by three fellows named Mead, Goodwin and Pollack in 1873, and for a while kept pace with Del Norte.

An old well north of Del Norte marks the spot of Loma today. The well used to be the Loma town well. Loma is Spanish for mist and the name is said to come from the appearance of mist rising from the plains.

## BIEDELL

Colorado mining history wouldn't be complete without mentioning Mark Biedell. A Frenchman who came to Colorado as a rancher, Biedell eventually became interested in mining. He invested in, and helped develop, several mining properties throughout southern Colorado. He was a guiding force in many a gold and silver camp (including Bonanza), and helped many of these camps and mines recover from depressions and disasters. He later became a merchant in Del Norte and was a leading figure in the development of that city.

It is well a city—although a ghost city—was named for him.

Biedell began ranching near here in 1865. When gold was found fifteen years later, he invested in the mining properties, and helped lay out the city. By 1883, 1,000 men were here and several mines were paying off handsomely, but the boom didn't last long and the camp was virtually empty by the late 80's.

## CARNERO

Carnero had a Spring Chicken mine and an Old Crow Literary Club. Otherwise, the camp was for the birds. The Spring Chicken came first. It was located in 1886, about the same time several other locations were staked out. The city grew from these locations. There were many businesses, a post office and the Old Crow Literary Club. A Catholic parish under Father John Brinker covered much of the area.

Carnero was also a stage stop on the run between Del Norte and Saguache. Carnero Creek was the fastest route to Cochetopa Pass, a busy pass in the settlement of Southern Colorado. There was also a Carnero Pass which paralleled Cochetopa Pass, and was also used quite a bit. Carnero was also a D & RG stop.

Carnero is Spanish for sheep, or mutton, the raising of which was also prominent in the region. The camp began to fade in the late 80's and died completely by 1900. The post office was later called Biedell. Then it was closed too.

*And Then There Were . . . . WILLOW CITY*, one of the first camps in the area, organized shortly before, and near, Weaver. A trace of the camp remains . . . . *AMETHYST,* believed to have grown around the Amethyst Mine on Bachelor Mountain, although some reports say it was predecessor of Jimtown. The Amethyst mine produced a million and a half in ore . . . . *CREEDEMOORE,* another camp near the junction of Rio Grande and Willow Creek, near *SOUTH CREEDE . . . . MEXICAN TOWN,* a small, temporary camp a short distance up the gulch from Embargo . . . . *CRYSTAL HILL,* a small camp alongside Biedell on Crystal Hill . . . . *CATHEDRAL,* once an important trading center, now little more than a post office village. It was named for the cathedral-like rock formation nearby.

## COMMODORE CAMP

This camp, located in a canyon at the foot of Mt. Blanca, was an outgrowth of activity in Creede. In 1899, Rene Steel, Gooch McClain, Rube Daniels, Elrick Schenck, and Steve Calkins located some free gold here "as large as wheat kernals." The find was made in a wild raspberry patch in Big Bear Canyon, where prospectors and others had come for a dozen years or so to eat their fill of the fruit.

The original location was named the Commodore. Its fame brought scores of others and the resultant camp was named after the first claim. There was a store, boardinghouse, and post office in the mouth of the canyon. Two saloons were owned and operated by Bob Wright and Lem Graves. Mr. and Mrs. George Grumley ran the boardinghouse, store, and meat market.

The first mail to the town came to the Zapata post office and was then taken in by horseback to Gard Howe's post office, which was named Hirst in honor of Mr. Hirst, then editor of the Alamosa newspaper.

Finally, everybody pitched in, including the county commissioners, and built a road through the pinons to Chimney Gulch and north into Big Bear Canyon. George Wheeler hauled passengers and freight in and out, as well as the mail. Ore was hauled out on pack mules.

All went well with the town for a short while until it was discovered that two separate groups claimed ownership of the Commodore. The lengthy litigation that followed closed the mine and spelled death for the town, despite activity at the Jumbo and other claims on Big Bear Lake, now called Como Lake.

In later years, some men from Mosca rigged up a crude aerial tram and hauled down some ore from the well-hidden old town.

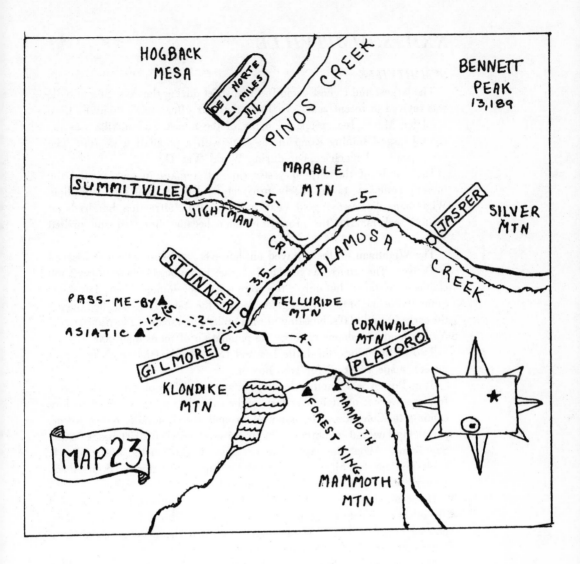

*MAP TWENTY-THREE*

SUMMITVILLE

Summitville
Platoro
Stunner (Conejos Camp, Loynton)
Gilmore
Jasper (Cornwall)

411

# XXII. SUMMITVILLE

## SUMMITVILLE

The largest and richest camp in the district during the 80's, Summitville was revived in recent years. In 1935, the year after the Summitville Consolidated Mines, Inc., reopened many of the mines, Summitville was the second largest mining camp in the state with a population of 700. The camp produced much copper during World War II.

The ghosts of the city of yesteryear still remain in and around the present company town. Early prospectors, led by James and William Wightman, discovered gold near here in 1870, attracting hundreds of fortune seekers. But the prospectors soon became disgusted and drifted away.

The Wightman brothers stayed on, however, and had some ore assayed in Denver. The report was good and another boom began. Soon some 2,500 claims were staked, but only a few were worth developing. These few made Summitville one of the largest gold camps in the state. It flourished during the early and mid-80's, boasting of nine mills, a newspaper, *The Summitville Nugget,* and 14 saloons to serve the population of more than 600.

Two of the mines, the Little Ida and Little Annie (the area's best producer), made a fortune for Tom Bowen.

Tom Bowen was another leading figure in early Colorado. He was a former governor of Idaho territory, and a carpetbagger in Arkansas, before coming to Colorado. He bummed around the Colorado boom towns, practicing law and gambling. Finally he was elected district judge in the San Juans. About the same time he struck it rich on the Little Ida. It made millions for him. He invested in many other mines. Some made money. Some didn't. But he didn't miss it.

He accumulated one of the biggest fortunes in southern Colorado. And like other carbonate kings, he turned to politics. Once a friend and poker-playing crony of H. A. W. Tabor, he defeated the Leadville King in a bitter battle for the GOP senate nomination.

Many stories have been woven about the man, the most popular of which was how he blocked the candidacy of Henry Wolcott for governor in 1882. Bowen was a leader of the anti-Wolcott faction. He had gathered a contingent of his supporters together, bound for Denver and the political convention. But the group missed the train in Del Norte by three minutes. A little thing like a missed train couldn't stop old Tom Bowen though. The group commandeered a hand-car and started pumping the long way to Denver. Hands blistered and out of breath, the group was about ready to give up. All except old Tom Bowen. He spied a locomotive on a siding.

This, too, he commandeered, and the group chugged into Denver in time to block Wolcott's candidacy. Good old Tom Bowen!

Summitville began fading in the late 80's and was deserted by 1893. The town was threatened by a huge forest fire in the area in 1882, but managed to escape with only negligible damage.

OTHER MINES: Major and Esmond (later called Aztec).

## PLATORO

One of the oldest and highest towns in the area. Platoro erupted during the 80's and hit its stride when a wagon road was built between it and Summitville in 1888. It had a population of 300 by 1890. But the ores couldn't carry the town indefinitely, and the miners slowly drifted away. There was a slight resurgence just after the turn of the century and again just before World War I, but the later booms didn't amount to much. Now the area is rapidly developing into a tourist region. And one of the tourist attractions is the old town of Patoro.

BEST MINES: Parole and Mammoth.

## STUNNER (Conejos Camp, Loynton)

Early residents believed Stunner had a great future ahead of it. It didn't.

Some prospecting was done here as early as 1879, but the first strike wasn't made until three years later. A town arose near the head of the Conejos River. It was first called Conejos Camp, then Loynton, and finally the name was changed to Stunner in 1887, for some reason or other.

A 45-mile toll road was built along the Conejos River to the site from Antonito. This boosted the area for a short while. The peak population was about 200 in the late 90's, but as the mines petered out, the miners slowly drifted away. Now only the debris from its past activity remains.

BEST MINES: Snow Storm, Merrimac, Log Cabin and Eurydice.

## GILMORE

A latter day camp founded when some ore was discovered in 1913. It died shortly thereafter, when the ore was found to be hardly worth the trouble. Only a trace of the site remains.

## JASPER (Cornwall)

Jasper died before it could learn how rich it might have been. Ten tons of ore were shipped to Denver for analysis in 1887, but the Denver smelter burned down before the assay was made—and Jasperites never knew. It is a town that could have been.

Good ore was found and some mining was done in the Sanger mine, about two miles above the city, and in the Miser and Perry lodes. But

413

much money was squandered in the early stages of its development and little was left to carry it through.

The site is now a haven for fishermen and summer tourists. The ruins of the "city that never knew" are a short distance away from the new tourist cabins. The town was originally called Cornwall for John Cornwall, the first postmaster.

# XXIII. THE SINGING SANDS

Winds whistle over Colorado's Great Sand Dunes, weaving eerie music and whispering endless legends of the past. It is natural that the grotesque formations, nestled in the pocket of some of Colorado's most majestic mountains, should be a mainspring of legend and ancient tales.

Some say the sand dunes represent the bed of an ancient ocean. However, most of Colorado was part of that ocean—where are the other sand dunes? Some believe the prevailing winds picked up all the ocean sand in this area between the mountain banks and deposited it at the foot of the mountains.

Endless Indian legend revolves around the sand dunes. The Spaniards, mountain men, and early explorer were amazed at the sight. Many tales are told of sheepherders, prospectors, and others who wandered onto the dunes and were never seen again.

The dunes are haunted by these lost strangers. The weird music of the wind and the sand are their moans and calls for help. When a person slides down the slopes, a deep rumbling can be heard, suggesting hidden caverns underground.

Wind and sand and the various lighting effects, especially at dawn and twilight, cause weird shadows to play upon the dunes. At these times, they say, giant ghostly horses can be seen against the horizon, their manes blowing in the wind and their heads raised high.

Forming a backdrop to the sand dunes are the magnificent Sangre de Cristo Mountains. The mountains were named when the Spanish explorer Valverde caught his first sudden view of the mountains just as the sun was rising. The sight took his breath away, and he was heard to mutter "Sangre de Cristo" (Blood of Christ).

Caves, known and hidden, high in these mountains add to the music and the legend of the area.

North of the Sand Dunes is, or was, the Luis Maria Baca Land Grant, the only grant in Colorado which had Spanish origin. It was originally called the Vegas Grant. The grant was petitioned for by Luis Cabeza de Baca in 1821, when this was Mexican territory. Later, the United States gave de Baca's heirs their choice of five grants of equivalent size—100,000 acres each. The heirs chose this grant in Colorado, and two grants each in New Mexico and Arizona.

Ownership of the grant became a hot issue in the last years of the 19th century when hundreds of prospectors rushed into the area, found precious metal, and established camps. After years of litigation, the Supreme Court upheld the provisions of the grant and booted the miners out.

Colorado's Governor William Gilpin acquired title to the grant, and still later, a Pensylvania company purchased the grant for $1,400,000. The firm continued to mine the precious metals for several years. Today the grant is one of the greatest cattle ranches in the west.

## MAP TWENTY-FOUR
### BONANZA-CRESTONE-SILVER CLIFF-ROSITA

Saguache
Bonanza (Bonanza City)
Sedgwick (Sedgewick)
Kerber City
Exchequerville, Claytonia and Bonita
Villa Grove and Valley View Hot Springs
Spook City
Orient (Oriental, Oriental City)
Bismarck (Bismark), Cotton Creek, Rito Alto, San Isabel, Sangre de Cristo
    and Short Creek
Wilcox
Crestone
Cottonwood
Julia City, Spanish, Teton, Lucky and Pole Creek
Liberty (Duncan)
Music City (Music Pass, Sand Creek)
Mosca
Hooper
Colfax (Blumenau)
Westcliffe (Clifton)
Silver Cliff
Ula (Ure)
Dora (Gove)
Querida (Bassick City, Bassickville)
Rosita (Brown's Spring)
Silver Park
Ilse
Galena (Camp Galena)
Greenwood
Custer City
Dawson City

And Then There Were .... SILVER CIRCLE, TRACY'S CABIN (or Tracy's Canyon), YORKVILLE, MIRAGE, NORTH CRESTONE, NEW LIBERTY, CLINTON, SHIRLEY (not on map), and OFER CAMP (not on map).

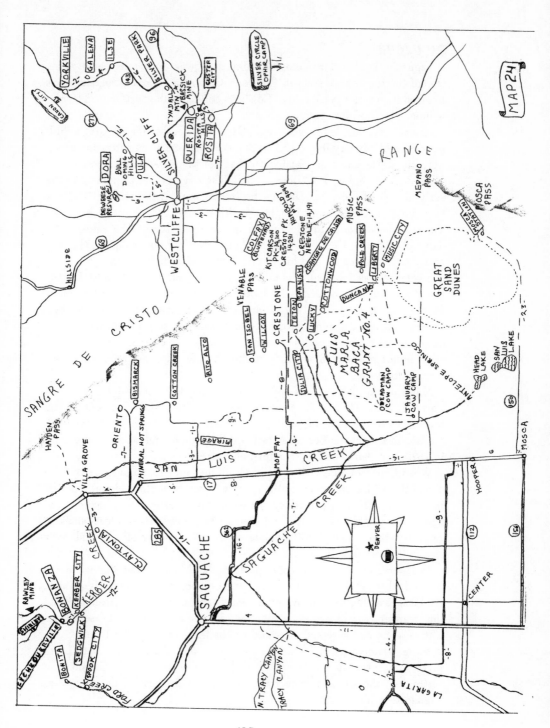

## SAGUACHE

Saguache is almost as colorful today as it was during its early years. One of the few county seats in Colorado without a railroad, Saguache has retained its frontier personality. Cowboys still dress the part here. The city is interesting and prosperous.

At one time, just a few years ago, Saguache boasted the greatest wealth per capita of any city in the United States. That was when cattle and sheep were king. The city's financial status has not sagged severely since.

Saguache is Indian for "Blue Earth." The red men are prominent in the early history of the area. During the Indian wars of the middle 1850's, a large body of U. S. troops caught up with a large Ute army led by Chief Tierra Blanca, leader of the Pueblo Massacre of 1854. The soldiers far outnumbered the Utes, so Tierra Blanca didn't stop to fight. Through crafty maneuvering he and his warriors escaped to fight again.

Saguache was founded about 1870, primarily as a supply post for the Los Pinos Ute Indian agency. It soon became important as a supply center for the mining camps in all directions, and for the cattle and sheep ranches.

Although never a mining town itself, Saguache's history was as colorful as any boom town. It was as rowdy a town as any on the frontier. Every other building was a saloon or gambling house. Girls and gunfights were fast and frequent.

Many of the first settlers were Germans mustered out of the army at Fort Garland. Their influence was important in the development of the town, even to the point of naming one of the streets "Sauerkraut Avenue."

Otto Mears got his business start peddling goods out of an adobe store in 1870, and married Mary Kampfshulte here.

When General Grant visited Colorado in the late 70's, Saguache gave him one of the wildest welcomes of the many wild welcomes the general received in the state. The feast, in which the whole town participated, included the best of the neighboring cattle and sheep, wild game of every sort, and one English settler donated 100 pounds of trout he caught at a neighboring stream the very day of the visit.

Horse racing was a favorite sport of the frontier, and Saguache enjoyed the best. The "big race of '79" is still being talked about. Red Buck, the local favorite, had taken on all comers and was still undefeated. Then the stranger from Texas rode into the city on an unknown horse named Little Casino and accepted the standing challenge to meet Red Buck.

Little Casino was given tremendous odds and the stranger was hard-pressed to cover all the bets. When the dust cleared, Little Casino won easily, and the stranger rode back to Texas with most of the money of Saguache in his pockets.

They say Saguache was voted county seat by just six votes. The opposition charged those six votes belonged to a team of oxen from a nearby farm. Despite the devious means by which the county seat was won, it found a permanent seat here.

## BONANZA (Bonanza City)

This city was named after a remark by the locater of a rich claim here: "Boys, she's a bonanza." And she was.

It was called the "new Leadville" of 1881, and fortune seekers flocked to the area by the hundreds. Founded a few months after Sedgwick and Kerber City, Bonanza soon outdistanced her neighbors and eventually absorbed them.

During the eighties Bonanza's population topped 1,500 and there were dozens of business houses. The *Bonanza News* was the best known of the town's newspapers. General Grant visited the city during one of his tours of Colorado. One of the best prospects was the Rawley. It sold for $100,000 in 1881, shortly after it was located.

A small mill was built in 1881, but it was only equipped to handle high grade ore and was little used. The Kelly and Company smelter was built the following year. But the high cost of shipping the ore, much of it low grade, almost spelled the end of Bonanza.

Then, town-saver Mark Biedell stepped in. His successful reorganization of the Michigan Mine and Mill Company soon made Bonanza pay, and the city was saved.

Before Bonanza was sure of its position as top city in the area there was great rivalry between the various camps. Most binges, especially on Saturday night, resulted in a raid on one of the other of the nearby camps. Some were killed and many were injured in the gang fights. But, of course, it was all good clean fun.

Activity lagged here as the price of silver fell, but the city never died out completely. In 1890, when the population dropped to 100, there was a revival. Another one took place in 1900, and there have been mild flutters off and on since, although, generally speaking, Bonanza fell far short of expectations because of the high cost of producing the generally low-grade ore.

The Empress Josephine, which produced seven millions in its day, was reopened in 1947 after forty years. The Bonanza, which ran continuously until it closed in 1898, was reopened two years later, and has produced off and on since.

The mines here had a unique problem in recent years when hoards of beavers invaded the area and penetrated as deep as two miles inside the mines, gnawing on timbers, interfering with the work, and endangering the lives of the miners. During the thirties experienced trappers were called into the area to rid it of the beavers, usually protected by the law.

The large Rawley Twelve Mine, about a mile beyond Bonanza and a short distance above Exchequerville, resumed operations in 1959, mining lead and zinc. The mine is owned by the Superior Mining Company, which now owns many of the mining properties in the area. The success of the Rawley "experiment" could determine whether or not the company will open more of the mines. Nonetheless, miners are now competing with the summer tourists for the cabins in Bonanza and Exchequerville.

BEST MINES: Rawley, Empress Josephine, Bonanza, Wheel of Fortune, Eagle, Defiance and Exchequer.

### SEDGWICK (Sedgewick)

Sedgwick was one of the first camps laid out along Kerber Creek in 1880. By the end of the year the camp had a population of 600. It grew rapidly and soon had several prosperous businesses, including a bowling alley, billiard hall, two large dance halls, several saloons, two hotels and a sawmill.

As Bonanza grew a short distance upstream, it soon absorbed Sedgwick and Kerber City, directly across the stream from Sedwick.

Sedgwick had the distinction of having the only brewery along the creek. It was located on Brewery Creek, which ran into the Kerber.

A mill was built at the site of Sedgwick in 1939, but it could not find suitable copper to process and was little used.

### KERBER CITY

Captain Charles Kerber was in command of Company I of the first Colorado Volunteers, which camped near here in 1865. It was the first settlement on the creek, which was named at this time. The mining camps along the creek didn't come into being until fifteen years later when gold and silver were discovered .

Kerber City was a smaller camp, directly across the creek from Sedgwick, both of which were absorbed by Bonanza.

### EXCHEQUERVILLE, CLAYTONIA and BONITA

Three of the smaller camps near Bonanza.

Exchequerville was believed to be the first camp in the area. It was, and is, located about a mile beyond Bonanza, a short distance below the large Exchequer mine. The town is situated at the junction of two roads, one leading to the newly-opened Raleigh Twelve, and the other going to the Exchequer and on up to Shirley. A few rejuvenated cabins remain in a small pocket in the mountains, to the right of the road as you come from Bonanza. Raleigh miners live in the cabins.

Claytonia was another camp along Kerber Creek, a few miles southeast of Bonanza. It was also an early camp, but didn't last very long before it lost to the bustling city to the north. Two cabins remain at the site of Claytonia.

Nothing remains at the one-time site of Bonita, a silver camp around the hill from Bonanza. The camp didn't last very long. Bonita is Spanish for neat or pretty, and was believed given as the name of the town for the scenic country surrounding it.

## VILLA GROVE and VALLEY VIEW HOT SPRINGS

Villa Grove was a vital supply point for the camps up Kerber Creek. Valley View Hot Springs was a resort. Villa Grove is now a ranching center. Valley View is still a resort.

Villa Grove, established in the 70's, became a terminus for the narrow gauge from Poncha Springs for a while. The population is about 100 now. The narrow gauge is gone. Don't miss Villa Grove's lonely little graveyard north of town, just off the highway.

Otto Mears built a seventeen-mile road from Villa Grove up Kerber Creek when the latter area was booming. Mears ran it as a toll road for some time. It was one of his earlier attempts at road-building.

## SPOOK CITY

This camp, located about two miles beyond Bonita, was apparently named for the Spook lode, and doesn't have the interesting story behind it one might expect. The Spook lode was a secondary location. The Lost Dickey was the better claim.

There was some activity here in 1879-80, but the biggest boom which caused the city to be named took place after 1893, when the Spook and the Lost Dickey were located.

The mines produced both gold and silver, but apparently not too much of either. A Danish syndicate purchased the claims in 1894 for $5,000, and gained from the Dickey, but little work was done on the Spook.

The site is a true Spook City, as nothing remains.

## ORIENT (Oriental, Oriental City)

Orient took its name from the Orient mine, Colorado's only commercial producer of limanite iron ore. The mine produced continuously for fifty years.

Orient was always an iron camp. During its heyday the camp shipped as much as 200 tons of iron ore per day to smelters in Pueblo and Durango.

The camp grew up in the late 70's. By 1880, there were two restaurants, a saloon, a milling company and several other businesses here. The popula-

421

tion was about 400 at the turn of the century. The mines were operated in later years by the Colorado Fuel and Iron Company.

## BISMARCK (or Bismark), *COTTON CREEK, RITO ALTO, SAN ISABEL, SANGRE DE CRISTO and SHORT CREEK*

Several towns once nestled at the western foot of the Sangre de Cristos. They all saw the prospectors but not all of them saw the gold or silver. Some became farm and ranch towns.

Bismarck, eight miles south of Villa Grove, saw a steady stream of prospectors during the 80's, 90's, and later, but few of them tarried. The town was a farm and ranch community, and little or no precious metal was found here. The town had some Germans among its early settlers and they named the community for the German leader.

Cotton Creek was a small mining town.

Apparently there were two Rito Altos, a small sheep and cattle-raising site on Rito Alto Creek on the western side of the range, and a mining camp just opposite it on the other side of the range. There are still some ruins left of the mining town. One of the towns had a post office as early as 1880. It was probably the mining town.

San Isabel was a gold town. It was nestled in a protected clearing and mining could be carried out both summer and winter. The mining wasn't too good, however, and San Isabel was better known as a cattle town. The peak population was about 400 persons.

Sangre de Cristo was a sheep and cattle town located at the headwaters of Cottonwood Creek. The population was small and composed mostly of Spanish Americans. There was a post office here for several years.

Short Creek was about a mile east of Liberty and was primarily a mining camp.

## WILCOX

A short-lived camp that arose out of a flutter of mining activity near the end of the 19th century and during a lull in the activity at Crestone. With the reopening of the big Cleveland mine in Crestone, Wilcoxites closed up their cabins and moved south.

## CRESTONE

The Crestone area has seen many faces in the past few hundred years. First there were the red men. The Comanches and Utes battled over possession of the area. Numerous arrow heads and old stone tools have been found here. Then came the Spanish in search of gold. Pike was the first Yankee. He and his party almost lost their lives in heavy snow near here.

The first prospectors came into the Crestone region in the late 70's. They found little to excite them and moved on. They came back in droves in 1890, however, when some free-milling gold was found. Before long, two thousand persons lived in the camp. A railroad spur was built to the site from Moffat. Crestone was well on its way toward being one of Colorado's top cities.

Then the Supreme Court decided to uphold the provisions of the Luis Baca Grant. The decision hit Crestone hard. The city was located right on the northern edge of the grant, and many of its best mines were within the grant proper. There was some violence as the Crestonites fought eviction, but eventually they moved a short distance out of the grant.

Shortly after the eviction, the Crestone mines within the grant were taken over by a private company. Many of the mines continued to produce until recent years. Millions were taken from them. Maybe they will produce again.

Meanwhile, Crestone is doing right nicely as a tourist center. It's not so exciting as mining, but it's steady. The major tourist interest is in the nearby Crestone needles, from which the community derives its name. Crestone is Spanish for Cock's Comb.

BEST MINES: Cleveland, Independent (located in 1901)

## COTTONWOOD

Cottonwood, one of the largest camps within the land grant, was just about hitting its stride when the miners were evicted. At the time of the eviction, Cottonwood had better than a thousand residents.

Shortly thereafter, a Philadelphia syndicate bought up the area and further developed it. Before long the syndicate was shipping $80,000 in bullion a month.

Some mining continued until the 20's. Cottonwood produced millions in gold, silver, copper, lead and iron. The best mine was the Independent.

Some cabins and foundations remain.

## JULIA CITY, SPANISH, TETON, LUCKY and POLE CREEK

Other camps located within the San Luis Baca Grant. Work stopped when the government upheld the provisions of the grant in 1900. The miners, however, bitterly opposed the eviction and there were some instances of violence.

Pole Creek, a little more than two miles south of Cottonwood, saw much activity before the eviction. There were three paying mines here and a stamp mill. There are still some ruins at the site, but it takes a hike to get there.

Spanish and Lucky were placer mining camps on Spanish Creek. There are some ruins at the site of Spanish, at the mouth of the creek.

Julia City was southwest of Crestone near the northern edge of the Luis Baca Grant.

## LIBERTY (Duncan)

When the miners of Duncan were booted out of the land grant in 1900, they simply moved their town a quarter of a mile east, just outside the grant, and founded the city of Liberty.

The Spanish were the first miners in the area and some of their ancient implements were found here.

William Gilpin, who later became a governor of Colorado, found gold here while traveling with the pathfinder, John Fremont. Gilpin returned to the area and helped develop it. But the ore didn't hold out for long, and Duncan was all but deserted again. Then in 1890, a richer strike was made, and Duncan saw its second, and largest, boom. During the 90's, Duncan had about 1,000 residents, a 40-student school, a newspaper, *The Golden Eagle*, mills and several businesses.

Duncan is now the site of a ranger station, and that's about all. There are some remains of Liberty, but not much, and the site is all but impossible to reach.

A hermit lived in Liberty until recent years, but now he's gone, and all is quiet.

## MUSIC CITY (Music Pass, Sand Creek)

Music City was located just north of the Sand Dunes at the foot of Music Pass. The Camp was just a small one, one of the many at the foot of the Sangre de Cristos. There was some mining here, but the camp didn't last long, so the mining must not have been too good.

Some say the pass received its name from the sighing sound of the winds off the sand dues. Others claim the name and the music come from the wind whistling through the caves along the pass. Perhaps it was a combination of both. Apparently when the wind blew, music abounded.

Legend says one of the caves was the "Cavern del Oro," a continuous passage under the Sangre de Cristos, which was said to contain an old Spanish mine. Although many have sought the mine through the years, it has never been found.

The pass itself was little used by trappers and traders because it was so arduous. It apparently had a lot of wind, too.

## MOSCA

Mosco was a stage station and supply center at the foot of Mosca Pass which crossed the Sangre de Cristo Range.

Although often called Roubidoux Pass for the latter-day adventurer Antoine Roubidoux, it was originally named for "Moscosca Alvardo," legendary Spanish explorer-captain who was said to have led the remnants of DeSoto's expedition from Pueblo to Santa Fe in 1542-43, probably over this pass.

The pass was a very important route in the early history of the westward movement and was traveled by many mountain men and explorers. Fur-trader Roubindoux drove a two-wheeled cart over the pass in 1837 to set up a fur-trading post on the Gunnison River. Ruxton, an English officer, crossed over the pass in 1846. Two years later, Fremont used the pass in one of his many thrusts into the mountains.

The route was improved upon and widely used in the development of southern Colorado. Later a modern highway was built over part of the old road. Mosca Pass lost its importance with the development of La Veta Pass.

Of course, long before the white men came, the pass was used extensively by the Indians. The section is important to Indian legend and history. Nearby "Lake of Souls" served as a reservoir of Indian life and death. According to Indian tradition, the soul emerged from the lake at birth and returned to it at death.

The ruins of an old stage station below Moffat mark the end of Mosca Pass.

## HOOPER

Hooper, once a proud railroad and trading town, is fighting extinction—and the womenfolk are at the wheel. A few years ago, when the railroad stopped running to Hooper, the town dwindled almost overnight. The population fell below 100. And one by one, those who remained over the years began drifting off.

Then, a couple of years back, the womenfolk decided to take a hand to stop the trend. The men said welcome to it. Women took over every office in the community. It isn't that they took over the high-paying jobs. Only one office is salaried—the clerk-recorder—and receives but five dollars a year.

The campaign hasn't shown any appreciable results as yet except that the population has remained constant—at about fifty—since the gals took over.

## COLFAX (or Blumenau)

In the years following the Civil War, the government developed many plans to encourage western immigration and settlement. Under one of the plans, a large colony of German veterans and their families from Chicago, under the leadership of Carl Wursten, were given land in the Wet Mountain Valley. The government even provided some equipment and the tents for the initial dwellings. Colfax was the German settlement, which, in 1869, was the first in the valley.

But the colonists couldn't get along and couldn't make a go of it before the first year was out. Some of their provisions were lost in an explosion. The town never got further than a tent settlement before most of the settlers, hungry and disgusted, moved on to other communities. The post office was moved to nearby Palmer Ranch. In 1872, the ranch settlement was named Blumenau. Shortly thereafter, the settlement was returned to its original site and resumed the name of Colfax. However, it was never more than a small ranching settlement. It lasted for years, before most of the settlers moved to other nearby towns.

## *WESTCLIFFE* (Clifton)

Legend says early Spanish soldiers filled a cave in Colorado full of Aztec treasure. Several mountain areas in Colorado claim the cave, but as yet it has not been discovered, and there is nothing clear-cut outside of legend that says the cave exists at all.

It is known the Spanish spent much time in the Sangre de Cristos, and a couple of findings have led natives to believe the fabled cave may be in the Westcliffe area.

A Captain Horn reported finding a skeleton in Spanish armor in 1869 on Horn Mountain. A Spanish cross was found nearby Marble Mountain (thirteen miles from Westcliffe) in the early 30's. The cave was thoroughly explored in 1934, but no trace of the Spanish treasure was found.

Anyway, it's an attractive legend.

Westcliffe was one of the many Colorado cities and communities created by the railroads. When the railroad was constructed into a new area, it often built its terminal a short distance away from the existing center of activity. Frequently the reasons for this were entirely practical—the selected site was better suited to the needs of the railroad, it was cheaper to end the railroad here than extend it over the rough terrain ahead, and so forth. But frequently, the railroad cut short the construction for no other reason than to increase the land value on that point and start a new city of its own.

Whatever the reasoning of the railroad, its action gave birth to many cities (Durango, Ridgeway, Salida, etc.) and destroyed many others (Animas City, Dallas, Cleora, etc.).

The construction of a railroad to within two miles of the booming city of Silver Cliff did not destroy that city, but did lessen its importance in the area, and gave birth to Westcliffe.

Records say the railroad stopped here to increase the land value of this point. But it is no secret that Dr. W. A. Bell may well have influenced the railroad's decision.

Dr. Bell traveled through here with his good friend General Palmer when

426

Palmer was searching for a southern route for the Denver and Rio Grande. Dr. Bell was so taken with this site he returned to it and settled here. In 1881, when the railroad arrived, Bell was instrumental in planning the city, which he named for his hometown, Westcliffe-by-the-Sea, England.

## SILVER CLIFF

Silver Cliff exploded on the Colorado scene in 1879, the year of the Leadville boom. And for a short while it threatened to outdistance the silver city to the north.

Within months of its founding, Silver Cliff was the third largest city in Colorado, trailing only Denver and Leadville. The population was estimated as high as 10,000, with hundreds more combing the hills in all directions. Silver Cliff was even being touted for state capitol.

But then the boom leveled off and Silver Cliff became just another city that had its day and then nestled back into the pages of history.

But what a day!

R. J. Edwards of Rosita made the first silver strike here in 1877. He had frequently noticed the curious rock and finally, out of curiosity, ripped off a piece of the cliff and had it assayed. The silver content was sufficient to encourage further development. His find brought hundreds of prospectors from Rosita and Bassickville (Querida). Silver still was not so attractive as gold, and the gold content of the area was practically nil. Before long most of the miners left, leaving the area once again to Edwards.

Edwards found some silver near the surface around the cliff, but something about the cliff continued to intrigue him, and he finally turned his attention back to it. A few feet under the hard wall of the cliff, Edwards found silver in tin-foil-like layers, assaying up to 740 ounces of silver to the ton.

The Silver Cliff boom was on for real.

Within weeks the entire area was covered with claims and prospect holes. Much workable silver was found near the surface, but the richer lodes were uncovered in small pockets a few feet under the surface. In the first year, the area produced more than two million in silver, and the best was yet to come.

Silver Cliff was one of the wildest of the many wild mining towns in the west. Saloons and gambling houses dominated the business scene and the only women in the city for the first few months were ladies of the street. Shootings and street fights were common and attracted only passing attention.

The first saloons were representative of the life in Silver Cliff. The saloons were little more than makeshift shelters with one long log bar. The

427

whiskey glasses were in use constantly and were washed but once a day. Water was dear but whiskey was cheap.

Despite the transient and rough nature of the first citizens, the town was laid out according to an elaborate and lasting plan. The plan called for ten miles of wide streets. After the water works was built, twenty-nine fire plugs were placed in strategic points throughout the city.

There were ten hotels, two banks, two daily and three weekly newspapers, several dance halls and gambling houses, twenty-five saloons, four stamp mills, two smelters and two concentration works, and scores of stores, selling everything from clothes to French pastry.

Shortly after the itinerant preachers began making the rounds of Silver Cliff, and the miners began sending for their wives and families, the city went legitimate. Churches and schools were built. A large and well-dressed police force went into action. A "chain gang" began to keep the streets in condition. And one of the best equipped and most efficient volunteer fire departments in the state was standing by.

The fire department was the pride of Silver Cliff. In those days there was an annual competition between fire departments throughout Colorado. Silver Cliff hosted the competition in 1882 and won it.

With the aid of Westcliffe, Silver Cliff won the county seat away from Rosita in a county election. But, as was often the case, the loser refused to give up the designation. So, a group of Silver Cliff citizens invaded Rosita one night and stole away all the county records. For Westcliffe's aid in winning the election, the county courthouse was built between the two cities. It still stands, although it is no longer in use.

Despite its fine volunteer fire department, Silver Cliff was virtually wiped off the map in a fire in 1880. The city was rebuilt, but threatened again by destruction two years later when fire broke out in a congested business area. Through heroic efforts on the part of the fire department and other citizens, the fire was finally brought under control after destroying the one business block.

The city began to fade during the mid-80s. It was only a shadow in 1893 when the silver panic all but pounded the nails in its coffin. But Silver Cliff has managed to survive, a sleepy little town of about 200 residents.

BEST MINES: Bull, Domingo (now combined), and Racine Boy.

SILVER DUST: Edwards' strike, named the Racine Boy for Edwards' hometown in Wisconsin, produced steadily for years and off and on after that . . . . two other big producers, Bull and Domingo, came into conflict over claims and the dispute almost resulted in armed warfare before a New York Company bought both claims for $325,000 . . . . the Bull, or Johnny Bull, was located quite by accident. It seems two prospectors had staked a claim ten years earlier but, after digging a ten-foot shaft, gave up on it. In 1878, Daniel Rarick, a Leadville prospector grubstaked to inspect this area, stumbled near the old claim. He drove his pick into the ground to help break his fall. He noticed galena specks on his pick and began to dig at the spot. At seven feet he struck solid galena ore. After Rarick's strike, the original claimants returned to re-claim their stake. A legal battle followed which soon involved the adjoining Domingo property and lasted until the New York firm took over . . . . before the water works was built, water was hauled in from springs several miles away and sold at forty cents a barrel . . . . Reverend Teitsworth is credited with preaching the first sermon in Silver Cliff—on the main street of the city. Another early preacher in Silver Cliff was Reverend Drummond, who walked the seven miles between Rosita and Silver Cliff once a week . . . . *The Weekly Prospector*, one of the many newspapers in Silver Cliff's history, was one of the most widely-read publications in southern Colorado . . . . during its heyday, Silver Cliff was said to be one of the most exciting places to live west of the Mississippi . . .highwaymen often cut off the city during its first years . . . . now the Silver Cilff area is the center of one of the best potato farming sections of Colorado.

## ULA (Ure)

Ula was settled a few months after Colfax and was therefore the first mining camp of any importance in the area. It was also the first county seat of Custer County. Some say the first settlers intended to name the town Ure after the Ute Indian Chief, but the name was either misspelled or misread by the post office department. Another theory is that the camp was named after the wife of one of the first settlers.

The camp was also known locally as "Britain's Paradise." Elaborate advertisements appeared in English newspapers telling of the plentiful game in this vicinity. The advertisements lured many a hunting-happy Englishman. The miners, impressed by the English ways of many of the settlers, referred to Ula as "a bit of ole England."

There were a number of claims staked out here around 1870, but only three amounted to anything. The peak population was around 100. In 1873, when Rosita soared in prominence, Ula-ites just upped and moved to the new boom city.

## DORA (Gove)

Dora, now covered by the DeWeese Reservoir, was another early city that was drenched with historical background. The site was favorite Indian hunting ground before the white man came. Lieutenant Pike was said to have explored near here. Other explorers followed and the site was well-known by Colorado's early hunters and trappers.

The site was ranchland before the boom hit the area. The town was platted in 1879 and was believed named for the wife of a nearby rancher. Because of its advantageous position at the head of Grape Creek, Dora prospered as a smelting center for a short time. The boom was aided by the construction of a branch of the Denver and Rio Grande.

The camp grew around the Chambers smelter, which worked about 20 tons of ore per day. Dora reached its peak about 1880, when more than 100 persons lived here. The name of the town was changed to Gove in 1885, but by that time hardly anyone cared.

*QUERIDA* (Bassick City, Bassickville)

There are many stories on the finding of the fabulous Bassick mine. All agree, however, it was an accident.

E. C. Bassick, a former sailor, worked at the Centennial Mining Company on nearby Tyndal Mountain. He crossed the site of his future discovery on the way back and forth to work almost every day. A man named John True had discovered some placer ore here a few years before but didn't develop his find.

Some say Bassick tripped over some unusual rocks on the way to work. Some say a rock broke off as he leaned against it. Anyway, it was an accident, and historians further agree, Bassick had the rock assayed just for the hell of it. The ores were worth $30. This was more than he made in one week as a miner, so he gave up his job and went to work on his location for real.

This was in 1877. They say his first carload of ore brought $10,000, and Bassick dug out more than a half-million in gold and silver before selling to an Eastern firm the following year. Under the management of the eastern company, the mine produced another million and a half before litigation set in, in 1885, slowing production and development of the mine.

The Bassick mine and other claims were worked only spasmodically from 1885 until 1903, when the Melrose Gold Mining Company took over most of the claims. After a few weeks the company found a rich lode near the surface which produced another two million dollars. The mine was worked off and on until 1915. Then, in 1923, the dumps were treated with cyanidation, which produced thousands of dollars more.

In all, the Bassick and the nearby claims produced several millions in gold and silver. At one time the ore was so rich it was shipped to Westcliffe with guards carrying sawed-off shotguns.

The city sprang up with the original discovery. It was first named Bassickville, then Bassick City. Some reports say the city was founded by David Livingston, nephew of Dr. Livingston of "I presume . . ." fame. Other reports say Livingston was just one of the founders and responsible for the name Querida. Querida is Spanish for "darling" or "beloved." Livingston selected the name because he dearly loved the site and was equally attracted to the word itself.

The peak year for Querida was 1882, when more than 1,000 persons lived here, and the city boasted a three-story hotel, sawmill and a big concentration mill.

430

The mine closed down temporarily in 1884, throwing 400 miners out of work. Litigation over conflicting properties began the following year, further adding to the downfall of the city. The city underwent several minor flutters of activity through the 90's and early 1900's, but for the most part Querida was dead. The city is silent today, its many buildings waiting patiently for another boom.

## ROSITA (Brown's Spring)

Rosita is silent and empty today, its romantic past only a memory. Its buildings which once sheltered the interesting people in her past are falling into ruin. Much has already turned to dust. It is a wonder a city so young and charming, could ever grow old—and die.

For Rosita was a Queen City in Colorado's early royal family.

A man named Daniel Baker was said to have made the first strike here. Others, including Dick Irwin (see Irwin), soon followed suit. The Hardscrabble mining district was organized in 1872. The city wasn't founded until the following year. Two of the best strikes weren't made until 1874—the Pocahontas and Humboldt.

There are two versions of how the city came to be named Rosita, Spanish for Little Rose. One story says Dick Irwin named the site Rosita for the many wild roses growing in profusion here. Another story tells of a Frenchman who drifted to the spot after the death of his Spanish sweetheart, and named the city in her memory.

Rosita hit its peak during the mid and late 70's, the population topping 2,000 persons. In addition to several hotels, saloons, processing mills and other businesses, the city had one of the largest breweries in the state, and a large cheese factory which produced up to 250 pounds of cheese a day—that is until the cattle got to eating too much wild garlic and their milk became contaminated.

It was a social town and a shooting town. There were many social organizations, which sponsored many a dance and other get-togethers.

Two drunks attempted to take over an Odd Fellows dance one night. Bouncers threw them out. A few minutes later the drunks returned with their "hardware" and shot the bouncers dead. The whole town participated in the "necktie party" given the hungover murderers the next day—a very sociable town.

An old-fashioned gun battle took place on the main street. It seems some city slickers moved in on the Pocahontas claim. To protect their property the slickers hired a bunch of thugs and toughs, led by the toughest thug of all—Major Graham, an escaped convict who was no more a major than you or I.

The citizens rose up against the slickers and their motley army, and in

431

the gun battle on the main street killed Graham and ran the rest of the slickers and the toughs out of town.

The Pocahontas was also involved in another battle over overlapping claims. The battle was called the "Pocahontas War" and threatened to explode into real violence before the miners court settled the dispute to the satisfaction of both sides.

"Commodore" Stephen Decatur (see Decatur) drifted into Rosita while it was still booming and attempted to gain back his lost fortune here. He didn't. He spent the last years of his life living on the charity of Rosita residents, and died penniless. He was buried in Rosita's cemetery, but his marker has long since disappeared.

The mining disputes, the pinching out of good locations, and booms in other nearby camps all contributed to the death of Rosita. Four business blocks of buildings were destroyed by fire in October, 1881, but the city was already well on the road to nothingness.

The city was a ghost by 1885. Only a few people who loved it stayed on, until one by one they died or drifted off. One of the few remaining citizens was Carl Wulsten, leader in the attempted founding of Colfax, the region's first settlement made by German veterans. Wulsten came to Rosita early and was one of its leaders during the city's boom. He remained in Rosita until he died in 1915.

BEST MINES: Senator (Baker's find), Pringle, Humboldt, Pocahontas.

GOLD DUST: The Humboldt and Pocahontas both produced $300,000 their first year. Silver was the top metal here, with estimated production running from two to three million . . . . the top newspaper was the *Index*, later named the *Sierra Journal* . . . . two stage lines ran daily service between Rosita and Silver Cliff until as late as 1881 . . . . the Hardscrabble district was named for Hardscrabble Gulch which was named for the hard scrabble the Indians had getting through it while being chased by soldiers after the Pueblo Massacre.

### SILVER PARK

There was a little mining at Silver Park, but not much. During its heyday, Silver Park served primarily as a stage station, post office and supply village for the activity around. It was located near the head of Hardscrabble Creek, nine miles northeast of Rosita.

### ILSE

The story of Ilse is the story of "the Eccentric Dutchman." The Dutchman struck paydirt here in 1878. They say he could have made a lot of money off his claim. Instead, he spent all he made and more in searching for the mother lode he was sure was here. It wasn't. And eventually the Dutchman skipped out on his creditors.

But the story doesn't end there. Years later, the Dutchman hit it rich in

Pack train entering Platoro. Picture taken in 1915. *U. S. Geological Survey photo.*

Bonanza around the turn of the century. It's still going. *State Historical Society of Colorado photo.*

Silver Cliff during its peak when it was the third largest city in the state and being boomed for the state capitol. *Historical Society of Colorado.*

434

Rosita then. *State Historical Society of Colorado.*

Querida and the Bassick Mine (on hill). *State Historical Society of Colorado.*

Custer City was going full blast in 1902 and 1903, but the promise of its "big day" never came true. Note statue of General Custer in background. *Denver Public Library Western Collection.*

Lonely marble blocks make a fitting headstone for the dead community of Custer City today. The main street of the town extended half way up the mound in the background. The mound is just north of the hill in the picture above.

Holocaust in Cripple Creek. Half the city was in panic while the other half looked on, unable to believe what was happening. Picture was taken during the early moments of the first fire in 1896. *State Historical Society of Colorado.*

437

Cripple Creek in 1903. Photo taken from Gold Hill. Mt. Pisgah in background. *U. S. Geological Survey photo.*

The Elkton. The story of its discovery and its naming is another Cripple Creek legend.

A lonely saloon at Midway, overlooking the Cripple Creek region.

The well-preserved houses at Winfield, built as headquarters and a show-place by Winfield Scott Stratton, one of Cripple Creek's most fabulous millionaires.

Altman as it looked during its peak. It was the highest incorporated city in the world and also an independent kingdom during the labor wars. *State Historical Society of Colorado.*

### DAWSON CITY

Dawson City, located in the Greenhorn Hills about four miles southwest of Canon City, lived and died within a period of two or three months, but had a furious time of it during that time.

It was late in 1898 when J. B. Hannum, D. W. Bonewitz, B. I. Dawson, and his two sons, B. X. and I. F. Dawson, uncovered a rich lode during a routine dynamite shot. The ore assayed at a fabulous $9,600 per ton. The men named their claim the Copper King and went to work.

But they weren't alone. The report of their strike virtually cleaned out Canon City. Everybody was in the hills staking claims as close to the Copper King as they could get, or putting up tents or cabins in the new campsite. More enterprising men were setting up restaurants, saloons, and boardinghouses in large tents. They did a booming business. It was estimated that more than 500 persons were here at its peak.

But, alas, the original find turned out to be little more than a lucky strike of a very rich, but very small, pocket of ore. Aside from this find, the Copper King was nothing but low-grade ore, hardly worth the effort. And nobody else found anything interesting there. In fact, the whole thing ended so suddenly that excitable money men didn't even have time to invest in the area and prolong its demise.

440

Idaho. And, the story goes, he spent much of the rest of his life tracking down all his creditors to pay them back five-fold.

The "Terrible," named when one miner claimed it had a "terrible big deposit," was the big mine at Ilse. It produced well from 1878 to 1888, and has been worked off and on since.

At its peak, Ilse had several hundred residents, a hotel, a large boarding house, a general store and three saloons. But the city had passed its peak in 1887 when fire destroyed most of the town. Little was rebuilt.

There have been several flutters of activity in later years. The biggest re-boom came in 1903 when a large mill was built. At peak capacity, the mill employed 100 men. The mill was later taken over by the Grant Smelting Company of Denver.

## GALENA (Camp Galena)

Galena got off to a good start, but fouled up somewhere along the way and didn't last very long. It had its beginnings in the late 70's, about the same time as Silver Cliff, and by 1880 some 300 people lived here. The camp boasted a hotel, post office, assay office and a few other businesses. It also served for a short while as a stage station between Canon City and Rosita.

The best mines were Slip Up and Star. A lone building marks the site today.

## GREENWOOD

A post office and railroad town established in 1872. The town was named for Colonel William Greenwood, a construction engineer, who was instrumental in getting the Denver and Rio Grande Railroad in from Canon City. A scant population still resides in Greenwood, which is now little more than a post office town.

## CUSTER CITY

High on a hill separating the once-bustling mining towns of Querida and Rosita, and not far off the old prospectors trail between the two towns, are two large but lonely marble blocks, set a few feet apart on a weed-blown field.

The marble blocks mark the center of what used to be Custer City. In all directions from the blocks, if one looks closely enough, are small foundations excavations where houses and buildings once stood. A shallow ditch runs from a place about halfway up a small rise behind the marble blocks to a point about 100 yards south of the blocks. Shallower and shorter ditches run from the main ditch to the house foundations. Fire hydrants once stood at either end of the main ditch, a distance of about three-fourths of a mile. A large galvanized pipe ran between them and small pipes carried water from the main pipe to the houses.

Custer City was a modern city . . . . although it had but a short life. In fact, one might say Custer City had but one big day.

That day was June 11, 1902.

It was long after Rosita and Querida got their start that the Maverick and Toledo were opened up and showed pretty good promise. It coincided with the time New England millionaires Col. Albert A. Poke, who made his money in bicycles, and envelope-maker G. Henry Whitcomb were casting about for some western enterprise in which to invest their money. They decided upon the Maverick and the Toledo.

Col. Poke and Whitcomb could teach those Madison Avenue boys a thing or two. They gave Custer City an opening day any public relations firm would be proud of.

The ceremonies got off to a rousing start with a short speech by Governor James B. Orman, and an equally short speech by Lt. Gov. Alva Adams. The marble statue of General George A. Custer was unveiled as the general's widow looked on.

Then the festivities started for real. Beer kegs were opened. The athletic events, including baseball, horseracing, and drilling contests, got underway.

But the most exciting part of the ceremonies was the actual erection of the town itself. The houses and buildings were built elsewhere, primarily in Pueblo, in sections and shipped to Custer City to be put together on the spot—the first pre-fabricated houses in Colorado.

One newspaper said hundreds of houses and buildings were built in this manner. But other newspapers were probably more correct when they said some 40 buildings went up. The buildings included a depot (that was never used), hotel, newspaper office, and bank. And, as one newspaper added as an afterthought, "neither have the saloons, churches and schools been overlooked."

By nightfall all the buildings were up and occupied, the first issue of the *Custer City Guidon* was on the streets, and the grand ball was underway. Here, on what was a bare hill that morning, stood a modern city. Plans were being made to run the local railroad up the hill, to make Custer City a shipping point for the "rich" mines around.

The sewage and waterworks were built. Electricty was installed. But the railroad never went up the hill. Custer City's other big dreams were never realized.

*And Then There Were* . . . . *SILVER CIRCLE* (not on map) was a hot spot in the late seventies. It seems some silver finds got a lot of ballyhoo. Shortly thereafter charges of "fraud" and "swindle" hit the fan. The prospectors claimed the strikes were the "richest in the area." There were some libel suits going. It was a heck of a place to end the story, but no more information was found on Silver Circle. It must have been a fraud after all. The camp was located in the Rosita area . . . . *TRACY'S CABIN* (or Tracy's Canyon) (not on map). An 1879 newspaper reported a Jacob Schucker hit paydirt "at the vicinity of Tracy's Cabin, about eight miles a little west of south of Saguache." The report predicted "a new Eldorado, with enough gold for hundreds, if not thousands." There is a Tracy's Canyon about eight miles southwest of Saguache. The correspondent for the newspaper report may have had marbles in his mouth and meant Trancy's Canyon rather than Tracy's Cabin. Or, possibly, there was a Tracy's Cabin and the canyon was named for Tracy, or vice versa. In any case, Tracy's Cabin or Canyon was not a new Eldorado after all. In fact, it was never heard from again as a gold section. . . . . *YORKVILLE*, a shortlived mining camp two miles from Galena. A few cabins were built here, but Yorkville was more of a tent settlement than anything else . . . . *MIRAGE*, another supply town and travel stop in the Saguache area. The town was once important to the livelihood of the region, but it is little more than a road stop today. It was reportedly named for the nearby sand formation that appears to be a body of water . . . . *NORTH CRESTONE* (not on map) and *NEW LIBERTY* (not on map), two towns listed as post offices around the turn of the century. They may have had something to do with all the mishmash about moving out of the land grant, but no information could be found about them . . . . *CLINTON*, a stage stop, saw mill and post office town about nine miles northeast of Silver Cliff on the road to Canon City . . . . *SHIRLEY*, an isolated camp around the Shirley mine, fourteen miles above Exchequerville. Only two buildings are left at the site. One is, or was, a boarding house. The site can be reached by standard auto, but it's a rough trip . . . . *OFER CAMP*, there was a small, short-lived camp on Ophir Creek between Querida and Rye. For some reason it was called Ofer Camp. There are the foundation ruins of a few old cabins near the top of the hill, about four or five miles up the Ophir Creek road.

# XXIV. THE BOWL OF GOLD

That Cripple Creek was a gold area in the first place and that it was discovered in the second place, are two of the strangest facts about this—the greatest gold district of them all.

The six miles square that make up the "Bowl of Gold" defy most geological theories. Cripple Creek sits on the edge of an ancient volcano. Belching volcanos frequently pick up gold, but seldom in such abundant quantities. But sometime in that dim ancient day a volcano burst forth in what was to be the center of Colorado. It scooped up a rich pocketful of gold, and sat back to cool and hide its treasure for a couple of million years.

The gold was well hidden. The Cripple Creek region, perhaps, looks less like a gold area than any other in Colorado. Unlike other gold districts, little float or gold dust was found on the surface. It was almost all underground. Most of the veins widened and became richer the deeper one dug.

These curious facts may account for the reason the Cripple Creek district got off to a number of false starts, and why people couldn't believe the gold when they saw it.

Once they did believe it, however, once the final, the real, rush began, it saved Colorado from going bust in the silver crash, helped the U. S. recover from the panic of 1893, and set the stage for one of the rip-roaringest sagas of any gold district in the world.

The goal of the gold rush to Colorado in 1859 was Pikes Peak, because, to an easterner, practically all Colorado lay at the foot of Pikes Peak. This exaggeration, or misconception, led many fortune seekers actually to seek gold at the foot of the towering mountain. They found some, not much. Anyhow, the real gold was found up north at Central City, or west at Fairplay or Oro City.

Cripple Creek became ranchland. One of the first ranchers in the area was William Womack. For years Womack and his son, Bob, saw the prospectors tramp across their land for the gold and silver hills in all directions. A member of the Hayden survey team discovered gold ore here in 1874. The find didn't seem worth developing. Cripple Creek was soon deserted again.

Ten years later some 3,000 gold-hungry prospectors rushed into the area when word got around that an old prospector named "Chicken Bill" was scooping nuggets out of the ground by the fistful. It was another "hoax" and the Cripple Creek hills were empty in four days. There was another false rush in 1887.

Three years earlier, Womack had sold his land. But his son stayed on to ride the range. The excitement of the early stampedes was in his veins. Bob Womack was more a prospector than a cowpuncher.

His discovery of gold is already legendary. The facts seem to become more obscure with each telling. One thing is consistent in all stories, however, and this one point is important to our tale: Bob Womack was a hard-drinking, loud-mouth cowpoke.

He often rode down into Colorado Springs for a blast. The more he drank the louder and more boastful he became. As early as 1878 he claimed he found float which assayed at $200 a ton. Several times he took ore specimens to the tavern to show around. He even put some on display in a store window. But the barroom crowd, knowing Bob Womack and the land he referred to, paid little heed.

Bob finally convinced a Colorado Springs dentist. Later he convinced a Colorado College geologist. They grubstaked Womack. Bob staked his claim on Poverty Gulch, dug a shaft ten feet deep. The ore he found assayed at $250 a ton.

Still nobody believed him.

In the late eighties, a Colorado College geology student, Edward de la Vergne, took a field trip up around Cripple Creek. He found some promising specimens and staked some claims.

Nobody was interested.

The whole thing came to a boil about 1891. Bob Womack was drinking more all the time, shouting his head off—almost going crazy trying to get people to believe him. De la Vergne, a dentist and a college professor, all honorable men, were interested in the possibilities of the Cripple Creek area. But they say the rush came when a loud, lush Bob Womack finally convinced a couple of well known prospectors who spread the word the gold was for real.

It was probably on the same drunk that Bob Womack shot out some street lights in Colorado Springs. One story goes that he woke up in jail the next morning to discover he had sold his claim, which produced millions, for a paltry $500. Another, less believable story, claims Bob Womack didn't want to mine anyway and sold his claim, after the rush had begun—during a sober bargaining session. He didn't want gold. He just wanted people to believe him.

Whatever the facts, the rush began in 1891, and the Cripple Creek saga erupted with the fury of an H-bomb.

The discoverer wound up penniless, but carpenters, pharmacists, and many others who knew little or nothing about mining became millionaires. People got rich just supplying the miners with their needs—all sorts of needs. Elder statesman Bernard Baruch was a hard rock miner here for a

444

while. Fred Stone, beloved actor of the nineties, was a resident here and played in the first touring troupe to come to the gold camp. The queen of the roaring twenties, Texas Guinan, once played the organ for Sunday school. Famed comics of the vaudeville circuit, Gallagher and Sheen, were motormen here. Lowell Thomas graduated from Victor High School. Damon Runyon went there too. A Jack Dempsey was killed in a mine accident. His brother, Bill, who also worked here, took over the name and became one of the nation's greatest champions. Another great champion, Jack Johnson, was a bouncer in a Cripple Creek saloon. Other champions fought or dug here. Tom Mix herded cattle near here.

And then there were the con men, gamblers, and ladies of the street . . . . the best. The only bull fight ever staged in continental U. S. fizzled in the Cripple Creek area, amid much publicity. Its promoters and participants were jailed and almost lynched. And Harry Orchard, one of history's most notorious cold-blooded mass killers, perfected his trade here.

There was more blood and booze spilt here than in any other small mining district in the world. And much of the violence centered around two of the bloodiest battles in labor history. There were two fires within five days that completely burned down the fabulous new city of Cripple Creek.

But despite all the extracurricular activity, the area produced nearly a half-billion dollars in gold—give or take ten or twenty million dollars for high-grading (a system by which the miners carried off some of the boss' best real estate in their pockets or anything else, including hollow-pick-handles).

And the Cripple Creek area is still producing. Who knows, prices may go up soon, or another strike may be made, bringing another rush to Cripple Creek and recalling the days when this was the greatest gold district of them all.

*MAP TWENTY-FIVE*

## CRIPPLE CREEK

Gillett

Cripple Creek (Fremont)

Anaconda (Barry, Squaw Gulch, Mound City)

Elkton (Arequa, Eclipse, Beacon Hill)

Victor

Lawrence, Dutchtown, Hollywood, Portland Station and Strong's Camp

Goldfield

Independence

Hull City (Macon)

Altman

Midway

Winfield (Stratton, Summit)

Cameron (Gassy, Grassy)

*And Then There Were . . . . WESTCREEK* (Given, Ackerman, North Cripple Creek) and *PEMBERTON* (both north of map), *TRUMBELL, TYLER, HAVERLY, HAYDEN, HAYDEN PLACER, HOOSIER, LOS ANGELES, JACKPOT, ECONOMIC JUNCTION, EAGLE JUNCTION, VISTA GRANDE, BADGER, DYER*, and *MANCHESTER.*

### GILLETT

Gillett did its part in adding to the Cripple Creek legend by staging the only Bull Fight ever held within continental United States. Joe "Arizona Charlie" Wolfe, amid much fanfare, scheduled the bull fight for 1895 at the Gillett race track. He imported real bulls and bull fighters from Mexico. He said they were the best. When the day came, celebrities from throughout the United States and Mexico jammed the city. The preliminaries were colorful, to say the least. The bullfight was anything but. Several defenseless bulls were slaughtered without a fair trial.

Some say the humane society got to Arizona Charlie before the fight, and some say the bulls were just tired from the long journey. Whatever happened, the 50,000 persons who jammed the race track and surrounding hills were looking for a fight, not excuses.

The bull fight ended in a riot. Arizona Charlie and the entire cast were jailed, more for their own protection than anything else. The scheduled three-day celebration ended with the first day, and everybody went back to where they came from, including Arizona Charlie and the "greatest matadors and toreadors in all Mexico." The story ended happily, however. The slaughtered bulls were cut up and passed out to the poor.

Some of the top horses of the day raced here and the track, despite the bull fight, was the pride of the entire area. But in 1911, after the stands

446

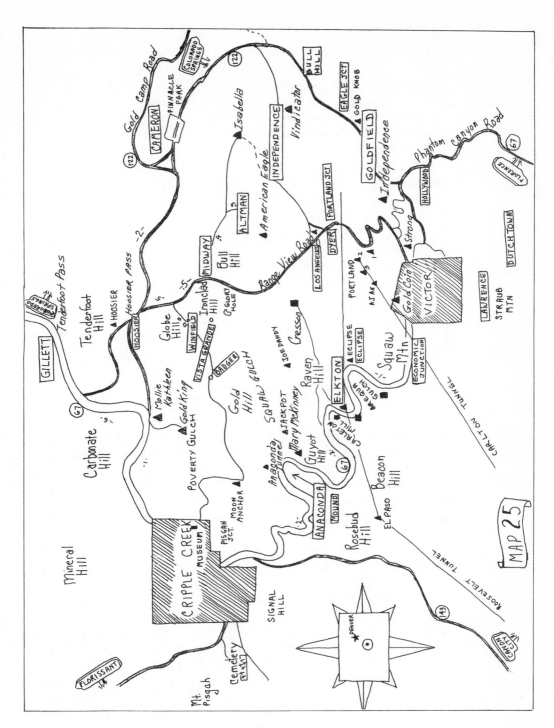

MAP 25

447

had been torn down, the track itself was plowed up and turned into farm-land.

Gillett was another family town, and a busy one. Some good mines were located nearby, the best of which was the Lincoln. A nearby reduction plant turned out 100 tons a day and employed nearly 100 men. The railroads also took advantage of the level ground on which Gillett was built for a terminal and freight yard.

The city had some of the best residential dwellings and many churches. Its own water system was supplied by the snow on Pikes Peak, and the city had its own hydrant system and electric light and power plant.

The city started disintegrating during the early years of this century. Now the ruins of an old church, located in the middle of a hay field west of the highway, and the old jail, near a small cluster of houses at a turn in the road, and an isolated hydrant or two are all that's left.

## CRIPPLE CREEK (Fremont)

Cripple Creek was the name given a small but rocky creek here many years before by ranchers and cowpokes whose cattle injured their legs while crossing the creek. The city wasn't so named until 1893, when two rival townships—Fremont and Hayden Placer—were consolidated. Estimates of the early population in the entire district have run as high as 100,000, but official figures run about half that amount. Cripple Creek's peak population was slightly more than 35,000 in 1900.

The site was a helter-skelter tent and cabin settlement the first few weeks, before cattlemen Bennett and Myers platted the town and sold lots, which were snapped up rapidly. Activity centered on the two main streets: Bennett Avenue, the main stem, was where the dignified business of the town was carried on, and Myers Avenue, one block south, which was equally as busy, although the business was of a different nature. Some of the top gamblers, prostitutes and saloon keepers in the business plied their trades here.

In 1916 an eastern dandy named Julian Street spent a week in Cripple Creek and wrote a lurid account of the city, emphasizing the social activities on Myers Avenue while glossing over the more prudish activities in other areas. Shortly after his story appeared in *Colliers*, the citizens of Cripple Creek, in protest against his slanted picture, renamed Myers Avenue Julian Street.

It was on this street that the first of Cripple Creek's devastating fires started. Legend-makers say the fire started when a young prostitute with a legend-like name—Jennie LaRue—tipped over a gasoline stove in a knock-down-drag-out fight with her boyfriend in a Myers Avenue parlor house. True or not, the fire did start in a parlor house. Fanned by a strong wind and despite the dynamiting of several buildings in its path in a vain effort to halt the blaze, the fire roared through the entire lower end of the town in just four hours. One-third of the business district was destroyed and some 300 buildings went up in smoke, including the postoffice, National Bank building and three churches. But despite the rapid advance of the fire, the many buildings dynamited, the scurry of frantic residents for safety, and the heroic dash of the Victor fire department over the dangerous road between the two towns, no lives were lost.

Cripple Creek had only begun to pick itself up from the first fire when—five days later—the second blaze erupted to destroy most of what was left of the city.

Again, accounts vary as to the origin of the fire. One account says the fire started when a pan of grease burst into flame in the kitchen of the Portland Hotel on Bennett Avenue. Another account says the fire was started by arsonists, since—although the main blaze started in the Portland Hotel—other fires developed simultaneously in other sections of the city. There have even been reports of arson suspects being lynched.

Once started, the fire roared through the town unabated. Dynamiting buildings in its path only added to the uproar. The second fire covered double the area of the first and the insurance loss was three times that of its predecessor. Every hotel and restaurant was demolished, 12 people were killed, scores were injured, and virtually eighty percent of the residents were homeless.

Fire departments as far away as Denver rushed to the scene in the vain effort to halt the blaze, and communities everywhere aided in the relief of the city. There were many stories of looting and scalping by wagon-masters in the mad dash for survival, but there were also many stories of heroism.

The overall story of the rebuilding of Cripple Creek is perhaps the most heroic story of all. Almost before the smoke had cleared, the people of Cripple Creek began to clear away the debris, and rebuild their town—much of it in brick.

The area was just reaching its stride when the fires broke, but little time was lost in mourning. Cripple Creek recovered rapidly and continued to progress, hitting its peak around 1900, and the boom lasted many years after the turn of the century.

Adding to the boom was the entrance upon the scene of railroads from every direction. The stories of the building of these railroads and the race between the Florence and Cripple Creek and the Colorado and Midland are stories in themselves. The Florence and Cripple Creek won the race but lost in the long run. The railway spent their profits repairing their trestles and other facilities which gave way frequently because of the hasty construction. The railroads brought in the tourists by the thousands, adding to the prosperity—and confusion—in the area. By 1903, two electric trolley lines between Cripple Creek and Victor, by way of the primary stations on the main lines, were operating and busy. Electricity replaced steam power. Huge pumps and tunnels were built to make the mining easier and safer.

By 1900, Cripple Creek had forty-one assay offices, ninety-one lawyers, eighty-eight doctors and dentists, fourteen newspapers, 139 saloons, three hospitals, thirty-four churches, twenty-five schools and one very busy undertaker.

The school and cultural life progressed as well. The Butte Opera House was sparkling nightly with some of the brightest stars of the day. New churches and meeting houses were being built every year, and some of the biggest names of the day—including Teddy Roosevelt—visited here.

And, despite rivalry from Victor over the honor, Cripple Creek became county seat of the newly formed Teller County in 1899.

Mining continued to improve year after year, and it didn't flag until well into this century. People as far away as London became rich because of Cripple Creek. Colorado has benefitted greatly, and many of the cultural and charitable institutions of Colorado Springs were built by Cripple Creek gold.

GOLD DUST: Poverty Gulch, where the first important strike was made, is just east of town. On the gulch is the Gold King mine which produced nearly eight million dollars, although its original owners purchased the claim from Bob Womack for $500 . . . . Bennett Avenue is paved with gold ore the early mine owners didn't think was worth processing . . . . nothing is left of the Bon Ton, Red Light, Crapper Jack's, and other notorious gambling and prostitution dens on Myers Avenue, but the Homestead parlor house was remodeled in 1953 and turned into a very respectable tourist home . . . . the Mt. Pisgah cemetery west of town is worth a visit, if only to see the most noted tombstone inscription: "He called Bill Smith a liar" . . . . Johnny Nolan's saloon, still standing at 3rd and Bennett, was the biggest gambling hall . . . . the station-turned museum at the entrance of town and the "meler-drama" at the Imperial Hotel during the summer are worth seeing . . . . the lavish National Hotel was opened for business in February, 1896, complete with elevators, turkish baths and its own electrical system . . . . before big business took over shortly after the turn of the century, there were more than 450 shipping mines in the area . . . . the peak year was 1900 when more than eighteen million dollars in gold was produced. It has been estimated that nearly 450 million has been produced in Cripple Creek, the fifth largest gold production of single areas in the world, more than the total production of the Comstock lode and about one-quarter of the total production of the entire Sierra Nevadas . . . . about thirty men, representing just about every walk of life, were made millionaires by Cripple Creek gold . . . . when the man responsible for it all, Bob Womack, suffered a stroke shortly after the turn of the century, the *Colorado Springs Gazette* attempted to raise $5,000 for the Bob Womack relief fund. After several front page editorials the total amount collected came to only $812. The fund collection was dropped . . . . Mount Pisgah was named after the mountain in Jordan from which Moses viewed the Promised Land.

## ANACONDA (Barry, Squaw Gulch, Mound City)

Huge log barriers holding back ore slack from the highway mark the site of Anaconda, a once bustling city of 2,000 persons. An old jail beside the road to the right and a few crumbling cabins down in the valley are all that remain of the city.

The town was supported chiefly by the Mary McKinney, which was once so rich it was said ore was plowed out by ox teams. The mine was just a prospect hole in 1898, but soon became one of the top producers in the region, yielding more than eleven million dollars in gold. The shafthouse of the mine was destroyed by fire.

The Carlton tunnel built to drain the lower levels of nearby mines is above the town (toward Cripple Creek) and the Anaconda tunnel outlet is near here.

Here, Texas Guinan—the Queen of the Roaring 20's—launched her career by playing an organ in an Anaconda Sunday School.

Another mine here was the Doctor Jackpot, behind the Mary McKinney mine southeast of town.

Anaconda was a composite of other camps: Squaw Gulch, Mound City and Barry.

The latter was in honor of Horace Barry, an important figure in the Cripple Creek story, although not a very stable one. Barry was a hard-drinking, poker-playing fool as well as being one of the best prospectors around. He located some of the best claims in the district but traded them off for bar tabs and poker debts.

He claimed Barry would be the cultural center of the Cripple Creek district. It never got that far, but it had its moments. Bright spot on the Barry cultural scene was the Squaw Gulch Amusement Club, boasting a membership of 400 of the elite in the district. Bob Womack was sergeant-of-arms of the club for a while.

Another club member and resident of Barry was Judge M. B. Gerry, the jurist who sentenced Packer in the only cannibalism trial held in the United States (see Lake City).

Mound City was farther down the gulch and grew around the Rosebud and Brodie Mills mines. The Brodie was one of the first cyanide reduction mills in the district. But generally, the Mound City mills couldn't compete with the other larger and more modern mills around, and the city began to fade about the turn of the century.

Anaconda had its peak in the mid-90's when it had better than a thousand residents and double that amount of tourists most every day.

451

*ELKTON* (Arequa, Eclipse, Beacon Hill)

Much of Elkton remains. In fact, two or three cabins are still occupied by miners who work in the famous Cresson mine a short distance behind the town.

The beginnings of the Cresson and Elkton mines are two more stories to add to the Cripple Creek legend. It seems a man named John W. Bernard, who knew nothing about prospecting, spent his first night in the Cripple Creek region sleeping on the ground. On awakening the next morning he staked the first likely rock pile he could find and named it for a pair of elk horns lying nearby.

The Elkton produced more than thirteen million dollars in its day. And Bernard gave half interest in the mine to two grocers in payment of a $36.50 grocery bill.

The Cresson mine, second largest producer in the area, had an equally haphazard beginning. A Chicago man named Harbeck bought the property around the turn of the century but did little about developing it. When he died, he left the property to his son, who knew as little about mining as his father did. However, the son asked a geologist, Richard Roelof, to investigate the claim and see if it was worth developing.

He did, and it was. The Cresson produced nearly 50 million dollars in gold and is still producing. In 1958, some 50 miners worked full time at the mine.

The first miners dug straight down in a never-widening shaft, year after year. In 1915, and at 1,200 feet, miners struck the famous Cresson Vug, a chamber of almost pure gold, thirty feet in diameter and twenty feet deep.

The ore was so rich that a vault door, similar to those used in banks, was placed over the opening of the chamber. Armed guards accompanied the ore on sealed box cars when it was shipped to Colorado Springs. One carload of the ore was said to have been worth a million dollars, a world record.

The mine was purchased by A. G. Carlton in 1916 for four million dollars. Carlton developed the property further, including the construction of the Carlton Tunnel, running from the mine to the Carlton Mill, standing below the town of Elkton.

The Carlton Mill was completed in 1951 at a cost of two million dollars. It produced more than four million dollars in gold bricks the first two years of operation. The mine is currently being operated by the Cresson Consolidated Gold Mining and Milling Company.

Elkton, the city, grew around the mine, and was also used by miners from the Cresson. Later, Elkton absorbed the nearby communities of Arequa, around the Arequa Mill across the road, Eclipse, and Beacon Hill.

The peak population was about 3,000 in 1905, ranking Elkton as one of the leading communities in the district.

Arequa Gulch was the site of Bob Womack's homestead. Bennett and Myers platted the homestead and sold lots at fancy prices. The total sale was $320,000.

In later years, as the mining tapered off and transportation was developed to a fine point in the district, most of the Elkton residents moved on, many moving around the hill to Victor. Ruins of the Arequa Mill are still visible, but for the most part, the Arequa, Eclipse and Beacon Hill sections of Elkton are all gone.

### VICTOR

Two or three hundred years before, Spanish explorers had searched the Colorado Rockies for the "City of Gold." They never found it. They just didn't stick around long enough.

Victor is Colorado's "City of Gold." Victor is built on gold ore. The Gold Coin mine, one of the richest in the area, was discovered while workers dug the foundation for a hotel. More gold was found under the high school athletic field, truly named the Gold Bowl. Victor's streets are paved with gold, since so much of ore nearby was so rich the city fathers didn't bother mining the "low-grade" stuff; it was used to make streets. In 1936 the town raised $5,000 by processing the ore from in front of the post office. Gold was dug in back yards. And the richest mines in this rich area are on the hill just above the city.

Victor bloomed just about the same time as did Cripple Creek, and since many of the richer mines were in Victor, the city rivaled Cripple Creek for many years. Much of the rivalry was bitter. In an effort to make Victor county seat of a county soon to be formed, some public-spirited citizens actually side-tracked a special train of state officials and dignitaries bound for Cripple Creek.

But in emergencies the rival cities stood together. Victor firemen risked life and limb in a mad dash to Cripple Creek over perilous Squaw Gulch when fire struck down Cripple Creek twice in one week. Victor citizens were among the first to offer relief after the fires had taken their toll. Cripple Creek repaid the favor three years later—in 1899—when fire destroyed much of Victor, causing a million dollars worth of damage and leaving 3,000 homeless.

Many of the mines in and around Victor were discovered in 1891 and 1892. During those years the entire area was covered by claims and prospect holes. Tents and shacks cluttered the landscape.

Finally, in 1893, the Woods Investment Company promoted the city. By the following year, some organization began to take shape among the tents

453

and cabins. Within months, Victor was the second city in the district and closely rivaled Cripple Creek. Its hotels, churches and homes were among the best in the region. Its 35,000 citizens were proud of the new city hall, large jail, and abundant facilities. It was the center of railroads and trolley cars. The area was unique among gold centers in that it was the only gold district in the world where a miner could go to and from the mines in trolley cars. During its peak years, nearly 60 trains and trolley cars passed through Victor daily.

The fire started in a gambling hall in August of 1899 and destroyed fourteen blocks within two hours. The citizens immediately began rebuilding in brick and stone.

But, sadly enough, Victor's glorious history is marred by two of the most violent labor wars in history, which centered in Victor and the mines above the city.

The Western Federation of Miners called the first strike in 1894, after several appeals to mine owners to correct the wage and hour inequalities at the mines. Some miners worked eight hours a day for their daily wage of three dollars. Others worked nine hours, and even more, for the same wage. When the miners objected, The Pharmacist and other mines attempted to correct the situation in their own way—by lowering the wage of an eight-hour day to $2.50. The miners finally issued an ultimatum: either establish an across-the-board basis of $3.00 for eight hours within ten days or a strike would be called. The mine owners ignored the ultimatum and the strike was called.

Picket lines were put up, and aside from a few minor skirmishes between pickets and scabs, and between owner-hired toughs and pickets, all was peaceful until six sheriff "deputies" were arrested in the union town of Altman on charges of carrying concealed weapons.

The sheriff asked for and got state troops, but a delegation of union miners met the troops and promised no violence, and the troops were withdrawn. By this time, however, nerves were on edge and the violence grew. Many were killed and injured (see Altman) until finally Governor Davis H. Waite personally intervened.

Governor Waite entered the battle with an open mind. The union was attracted by his fairness and authorized him to be sole arbitrator for the miners. After a few meetings with the mine owners, Governor Waite brought about a settlement of the strike, and a standard wage of $3.00 for eight hours was established and maintained.

In June of 1894, General Thomas J. Tarsney, adjutant general of Colorado, disliked by the union miners for leading action against them, was kidnapped in Colorado Springs, taken a short distance out of town, and tarred and feathered.

Governor Waite offered a reward of $1,000 for the vandals, but although many suspects were arrested, the culprits were never found. General Tarsney later refused to return to Colorado Springs and testify before the grand jury, claiming the jury was a farce which was suppressing rather than investigating the incident.

The second strike, called in August, 1903, was more violent and resulted in the downfall of the union. A different governor worked with the mine owners against the miners. Two union men in a mill in Colorado Springs were fired for their union activity. The mill workers struck and within hours the Western Federation of Miners in the Cripple Creek district struck out of sympathy. The mine owners immediately ordered a general closedown of the mines, throwing nearly 4,000 miners out of work. A few days later the mines were reopened, using non-union help heavily guarded by "toughs" deputized by the mine owners.

The violence, as in the first strike, grew from minor skirmishes to open warfare with many deaths and injuries. A train was wrecked, two mine officials were killed in an explosion of the Vindicator (see Independence), and an elevator car carrying scabs to work at the Independence mine was "tampered with" and 15 scabs fell to their death.

Governor James Peabody declared martial law and sent the state militia into the area. The mine owners took full advantage of the situation, thus writing one of the sorriest stories of Colorado history. Union men by the hundreds were rounded up and herded into "bull pens," little different from wartime concentration camps. Union leaders were beaten and run out of camp.

However, the mine owners carried things too far. The next spring, Governor Peabody suddenly withdrew his troops and placed the responsibility back on the mine owners. But the damage had been done.

The union miners struck back with a vengeance. On June 6th, the station at Independence exploded, killing nineteen scabs and injuring several more (see Independence); a riot broke out in Victor, two were killed and many injured. Shootings and beatings were rampant throughout the area.

And the Colorado National Guard was called out again by Governor Peabody and martial law was declared. Union men were rounded up again and placed in bull pens in Victor, Goldfield and Independence without any charges filed. Union leaders by the scores were "deported" to Kansas or New Mexico.

Within days the union was broken and the troops were withdrawn. The mine-owners had won. The card system of employment was installed whereby a miner needed a card issued by the mine operators to gain employment anywhere in the area. No card, no job. Cards weren't issued to union men, sympathizers or trouble makers—whether the label was just or not. The Cripple Creek area and the Western Federation of Miners never completely recovered from the strikes. The history of labor-management relations suffered a major setback.

GOLD DUST: Drainage tunnels begun in the 90's and completed in 1914 lowered the entire water level of the district by 700 feet . . . . the Carlton Tunnel was completed in 1941 at a cost of a million and a half dollars. The seven-mile bore connected the Portland, Cresson, Ajax and Vindicator shafts, and drained all the properties dry in two days . . . . William (Jack) Dempsey worked in the Portland mine . . . . Lowell Thomas graduated from Victor High School . . . . west of Victor is the Economic Gold Extraction Company plant, the largest ore reduction plant in the country . . . . the Strong Mine, just above the city, produced more than twenty million dollars in gold and is still producing . . . . the Gold Coin mine and miners club house is located in the center of the city. Much of the structure was razed to avoid taxation, and the club house is now a private house . . . . the population of Victor is about 400 today . . . . Victor was laid out on Mount Rosa Placer property . . . . Teddy Roosevelt, here to boost McKinley's chances among the Colorado miners, was almost mobbed by angry Victor citizens who, as virtually all Colorado miners, were bitter about what the administration did to the price of metals. Roosevelt was rescued from the mob—and possible death—by Danny Sullivan, who pushed the vice president into a waiting train at the last minute. Said Roosevelt to Sullivan: "Sir, you have saved my life." Whereupon, Roosevelt presented Sullivan with a ring. Sullivan, who became a well-known Colorado civil servant, wore the ring from that day on.

## LAWRENCE, DUTCHTOWN, HOLLYWOOD, PORTLAND STATION, STRONG'S CAMP.

All suburbs absorbed by Victor.

Lawrence was platted a short time before Victor. It might have outdistanced Victor, had not the latter had a more convenient location.

Lawrence was platted in January, 1892, on the homestead of Victor C. Adams. Lawrence had an experimental chlorination plant, built by Joe Lamar, Utah mining king. The chlorination process, imported from Transvaal, did not work at first in Cripple Creek, but its further development greatly boosted the mining industry in Colorado.

Portland Station and Strong's Camp were small communities around the big mines in Victor.

Hollywood and Dutchtown were residential and milling suburbs of Victor.

*GOLDFIELD* (with Independence)

The third largest city in the area during its heyday, Goldfield was considered a family town. In 1894, the site was a pasture, albeit a "well-worked" pasture. Surface locations covered the area and the nearby hills were honey-combed with mines. The city soon grew around the diggings. The population in 1900 was 3,500.

The town was originally established by the owners of the Portland Mine in 1895.

Goldfield was another strong union town. Many of the town officials were union officials as well. It is little wonder the city was heart of the labor wars of 1894 and 1903 (see Victor). But when the union was broken and many of its leaders ousted in the last labor battle, mine owners came into control of the city.

Since Goldfield was laid out on level ground and was near many of the big mines, all three of the railroads maintained stations and freight yards here. Three-fourths of all the ore mined in the district was shipped from here.

The Portland Mines were the biggest shippers in the area and have produced more than sixty million dollars in gold. The story of the founding of the original Portland Mine is another Cripple Creek story that reads like a fable.

In 1892, two Irishmen—one a plumber and the other a carpenter—staked one-sixth of an acre on Battle Mountain and began digging. The two—James Burns, the plumber, and James Doyle, the carpenter—soon ran out of funds, so they took on another partner, John Harnan, a drifter and doer of odd jobs. The three men sank a shaft and at the six-foot level they hit ore that "made their eyes bug out." Fearing trouble from nearby claims, they worked only at night. But their secret got out and in no time other claims were made on the property. With the aid of Winfield Scott Stratton (see Winfield) and money from the ore they had already scooped up, they successfully fought the suits. By 1894, the men formed the Portland Gold Mining Company and bought off other desirable claims nearby. At one time their holdings were valued at nearly $100,000,000.

The ore was so rich, some carloads were valued at $50,000, and the mine produced $30,000,000 in gold by 1911.

As Goldfield grew toward Independence, the two towns consolidated with a total population of 3,000.

Much of the city is still standing, but it is nothing compared to how it used to be. Looking down from the vicinity of Blue Bird Mine, one can see the vague pattern of streets, now obscured and empty, but once lined with homes and businesses.

457

## INDEPENDENCE (with Goldfield and Hull City)

Independence is perhaps most noted for the violence that occurred here during the labor wars. The explosion which destroyed the station killed nineteen scabs and injured many more.

But the once-prosperous city was more than just one explosion. There were two.

The Vindicator mine, in the town, was the fourth largest producer in the region, turning out more than twenty-seven million dollars in gold. The mine closed down only in recent years. Nearby are the remains of the Hull City Placer, another top producer.

Harry Orchard, stage director of the Independence station blast, conducted a dress rehearsal within the Vindicator mine. The story goes, Harry, who usually did things up thoroughly, planned to blow up an elevator of scabs during a shift change within the big mine. But Harry got lost inside the mine and set the explosion on the wrong level. The explosion only killed two mine officials, and the scabs lived to work again.

Harry often went after big game. He was foiled in attempts to blast Governor Peabody, Colorado Supreme Court Chief Justice William H. Gabbert and Justice Luther M. Goddard. However, he was later successful in blowing up the former governor of Idaho and spent the remainder of his life in Idaho State Prison.

Two or three of the many houses remaining in Independence are still occupied. The rest are empty and dilapidated.

## HULL CITY (Macon)

The site was platted in 1895 on Hull City Placer ground, and soon obtained a post office under the name of Macon. It was first a part of Goldfield, although Goldfield was a mile away. Later the land was purchased by the Independence Town and Mining Company, and Hull City—or Macon—soon became part of the growing city of Independence.

Hull City's best known character and perhaps the most scaggly character in the Cripple Creek region was a Missouri farmer named A. G. Smith. Smith was considered a tramp. They say he had more tobacco stains on his shirt than buttons. He was the source of another good laugh when he staked out a claim covered with surface rock.

You guessed it. At 120 feet, Smitty hit a rich lode and realized more than three-quarters of a million dollars from it.

## ALTMAN

One of the most bustling cities in the region around the turn of the century, Altman was composed almost exclusively of union miners, and was one of the union headquarters during the bloody strikes (see Victor) and the center of much of the violence. During the strike, Altman was declared an independent kingdom by "King Calderwood," leader of the Western Federation of Miners. Passports were needed to enter the town and the King conducted his own diplomatic relations with the mine owners.

Calderwood was a forceful leader of the union in Cripple Creek. He had a genius for organization and was a rock against the tyranny of the mine owners. They say it was Calderwoods' backroom scheming with Governor Waite that brought about a fair settlement in the first strike. True or not, Calderwood first went down into the mines at the age of nine—in Scotland. He put himself through college while working in the mines in Pennsylvania. A fighting liberal, Calderwood was a member of the Mollie MacGuires, early-day Wobblies, and was one of the founders of the Western Federation of Miners. Not as well-remembered, perhaps, as Eugene Debs or "Big Bill" Haywood, Calderwood was nonetheless one of the guiding spirits in the labor movement.

Since the city was a union stronghold, the mine owners rounded up an army of 1200 "deputies" to attack the mountain kingdom. The miners constructed a rude fort and waited for the attack. When the attack didn't come, the miners took the offensive. Many were injured and some killed on both sides during the skirmish and the counterattack the following day. When the smoke had cleared, the miners had possession of the Strong Mine above Victor.

This tragic "war" and an incident a short while later, when a justice of the peace from Anaconda was beaten up in Altman, were decisive in influencing Governor Peabody to call out the militia and declare martial law in the Cripple Creek district.

Violence was so common at one time, a busy undertaker offered to give group rates for funerals if all killings were done on Saturday.

Altman was the highest incorporated town in the United States in its day and was named for Sam Altman, who built the first stamp mill in Cripple Creek. The town covered the entire top of the hill, had several hotels, restaurants and saloons, and boasted of not having or needing a hospital or slum area.

The American Eagle mine dominated the site, and still does as only a few of the cabins and the foundations of the city (below the mine) remain.

Other nearby mines were the Buena Vista, Victor and Pharmacist. They say the Pharmacist was located by two druggists who knew nothing about mining but located the rich lode by throwing a hat in the air and staking out the spot on which it landed.

Altman had two of the top lawmen. Sheriff Mike McKinnon died with his boots on while shooting it out with six Texas hoodlums. The story goes all six bit the dust before McKinnon drew his last breath.

Marshall Jack Kelly chopped down the leader of the notorious Smith gang that terrorized and excited Cripple Creek for years. It seems "General" Jack Smith got boozed up in Cripple Creek one night and proceeded to take over the town of Altman. His reign of terror was climaxed by the release of all the prisoners in the Altman jail. Smith had pulled a number of similar "pranks" in the past. They were laughed off and forgotten. But this rubbed Kelly the wrong way. He swore out a warrant for Smith's arrest.

Smith put up bail and, on his release, stationed himself in a bar and waited for Kelly. Some say Smith hoisted a few while he was waiting. This might explain why he missed Kelly as the marshall walked through the door. The shot killed one of Smith's own men. Kelly didn't miss. He killed Smith with the first shot.

The gang was run by one of the molls for a while. She did plan a cagey Wells Fargo robbery at Grassy (Cameron). The gang made off with $16,000. But they had help. The driver was a member of the gang.

The gang went down hill rapidly after that. Some, including the moll, were tracked down and captured in Leadville. Two other members were killed in a barroom brawl. Another committed suicide. Tough cop Frank Lupton collared the last leader of the gang, Henry McQuaan, in Victor. Another gang member attempted to break up the arrest. Lupton used McQuaan as a shield and took the other in tow. He met trouble a couple of times on the way back to Cripple Creek, but he got his prisoners there.

## MIDWAY

A couple of old cabins and a tumbledown saloon, its glassless windows providing a majestic view of row upon row of Colorado mountains, is all that remains of Midway. It must have been a wonderful town to live in. Today it is a wonderful ghost town to visit—and to look out from.

In its day, Midway was a residential and tourist town, generally considered a part of Altman when that city overran the hilltop. They say Harry Orchard, in cahoots with another terrorist, Steve Adams, began preparations here for blowing up the Independence station. Otherwise, the good city of Midway was used for easy living and wonderful looking.

Around the hill from Midway at the top of Squaw Gulch is Glory Hole, the largest hole in the district, where miners actually mined up rather than down. The hole, some 150 feet deep, is the result of planned cave-ins to get at the ore in the mountains.

The nearby mill is the Kavanaugh Mill.

### WINFIELD (Stratton, Summit)

Just off the road to the right, about a half mile from Midway, is the lavish spread built by Winfield Scott Stratton, the area's first millionaire. The buildings, kept in good repair, served both as operation offices for Stratton's vast holdings and as a show place.

Stratton drifted into Cripple Creek district during the early days of the rush, after failing to win his fortune in many other boom camps in Colorado. He was by trade a carpenter, and he paid his way from camp to camp by plying his trade, while spending as much time as he could prospecting.

Stratton tried Silver Cliff in 1881, Red Cliff in 1882, Aspen in 1883, Tincup in 1884, and Breckenridge in 1885. He always wintered in Colorado Springs, and in 1885 he went to Colorado College to study mining and geology.

Shortly after coming to Cripple Creek, Stratton found some granite ore about six miles away from most of the other diggings. But the short course he had taken in mineralogy told him the outcroppings weren't worth bothering with. He staked other claims in the vicinity and worked on them, but he frequently returned to his original site. He did some work on the spot, until—on Independence Day, 1891—he struck what he called the Independence lode.

The lode was so rich he passed by ore valued up to $5,000 a ton just to get the "good stuff." The story goes Stratton did not push development of the Independence, and the nearby Martha Washington, which he staked at the same time, because he feared "the banks would go bust." He preferred to let the gold remain in the ground until it was needed. He sold his workings to an English syndicate eight years later for eleven million dollars. The Independence produced more than twenty-five million dollars in gold up until 1915, when the property became part of the Portland property.

Stratton spent much of the remainder of his life and much of the money he gained from the Cripple Creek gold fields in philanthropic pursuits. His most notable work involved the Myron Stratton home for the physically handicapped near Colorado Springs. On his death in 1902, he willed four million dollars to the institution.

The one million dollar commission paid Vernon Z. Reed of Denver for negotiating the sale of the Independence and Washington mines to the London syndicate established another Colorado fortune.

461

*CAMERON* (Gassy, Grassy)

Plans were underway in 1958 to reopen the Cameron Mine after twelve years of inactivity. If Cameron is reborn, it will have to start from scratch. Not one trace of the once-prosperous city exists.

Although never a large community, Cameron served as a recreation center for the entire Cripple Creek area, as well as being a mining and important railroad center. In fact, there was a time the city fathers planned to call the site Cripple Creek, but a larger settlement a short distance away discarded the name Fremont about the same time and took Cripple Creek for its own.

A report says a small ranching community was the first settlement here. It was named Gassy for a nearby rancher and his gastronomical condition.

About 1892, the Bennett and Myers Company laid out a city on the site and called it Grassy, for the meadowland. For a short while the city served as a terminal for the Short Line R.R. But as the railroad moved on, so did most of the residents. Eventually the mining activity in the district moved toward the site. The Lansing had already produced a quarter of a million, and other strikes were made here.

In 1899, the Woods Investment Company purchased the townsite for $123,000 and laid out the city of Cameron. Part of the city's development was Pinnacle Park, and therein lies Cameron's fame.

The park covered 30 acres just south of town and served as an amusement center for the entire district. The park included a large dance pavilion, band stand, zoo, playground, picnic and athletic field—Cameron's pride and joy. The stadium seated 1,000 people, and was often overflowing with those wishing to witness some of the most boisterous baseball and football games in early Colorado history.

Although the population of Cameron never exceeded 500, hundreds more would descend upon the community every week-end and on the holidays. The park's biggest day was on Labor Day, 1900, when more than 9,000 persons paid their ten cents to pass through the turnstiles into Pinnacle Park.

Although small, Cameron itself was one of the most progressive communities in the district. It had a modern school, escape-proof jail and perhaps the best city hall in the district.

But, alas, its prosperity was a fleeting thing. Its mines were not the best and soon gave out. The bitter labor wars of 1903-04 did much to hasten the death of the city. Eventually, its residents moved elsewhere and its attractive homes and buildings were torn down or moved.

It is important today only as the beginning to the harrowing but beautiful back-door trip to Colorado Springs over the old Short Line railroad grade. The dusty and sometimes narrow railroad roadbed traverses some of the most beautiful but least seen country in Colorado—described once by Teddy Roosevelt as a beauty that "bankrupts" the English language.

BEST MINES: Elsmere, Isabella, Victor, Wild Horse, Damon, Jerry Johnson, Hoosier, Lansing, Morning Star and Blanche.

*And Then There Were* . . . . *WESTCREEK* (Given, Ackerman, North Cripple Creek) and *PEMBERTON* (north of map) two once-large communities that grew out of a number of camps about forty-five miles north of Cripple Creek. Only Westcreek is shown on most standard maps now, although it is believed to be the actual site of Pemberton of yesteryear, and the ruins of Westcreek a short distance away. The area was active during the nineties and a few years into this century when some gold ore was found here. At first, they thought it might be another Cripple Creek and more than 5,000 prospectors rushed into the area. But the ores were not so rich as those found around Cripple Creek and Westcreek-Pemberton sputtered for a while—and then died. The area's most remembered achievement was the joint development of the best properties by the miners. Seeing the properties were not so good as they could be, the miners worked together to develop the best claims, including the construction of a 500-foot tunnel . . . . *TRUMBULL* and *TYLER* (not on map) two of the many camps around Westcreek and Pemberton. Tyler was named for Captain George F. Tyler, a local rancher on whose land the Westcreek locations were made . . . . *HAVERLY* (not on map) theatrical promoter Jack Haverly had a sidelight—promoting towns. He wanted to become immortal by having a Colorado city named after him. He met with bad luck in the Irwin area (see Ruby) but that didn't stop him. He planned an elaborate town for a site on the edge of the Cripple Creek area, promised the construction of several buildings, and sold several lots at a fancy price. Then he up and skipped town. Since the same story is told around Irwin, and since Haverly was there, too, chances are only one of the stories is true. If we must choose one specific site for our little swindle, this writer thinks we would fare better if we chose Cripple Creek. The Cripple Creek records are more recent and more detailed, and it is doubtful that Haverly would be able to get away with the stunt at Cripple Creek if he had pulled it earlier in the Irwin area. But then, again, perhaps someone else pulled the swindle at Irwin and Haverly learned the tricks of the trade then . . . . *HAYDEN PLACER* (not on map) a camp on the site of Cripple Creek but one year earlier (1891). Some say Hayden Placer was not more than a tent and shanty settlement and died within the year, while others claim it was the predecessor of Cripple Creek and was absorbed by that city . . . . many small and/or temporary towns sprang up in the 90's and early 1900s throughout the Cripple Creek vicinity. The towns were at the sites of mines and mills. Among these were the *HOOSIER*, near the Hoosier mine; *LOS ANGELES* and *JACKPOT* near the Los Angeles and Jackpot mines respectively; *ECONOMIC JUNCTION*, near the Economic Mill, and *EAGLE JUNCTION* near the Eagle Sampler. Other towns were at important junctions or other railroad facilities, such as *VISTA GRANDE, BADGER* and *DYER*. But as transportation improved in the area, or activity tapered off, only skeleton crews remained at the sites, and the others moved to the excitement of the cities. Nothing remains of these towns save the mines and mills around which they were built, or the beds of the once-busy railroad.

. . . *MANCHESTER* (north of map), a little-known although fairly important, mining town about 19 miles north of Cripple Creek and nine miles south of Pemberton. The town is inaccessible even to jeeps now.

# XXV. FROM DUST TO DARKNESS

The following towns or camps were mentioned here and/or there in the course of my research, but little or nothing could be found on them beyond their names. They may have been no more than tent settlements or proposed townsites. Some may have been alternate names for known camps. Many may have been little more than stage or railway stops. Some, however, were important enough to have post offices. The rest are listed here for the first time. The names in parentheses are the nearest known towns to the elusive sites or the counties in which they were contained.

Aberdeen (Chance)
Albany (Ouray)
Altman's or Alton's Camp (Monarch)
Anson (Boulder)
Apex (Leadville)
Arizona Bar (Hahns Peak)
Ash (Ouray)
Aureo (Gunnison)
Aurora (Ouray)
Belleview (Gunnison)
Bilk (Telluride)
Camp Ideal (Gunnison)
Carpenter Hill (Gunnison)
Columbus (Monarch)
Copperville (Gunnison)
Cottage Grove (Alma)
Cousden (White Pine)
Crookton (Saguache)
Cross Mountain (Tin Cup)
Dailey (Silver Plume)
Dana (Chaffee County)
Dawson City (Westcliffe)
Dayton (Spencer)
Deen (Leadville)
Eagle Sampler (Independence)
Elko (Silver Cliff)
Elk Park (Silverton)
Elkton (Gothic)
Fisher (St. Elmo)
Foosel or Fooses (Monarch)
Galena (Schofield)
Givens (Bowerman)
Glencliff (St. Elmo)
Grassy Hill (Silverton)
Green's Gulch (Monarch)
Hamilton (Winfield)

Hangman Camp (Buena Vista)
Hartz (Monarch)
Hecla (Salida)
Henry (Leadville)
Hermit (Lake City)
Hill (Boulder)
Hillsdale (Fairplay)
Jennings (Monarch)
Keeldar (Leadville)
Leon (Crested Butte)
Leopard (Telluride)
Lotus (Ouray)
Marion (Spencer)
Marshalltown (Gunnison)
Mason (Grand Lake)
Maurice (Powderhorn)
Minersville (Querida)
Missouri Gulch (Clear Creek County)
Moscow (Gunnison)
Mounds (Gunnison)
New Liberty (Saguache)
North Crestone (Saguache)
Ofer or Ophir (Empire)
Omega (Telluride)
Ophir Camp (Rosita)
Oversteg (Jack's Cabin)
Park City (Grand Lake)
Park City (Leadville)
Parkville (Saguache)
Perins (Durango)
Permit (Westcliffe)
Pole Creek (Lake City)
Pomeroyville (Georgetown)
Rathbone (Aspen)
Red Mountain (Gunnison)
Red Rock (Boulder)

Rogers (Crested Butte)
Sewell (Carbondale)
Sillsville (Chance)
Silver Circle (Custer County)
Silver Creek (Custer County)
Silver Hill (Summit County)
Silvery City (Summit County)
Slavonia (Hahns Peak)
Sugar Hill (Gunnison)
Sunnyside (Ward)
Sunset City (Westcliffe)

Timberline Town (Montgomery)
Tracy's Cabin (Saguache)
Two-Bit Gulch (Twin Lakes)
Valley Spur (Pitkin)
Vanguard (Gunnison South)
Waco (Twin Lakes)
Watson (Aspen)
Wood Mountain (Wall Street)
Woodstock (Bowerman)
Wortman (Leadville)
Yankee Bar (Black Hawk)

# XXVI. GLOSSARY

*Arastra,* rather primitive method of grinding out quartz and precious ore particles by heavy stones on a large circular stone bed. The large stones were often dragged by a mule, led on a circular path by a rotating shaft. Arastras used widely by early Spanish miners and by some early Yankee miners in Colorado. Remains of some Spanish arastras found near Fairplay. Some Yankee arastras were built near Silverton and other areas.

*Argentum,* Latin for silver. Derivation of argentiferous meaning producing or containing silver, such as ore.

*Assay,* measuring proportion of gold or silver content in ore.

*Bar,* a bank of sand or gravel along a stream.

*Bedrock,* solid rock underlying or forming a solid bottom for the superficial upper layer.

*Blossom rock,* outcropping or a vein.

*Claim,* see Staking a claim.

*Carbonates,* ores rich in lead content.

*Concentration works,* a process of separating the valuable parts of the ore from the other elements found in the rock.

*District* (mining), an area which usually comprises all or most of the locations made in a new boom area and which marks the boundaries in which the specific mining laws of that area apply.

*Dredge* (mining), similar to the dredges used in scraping and scooping out river bottoms for sand and mud traps. Mining dredges scoop out the sand and gravel along the stream bed, washes through what it collects, returning the unwanted particles to the stream and depositing the heavier metal particles on a pontoon.

*Fissure,* narrow gap or crack in the rock which often contains valuable metals.

*Float,* fragments of ore that had broken off a main vein to become buried rock outcropping.

*Galena,* commonest form of lead sulphide, frequently containing silver.

*Glance,* ore with a lustre indicating metal content.

*High grading,* a method perfected by miners for carrying off rich ore from the mines and selling it themselves. The ore would be carried out in pockets, real or makeshift, in the clothing, lunch buckets, false helmet brims, hollow pick handles, false soles and heels in shoes, and everything else they could think of. High grading at Cripple Creek got so bad mine owners set up some of the first shower and locker rooms in the mining business and required the miners to wash and change clothes before leaving the mine. Even at that, inspectors were posted at the exits to inspect the miners and their possessions before leaving. It has been estimated that more than twenty million dollars worth of ore was carted off by high grading in the Cripple Creek mines.

*Hydraulic mining,* a process of washing ore from its bed with powerful jets of water.

*Iron pyrite,* better known as fool's gold because of its resemblance to the real thing.

*Jump a claim,* a method of taking over a good mining claim after it had been staked out by someone else. This was usually, but not always, done before the claim was registered.

*Location,* boundaries of a claim, fixed by the limits set by the mining laws of the district.

*Lode,* a deposit of ore containing gold, silver and other precious metals found in vein or fissure in quartz and other rocks.

*Mother lode,* the primary deposit or vein.

466

*Nugget*, a lump of native or pure gold found in deposits and placer mines.

*Outcropping*, the emergence of layers of rock appearing above the surface of the ground, as strata of rock.

*Pan*, basic method of washing metal particles from gravel and sand in a miners' pan, somewhat similar in appearance to a pie pan.

*Placer*, loose surface soil containing gold and silver particles.

*Placer mining*, washing the surface soil, carrying away the light worthless particles while leaving the heavier metals.

*Platting* (a townsite), planning or mapping a townsite, designating lots.

*Quartz*, hard, transparent to opaque, minerals, one of the commonest known.

*Reduction works*, mill for separating metals from substances combined with it.

*Rocker*, crude, usually wooden, apparatus for washing metal particles from gravel. It works on much the same principle as a pan, but on a larger scale.

*Ruby silver*, a silver-arsenic sulphide mineral.

*Sampler*, a plant equipped to determine the value of the ores.

*Sluice*, an inclined trough, usually made of wood, for washing gold ore. The flow of the water is regulated by flood gates.

*Stake a claim*, marking the boundaries of one's location in accordance with the limits set down by the mining laws of the district.

*Stamp mill*, a mill containing heavy stamping apparatus for crushing ore to separate the particles.

*Stope*, an excavation from which ore is extracted in series of steps or ledges.

*Sulphuret*, undecomposed metallic ores, usually sulphides.

*Sylvanite*, native telluride of gold and silver. Valuable ore of gold.

*Telluride*, several native compounds of tellurium and gold and silver, highly valued as ores.

*Tellurium*, a rare metallic element, often combined with gold and silver in sylvanite.

*Vein*, a fissure or elongated ore mass, richer than the surrounding rock. Some veins in Colorado ran for several miles in a fairly straight line. Many mines and even a few mining districts could be located on one vein.

*Vug*, a hollow or cavity in a rock, often lined with crystalline material.

*Wire silver*, native silver appearing in the form of threads or wire.

# XXVII. ACKNOWLEDGMENTS

It would be impossible to list all the people who contributed to this book. Many didn't even know they were helping. Being new to book writing, I was negligent at first in taking down names of those I talked with, who provided me with information. I thank these nameless people throughout the state. Next time around I will be more considerate and take down the names as well as the information.

Some persons, however, were so helpful I couldn't neglect their names.

First of all, thanks to Mrs. Agnes Wright Spring and others at the State Historical Museum who gave me the run of the place back in 1951 when I was a guide and when this book got its start. Thanks for contemporary help from Mrs. Laura Ekstrom, assistant librarian.

Much thanks to Mrs. Alys Freeze, Mrs. Opal Harber, Mrs. Margaret Howie, Mrs. Mary Hanley, Mrs. Katherine Hawkins and Jim Davis at the fine Western History Section of the Denver Public Library who patiently helped me find material and offered many good suggestions.

Thanks to Hal Haney and the Colorado Publicity Department; the Denver and Colorado Springs Hospitality Centers; the State Fish and Game Department; U. S. Forest and National Park service; and the highway and post office departments, U. S. Geodetic Survey, and U. S. Bureau of Mines.

Personal thanks to Mrs. John Burgener, Mr. and Mrs. Kenny Reynolds, R. M. Hagerman, Pinky Warell, Harold Ellithorpe, Mr. and Mrs. Donald Orth, Francis B. Rizzari, H. M. McMillan, Jim Ward, Mrs. Ruth Alley, Robert Dunne, Mervin Snow, A. A. Kelly, Richard Marvin, Wilbur F. Shafto, Jack Foster, Dean Mundorf, John Chick, Jim Wetherill, Sandra Dallas Atchison, Dale Finch, E. J. Tallant, and others who provided special information and help.

Last but far from least, my heartfelt thanks to my wife, Sandy, and to my mother, Mrs. Eve Bennett Haberl. I wanted to make this book read "by Sandy and Perry Eberhart," but my wife would have none of it. Nonetheless, she did the dirty work, typing, re-typing and typing again, some editing, while offering suggestions and lending much-needed encouragement. This book would not have been published without her. My mother was a great help in editing the book, particularly in marking out a few thousand "fabulouses," "lavishes" and "booms" (sometimes I get carried away—it's the subject). She, too, offered many suggestions and gave encouragement.

A number of publications were especially helpful in the compilation of this book. Early newspapers, particularly the *Rocky Mountain News*, were extremely helpful. If only I had the time to read them all, page by page! Not only are they tremendously interesting, they contain an endless reservoir of information. Some of the most interesting facts concerning early Colorado are still hidden in these papers. Both the State Historical Museum and the Western History section of the Denver Public Library have excellent files of these newspapers. All modern books on Colorado mining history and ghost towns begin with Muriel Sibell Wolle's wonderful book, *Stampede to Timberline*. No study of Colorado could be undertaken without it. Priceless information was also obtained from the State Historical Society's *Colorado Magazine*; the Works Progress Administration's *Colorado, A guide to the highest State; The Westerner's Brand Books*; Don and Jean Griswold's recent *Colorado Century of Cities*, and a couple of old books, George Crofutt's *A Grip-Sack Guide to Colorado*, and Axel Silversparre's *Appendix to a new map of Colorado*, published in 1882 and 1881 respectively.

And, finally, thanks to the thousands of people, all kinds of people, who scampered over the Colorado Rockies the past one hundred years and made this book so interesting to write.                                                                         P.E.

# XXVIII. BIBLIOGRAPHY

Atwood, Wallace W., *The Rocky Mountains*. New York, Vanguard Press, 1945.

Baggs, Mae Lacy, *Colorado, the Queen Jewel of the Rockies*. Boston, Page Co., 1918.

Bancroft, Caroline, *Famous Aspen*. Golden Press, 1957.

Bancroft, Caroline, *Gulch of Gold*. Denver, Sage Books, 1958.

Bancroft, Caroline, *Historic Central City*. Denver, World Press, 1951.

Bennett, *Gazetteer of Colorado*. 1902.

Brandon, William, *The Men and the Mountain*. New York, William Morrow & Co., 1955.

Brigham, Lillian Rice, *Colorado Travelore*. Denver, Peerless Printing, 1938.

Buchanan, John W. and Doris G., *The Story of Ghost Town Caribou*. Boulder, Boulder Publishing, Inc., 1957.

Cairns, Mary Lyons, *The Olden Days*. Denver, World Press, 1954.

Carhart, Arthur H., *Colorado*. New York, Coward-McCann, Inc., 1932.

Chapman, Arthur, *The Story of Colorado*. New York, Rand McNally & Co., 1924.

*Colorado Magazine, Place Names in Colorado*. Denver, Colorado State Historical Society, Jan. 1940 through May, 1943.

Colorado State Historical Society, *Colorado Magazine*. Denver, 1923 through 1958.

Corbett, Thomas B., *Colorado Directory of Mines*. Denver, Rocky Mountain News Printing Co., 1879.

Crofutt, George A., *A Grip-Sack Guide of Colorado*. Omaha, Overland Publishing Co., 1881.

Crum, Josie Moore, *The Rio Grande Southern Story*, Durango, Colorado, Railroadiana, Inc., publishers, 1957.

Darley, Rev. George M., *Pioneering in the San Juan*. New York, Fleming H. Revell Co., 1899.

Denver Posse of Westerners, *Westerners Brand Books*. Denver, Artcraft Press, 1946-48; Golden Press, 1949; U. of Denver Press, 1950; Denver, Artcraft, 1951; Denver, Arthur Zeuch, 1952; Boulder, Johnson Publishing Co., 1953-1956.

Dyer, Rev. John L., *The Snow Shoe Itinerant*. Cranston & Stowe, 1890.

Ellis, Amanda M., *Bonanza Towns*. Denver, Denton Printing Co., 1954.

Fossett, Frank, *Colorado, Its Gold and Silver Mines*. New York, C. G. Crawford, 1880.

Fossett, Frank, *Colorado*. New York, C. G. Crawford, 1880.

Fowler, Gene, *Solo in Tomtoms*. New York, Viking Press, 1946.

Fowler, Gene, *Timberline*. New York, Covici, Friede, 1933.

Fritz, Percy C., *Colorado, The Centennial State*. New York, Prentice-Hall, 1941.

Fritz, Percy S., *Mining Districts of Boulder County*. Unpublished Doctor's Thesis, Colorado University, 1927, Denver Public Library.

Gannett, Henry, *Gazetteer of Colorado*, Washington, Government Printing Office, 1906.

Gibbons, Rev. J. J., *On the San Juan, Colo*. Denver Public Library, 1898.

Gimlett, F. E., *Over Trails of Yesterday*. Published by author, 1951.

Griswold, Don and Jean, *A Carbonate Camp Called Leadville*. U. of Denver Press, 1951.

Griswold, Don and Jean, *Colorado Century of Cities*. Denver, Smith-Brooks, 1958.

Hafen, LeRoy, *Colorado and Its People*, (four vols). New York, Lewis Historical Publishing Co., Inc., 1948.

Hafen, LeRoy, *The History of Colorado*. Denver, Linderman Co., Inc., 1927.

Hall, Frank, *The History of Colorado*. Chicago, Blakely Printing Co., 1889-1895.

Hearld, Weldon, *Scenic Guide to Colorado*. Boulder, H. C. Johnson, 1952.

Hunt, Inez and Wanetta W. Draper, *Ghost Trails to Ghost Towns*, Denver, Sage Books, 1958.

Jackson, Clarence S. and Lawrence W. Marshall, *Quest of the Snowy Cross*. U. of Denver Press, 1952.

Lavender, David, *The Big Divide*. Garden City, Doubleday and Co., Inc., 1948.

Lavender, David, *One Man's West*. Garden City, Doubleday and Co., Inc., 1956.

Lovelace, Leland, *Lost Mines and Hidden Treasure*. San Antonio, Naylor Co., 1956.

McLean, Evelyn Walsh, *My Father Struck It Rich*. London, Faber & Faber, 1936.

Matthews, Ruth Estelle, *A Study of Colorado Place Names*. Unpublished Masters Thesis, Denver Public Library, 1940.

Mazulla, Fred and Jo, *Cripple Creek and the Pikes Peak Region*. Denver, A. B. Hirschfield, 1956.

Montgomery, Mabel Guise, *The Story of Gold Hill, Colorado*. Published by author, 1930.

Mumey, Nolie, *Creede*. Denver, Artcraft Press, 1949.

Ormes, Robert M., *Guide to Colorado Mountains*. Denver, Sage Books, 1955.

Parkhill, Forbes, *Wildest of the West*. Denver, Sage Books (re-issue), 1958.

Parson, Eugene, *A Guide Book to Colorado*. Boston, Little Brown & Co., 1911.

Pearl, Richard M., *Colorado Gem Trails*. Denver, Sage Books, 1951.

Quiett, Glenn Chesney, *They Built the West*. New York, D. Appleton-Century Co., Inc., 1934.

Rockwell, Wilson, *Sunset Slope*. Denver, Big Mountain Press, 1956.

Schader, Conrad F., *Tin Cup, Colorado*. Denver, Lynn Publishing, 1953.

Shoemaker, Len., *Roaring Fork Valley*. Denver, Sage Books, 1958.

Silversparre, Axel, *Appendix to a New Map of Colorado*. Chicago, J.M.W. Stationery and Printing Co., 1882.

Sprague, Marshall, *Money Mountain*. Boston, Little Brown & Co., 1953.

Stone, Irving, *Men to Match My Mountains*. Garden City Doubleday & Co., 1956.

Stone, William Fiske, *History of Colorado* (four vols). Chicago, S. J. Clark Publishing Co., 1918.

Taylor, Bayard, *Colorado*. G. P. Putnam & Son, 1867.

Vickers, W. B., *History of the City of Denver*. Chicago, Baskin & Co., 1880.

Waters, Frank, *Midas of the Rockies*. Denver, Sage Books, 1946.

Wentworth, Frank, *Aspen of the Roaring Fork*. Lakewood, Francis Rizzari Pub., 1950.

Williams, Albert N., *Rocky Mountain Country*. New York, Duell, Sloan & Pearce, 1950.

Willison, George, *Here They Dug the Gold*. New York, A. L. Burt Co., 1931.

Wolle, Muriel Sibell, *Stampede to Timberline*. Published by author, 1949.

Works Progress Administration, *Colorado, A Guide to the Highest State*. New York, Hastings House, 1941.

Works Progress Administration, *Ghost Towns of Colorado*. New York, Hastings House, 1947.

MAGAZINES AND PAMPHLETS: *Mining and Industrial Report* (1887-1889); *Camp and Plant; Colorado Mineral Resources* (1904); *Rocky Mountain Life Magazine; Colorado Wonderland; Directory of Post Offices; Publications of the Geological Survey; Publications of the U. S. Bureau of Mines;* Tourist pamphlets from Denver, Aspen, Colorado Springs, Cripple Creek, Leadville, Fairplay, Georgetown, and Silverton; *Colorado Outdoors.*

NEWSPAPERS: (Denver) *Rocky Mountain News, Denver Post, Denver Times, Denver Republican, The Central City Daily and Weekly Register-Call, Caribou Post, Solid Muldoon, Apex Pine Cone, Fort Collins Courier, Tin Cup Times, White Pine Cone, The Silver World, The Mining Journal, Fairplay Flume, Alamosa Empire, The Mining World, Leadville Chronicle, Leadville Herald Democrat, Breckenridge Journal.*

# INDEX OF TOWNS

471

473

477